FAREWELL TO THE PRIESTLY WRITING?

ANCIENT ISRAEL AND ITS LITERATURE

Thomas C. Römer, General Editor

Editorial Board:
Susan Ackerman
Thomas B. Dozeman
Alphonso Groenewald
Shuichi Hasegawa
Annette Schellenberg
Naomi A. Steinberg

Number 38

FAREWELL TO THE PRIESTLY WRITING?

The Current State of the Debate

Edited by

Friedhelm Hartenstein and Konrad Schmid

Translated by

Wesley Crouser, Paavo N. Tucker,
Henry Heitmann-Gordon, and David Cloutier

SBL PRESS

Atlanta

Copyright © 2022 by SBL Press

Originally published as *Abschied von der Priesterschrift? Zum Stand der Pentateuchdebatte.* ©2015
Negotiated by Evangelische Verlagsanstalt GmbH, Leipzig

All rights reserved. No part of this work may be reproduced or transmitted in any form or by any means, electronic or mechanical, including photocopying and recording, or by means of any information storage or retrieval system, except as may be expressly permitted by the 1976 Copyright Act or in writing from the publisher. Requests for permission should be addressed in writing to the Rights and Permissions Office, SBL Press, 825 Houston Mill Road, Atlanta, GA 30329 USA.

Library of Congress Control Number: 2022948061

Contents

Foreword...vii

Abbreviations...ix

The Priestly Writing as a Source: A Recollection
    Christoph Levin...1

Once Again: The Literary-Historical Profile of the P Tradition
    Erhard Blum..27

Genesis 5: Priestly Redaction, Composition, or Source?
    Jan Christian Gertz 63

The Literary Character of the Priestly Portions of the Exodus
    Narrative (Exod 1–14)
    Christoph Berner...95

From the Call of Moses to the Parting of the Sea: Reflections on
    the Priestly Version of the Exodus Narrative
    Thomas Römer 135

The Priestly Writing and Deuteronomy in the Book of Leviticus:
    On the Integration of Deuteronomy in the Pentateuch
    Eckart Otto...165

The Holiness Legislation and the Pentateuch: Tradition- and
    Composition-Historical Aspects of Leviticus 26
    Christophe Nihan..193

Bibliography..235

Contributors...263

Ancient Sources Index 265
Modern Authors Index 280

Foreword

Identifying the Pentateuch's Priestly Code as an originally independent source is one of the most prominent and recognized results of historical biblical scholarship. The success of this hypothesis is due to three basic observations, which have been described and expressed many times ever since biblical criticism's beginnings. First, there are the notable doublets of certain narrative materials. Second, the theological conception of אלהים is a characteristic of these writings, which, like the first feature of doublets, is essentially limited to Genesis and the first part of the book of Exodus. And third, linguistically and theologically peculiar concepts have greatly supported the identification of Priestly text segments. Particularly striking is how frequently these first two observations overlap, with traditions of doublets often using אלהים terminology in one of the versions.

However, the last forty years have witnessed significant developments in discussions of the Priestly literature in the Pentateuch. Since the work of Frank Moore Cross and Rolf Rendtorff, P's character as an independent source has been questioned, and since the work of Lothar Perlitt and Thomas Pola, the problem of its literary ending has become increasingly controversial. In current research, one can no longer presume that the Priestly texts were a formerly independent source, nor that P extends from Gen 1 to Deut 34.

Regardless of how one assesses these debated questions, it remains true that the response to them will impact one's model of the Pentateuch's composition in fundamental ways. Many foundational judgments regarding the Pentateuch's development, as well as ancient Israel and Judah's history of religion and theology, depend on literary-critical assessments of the Priestly texts. Both the older and newer documentary hypotheses have considered it the Grundschrift of the Pentateuch, and some more recent approaches to the Pentateuch's composition argue that it either inaugurates or at least propagates the canonical portrait of a transition from the ancestral to the exodus narratives. The Priestly Code is thus at

-vii-the center of crucial literary-historical theories about the formation of the Hebrew Bible.

Whether one maintains, abandons, or modifies the hypothesis of the Priestly Code, the essays in this volume offer observations and arguments in favor of each of these positions, which should inform scholarly decisions in either direction.

The present volume contains proceedings from the conference "Farewell to the Priestly Code? On the State of the Pentateuchal Debate," part of the Hebrew Bible/Old Testament section at the Wissenschaftlichen Gesellschaft für Theologie, which took place in Stuttgart-Hohenheim on 17–19 May 2012.

We thank the speakers Christoph Levin (Münich), Erhard Blum (Tübingen), Jan Christian Gertz (Heidelberg), Christoph Berner (Göttingen, now Kiel), Eckart Otto (Munich), Christophe Nihan (Lausanne), and Thomas Römer (Lausanne and Paris) for their contributions that supply a picture of the current state of discussions about the Priestly texts in the Pentateuch. We also thank Wesley Crouser, Paavo N. Tucker, Henry Heitmann-Gordon, and David Cloutier for translating the essays from the German original, which was published as *Abschied von der Priesterschrift? Zum Stand der Pentateuchdebatte* in 2015 by the Evangelische Verlagsanstalt in Leipzig. Finally, our thanks go to Samuel Arnet, Jordan Davis, and Hans Decker, who prepared the manuscript, and to SBL Press, especially Bob Buller and Nicole L. Tilford, and to the editors of the Ancient Israel and Its Literature for accepting this book for their series.

Friedhelm Hartenstein and Konrad Schmid
Munich and Zurich, July 2022

Abbreviations

ÄAT	Ägypten und Altes Testament
AB	Anchor Bible
ABG	Arbeiten zur Bibel und ihrer Geschichte
AIL	Ancient Israel and Its Literature
AnBib	Analecta biblica
AOAT	Alter Orient und Altes Testament
ATANT	Abhandlungen zur Theologie des Alten und Neuen Testaments
ATAT	Arbeiten zu Text und Sprache im Alten Testament
ATD	Das Alte Testament Deutsch
AYBRL	Anchor Yale Bible Reference Library
BA	La Bible d'Alexandrie
BBB	Bonner biblische Beiträge
Ber. Rab.	Bereshit Rabbah
BETL	Bibliotheca Ephemeridum Theologicarum Lovaniensium
Bib	*Biblica*
BibInt	Biblical Interpretation Series
BKAT	Biblischer Kommentar, Altes Testament
BN	*Biblische Notizen*
BThSt	Biblisch-theologische Studien
BWANT	Beiträge zur Wissenschaft vom Alten (und Neuen) Testament
BZ	*Biblische Zeitschrift*
BZAR	Beihefte zur Zeitschrift für altorientalische und biblische Rechtsgeschichte
BZAW	Beihefte zur Zeitschrift für die alttestamentliche Wissenschaft
CAT	Commentaire de l'Ancien Testament
CBET	Contributions to Biblical Exegesis and Theology

ConBOT	Coniectanea Biblica
DJD	Discoveries in the Judaean Desert
ECC	Eerdmans Critical Commentary
EstBib	*Estudios bíblicos*
EvT	*Evangelische Theologie*
FAT	Forschungen zum Alten Testament
FB	Forschung zur Bibel
FRLANT	Forschungen zur Religion und Literatur des Alten und Neuen Testaments
GKC	Kautzsch, Emil, ed. *Gesenius' Hebrew Grammar*. Translated by Arther E. Cowley. 2nd ed. Oxford: Clarendon, 1910.
HAT	Handbuch zum Alten Testament
HBS	History of Biblical Studies
HeBAI	*Hebrew Bible and Ancient Israel*
HEN	*Henoch*
HKAT	Handkommentar zum Alten Testament
HTR	*Harvard Theological Review*
IEKAT	International Exegetical Commentary on the Old Testament
KeH	Kurzgefasstes exegetisches Handbuch zum Alten Testament
KHC	Kurzer Hand-Commentar zum Alten Testament
JAJ	*Journal of Ancient Judaism*
JBT	*Jahrbuch für biblische Theologie*
JDT	*Jahrbuch für deutsche Theologie*
JPSTC	Jewish Publication Society Torah Commentary Series
JSJSup	Journal for the Study of Judaism Supplement Series
JSNTSup	Journal for the Study of the New Testament Supplement Series
JSOTSup	Journal for the Study of the Old Testament Supplement Series
JTPh	*Jahrbücher für protestantische Theologie*
Jub.	Jubilees
LHBOTS	Library of Hebrew Bible/Old Testament Studies
LXX	Septuagint
MT	Masoretic Text
NICOT	New International Commentary on the Old Testament
OBO	Orbis Biblicus et Orientalis

Abbreviations

ÖBS	Österreichische biblische Studien
OTL	Old Testament Library
OTS	*Oudtestamentische Studiën*
RB	*Revue biblique*
RBS	Resources for Biblical Studies
RGG	Betz, Hans Dieter, ed. *Religion in Geschichte und Gegenwart.* 4th ed. Tübingen: Mohr Siebeck, 1998–2007.
RHPR	*Revue d'histoire et de philosophie religieuses*
SamPent	Samaritan Pentateuch
SBAB	Stuttgarter biblische Aufsatzbände
SBS	Stuttgarter Bibelstudien
SCS	Septuagint and Cognate Studies
SEÅ	*Svensk exegetisk årsbok*
Sem	*Semitica*
ST	*Studia Theologica*
StudBib	Studia Biblica
SymS	Symposium Series
TB	Theologische Bücherei: Neudrucke und Berichte aus dem 20. Jahrhundert
TDOT	Botterweck, G. Johannes, and Helmer Ringgren, eds. *Theological Dictionary of the Old Testament.* Translated by John T. Willis et al. 8 vols. Grand Rapids: Eerdmans, 1974–2006.
TP	*Theologie und Philosophie*
TRE	Krause, Gerhard, and Gerhard Müller, eds. *Theologische Realenzyklopädie.* Berlin: de Gruyter, 1977.
TRu	*Theologische Rundschau*
TT	Theologisch Tijdschrift
UTB	Uni-Taschenbücher
VGTh	Veröffentlichungen der Wissenschaftlichen Gesellschaft für Theologie
VT	*Vetus Testamentum*
VTSup	Supplements to Vetus Testamentum
WBC	Word Bible Commentary
WMANT	Wissenschaftliche Monographien zum Alten und Neuen Testament
ZAR	*Zeitschhrift für Altorientalische und Biblische Rechtsgeschichte*
ZAW	*Zeitschrift für die alttestamentliche Wissenschaft*

xii Abbreviations

ZBK.AT	Zürcher Bibelkommentare Alten Testament
ZKT	*Zeitschrift für katholische Theologie*
ZTK	Zeitschrift für Theologie und Kirche

The Priestly Writing as a Source: A Recollection

Christoph Levin

The subtitle "a recollection" permits the following to be read either as an obituary of the Priestly writing as a source of the Pentateuch or as a view toward its revival. Both readings can be justified. That this essay is no more than a recollection further indicates that there is nothing new to be said. After two and a half centuries of modern research all conceivable arguments have been brought to the table.

1. The Problem of the Documentary Hypothesis

When the research community was celebrating the 250th anniversary of Robert Lowth's *De sacra poesi* and Jean Astruc's *Conjectures* in 2003,[1] Rudolf Smend said the following in a ceremonial address:

> The books of the two illustrious dilettanti contain ... two discoveries that are so obvious that one wonders why they had to be made at all...: in Lowth's, the discovery of the *parallelismus membrorum* ... as the main feature of Hebrew poetry; in Astruc's, the discovery that in Genesis two sources [*mémoires*] can be separated by the fact that they have different names for God, Elohim/God being the one, Jehovah/Yahweh/the Lord the other.[2]

---

1. Robert Lowth, *De sacra poesi Hebræorum prælectiones academicæ Oxonii habitæ* (Oxford: Clarendon, 1753); Jean Astruc, *Conjectures sur les mémoires originaux Dont il paroit que Moyse s'est servi pour composer le livre de la Genese: Avec des remarques, qui appuient ou qui éclaircissent ces Conjectures* (Paris: Fricx, 1753).

2. Rudolf Smend, "Das alte Israel im Alten Testament," in *Bibel und Wissenschaft: Historische Aufsätze* (Tübingen: Mohr Siebeck, 2004), 1–14, esp. 1 (my translation).

One of these two conclusive facts, the *parallelismus membrorum*, has not, at least for now, been called into question. The same cannot be said for the Documentary Hypothesis.

The problem of the Documentary Hypothesis was and remains that it is so obvious. This has hampered the appreciation of the fact that the combination of two (or more) large narrative works can only have been an exception in the literary history of the Old Testament and presupposes exceptional, unrepeatable circumstances.

Since the (older) Documentary Hypothesis is so clearly apparent in Genesis and especially the primeval history, one did not always take sufficient note of the historical and literary-technical preconditions this hypothesis necessarily requires. Even today, it can happen that the real or apparent self-evidence of a critical analysis causes us to forget the synthesis this invariably implies. This synthesis, however, is crucial in supplying a frame to the analysis. No matter how convincing it may seem, an analysis that cannot be made plausible from the point of view of the scribes and disregards their literary means and their theological and historiographic aims is worthless.

A closer look at the beginnings of modern Pentateuch criticism reveals that all proposals presented were originally more nuanced than they may appear in hindsight. The text never submitted to the simplistic game of J-E-P that older exegesis is generally accused of. Even the oldest versions of the Documentary Hypothesis as formulated by Astruc and Johann Gottfried Eichhorn depended on the Fragmentary Hypothesis. As such they were, at least as far as the two pre-Mosaic histories are concerned (which correspond more or less to what we today call "Priestly writing" [P] and "Yahwist" [J]), hypotheses similar to those that are current in exegesis today.[3] It was not P and J (as later research has called them) that were the "documents" of the older Documentary Hypothesis but the sources used by P and J. Just like the idea of *Elohist as narrator*, the Yahwist as narrator is a creation only of the nineteenth century and has, like the former, come to be exposed as a "wrong track of Pentateuch criticism."[4]

---

3. In Astruc's view, the authors of the two great histories A and B integrated a great number of independent literary documents into their works. He further assumed ten additional fragments that he declined to assign to either A or B because the criterion of the divine names was not applicable. He called them C (in the flood narrative) or D. A similar approach was taken by Johann Gottfried Eichhorn, *Einleitung ins Alte Testament*, 3 vols. (Leipzig: Weidmann & Reich, 1780–1783), 2:294–381.

4. See Paul Volz and Wilhelm Rudolph, *Der Elohist als Erzähler: Ein Irrweg der*

The Priestly Writing as a Source: A Recollection   3

2. Ilgen and de Wette: Documentary or Supplementary Hypothesis

Karl David Ilgen, who made great advances in identifying the documents in Genesis, remarked already in 1798 that:

> Discerning and separating out the documents the first book of Moses is compiled out of is such a distinct business, and so unique in its nature, that no pursuit of that form of criticism which is known as the *higher* is comparable.[5]

It was, however, Ilgen himself, who set the wrong course in increasing the number of sources. His exegetical ensemble consisted of a compilator and seventeen documents, which he assigned to three authors, in place of the two identified by Astruc and Eichhorn:

> All the dissected parts I have combined into *seventeen* self-sufficient documents, of which *ten* belong to [Eliel] Harischon, *five* to Eliel Haschscheni, and *two* to Elijah Harischon.[6]

By distinguishing between *Eliel Harischon* and *Eliel Haschscheni*, Ilgen anticipated the later distinction between Priestly writing and Elohist, though he assigned the textual material differently. The third author, *Elijah Harischon*, corresponds to the later Jehovist or Yahwist. Moreover, Ilgen completed his puzzle by adding in the option of a second Yahwist, Elijah Haschscheni, even if this figure remained a theoretical one.

The ten documents of the first first Elohist—that is, the Priestly writing (in later terms)—follow the *toledot*-formula in Genesis. Five documents

---

Pentateuchkritik? An der Genesis erläutert, BZAW 63 (Gießen: Töpelmann, 1933). That this implies "the definitive 'farewell to the Yahwist,'" as has been claimed by Erhard Blum, "Die literarische Verbindung von Erzvätern und Exodus," in *Abschied vom Jahwisten: Die Komposition des Hexateuch in der jüngsten Diskussion*, ed. Jan Christian Gertz, Konrad Schmid, and Markus Witte, BZAW 315 (Berlin: De Gruyter, 2002), 119–56, esp. 121, is the most recent wrong track ("Irrweg") in Pentateuch criticism.

5. Karl David Ilgen, *Die Urkunden des Jerusalemischen Tempelarchivs in ihrer Urgestalt*, vol. 1 (Halle: Hemmerde & Schwetschke, 1798), 341 (my translation). On Ilgen, see Bodo Seidel, *Karl David Ilgen und die Pentateuchforschung im Umkreis der sogenannten Älteren Urkundenhypothese*, BZAW 213 (Berlin: De Gruyter, 1993).

6. Ilgen, *Urkunden*, 494: "Ich habe die sämmtlichen zerlegten Theile zu *siebzehn* für sich bestehenden Urkunden verbunden, davon *zehn* Harischon, *fünf* Eliel Haschscheni, und *zwey* Elijah Harischon gehören." He means: "zehn *Eliel* Harischon."

4   Christoph Levin

are given to the second Elohist, including the entire non-Priestly text of the primeval history, and two to the Jehovist. The first Jehovist document begins with Gen 12 and ends with Gen 33, while the second consists of Gen 38. The story of Joseph is divided between the two Elohists. In sum, that once again means that the Documentary Hypothesis merges with the Fragmentary Hypothesis. For Ilgen, the source writings derive not from authors in the strict sense but from collectors and compilers—or, one could say, from redactors.

That said, the methodological constraints become visible in the details. A good example is Ilgen's treatment of the scheme of seven days in the first creation account—specifically the account's orientation toward the Sabbath, which Werner Carl Ludewig Ziegler and Johann Philipp Gabler had identified as the product of literary reworking.[7] In assigning this revision to the second Elohist, Ilgen used the Documentary Hypothesis to guide his interpretation, rather than applying the Supplementary Hypothesis, as would have been appropriate.[8] To do so, he had to assume that the majority of the supposed document is lost in the chapter. Such *argumenta e silentio* later became common among scholars separating sources.

Ilgen's *Urkunden des Jerusalemischen Tempelarchivs* was followed by Wilhelm Martin Leberecht de Wette's *Kritik der Mosaischen Geschichte*. De Wette is considered the originator of the Supplementary Hypothesis. He disputed that the change from Elohim to Yahweh could be used as a criterion in distinguishing documents: "The names Elohim and Jehovah are not the distinguishing property of two different writers but probably of two different periods or religious schools."[9] The power of Ilgen's main criterion, which was based on Astruc's discovery and had been popularized by Eichhorn, had thus been dampened. In its place, de Wette now for the first time based himself on the work we now call the Priestly writing.

---

7. Werner Carl Ludewig Ziegler, "Kritik über den Artikel von der Schöpfung nach unserer gewöhnlichen Dogmatik," in *Magazin für Religionsphilosophie, Exegese und Kirchengeschichte*, ed. Heinrich Philipp Conrad Henke, vol. 2 (Helmstädt: Fleckeisen, 1794), 1–113; Johann Philipp Gabler, *Neuer Versuch über die Mosaische Schöpfungsgeschichte aus der höhern Kritik: Ein Nachtrag zum ersten Theil seiner Ausgabe der Eichhorn'schen Urgeschichte* (Altdorf: Monath & Kußler, 1795).

8. See Christoph Levin, "Tatbericht und Wortbericht in der priesterschriftlichen Schöpfungserzählung," *ZTK* 91 (1994): 115–33.

9. Wilhelm Martin Leberecht de Wette, *Kritik der Mosaischen Geschichte*, vol. 2 of *Beiträge zur Einleitung in das Alte Testament* (Halle: Schimmelpfennig, 1807), 29–30 (my translation).

The Priestly Writing as a Source: A Recollection 5

Genesis and the beginning of Exodus are originally based on an original whole, a kind of epic poem, that, earlier than almost all other pieces and at the same time the original of these, as it were, served as a the foundation to the collection of documents about this part of the history, to which the others are added on as explications or supplements. This we must seek to emphasize and characterize. If we are successful, this will shed light on the other pieces appended to it; we will understand those only through this.[10]

However, de Wette was not able to make the Priestly writing plausible as the basic text of the entire Pentateuch, a fact Hermann Hupfeld later drew attention to.

With true critical caution and austerity, he [de Wette] confined himself to pursuing the *Urschrift* he sought only in *broad strokes* and in its *sure* traces, without attempting, as usual, a complete assignment of the individual parts, which at that stage could not be achieved without arbitrariness and vague conjectures; as such, he assigned to the *Urschrift*, besides the main stages—creation, deluge, and the call of Abraham— and the tribal registers that fill the gaps, with certainty only chapter 23; 35:9–15; 46:2ff; 48:1–7; 49:29–33; 50:12, 13 (also, as it seems, the Elohim source of the Joseph-story ...). From this he distinguishes with fine sense ... later *imitations* and *embellishments....* And certainly the form of the *Urschrift* would have emerged even more definitely from these and other utterances of that first work even then, if that had been his goal and his intention had not chiefly been to prove the mythical (unhistorical) character of the narration.[11]

De Wette had no interest in literary history in the narrow sense. He was primarily focused on defining the *genre* of the Mosaic story, that is, on demonstrating that it was not a historical source in the strict sense but a myth. As such, he was able to confine himself, after Gen 17, to a rather general treatment of the text.

The Supplementary Hypothesis had a strong impact on Heinrich Ewald, Friedrich Tuch, August Knobel, and others.[12] In the preface to his

---

10. De Wette, *Kritik der Mosaischen Geschichte*, 28–29.

11. Hermann Hupfeld, *Die Quellen der Genesis und die Art ihrer Zusammensetzung* (Berlin: Wiegandt & Grieben, 1853), 3–4 (my translation).

12. Heinrich Ewald, *Die Komposition der Genesis kritisch untersucht* (Braun-

6   Christoph Levin

Genesis commentary, Knobel describes the supposed foundational text ("Grundschrift") as follows:

> The ancient document, on which the books of Moses and Joshua are founded, easily reveals itself to the critical eye by its firm purpose and plan and its invariably stable manner and language. In my view, it can be detected with some certainty, especially since it seems to be fully preserved with the exception of a small number of statements. The business of criticism is more challenging by far, however, for those pieces, which have been added to the old *Grundschrift* by the editor's hand. They show no such unity as do the parts of the *Grundschrift*.[13]

The disposition of the Pentateuch could thus most easily be explained by a single document that was later supplemented. The elegant simplicity of this explanation caused the obvious gaps of the *Grundschrift* to be tolerated. Here lies the key weakness of the Supplementary Hypothesis.

3. Hupfeld and Nöldeke: The Newer Documentary Hypothesis

As a result, the Documentary Hypothesis gained the upper hand once more, and it was Hermann Hupfeld (1853) who set the course. He turned the three writers Ilgen had posited into three sources. The first crucial prerequisite for his hypothesis was that Hupfeld developed the profile of the "Urschrift," as he now judiciously called what is today the Priestly writing, with greater precision, in order to separate from it the text of the other documents, which we now call Elohist and Yahwist.

> Such is the *first* task of this work, which has the purpose first and, on the one hand, of *proving a number of previously overlooked parts of the Urschrift* and in doing so establish their coherence; on the other hand, and primarily, of *rejecting a number of later pieces with which it has been wrongly burdened* and thereby to free its image of foreign traits and establish it in its *purity*. This is followed by a *second*: the study of the *later sources*, especially of the pieces designated by the name *Yhvh*, of their historical character and connections, as well as the mode by which

---

schweig: Ludwig Lucius, 1823); Friedrich Tuch, *Kommentar über die Genesis* (Halle: Buchhandlung des Waisenhauses, 1838).

13. August Knobel, *Die Genesis erklärt* (Leipzig: Hirzel, 1852), from the preface (my translation).

The Priestly Writing as a Source: A Recollection   7

they were assembled into a whole together with the *Urschrift*, that is, the mode of *redaction*.[14]

Hupfeld clearly rejected the Supplementary Hypothesis:

> In this quest for unity and simplification of the process of composition and redaction of the components, one has now come to assume in the Pentateuch … only *one single* independent *written source*, the *Urschrift Elohim*, and to assign the *Yhvhistic* components—apart from a few special documents—to the *redactor*, or rather *author* of the book itself, who supplemented the basic document, that is, extended and embellished it according to later points of view and needs, and thus created the present work; he is hence called after this activity the *"supplementer"*.… It is the natural impetus and consequence of this view, that first, as the gaze seeks everywhere after connection, relation and relationship, the *peculiarities* and *differences* are easily *overlooked* or neglected; and second, that involuntarily the impact of the *Yhvhist* as supplementer is supposed to be as *slight and insignificant as possible*: because additions that contain indispensable constituents of the story or substantial deviations from the written source available to him (as well as, on the other side, mere repetitions of what is said) would prove damaging to his character as a mere supplementer and make the whole assumption unlikely. For this double reason one cannot avoid *burdening the Urschrift with as much and as diverse material as possible*.[15]

Hupfeld recognized that in order to make the Supplementary Hypothesis possible at all, the Priestly writing had been assigned too much text and its profile effaced in the process.

Hupfeld's skill is apparent in the fact that he not only separated the documents but also considered their mode of composition at the same time:

> In general, the redaction of Genesis from the three established documents is comparable to the project of composing a *gospel harmony* out of the gospels, especially the first three, as was attempted already early on; and had the sources from which they are composed been lost and forgotten, the case would be quite the same. But the fact that the project in our book was not unsuccessful is proved already by the fact that it has for so long hidden its origin from such diverse component parts and

---

14. Hupfeld, *Die Quellen der Genesis*, 5.
15. Hupfeld, *Die Quellen der Genesis*, 78–79.

8   Christoph Levin

could be regarded as a unified work and is still considered such by many to this day; and yet, at the same time, it has made it possible to recent criticism to separate the sources woven together in it more or less clearly and exactly.[16]

This comparison to Tatian's gospel harmony has since been occasionally repeated, with particular emphasis by Herbert Donner.[17]

Hupfeld's impact was significant. Theodor Nöldeke, who is generally seen as a key figure in identifying the Priestly writing, followed his work,[18] as did later Abraham Kuenen and Julius Wellhausen. Ever unpretentious, Kuenen describes the Priestly writing of the Documentary Hypothesis as follows:

> We have no difficulty in discovering in certain Elohîm-passages in Genesis the now scattered segments of a systematic work that begins with the creation in six days, followed by a genealogy from Adam to Noah; describes the deluge and the covenant of Elohîm with Noah and his posterity; passes by another genealogy (from Shem to Terah) on to the tribal fathers of Israel, Abram, Isaac, and Jacob; and continues their history down to the death of Jacob in Egypt. All this has come down to us nearly, but not quite, complete. There are some few verses and passages of which we cannot yet determine whether they do or do not belong to the work, for it is only the study of the other elements of the Hexateuch and of the method of its redaction that can settle the point. But, generally speaking, the now scattered portions so obviously belong to each other and resemble each other so closely in language, style, and character that there is no room for the smallest doubt as to their common origin, so that, in point of fact, almost complete agreement exists on the subject.[19]

---

16. Hupfeld, *Die Quellen der Genesis*, 195.

17. Herbert Donner, "Der Redaktor: Überlegungen zum vorkritischen Umgang mit der Heiligen Schrift," *Hen* 2 (1980): 1–29.

18. Theodor Nöldeke, "Die s. g. Grundschrift des Pentateuchs," in *Untersuchungen zur Kritik des Alten Testaments* (Kiel: Schwers'sche Buchhandlung, 1869), 1–144.

19. Abraham Kuenen, *An Historical-Critical Inquiry into the Origin and Composition of the Hexateuch*, trans. Philip H. Wicksteed (London: Macmillan, 1886), 65–66. Dutch original: Kuenen, *De Thora en de historische boeken des Ouden Verbonds*, vol. 1 of *Historisch-critisch onderzoek naar het ontstaan en de verzameling van de boeken des Ouden Verbonds*, 2nd ed. (Leiden: Engels, 1885), 66.

The Priestly Writing as a Source: A Recollection 9

4. Wellhausen and Kuenen: From the Supplementary Hypothesis to the Documentary Hypothesis (and Back Again)

In 1871, Wellhausen drew not on Hupfeld but on his teacher Ewald and thus on the Supplementary Hypothesis:

> Also in the Pentateuch no two or more large historical works with the same subject were originally written independently of each other, so that the later takes no note of the earlier. Instead, partly smaller pieces were attached to a core, in which for the first time the hitherto isolated oral and written stories had been joined together ..., partly the whole was reworked in light of this new connection, perhaps in such a way that it itself in its essential content remained incorporated into the new edition right from the start, or in such a way that only the basic elements of its plan were significant for the latter, which made it possible for a later redactor to combine the old and the new—there is much to be said for both possibilities.[20]

If Wellhausen was soon to abandon the Supplementary Hypothesis, this was due less to insights gained from literary history and more to his interest in the history of religion. Since the Priestly writing was the youngest element of the Pentateuch, as Wellhausen had undertaken to show, it could not have acted as the *Grundschrift* for the literary history of the text. The text needed a new foundation. This was provided by the other sources, as offered by Hupfeld. Wellhausen merely changed the sequence: instead of P-E-J, it became J-E-P. Since Deuteronomy (Dt) was able to act as the fulcrum in the history of tradition, it was assigned a key role in the argument.

In 1877 Wellhausen summarized his views in his *Composition des Hexateuchs* before embarking on his *Geschichte Israels I*, from 1878, which he called *Prolegomena zur Geschichte Israels* from the second edition onward.

> Having reached the conclusion of my investigation, I shall briefly summarize its results once more. From J and E derived JE, and Deuteronomy was later connected with JE; an independent work beside it is Q.[21] Extended into the Priestly writing, Q is now united with JE + Dt and this created the Hexateuch. For the sake of simplicity, I usu-

---

20. Julius Wellhausen, *Der Text der Bücher Samuelis* (Göttingen: Vandenhoeck & Ruprecht, 1871), x–xi, my translation.

21. Q (*liber quattuor foederum* = book of four covenants) was Wellhausen's first

10 Christoph Levin

ally abstract from the fact that the literary process was in effect more complicated, and the so-called Supplementary Hypothesis therefore does still find its application in a subordinate manner. J and E probably experienced several enlarged editions (J¹ J² J³, E¹ E² E³) and were worked together not as J¹ and E¹ but as J³ and E³; the same applies to JE, Dt, and Q, before they were combined with the larger entities in question. But I am convinced that, apart from Deuteronomy, there are only three independent writings that fully presented the matter, J and E and Q. Admittedly, I have not succeeded in following the thread of J and E through the whole.[22]

In university textbooks, this is usually given in a shortened and simplified form. This obscures the extent to which the Supplementary Hypothesis remained significant to Wellhausen. After all, Wellhausen willingly corrected himself in an exchange with Kuenen:

> I am by no means wedded to the views I expressed about the composition of the Hexateuch—except for the principle that except for the main sources there were all kinds of excrescences, that the Supplementary Hypothesis can be justified, and that the mechanical mosaic hypothesis is absurd. Kuenen's essays are corrections in line with my own intentions; in this respect, I admit all he says, even what he did not yet say.[23]

What this can mean for the analysis of the texts can be observed by looking at the supplements added to the *Die Composition des Hexateuchs* in 1885. There the Supplementary Hypothesis is extensively used:

> I have been led by textual criticism to literary criticism, because it turned out that sometimes there was no boundary to be found between where the glossator's work ceased and that of the literator began. Already early on, this made me suspicious of the manner in which the Hebrew history books were regarded as a mere mosaic…. In examining the composition of the Hexateuch, I realized that there are indeed three independent narrative threads running through it, but that these grand arcs have not merely been cut to size and lightly sewn up but have, before, upon,

---

siglum for the Priestly writing; see Julius Wellhausen, "Die Composition des Hexateuchs," *JDT* 21 (1876): 392–450; *JDT* 22 (1877): 407–79, esp. 392.

22. Wellhausen, "Die Composition des Hexateuchs," 478–79 (my translation).

23. Julius Wellhausen to Adolf Jülicher, 8 November 1880, published in *Briefe*, ed. Rudolf Smend (Tübingen: Mohr Siebeck, 2013), 78 (no. 94) (trans. Margaret Kohl).

The Priestly Writing as a Source: A Recollection   11

and after their unification (which did not occur at the same time), been greatly increased and revised, that, in other words, the literary process by which the Hexateuch originated was very complicated and that the so-called Supplementary Hypothesis does indeed find its application though in a different sense than originally formulated. However, the last layer of sediment, which superficially covers the whole bedload, I have not properly appreciated, at least in the narrative parts, especially where it is strikingly prominent. Here Kuenen has, as I have already gratefully said elsewhere, freed me from the leftover remnants of the old leaven of the mechanical separation of the sources.[24]

With regard to the text's composition, Wellhausen maintained the notion that P acted as its basis. In doing so, he recognized that the nature of the sources and their relative age are not necessarily connected. He further saw the difference between the history of tradition and the history of religion, on the one hand, and the place of the sources in the text's redaction history, on the other. All in all, however, literary history was a means to an end to him, as it had been for de Wette: a way of reconstructing history and history of religion.

5. Budde and Smend: The Newest Documentary Hypothesis

Wellhausen's rejection of the "mechanical mosaic hypothesis" has not prevented others from using his observations to separate the sources with greater precision. One example, itself a book with admirable exegetic acumen, is Karl Budde's *Urgeschichte* of 1883.[25] Budde wanted to penetrate the complex literary-historical process by using the example of Gen 1–11 and to establish Wellhausen's hypothetical entities J^1 J^2 J^3 as precisely as possible. In doing so, he made a wealth of apt observations. But whenever he merged the Supplementary and Documentary Hypotheses and combined the sequence of the versions with some sort of concurrency, in such a way that the differently edited versions had later been combined into a new literary whole, he went too far.[26]

---

24. Julius Wellhausen, *Die Composition des Hexateuchs* (Berlin: Reimer, 1885), 314–15 (my translation).

25. Karl Budde, *Die Biblische Urgeschichte (Gen. 1–12, 5) untersucht* (Gießen: Ricker, 1883).

26. Budde later proceeded similarly in his analyses of Judges and Samuel. See Karl Budde, *Die Bücher Richter und Samuel, ihre Quellen und ihr Aufbau* (Gießen: Ricker,

12   Christoph Levin

Wellhausen voiced his opinion of Budde's approach in a letter to William Robertson Smith:

> I find Pentateuch criticism the more repugnant the more people generally are grimly determined to undertake it. It is really high time that they were offered some other subject. I do not much care for Budde's analysis of Gen 1 ff. either, even in its refined form. The very fact that the matter is probably so extremely complicated, should make one modest in one's claims. But Kuenen seems delighted with the book.[27]

In his great commentary on Genesis (1st ed. 1901; 3rd ed. 1910), Hermann Gunkel separated the sources using a "zipper principle" that often produced implausible results in terms of literary history. A drastic example are the nine verses of the tower of Babel narrative (Gen 11:1–9), which he divided into two parallel sources: a city recension that ended in the confusion of the languages and a tower narrative that told of the dispersion of mankind across the earth.[28]

In his 1912 *Erzählung des Hexateuch*, Rudolf Smend Sr. understood the composition of continuous narratives that were intended to supersede their older predecessors and nevertheless were later combined with them as the rule:

> The compilation of the younger narrative works with the older ones was not intended by their authors. Of course, J^2 was dependent on J^1, and E dependent on J, but J^2 wanted to replace J^1, and E the compilation J. Nonetheless, J^2 was compiled with J^1 and E with J. This peculiar process has been repeated in the history of the Hexateuch ever since.[29]

The result can be best observed in Otto Eißfeldt's *Hexateuch-Synopse* of 1922. Eißfeldt took Smend's results and presented them in synoptic columns. The method is strikingly mechanical:

1890); Budde, *Das Buch der Richter erklärt*, KHC 7 (Tübingen: Mohr Siebeck, 1897); Budde, *Die Bücher Samuel erklärt*, KHC 8 (Tübingen: Mohr Siebeck, 1902).

27. Julius Wellhausen to William Robertson Smith, 30 December 1883, published in Smend, *Briefe*, 138 (no. 177) (trans. Margaret Kohl).

28. Hermann Gunkel, *Genesis Translated and Interpreted*, trans. Mark E. Biddle (Macon, GA: Mercer University Press, 1997), 94–95.

29. Rudolf Smend, *Die Erzählung des Hexateuch auf ihre Quellen untersucht* (Berlin: Reimer, 1912), 342–33 (my translation).

The Priestly Writing as a Source: A Recollection 13

In the Hexateuch, with D excluded once again, one can point to about fifty passages, in which fourfold elements appear; if one succeeds in arranging these fifty times four items into four rows of items, or rather, if comprehensive observation of the facts urges one toward this order; and if in the process the whole substance of the Hexateuch is almost completely used up: then the assumption of a fourfold narrative thread may be considered proven.[30]

If one reads the parallel columns that result from these premises, one will find many cases in which a meaningful narrative sequence fails to emerge. Contrary to its intent, the Hexateuch synopsis fails to demonstrate the documentary hypothesis and in fact involuntarily provides a counter-argument.

6. From Klostermann to Blum: A Farewell to the Priestly Writing

In the meantime, Wellhausen's opponents had sounded the charge. The first victim was the Priestly writing. Its late dating by Karl Heinrich Graf, Kuenen, and Wellhausen would, sooner or later, call into question its status as the *Grundschrift* in the literary history,[31] and the lack of continuous literary coherence is much more evident in P than in J. In 1893, August Klostermann voiced his opinion quite clearly:

I think it is among the most brilliant attestations of his taste and his fine sense of the natural that Wellhausen finally admitted that the narrative of Q, as criticism has unearthed it, did not exist for itself and could be explained only by its direct relation to the Jehovist narrative, moreover,

---

30. Otto Eißfeldt, *Hexateuch-Synopse: Die Erzählung der fünf Bücher Mose und des Buches Josua mit dem Anfange des Richterbuches* (Leipzig: Hinrichs, 1922), 6 (my translation).

31. Upon closer inspection, the foundations of this were laid already by Karl Heinrich Graf, when he drew conclusions for the narrative of the Pentateuch from the proof that the laws of the Priestly writing are to be dated late (Karl Heinrich Graf, "Die Bestandtheile der geschichtlichen Bücher von Genes. 1 bis 2 Reg. 25 [Pentateuch und Prophetae priores]," in *Die geschichtlichen Bücher des Alten Testaments: Zwei historisch-kritische Untersuchungen* [Leipzig: Weigel, 1866], 1–113; Graf, "Die s. g. Grundschrift des Pentateuchs," in *Archiv für wissenschaftliche Erforschung des Alten Testamentes*, ed. Adalbert Merx, vol. 1 [Halle: Buchhandlung des Waisenhauses, 1869], 466–77). He nevertheless maintained the term *Grundschrift*: "This solution is simply that the so-called *Grundschrift* text forms that part of the Pentateuch that was added last and with the insertion of which the redaction was completed" (468, my translation).

14 Christoph Levin

that what was omitted from Q by R and replaced with elements from JE was parallel to these and probably not much different from them.[32]

Once again, the Supplementary Hypothesis comes into play, with JE now acting as *Grundschrift*. Klostermann was not to remain a solitary voice. In 1908, Bernardus D. Eerdmans in Leiden contended:

> The so-called Priestly, historical-legislative writing, which began with Gen 1, demands much in the way of critical good faith. It seems quite peculiar that such great agreement has been reached precisely in distinguishing these Priestly parts.[33]

> The so-called P-elements are not fragmented parts of a certain writing but traditions of various origins, which cannot be plausibly said to have been assembled by a priestly, exilic, or postexilic writer as an introduction to a legal work.[34]

Johannes Dahse (1912) also attempted to make the Supplementary Hypothesis plausible for the Priestly writing:

> Surely there can no longer be any doubt that our compiler and exegete is Esra the scribe who made "the book" suitable for the practice of preaching at the service. He was concerned not with adding something new to the traditional scripture but to "clarify the meaning so as one might understand what had been read'" [cf. Neh 8:8] and that the community would be edified by it. *Genesis, as we now have it, is an adaptation of an older narrative type for the purposes of worship; in most of the so-called P-fragments, but also in other sentences, we are dealing, as it were, with liturgical frills....* In conclusion, I may be permitted to draw on the analogy that would arise in our German Bibles if the chapter headings were to be rendered unrecognizable as such and printed together with the rest of the text. Then a new "P" would be created in our Bibles.[35]

---

32. August Klostermann, *Der Pentateuch: Beiträge zu seinem Verständnis und seiner Entstehungsgeschichte* (Leipzig: Deichert, 1893), 10 (my translation).

33. Bernardus D. Eerdmans, *Die Komposition der Genesis.* Vol. 1 of *Alttestamentliche Studien* (Gießen: Töpelmann, 1908), 2 (my translation).

34. Eerdmans, *Die Komposition der Genesis*, 33 (my translation).

35. Johannes Dahse, "P in Genesis 12–50," in *Textkritische Materialien zur Hexateuchfrage*, vol. 1 (Gießen: Töpelmann 1912), 144–74, here 161–62 (my translation).

The Priestly Writing as a Source: A Recollection 15

Such a position is not altogether devoid of eccentricity, but the observations put forward still have some merit.

Another exponent of such criticism was Max Löhr (1924), who could already draw on Eißfeldt's Hexateuch synopsis:

> Finally, it is questionable whether what is ascribed to P in Genesis can really be taken out of its context and, however much the redactions may have suppressed, can be regarded as the substance, in content and arrangement, of an independent source text.... It seems more natural to me to suppose that the diverse material of Genesis, at least for the most part, is assembled for the first time by *one* man and his assistants, with a definite plan and a definite purpose, than to postulate the very complicated process of assembling a series of independent source texts.... There are also endless glosses and changes in detail.[36]

A similar line was taken by Paul Volz (1933), who regarded not only the Elohist but also the Priestly writing as a "wrong track of Pentateuch criticism":

> The theory of source separation assumes that, besides J and E, P too had provided a continuous narrative of the primeval history and the history of the patriarchs, so that a threefold (to some even a fourfold) work of parallel narratives existed and that in some stories J, E, and P are now intertwined. This assumption can hardly be maintained with regard to P, any more than that of the narrative work E. It can be only laboriously asserted even by the adherents of the source theory.[37]

Frank Moore Cross (1973) may serve as an important Anglophone voice here:

> The Priestly Work was composed by a narrow school or single tradent using many written and, no doubt, some oral documents. Most important among them was the Epic (JE) tradition. The Priestly strata of the Tetrateuch never existed as an independent narrative document. The Priestly tradent framed and systematized JE with Priestly lore, and, especially at points of special interest, greatly supplemented JE. The Priestly work had as its central goal the reconstruction of the covenant of Sinai

---

36. Max Löhr, *Der Priesterkodex in der Genesis*, vol. 1 of *Untersuchungen zum Hexateuchproblem*, BZAW 38 (Gießen: Töpelmann, 1924), 1, 30, 31 (my translation).

37. Paul Volz, "Anhang: P ist kein Erzähler," in Volz and Rudolph, *Der Elohist als Erzähler*, 135–42, here 135 (my translation).

16 Christoph Levin

and its associated institutions. At the same time, it was a program written in preparation for and in hope of the restoration of Israel.[38]

In his study of the patriarchal narrative, Erhard Blum (1984) argued:

> In fact, it seems quite astonishing to me that the textual material in Gen 12–50 that has been claimed for "P" did not lead to a general problematization or questioning of the hypothesis of an independent P-narrative. This rather more than thin and "patchy" thread … is a caricature of a narrative rather than a patriarchal story."[39]

These observations all support a Supplementary Hypothesis in the form of an edition.

7. Von Rad and Noth: From Tradition History to Redaction Criticism

The fact that the flaws of the P-hypothesis did not become ever more pronounced is probably due to the shift in interest toward the history of tradition, which dominated Old Testament studies from the 1920s onward. Once one had decided that the historiographical concept of the Pentateuch was based on orality and certain Sitze im Leben ("discursive frames"), the question as to why the hypothetical sources could have one and the same outline—which is most easily answered using the Supplementary Hypothesis—lost much of its urgency. The literary history was relegated to second string.

The "Short Historical Creed" (Deut 26:5b–9; 6:20–24; Josh 24:2b–13) Gerhard von Rad postulated as the reason for the uniform disposition of the Pentateuch sources soon turned out to be a late summary.[40] Even the

---

38. Frank Moore Cross, *Canaanite Myth and Hebrew Epic: Essays in the History of the Religion of Israel* (Cambridge, MA: Harvard University Press, 1973), 324–25.

39. Erhard Blum, *Die Komposition der Vätergeschichte*, WMANT 57 (Neukirchen-Vluyn: Neukirchener Verlag, 1984), 426–27 (my translation).

40. Gerhard von Rad, "The Form-Critical Problem of the Hetateuch" (1938), repr. in *From Genesis to Chronicles: Explorations in Old Testament Theology*, ed. E. W. Trueman Dicken (Minneapolis: Fortress, 2005), 1–58, esp. 3–7. See Leonhard Rost, "Das kleine geschichtliche Credo," in *Das kleine Credo und andere Studien zum Alten Testament* (Heidelberg: Quelle & Meyer, 1965), 11–25; Wolfgang Richter, "Beobachtungen zur theologischen Systembildung in der alttestamentlichen Literatur anhand des 'Kleinen geschichtlichen Credo,'" in *Wahrheit und Verkündigung: Michael Schmaus*

The Priestly Writing as a Source: A Recollection 17

entity G that Martin Noth envisaged behind J and E[41] has been laid to rest by the Elohist's gentle demise.[42] Since the 1960s at the latest, scholars had to focus on redaction history, as one can see already in Noth's work in 1943:

> The most important point to grasp, in my opinion, is that in terms of the overall structure of his narrative P unmistakably follows older tradition just as we have it in fixed literary form, primarily in J. This does not mean that J has to have been used by P as a literary *Vorlage*. The situation is rather that the structure of the tradition concerning the pre-history of Israel as we encounter it in J was undoubtedly determinative for P as he shaped his work.[43]

This shift toward redaction history then occurs explicitly with Hans Walter Wolff's *Kerygma des Jahwisten* (1964).[44]

8. The Dilemma of the Priestly Writing: Edition or Source?

In spite of the wealth of exegetic counter-arguments, the Priestly writing continues to be thought of by many as the "Archimedean point of Pentateuch scholarship."[45]

---

zum 70. Geburtstag, ed. Leo Scheffczyk et al., vol. 1 (Munich: Schöningh, 1967), 175–212; Brevard S. Childs, "Deuteronomic Formulae of the Exodus Traditions," in *Hebräische Wortforschung: Festschrift zum 80. Geburtstag von Walter Baumgartner*, ed. Benedikt Hartmann et al., VTSup 16 (Leiden: Brill, 1967), 30–39; Norbert Lohfink, "Zum 'kleinen geschichtlichen Credo' Dtn 26,5-9," *TP* 46 (1971): 19–39.

41. Martin Noth, *Überlieferungsgeschichte des Pentateuch* (Stuttgart: Kohlhammer, 1948), 40–44.

42. Volz and Rudolph, *Der Elohist als Erzähler*; Wilhelm Rudolph, *Der "Elohist" von Exodus bis Josua*, BZAW 68 (Berlin: Töpelmann, 1938).

43. Martin Noth, *The Chronicler's History*, trans. Hugh G. M. Williamson, JSOTSup 50 (Sheffield: JSOT Press, 1987), 136; German original: *Überlieferungsgeschichtliche Studien* (Halle: Niemeyer, 1943), 207.

44. Hans Walter Wolff, "Das Kerygma des Jahwisten" (1964), repr. in *Gesammelte Studien zum Alten Testament*, 2nd ed., TB 22 (Munich: Kaiser, 1973), 345–73.

45. Konrad Schmid, "Differenzierungen und Konzeptualisierungen der Einheit Gottes in der Religions- und Literaturgeschichte Israels," in *Der eine Gott und die Götter: Polytheismus und Monotheismus im antiken Israel*, ed. Manfred Oeming and Konrad Schmid, ATANT 82 (Zürich: Theologischer Verlag, 2003), 11–39, esp. 19.

18   Christoph Levin

> Since its critical separation out of the Pentateuch by Theodor Nöldeke, the Priestly writing (= P) has been the starting point and foundation of all literary-historical theorization of the Pentateuch. Establishing its relations to the nonpriestly pieces of the Pentateuch sets the course for their assessment.[46]

Ploughing on in a rut that should have been abandoned in the nineteenth century, scholars continue to insist that P is the *Grundschrift* and the remaining text is characterized by not being part of the Priestly writing.[47] In fact, however, the Priestly writing poses a dilemma so thorny, it can hardly be resolved.

(A) A number of established reasons make it difficult to accept the Priestly writing as an independent source.

(1) Its independence is called into question mainly by the fact that the narrative is not a continuous sequence. It presupposes significant amounts of material that is found only in the non-Priestly text: the destruction of Sodom (for Gen 19:29); the marriage of Isaac and Rebekah (for Gen 25:20); Jacob's wealth in flocks that he gained from Laban and his flight (for Gen 31:18); the story of Joseph and the move of Jacob's sons to Egypt (for Gen 37:2; 41:46; 46:6–7; 47:27–28).

Even if one presupposes that in these cases the redaction R^{JP} ignored the text of the Priestly writing in favor of the parallel account, keeping only the dates in Gen 16:16; 21:5; 25:26; 50:22, the supposed omission remains a serious flaw. Exegesis has long overlooked this problem with surprising ease by interpreting the Priestly writing as "the scarlet thread on which the pearls of JE are hung."[48]

> One of the most secure results of a literary-critical analysis of these books is that both in general and in matters of detail the redactor took the P-narrative as his starting point and worked the older sources into it. Whenever possible, this was done without anything being cut out, but

---

46. Eckart Otto, "Forschungen zur Priesterschrift," *TRu* 62 (1997): 1–50, here 1 (my translation).

47. The term *non-P* is now gaining traction mainly because one has grown so eager to avoid the term *Yahwist*. The cost this simplification incurs, in that such a negative definition is hardly satisfactory, especially given that it glosses over the complex literary evidence, is being paid with surprising willingness.

48. Julius Wellhausen, *Prolegomena to the History of Ancient Israel*, trans. J. Sutherland Black and Allan R. Menzies (Edinburgh: Black, 1885), 332.

The Priestly Writing as a Source: A Recollection   19

if the need arose the older sources were cut and rearranged in favour of the P-narrative which was being used as the basis. This method of the redactor, which is too well known to require any more precise exposition, was not only determinative for the combination of the sources in individual cases of greater or lesser significance. By extension, it was also responsible for the delimitation of the larger whole which emerged from this redactional process.[49]

It is not for nothing that these claims remain without a "precise exposition" that gives textual evidence to support them. In fact, the Priestly writing has substantial gaps in the patriarchal history. Without this history, however, the Priestly writing is unimaginable as an independent literary work, since it would lack the necessary literary coherence from the Creation to the Sinai.

(2) The thorniest problem is that essential information is not provided. An example is Moses, who suddenly appears in Exod 6:2 without having been introduced.

(B) On the other hand, is also impossible to read the Priestly writing as a mere supplement to the older, non-Priestly text. The most important arguments are as follows:

(1) The primeval history Gen 1–11 and the story of Moses's calling in Exod 6 up to and including the miracle at the sea in Exod 14 can be adequately understood only if one presupposes two parallel narratives. This has been demonstrated aplenty.[50]

(2) The Documentary Hypothesis clearly applies to the flood narrative in Gen 6–9 and the miracle at the sea in Exod 14.[51] Already Eichhorn began his attempt to prove that Genesis was a compound of two histor-

---

49. Noth, *Chronicler's History*, 138.

50. For the primeval history most recently in several contributions by Jan Christian Gertz, e.g., "Beobachtungen zum literarischen Charakter und zum geistesgeschichtlichen Ort der nichtpriesterschriftlichen Sintfluterzählung," in *Auf dem Weg zur Endgestalt von Genesis bis II Regum: Festschrift Hans-Christoph Schmitt*, ed. Martin Beck and Ulrike Schorn, BZAW 370 (Berlin: De Gruyter, 2006), 41–57; Gertz, "Source Criticism in the Primeval History of Genesis: An Outdated Paradigma for the Study of the Pentateuch?," in *The Pentateuch: International Perspectives on Current Research*, ed. Thomas B. Dozeman, Konrad Schmid, and Baruch J. Schwartz, FAT 78 (Tübingen: Mohr Siebeck, 2011), 169–80; Gertz, "The Formation of the Primeval History," in *The Book of Genesis: Composition, Reception, and Interpretation*, ed. Craig A. Evans, Joel N. Lohr, and David L. Petersen, VTSup 152 (Leiden: Brill, 2012), 107–36.

51. On Exod 14, see Christoph Levin, "Source Criticism: The Miracle at the Sea," in *Method Matters: Essays on the Interpretation of the Hebrew Bible in Honor of David*

20 Christoph Levin

ical works by discussing Gen 6–9.[52] The analysis of the flood narrative has since become ever more nuanced.[53] The best argument in favor of the Documentary Hypothesis is that those exegetes who wanted to make the Supplementary Hypothesis evident have taken both P and J (and vice versa) as either core or supplement. Either one doubts that the Priestly writing can provide an independent account, or one makes the same claim for the Yahwist's version.[54] There can be no stronger proof that two independent accounts have been combined here.

(3) In the account of the plague of frogs, there is a gap between Exod 8:3 and 11aβ. Such gaps, like the objectless reference to the act of building a window in the ark in the Yahwist's flood narrative (Gen 8:6b), provide strong evidence against the Supplementary Hypothesis. Not that they are fully preserved, but that they have been damaged in the process of merging the sources, most clearly demonstrates that the current text was preceded by two independent narrative works.

(4) In several cases where the P-thread is thin and has been mutilated in the process of merging the sources, it can nevertheless be traced with relative ease. The best examples are Abraham's journey and his separation from Lot (Gen 12:5; 13:6, 11b–12bα; 19:29abα) and the suffering of the Israelites in Egypt (Exod 1:13–14; 2:23aβ–25; 6:2ff.).

(5) A strong indicator in favor of former literary independence is that such fragments show traces of literary growth that is restricted specifically to this literary level. In the depiction of Abraham and Lot one reads:

L. Petersen, ed. Joel M. LeMon and Kent Harold Richards, RBS 56 (Atlanta, GA: Society of Biblical Literature, 2009), 39–61.

52. Eichhorn, *Einleitung ins Alte Testament*, 2:301–9, 311–18. The two creation accounts were not particularly significant to Eichhorn, since he considered Gen 2:4–3:24 a separate document, due to its use of the divine name "Yahweh Elohim": "Already the second chapter from the fourth verse and the third one make up a separate document."

53. See esp. Hupfeld, *Die Quellen der Genesis*, 6–16, 132–36; Eberhard Schrader, *Studien zur Kritik und Erklärung der biblischen Urgeschichte* (Zürich: Meyer & Zeller, 1863), 136–48; Budde, *Die biblische Urgeschichte*, 248–76; Gunkel, *Genesis Translated and Interpreted*, 138–42; Christoph Levin, *Der Jahwist*, FRLANT 157 (Göttingen: Vandenhoeck & Ruprecht, 1993), 112–14.

54. For arguments that the Priestly writing does not have an independent account, see Erhard Blum, *Studien zur Komposition des Pentateuch*, BZAW 189 (Berlin: De Gruyter, 1990), 281–85; and others. For the same claim about the Yahwist, see Jean Louis Ska, "El Relato des Diluvio: Un Relato Sacerdotal y Algunos Fragmentos Redaccionales Posteriores," *EstBib* 52 (1994): 37–62; and others.

The Priestly Writing as a Source: A Recollection

^{12:5} And[55] Abram took Sarai his wife, and Lot his brother's son, and all their possessions which they had gathered
and the persons that they had gotten
in Haran; and they set forth to go to the land of Canaan. And they came to the land of Canaan. ^{13:6} And the land could not support both of them dwelling together;
for their possessions were so great that they could not dwell together. ^{11b} Thus they separated from each other. ¹² Abram dwelt in the land of Canaan, while Lot dwelt among the cities of the Plain. ^{19:29} So it was that, when God destroyed the cities of the Plain, God remembered Abraham, and sent Lot out of the midst of the overthrow.[56]

The redundancies are not simply due to the style of the Priestly writing but derive from parentheses and restatements.

^{1:13} The Egyptians became ruthless in imposing tasks on the Israelites, ¹⁴ and made their lives bitter with hard service in mortar and brick and in every kind of field labour.
They were ruthless in all the tasks that they imposed on them. ^{2:23aβ} The Israelites groaned under their slavery, and cried out.
Out of the slavery their cry for help rose up to God. ²⁴ God heard their groaning, and God remembered his covenant with Abraham, Isaac, and Jacob. ²⁵ God looked upon the Israelites, and God took notice of them. ^{6:2} God spoke to Moses and said to him: I am Yahweh. ³ I appeared to Abraham, Isaac, and Jacob as El Shadday, but by my name Yahweh I did not make myself known to them.

Taken together, the arguments in favor of independence should outweigh the others not only in number, but also in their significance—unless, of course, one were to follow Erhard Blum, who considered the Priestly writing neither a source, nor an edition.[57] It is questionable, however,

---

55. The dating in Gen 12:4b is not necessarily part of the chronological system of the Priestly source. It may have been added after the sources were merged; see Smend, *Die Erzählung des Hexateuch*, 12.

56. Contrary to what is usually assumed, not all of verse Gen 19:29 is part of the Priestly writing. "The last part of the verse 'when he overthrew the cities where Lot had settled,' is a note on the first part of the verse." Verse 29bβγ is probably a parenthesis of redaction R[JP].

57. Blum, *Studien zur Komposition des Pentateuch*, 232. See also the considerations of Wellhausen above.

22 Christoph Levin

whether this response could provide a way out of the dilemma posed by
the literary history without ultimately abandoning the literary unity of
the Priestly writing.

9. The Priestly Writing as a Special Case of Tradition History

If the Priestly writing was once an independent account of the early history, it is exceptional in its relationship to the older tradition, since there
is no other case in the literary history of the Old Testament in which an
older tradition is replaced in this way: it is always continued, updated,
and supplemented to reflect the changed circumstances of the day.[58] What
could have caused the Priestly writing to be written as a new, alternative
account, rather than as a reworking of the existing one?

The only possible answer is that the conception of history that the
Priestly writing formulates involves such drastic change that it could not
simply be superimposed on the older account. As a first step, the reasons
that may have informed this new approach can be determined by elimination. They are not to be found in (1) the chronological system of the
Priestly writing. The system could have been added onto the older text
without difficulty and was indeed probably partly created this way.[59] They
are also not to be found in (2) the system of the *toledot*, which has not
unreasonably been claimed to have been layered on top of older narratives and genealogies and that is in some cases clearly secondary.[60] They
are not even to be found (3) in the promises made to Noah in Gen 9:9,
11b, to Abraham in Gen 17:7, and to Moses in Exod 6:5–7; 29:45–46, even
though these four promises of covenant provide a structure[61] with a theo-

---

58. This changes only with apocryphal books, such as the book of Jubilees. The
Chronicler's narrative that paralleled the Enneateuch may also fit here.

59. See Smend, *Die Erzählung des Hexateuch*, 14: "Originally, P had, at most, information about the age of the patriarchs, and even that is not necessary to assume.…
The world era of the Hexateuch … also requires a connection between the Hexateuch
and the books of Judges, Samuel, and Kings, which tell the story of Israel in chronological order."

60. Not in Gen 2:4a, but certainly in 10:1 and 36:9. See Smend, *Die Erzählung
des Hexateuch*, 16: "Given all this, the אלה ת' in Genesis derives in many places from
a glossator, who wanted to emphasize the genealogical structure of the Genesis narrative, but acted without the necessary rigor and prudence and occasionally put the
formula in the wrong place."

61. See Thomas Pola, *Die ursprüngliche Priesterschrift: Beobachtungen zur Liter-*

The Priestly Writing as a Source: A Recollection   23

logical significance that is most clearly evident in the independent Priestly writing. The addition of the covenant scene of Gen 15[62] shows that this covenant theology could have been introduced also into the older account.

There are two peculiarities of the Priestly writing that are incompatible with the older account, and these played a crucial part in separating the sources from the very beginning. The first is the step-by-step system of the revelation of God's name, beginning with Elohim in the primeval history, followed by El Shaddai in the patriarchal history from Gen 17[63] to the final revelation of the divine name Yahweh to Moses from Exod 6:2 on. These tiers could not have been realized on the basis of the older version; for in that, the Yahwist uses the divine name already in Gen 2:5, and Gen 4:26 clearly notes the beginning worship of Yahweh: "At that time people began to invoke the name of Yahweh." In the Priestly writing, by contrast, worship of Yahweh is tied to the residence the Israelites are to build in the desert and where Yahweh's glory will be made apparent. Hence, Yahweh reveals himself with his name only during the Exodus. This sequence could not have been created on the basis of the older version.

This ties into a second peculiarity. The Yahwist stresses that Yahweh is effective and can be worshipped everywhere and especially in foreign lands. In that he responds to the concerns of the diaspora, which were incompatible with the demands of Deuteronomy that tied worship of Yahweh to the sanctuary in Jerusalem (Deut 12:13–14). Already Cain and Abel, the sons of the first human couple, offer sacrifices to Yahweh (Gen 4:3–4), as does Noah (Gen 8:20), who is forced to take a surplus of pure animals into his ark for this very purpose (Gen 7:2). Abraham demonstratively builds altars throughout his journey (Gen 12:7–8; 13:18), and Jacob is even said to have founded the sanctuary at Bethel (Gen 28:11–19)—the nightmare of the Deuteronomists.

---

arkritik und Traditionsgeschichte von Pg, WMANT 70 (Neukirchen-Vluyn: Neukirchener Verlag, 1995), 277, following Christoph Levin, *Die Verheißung des neuen Bundes in ihrem theologiegeschichtlichen Zusammenhang ausgelegt*, FRLANT 137 (Göttingen: Vandenhoeck & Ruprecht, 1985), 222–34.

62. See Christoph Levin, "Jahwe und Abraham im Dialog: Genesis 15," in *Gott und Mensch im Dialog: Festschrift Otto Kaiser*, ed. Markus Witte, BZAW 345.1 (Berlin: De Gruyter, 2004), 237–57.

63. Gen 17:1; 28:3; 35:11; Exod 6:3. The other instances are later additions: Gen 43:14; 48:3; 49:25.

24 Christoph Levin

In the Priestly writing, on the other hand, Noah's sacrifice is notably absent.[64] Without the central cult site, it was unthinkable. Already in the creation account, the Priestly writing is looking toward the sanctuary that will be created at the Sinai. This is the reason why it was impossible to graft this conception onto the older one—that is, the Yahwist. They are simply mutually exclusive, also at the literary level. These historical accounts were combined only at a later stage. The result are the familiar difficulties and contradictions that were used to separate the sources ever since.

10. Preconditions of the Documentary Hypothesis: Ten Theses

(1) The demanding endeavor of merging two parallel accounts of the salvation history into a third, composite entity is conceivable only if there were compelling theological reasons to undertake it. J and P were considered "unanimous in relation to the truth, and this unanimity was to be preserved and made visible through compilation."[65]

(2) It follows that the redaction that combined the two sources—one should call it not "final redaction (R)", but rather "redaction R^{JP}"—preferred neither of them. To R^{JP} the Priestly writing was no more canonical than the Yahwist. The common claim that R was particularly close to P cannot be upheld. The precondition for the combination of the sources was their equal religious weight.

(3) It further follows that the new composition had to preserve the two sources as much as possible. This explains the many repetitions and difficulties that allow the sources to be separated. "This is due ... to the strict *fidelity* with which the redactor or author of the book ... joined his sources verbatim and in full, and compiled them while retaining all their peculiarities."[66]

(4) This does not necessarily mean that the *exact wording* of both sources had to remain unharmed. It would in any case be both maintained and dissolved within the new literary entity. The redaction aimed only to preserve the theological and historiographical substance. While any attempt to restore the exact wording of the two sources in full is therefore doomed, this restriction does not argue against the practice of separating the sources in itself.

---

64. The sacrifice offered by the surviving hero of the flood is an indispensable part of the narrative also in the Mesopotamian versions.

65. Donner, "Der Redaktor," 26.

66. Hupfeld, *Die Quellen der Genesis*, 195–96.

The Priestly Writing as a Source: A Recollection   25

(5) The two sources could only be unified because their historiographical sequences agreed. The structure of the older history, as well as a number of details, must have been known to the younger account, regardless of how this was accomplished.

(6) The procedure in unifying the two sources must have been as simple as possible. The parallel sources were presented one after the other, passage by passage. The zipper principle was used only in two exceptional cases and for good reason: in the flood narrative Gen 6–9 and the miracle at the sea Exod 14.

(7) In the actual process of unification of the two sources, the Documentary Hypothesis transforms into the Supplementary Hypothesis: one of the two sources is the basis, the other is added in, and vice versa. There was no preference for one source or the other. The procedure was determined by the structure and/or the amount of text. While in the primeval history the Priestly writing provides the basis, it becomes the supplement in the patriarchal narrative. P takes back the lead only from Exod 6 onward. Also in the sequence of the first and second part of the Sinai pericope (Exod 19–24; 32–34), the Priestly writing (Exod 25–29 with appendices) is an addition rather than the base.

(8) The sources J and P were combined in an early stage of the Pentateuch's literary history. The majority of the text was added only after these sources were combined. For the primeval history alone, at least a quarter of the current text derives from this later stage.[67] In Gen 12–50 it is presumably around half. This becomes clear if one considers chapters 14; 15; 18B; 20–22*; 23; 34; 38; 48; 49, all of which are of late date either in full or in large parts. In the middle books of the Torah, such later additions are even more substantial. "The redaction of the Hexateuch, then, assumes the form of a continuous diaskeue or diorthosis."[68]

(9) The fact that the significant majority of the current text presupposes the combination of J and P does much to diminish the plausibility of mechanical source separation. On the other hand, this also provides the reason for the coherence of the current history. The Supplementary Hypothesis probably applies everywhere unless there is clear data to the contrary. Not the Pentateuch sources, but supplements are the rule. One

---

67. See Christoph Levin, "Die Redaktion R[JP] in der Urgeschichte," in Beck and Schorn, *Auf dem Weg zur Endgestalt*, 15–34.

68. Kuenen, *Historical-Critical Inquiry*, 315; Dutch original 305.

26   Christoph Levin

can separate the sources successfully only if one also attempts to reconstruct their original form (P^G und J^{Q+R}).

(10) The final form is the result of the literary stream of tradition gradually running dry and not of a conscious decision. The book form of the Torah was not made but *grew* over time,[69] in a fashion only appropriate to a religious text of such great significance. "Provocatively put: There is no such thing as 'the final redaction.'"[70]

---

69. See Bernhard Duhm, *Das Buch Jeremia*, KHC 11 (Tübingen: Mohr Siebeck, 1901), xx.

70. Blum, *Studien zur Komposition des Pentateuch*, 380.

Once Again:
The Literary-Historical Profile of the P Tradition

Erhard Blum

The substantial and unusually stable consensus regarding the delimitation of the so-called Priestly textual elements in the Pentateuch, as it has stood since Theodor Nöldeke,[1] speaks for itself and constitutes a valuable asset for our discipline. In view of this basic consensus, the options for the literary-historical profile of the P tradition discussed in this essay may seem to be rather marginal variants. The effects of the various positions on the interpretation of individual texts remain limited indeed. However, when we are dealing with broader textual issues, we may get a different picture, and the implications may be wide-ranging.

In substance, there seems to be a simple and clearly defined alternative: either P (or, more precisely, an initial version of P, labeled P^G, where the G stands for "Grundschrift") constituted an independent source or document—a position held by the majority of scholars—or P consisted in one or several redactional expansion(s) of a preexisting pentateuchal tradition, a position which has been and continues to be held by a minority.[2] This binary opposition gets taken for granted to such an extent that

---

1. Theodor Nöldeke, "Die s. g. Grundschrift des Pentateuchs," in *Untersuchungen zur Kritik des Alten Testaments* (Kiel: Schwers'sche Buchhandlung, 1869), 1–144.

2. For an overview of this minority position in earlier research cf. Norbert Lohfink, "Die Priesterschrift und die Geschichte," in *Congress Volume Göttingen*, ed. Walter Zimmerli, VTSup 29 (Göttingen: Brill, 1977), 197 n. 28; Erhard Blum, *Die Komposition der Vätergeschichte*, WMANT 57 (Neukirchen-Vluyn: Neukirchner, 1984), 425–26; and Otto Kaiser, *Einleitung in das Alte Testament: Eine Einführung in ihre Ergebnisse und Probleme*, 5th ed. (Gütersloh: Gütersloher Verlaghaus, 1984), §10. Karl Heinrich Graf, "Die s. g. Grundschrift des Pentateuchs," in *Archiv für wissenschaftliche Erforschung des Alten Testamentes*, ed. Adalbert Merx (Halle: Buchhandlung des Waisenhauses, 1869), 1:466–77, already argued that the narrative parts of P

28   Erhard Blum

there is a tendency to classify under one of these alternatives hypotheses that are even incompatible with them. This applies, among others, to a suggestion of mine, which has often been placed in the category "P as redaction," although it was published with the (deliberately) striking title "Die priesterliche Schicht: weder 'Quelle' noch 'Redaktion'" ("The Priestly Layer: Neither 'Source' nor 'Redaction'").[3] Yet an open look at *verifiable* textual productions should suffice to see that there is a multitude of possi-

---

in Genesis, Exodus, and Numbers did not constitute an independent textual stratum, thus confirming his view that "the so-called 'Grundschrift' of the Pentateuch does not constitute the basis of its story [i.e. of the Pentateuch], but rather consists in later additions made to the Yahwistic work" (474). In the more recent discussion on the formation of the Pentateuch, the reference works are Frank Moore Cross, "The Priestly Work," in *Canaanite Myth and Hebrew Epic: Essays in the History of the Religion of Israel* (Cambridge, MA: Harvard University Press, 1973), 293–325; John Van Seters, *Abraham in History and Tradition* (New Haven: Yale University Press, 1975), 279–95; Van Seters, *The Life of Moses: The Yahwist as Historian in Exodus–Numbers* (Louisville: John Knox, 1994); Van Seters, *The Pentateuch: A Social-Science Commentary*, Trajectories 1 (Sheffield: Sheffield Academic, 1999), 80–86, 160–89; and Rolf Rendtorff, *Das überlieferungsgeschichtliche Problem des Pentateuch*, BZAW 147 (Berlin: De Gruyter, 1976). Corresponding positions in the most recent German-speaking context are held by Christoph Berner, *Die Exoduserzählung: Das literarische Werden einer Ursprungslegende Israels*, FAT 73 (Tübingen: Mohr Siebeck, 2010) and Rainer Albertz, *Ex 1–18*, vol. 1 of *Exodus*, ZBK.AT 2.1 (Zürich: TVZ, 2012), who speaks of several "priesterliche Bearbeitungen." Concerning the range of texts discussed in this article, see especially Jakob Wöhrle, *Fremdlinge im eigenen Land: Zur Entstehung und Intention der priesterlichen Passagen der Vätergeschichte*, FRLANT 246 (Göttingen: Vandenhoeck & Ruprecht, 2012).

3. Erhard Blum, *Studien zur Komposition des Pentateuch*, BZAW 189 (Berlin: De Gruyter, 1990), 229–85. This pointed formulation was also intended to emphasize the contrast to my earlier position in Blum, *Die Komposition der Vätergeschichte*. See also, for instance, Ivan Engnell (*Gamla Testamentet: En traditionshistorisk inledning*, vol 1. [Stockholm: Svenska Kyrkans Diakonistyrelses Bokförlag, 1945]; Engnell, "The Pentateuch," in *A Rigid Scrutiny: Critical Essays on the Old Testament* [Nashville: Vanderbilt University Press, 1969], 50–67), who attributed the Tetrateuch to a circle of priestly collectors who used primarily oral traditions, is sometimes presented as a forerunner of the redactional hypothesis (also by myself in Blum, *Die Komposition der Vätergeschichte*). On the other side of the divide, Israel Knohl's distinction between "PT (Priestly Torah)" and "HS (Holiness School)" gets easily (mis-)understood as another version of the distinction between P^G and P^S, although his Priestly Torah did not constitute a continuous work, but rather existed "in the form of individual scrolls, and it was HS that edited and combined them" (Israel Knohl, *The Sanctuary of Silence: The Priestly Torah and the Holiness School* [Winona Lake, IN: Eisenbrauns, 1995], 101).

Once Again: The Literary-Historical Profile of the P Tradition   29

bilities aside from source and redactional expansion. For instance, neither Chronicles in the Hebrew canon, nor the Synoptic Gospels, nor Josephus's *Antiquitates* fit neatly in one of these two models.

The following analysis tries to determine, once again, which textual evidence (primarily in the ancestral history) is under discussion and what may be inferred from this evidence for the textual formation of P. Due to both the history of research on this topic and the nature of the problem at hand, this analysis will use the binary opposition mentioned above, or more precisely, the basic understanding of the independence of texts (which this opposition presupposes) as a starting point.

1. The Criteria

How can one show that a given diachronic textual stratum—under the assumption that there is a broad consensus concerning its definition for the sake of simplicity—once constituted an independent source? Most likely by proving, or at least by making a plausible argument, that the supposed textual composition as a whole is complete and that the text sequence that may be reconstructed is consistent and coherent. Since the completeness of a stratum and its coherence cannot always be evaluated apart from each other, both aspects may become intertwined. Furthermore, since we are dealing with historical processes in the formation of traditions with their intentional and contingent components, we should not expect to easily achieve clear results. For instance, it is not improbable that parts of a presumed source in a composite work were lost—unless there are, on the other hand, historical and philological reasons against this assumption.

At the very least, a probability criterion seems to be unproblematic: the more unified and coherent the reconstructed source is, the higher the probability of the corresponding hypothesis. This rule can also be applied in the opposite direction to argue for the dependence of a textual stratum: the more incomplete and incoherent its diachronically delimited elements appear to be, the higher the probability of its diachronic dependence.

Either way, one becomes admittedly entangled in discussions of how to assess the evidence, which can lead in cases with inconclusive results to a *non liquet*. This is why it is important to clarify the character of the gaps/incoherent elements and to thoroughly examine different options to explain them.

In addition, it would be desirable to supplement the probability criterion with further ones. Two *significance criteria*, which complement each

30   Erhard Blum

other in certain respects, seem worthy of consideration in this regard. The one criterion (1) states that such cases, in which a (clear) narrative coherence becomes recognizable only when the textual material that is diachronically distinct is disregarded, should be considered especially significant. In other words: if diachronically distinct material interrupts an otherwise coherent and continuous context, this speaks for the independence of the context in relation to the material causing the interruption. The other criterion (2) states that such cases should also be considered especially significant, in which not just a gap or a substantial incoherence is found, but in which the textual evidence can only be convincingly explained together with the textual elements which have been discarded as diachronically distinct. In other words: if substantial elements of the stratum under discussion seem to have been formed while taking an older context into account, this calls into question its independence.

2. The Completeness and Coherence of the P Stratum in the Patriarchs' Narrative

Chains usually break at their weakest link. In discussions on the existence of an independent Priestly work, opponents of this hypothesis have identified parts of the ancestral history as such a weakness from the start. Its proponents find the same evidence to be explainable or not significant (enough). This is why the following analysis focuses on this material. The textual basis for the analysis is displayed in table 1 (see page 53).

2.1. Coherence Test No. 1: Narrative Gaps and Their Explanation

It is necessary to examine the unity and completeness of the P narrative as an independent narrative within the framework of the Priestly source hypothesis, not only because of fundamental issues of method, but also because of the view widely held in the German-speaking context that P and the older sources were not intertwined as an addition of equally ranked narrative threads in the main redaction. Instead, the redactor "made the P narrative the *basis* of his work and *enriched* it by suitably inserting here and there parts of the other narrative."[4] This picture implies explicitly that

---

4. Martin Noth, *A History of Pentateuchal Traditions*, trans. Bernhard W. Anderson (Chico, CA: Scholars Press, 1981), 12 (the German original was published in 1948). But see already Julius Wellhausen, *Die Composition des Hexateuchs und der*

Once Again: The Literary-Historical Profile of the P Tradition   31

"only the P narrative is preserved completely in its original extent and that therefore the identified P elements connect smoothly with each other."[5]

However, in contrast to what these quotes might suggest, there are obvious and indisputable gaps especially in the ancestral history, in any case from Gen 25 onward.

First, P does not have any Isaac narrative of its own, a point that we will have to address later.[6] But the Jacob narrative in P also begins with a lacuna between Gen 25:20 and 26b: the birth of the twins is missing. Furthermore, the span of twenty years in Isaac's life between his wedding and the birth of his children conveys the childlessness of the couple at the beginning of their married life, a detail that is not mentioned in P. In other words, the short notes in P fit perfectly well in the plot of the pre-Priestly story. Nevertheless, the *possibility* of redactional omissions in order to use corresponding passages from the pre-Priestly story cannot be dismissed out of hand.[7]

Between Gen 28:9 and 31:(17–)18,[8] Jacob's arrival and stay at Laban's home are missing. Even if we took the pattern of the allegedly complete P narrative about Abraham (more on that below) as a basis, in which no plot can be found except for itineraries and birth notices (with Abraham's age provided on every occasion), we would expect to see at least the weddings of Laban's daughters and the birth of their children before 31:17–18.[9] In this case, Martin Noth's renewed assumption of a redactional omission is not plausible, because there would be no explanation for the list of Jacob's sons with their mothers which P provides at a later point in Gen 35:22b–26.[10] This list seems rather to show that the

---

historischen Bücher des Alten Testaments, 3rd ed. (Berlin: Reimer, 1899), 3, concerning Gen 1–11: "Q is used as the basis; JE gets conformed to it."

5. Noth, *History of Pentateuchal Traditions*, 17.

6. See section 3 below.

7. See Noth, *History of Pentateuchal Traditions*, 14, who sees here an example of "exceptional cases" in which "the weight of the detailed narratives in the old sources induced the redactor to cut the P narrative."

8. Contra Noth and others, there is no convincing reason to separate v. 17 and 18.

9. The sentences in 29:24, 28b, 29, and 30:4a, 9b extracted by Otto Eißfeldt, *Hexateuch-Synopse: Die Erzählung der fünf Bücher Mose und des Buches Josua mit dem Anfange des Richterbuches* (repr., Darmstadt: Wissenschaftliche Buchgesellschaft, 1962), 55*–57*, following other scholars, have nothing to do with P and cannot fill the void anyway.

10. Noth, *History of Pentateuchal Traditions*, 14. This problem could only be

32 Erhard Blum

arrangement of short notes in P was aligned with the preexisting story from the start.

The Joseph story holds, in the words of Nöldeke, the "most painful gap in the whole *Grundschrift*."[11] After the introduction in Gen 37:1–2ab (where the attribution of v. 2* to P is not reliable at all, except for the toledot heading and Joseph's age [?]), there is the isolated statement on Joseph's age "when he stood before Pharaoh" in 41:46a (integrated in the text through the resumptive repetition of v. 45b in v. 46b) and then the short note depicting the family move to Egypt (46:6–7).[12] (46:8–27 constitutes a continuation written by more recent P scribes.) The source of the scene in which Jacob gets an audience with the Pharaoh in 47:(5–)7–11 remains controversial. Noth omits the whole passage with regards to P, including the statement in verse 9 concerning Jacob's age, although it is integrated in the Priestly chronology; others would assign verses *5–11, the longer version of the LXX, or 47:7–10, 11* to P.[13] However, these hypotheses pay too

---

avoided with the drastic solution of Hermann Gunkel, *Genesis*, HKAT 1.1, 3rd ed. (Göttingen: Vandenhoeck & Ruprecht, 1910), 388, who moves Gen 35:22b–26 before 31:18, although he did not see that these verses provide the information concerning Jacob's family in retrospect, as Noth, *History of Pentateuchal Traditions*, 17 n. 50, noticed. Benjamin's position in the list does not give any reason either for such a textual rearrangement: the scribe (be it P or Rp), who put 35:22b–26 after 35:16–20, simply did not see the necessity of distinguishing Benjamin from his brothers in the caption in v. 26b.

11. Nöldeke, "Die s. g. Grundschrift des Pentateuchs," 31.

12. Genesis 46:5 constitutes a complex and important case for the problem under discussion: On the one hand, 46:5–7 and 31:17–18 were unmistakably laid out in a parallel fashion; cf. the synopses in Blum, *Die Komposition der Vätergeschichte*, 248, 332 and David Carr, *Reading the Fractures of Genesis: Historical and Literary Approaches* (Louisville: John Knox, 1996), 104–5 with 106–7. On the other hand, 46:5 continues the narrative thread of the Joseph Story from 45:19, 21, 27. Genesis 46:5b even seems to have constituted the original narrative continuation of 45:28 before the younger Beersheba scene was added. This knot may come untied if we reckon with the possibility that the P scribes wrote 46:6–7 as the continuation of the preexisting short note about the departure in 46:5 and aligned 31:17–18. with the resulting passage 46:5–7 (Blum, *Die Komposition der Vätergeschichte*, 333). Incidentally, this observation constitutes an additional piece of evidence for the attribution of Gen 46:1–5a to a pre-Priestly composition (297–301, 339–61).

13. For verses *5–11, see most recently Rüdiger Lux, "Geschichte als Erfahrung, Erinnerung und Erzählung in der priesterschriftlichen Rezeption der Josefsnovelle," in *Erzählte Geschichte: Beiträge zur narrativen Kultur im alten Israel*, ed. Rüdiger Lux, BThSt 40 (Neukirchen-Vluyn: Neukurchner, 2000), 147–80, here 165–71. The ring structure in 47:5*–6a, 7–11 described in Blum, *Die Komposition der Vätergeschichte*,

Once Again: The Literary-Historical Profile of the P Tradition   33

little attention to the parallel structuring with 41:46, not only with regards to the contents (Joseph/Jacob "stand" [עמד] before the Pharaoh and their age is given) but also with regards to the wording (ויצא ... מלפני פרעה) and the redactional technique used (resumptive repetition). Based on the latter, it is most likely that 47:8–10 belong to P.[14] Furthermore, I would attribute (against Noth et al. but with Rüdiger Lux) 47:27–28 completely to P, for verse 27a, 37:1, and 36:8 provide the evidence.[15]

Genesis 48:3–7 deals then with the status of Joseph's sons, Ephraim and Manasseh, whose birth notice is missing (!) from P, but who are raised through adoption to the rank of direct sons of Jacob (v. 5: כראובן ושמעון יהיו לי; לי הם), which means that they are included in the blessing and promise that were granted to Jacob's family line according to verse 4 (this inclusion being made explicit with ועתה at the beginning of v. 5). Verse 6 excludes sons of Joseph which would eventually be born later[16] (לך יהיו) from attaining this rank (especially in terms of inheritance). The emphatic pronoun ואני in verse 7 creates a link over and above verse 6 back to verse 5 (לי הם) and also begins the explanation for the special status of both sons of Joseph: Jacob lost Joseph's mother Rachel prematurely, which implies that he (in contrast to Joseph according to v. 6![17]) would never again have the

---

165 n. 57, is the result of P expanding the text, as I am about to show. For the longer version of the LXX, see Claus Westermann, *Genesis 37–50*, BKAT 1.3 (Neukirchen-Vluyn: Neukirchener, 1982), 188 with older secondary literature and a reference to Wilhelm Rudolph, "Die Josefsgeschichte," in *Der Elohist als Erzähler: Ein Irrweg der Pentateuchkritik? An der Genesis erläutert*, ed. Paul Volz and Wilhelm Rudolph, BZAW 63 (Giessen: Alfred Töpelmann, 1933), 165–67, who sees the Septuagint (or its Vorlage) as the result of an attempt at correcting the text by interpretation. For 47:7–10, 11*, see Westermann, *Genesis 37–50*, ad loc.

14. One exception was, unsurprisingly, Benno Jacob, *Das Buch Genesis* (repr. Stuttgart: Calwer, 2000), ad loc. See also Blum, *Die Komposition der Vätergeschichte*, 252–53 n. 56. In 47:11, I attribute the sentence ויתן להם אחזה בארץ מצרים in v. 7 and maybe the expression ויעמדהו (cf. 41:46a) to P. The short meeting between Jacob and the pharaoh as the conclusion of the pre-Priestly audience scene, which began in 47:1, shows Jacob as the active side (blessing) and preserves the dignity of the old father in an impressive manner.

15. Lux, "Geschichte," 159–60, with n. 40.

16. The *qatal* form הולדת in v. 6a offers a nice example of the use of the perfective aspect to express a relative anteriority to a situation or event (situated in the future) presented with the imperfective aspect.

17. The striking introduction of a purely theoretical possibility for Joseph according to v. 6—the Old Testament does not know of any further sons of Joseph—under-

34 Erhard Blum

opportunity to father other sons with the wife he loved. Now Ephraim and Manasseh are put in this very position! In accordance with the inner logic of verses 3–7, verse 7 must therefore belong to the preceding P section of text as its conclusion.[18] Conversely, this verse is understandable only in combination with its preceding context.[19] The notorious difficulties that many interpreters have with 48:7 stem from their apparent conviction that a P text cannot quote or refer to the pre-Priestly passage Gen 35:16–19 from a source-critical point of view.

Similarly, the third to last sentence (v. 33ab) of the coherent P section Gen 49:29–33 would have been left in place if not for the fact that it refers back to 48:2b (pre-P). On the other hand, 49:1a gets generously attributed to P, although there is no reason for this apart from the fact that it allows us to complete the P narrative with a sentence.

With regards to Gen 50:12–13, it would be advisable to follow scholarly tradition. The new suggestion to add verse 14 as well to P leads to insurmountable problems.[20] However, following David Carr and Lux (but in contrast to the previous consensus), we should attribute 50:22a (cf. 37:1; 47:27–28) to the P line.[21] On the other hand, the following sentence

---

lines not just the special provision concerning Ephraim and Manasseh, but also draws attention to the *im*possibility for Jacob implicit in v. 7.

18. In the broader context of P, the reference to Rachel's death and grave constitutes the necessary counterpart to the mention in 49:31 of Leah's burial in the family grave at Mamre. In this respect, Anneli Aejmelaeus and Ludwig Schmidt, *The Traditional Prayer in the Psalms / Literarische Studien zur Josephsgeschichte*, BZAW 167 (Berlin: De Gruyter 1986), 121–97, esp. 254–55, is right. On the discussion with Schmidt, cf. Blum, *Studien zur Komposition des Pentateuch*, 229–30 n. 4.

19. Lux, "Geschichte," 174–75, proposes another interpretation: "Did P want to suggest to its readers, through the recollection of Rachel's early death on the way from Paddan to the promised land, that it can also be too late to return home? Did it want to hint that Rachel, not least because of the long years in which she allowed herself to linger abroad with Jacob and his family, could only find a grave in the promised land, that she died before she actually arrived in it?" This raises some questions: in what respect should Jacob's family have actually not arrived yet in southern Benjamin ("on the way, a little distance from Ephrath")? According to the reference text 35:16–20, Rachel died in childbirth. Where's the connection with staying abroad?

20. See Erhard Blum, "Zwischen Literarkritik und Stilkritik: Die diachrone Analyse der literarischen Verbindung von Genesis und Exodus—im Gespräch mit Ludwig Schmidt," *ZAW* 124 (2012): 503–4, with n. 45.

21. See Carr, *Reading the Fractures of Genesis*, 109–10 (with a reference in n. 63 to Hermann Hupfeld, *Die Quellen der Genesis und die Art ihrer Zusammensetzung*

Once Again: The Literary-Historical Profile of the P Tradition   35

giving Joseph's age is definitely not Priestly because of the number's syntactic make-up.[22] The P note here was probably rephrased in the course of a post-Priestly remodeling of the transition from Genesis to Exodus.[23]

How can we summarize our findings in the Joseph story? The short and scattered P notes presuppose the plot of the Joseph story in its catastrophic features (47:9!) and in its big turns (41:46), but this plot does not get told *in P itself*! Can we plausibly explain this observation with the assumption that this is the result of considerable redactional omissions (for instance, because of contradictions or repetitions)?[24] This assumption is difficult to maintain when we compare with the remaining P context. First, the scribes did not shy away otherwise from inserting P traditions with hard contradictions and striking repetitions in the material at their disposal. Secondly, a fully developed Joseph story in the narrative sense would completely contradict P's literary paradigm as discernible in the narratives of the Patriarchs, which is characterized by a drastic reduction of the plot to mere notices of pregnancies, births, and travel. Furthermore, it would be the only time in the P material that the scribes would have gotten involved in a suspenseful and intricate plot.

If we also consider the fact that several P elements not only factually presuppose the pre-Priestly story but are also impossible without the literary context (cf. significance criterion 2 above),[25] we come to the first provisional conclusion that the existence of an independent P thread is very unlikely in the range of text we discussed (mainly Gen 25–50).

[Berlin: Wiegandt & Grieben, 1853]); Lux, "Geschichte," 159–60; Jan C. Gertz, "The Transition between the Books of Genesis and Exodus," in *A Farewell to the Yahwist? The Composition of the Pentateuch in Recent European Interpretation*, ed. Thomas Dozeman and Konrad Schmid, SymS 34 (Atlanta: Society of Biblical Literature, 2006), 78–79, also considers the possibility that v. 22a might belong to a redactional layer connecting P with the Joseph story and links this with a supposition that v. 22a might be a "graphic *Wiederaufnahme*" of v. 14a. But is there such a thing as a "graphic *Wiederaufnahme*"?

22. See Blum, *Studien zur Komposition des Pentateuch*, 364 n. 14. Astonishingly, the authors in the preceding footnote begin their analysis with the supposedly clear Priestly character of v. 22b.

23. See Blum, "Zwischen Literarkritik und Stilkritik," 509–10 with n. 65 (N.B.: before n. 65, "Jdc 1,6" should be corrected to "Jdc 2,8").

24. This was the approach that suggested itself within the framework of the documentary hypothesis already in Nöldeke, "Die s. g. Grundschrift des Pentateuchs," 31.

25. See the remarks above on 48:3–7 (49:33*), as well as Gen 46:5, 6–7 with 31:17–18. The toledot heading in 37:2, which still has to be discussed, also belongs to this set.

2.2. Coherence Test No. 2: Seamless Connections of Reconstructed P Pieces

It is well known that there is a series of passages in which text elements that are attributed to P can be seamlessly connected and read together in a continuous fashion. Such passages are found in the Primeval History, at the beginning of Exodus (with qualifications), but also within the ancestral history. This evidence probably constitutes the strongest argument for an independent P source (cf. criterion 1 above). Therefore, a more thorough examination of the relevant passages is necessary.

We have little to expect from the Jacob story in that regard because of the fragmentary character of its P thread. Nevertheless, one of the most significant examples is to be found here: the short notes in 26:34–35 and 27:46–28:9 concerning Isaac's and Rebekah's grief because of Esau's Canaanite wives, which in P brings the focus on Jacob as the promise bearer. The direct connection between both passages at the thematic and narrative levels is obvious, but in the tradition as it now stands, they are separated from each other by the long episode of Gen 27.

The beginning of the Abraham story in P before Gen 17, whose traditional delimitation is Gen 11:27–28, 31–32, 12:4b–5, 13:6, 11b(?), 12abα, and 16:1a(?), 3, 15–16, is characteristic in other respects.[26] These verses may be read, to a large extent,[27] consistently as a series of events. At the same time, the nonnarrative character of the portrayal is striking: the plot time remains uniform, without any distinctiveness (cf. the transition 12:15/13:6). In comparison with the corresponding material from non-Priestly sources, it is clear that both P and non-P follow the same path, but the P elements seem like boiled down versions of non-P scenes/episodes, which were shrunk down to a succession of plain facts whose chronologi-

---

26. In Gen 16, the allocation of v. 1a is not clear at all; v. 15 is also controversial (Rendtorff, *Das überlieferungsgeschichtliche Problem des Pentateuch*, 125), but the clear parallel in 21:3 supports P.

27. Interestingly, Graf, "Die s. g. Grundschrift des Pentateuchs," 471 saw a problem in 12:4. According to him, "the remark 12:4b presupposes the presence of the Jahwistic piece 12:1–4a." This is not without reason, because the statement giving Abram's age in 12:4b has the same syntactic structure (nominal clause with *be* + inf.) as Gen 21:5, 25:26 or 41:46, where, as should be expected from such a nominal clause, it follows the description of the events to which the infinitive refers. In the P context of 12:4b–5, however, the statement of Abram's age would come before those events; there is no such problem if we take into consideration the context (12:4a) that does not belong to P (cf. Graf).

Once Again: The Literary-Historical Profile of the P Tradition   37

cal relationships are marked only with dates and statements on the age of the characters as in 12:5b or 16:3.[28]

In sharp contrast to the findings in 2.1, the last two examples suggest that the specific character of the P story is only recognizable when these passages are read in isolation. This would indicate an independent literary source. How do things stand in other passages?

The P note Gen 19:29 about the destruction of the cities of the *kikkar* constitutes a problematic case.[29] According to the leading opinion since Nöldeke, this is "one instance in which the original sequence of the elements within the P narrative had to be modified [by the redactor, EB]."[30] The original position of 19:29 is unanimously considered to be in continuation of 13:12.[31] The verse about Lot's rescue from the destruction of the cities does indeed fit smoothly there.[32] This summarizing note—shaped in a poetically redundant chiasmus—unmistakably presupposes some knowledge of the Sodom/Lot story on the part of its readers. However, two things remain unclear here: one is the explanation given for Lot's rescue, which is that God "remembered" (זכר) Abraham. In general, the P pieces had not mentioned God since Gen 11:27, and Abraham's special relationship with God is established in Gen 17. Verse 19:29a only makes sense after the encounter in chapter 17, and that is why it should remain where it is. However, 19:29 would admittedly seem lost, from a narrative point of view, within a separate P thread between Gen 17 and 21:*1–5; it needs the context of Gen 17–19.[33] The other unclear point concerns Lot as a character. Why does he get introduced to such an extent in P at the beginning of the Abraham tradition? The only conceivable answer would be his genealogical-etiological importance with regard to the neighboring nations Ammon and Moab; that is in fact the whole point of Lot's connection with Sodom in the pre-Priestly story. However, Lot would remain an isolated motif in an independent P thread, particularly since Ammon

---

28. For an attempt at a theological interpretation of the isolated P thread in the Abraham Story (which I find at times too daring), see Herbert Specht, "Von Gott enttäuscht—Die priesterschriftliche Abrahamsgeschichte," *EvT* 47 (1987): 395–411.

29. See already Graf, "Die s. g. Grundschrift des Pentateuchs," 471–72 ad loc.

30. Noth, *History of Pentateuchal Traditions*, 13.

31. See already Nöldeke, "Die s. g. Grundschrift des Pentateuchs," 22; Noth, *History of Pentateuchal Traditions*, 13.

32. Notice the anaphora of ערי הככר from 13:12bα in 19:29a.

33. Moreover, it fits well there stylistically as a poetic summary.

38   Erhard Blum

and Moab are absent from P texts.[34] These problems are naturally avoided if the pre-Priestly narrative context was present at the time when the Lot elements where formulated.

Finally, we have to examine the best-known join of separate P pieces, which lies at the beginning of Exodus, where the P story, usually defined as Exod 1:1–5, 7*, 13–14, 2:23aβ–25, and 6:2–9, provides basic information on the background and the beginning of the events in a continuously readable manner. The passages Exod 2:23aβ–25 and 6:2–6, which are separated by several chapters, fit especially well together:

> Exod 2:23 And the Israelites moaned because of their forced labor.
> They cried out and their cry went up to God from the forced labor.
> 24 God *heard their groaning*.
> And God <u>remembered his covenant</u> with Abraham, with Isaac and with Jacob.
> 25 And God saw the Israelites,
> and God *knew* it (MT) // he *let himself be known* to them (LXX).[35]

> Exod 6:2 And God spoke to Moses and said to him:
> I am YHWH.
> 3 I appeared to Abraham, Isaac and Jacob as El Shaddai, but I have not *let myself be known* to them under my name YHWH.
> 4 I have also established my *covenant* with them, to give them the land of Canaan, the land of their residence, in which they lived.
> 5 Moreover, I *heard the groaning* of the Israelites,
> how the Egyptians oppressed them with work;
> and I <u>remembered my covenant</u>.
> 6 Therefore, tell the Israelites:

---

34. Nöldeke (and Graf) still considered this question: "By the way, we must first notice here, with certainty, a gap in the Grundschrift. This [missing passage] tied without a doubt both nations Moab and Ammon to Lot, who has no significance of his own" (Nöldeke, "Die s. g. Grundschrift des Pentateuchs," 22). Graf (see 37 n. 29 above) inferred from this that P was conceived as an addition to its context. Nöldeke suspected that the redactor had left something out. However, it would not be easy to imagine a corresponding genealogical note in P: it would have had to explain the connection with the destruction of Sodom, why the genealogical line did not continue through Lot's sons, etc., aspects which would have forced P to an exposition which it has otherwise avoided.

35. The Septuagint version might be preferable (cf. Werner H. Schmidt, *Exodus*, BKAT 2 [Neukirchen-Vluyn: Neukirchner Verlag, 1974], ad loc.); I held another position in Blum, *Studien zur Komposition des Pentateuch*, 240 n. 43.

Once Again: The Literary-Historical Profile of the P Tradition   39

Both partial texts seem even more to have been formulated in relationship to one another than the short notes on Esau before and after Gen 27 (see above) and indicate therefore a primary literary connection. However, the transition between them has a narrative deficiency which led Abraham Kuenen to conclude: "Ch. vi. 2 sqq. is not the direct continuation of ii. 23b–25, for Moses appears as already known to the reader."[36] Such an unprepared appearance of a protagonist who happens to be not just any figure, but the main character himself, would indeed be unimaginable in an intact story.[37] This problem can be solved only by postulating the loss of a P text before Exod 6:2,[38] which would weaken the argument that this verse fits perfectly right after the end of Exod 2, or by referring to the pre-Priestly narrative context, which is used as an argument for the supplementary hypothesis since Karl Heinrich Graf.[39]

The phenomenon of a continuously progressing textual thread in P, provided that this thread can be reconstructed, has been confirmed in many passages, although not with such consistency as is often assumed. Nonetheless, these findings are sufficient to come to the second provisional conclusion: the definition of P as a redaction/*Bearbeitung* in the sense of a *Fortschreibung* of given texts has to be ruled out.

---

36. Abraham Kuenen, *An Historical-Critical Inquiry into the Origin and Composition of the Hexateuch*, trans. Philip H. Wicksteed (London: MacMillan, 1886), 329.

37. The question is not whether the figure is known by the readers but how the narrative introduces its main character. The reference of Klaus Koch ("P—kein Redaktor! Erinnerung an zwei Eckdaten der Quellenscheidung," *VT* 37 [1987]: 465) to the following genealogy in Exod 6:14–27 (cf. already Nöldeke, "Die s. g. Grundschrift des Pentateuchs," 37) does not help in this case, because it is mainly directed at Aaron and his sons and at further future protagonists like Korah. Furthermore, it proves to be inserted in the context of 6:2–23 and 7:1–6, together with its frame (6:13 + 26–27), through a large resumptive repetition of 6:10–12 in 6:28–30 (cf. Bruno Baentsch, *Exodus—Leviticus—Numeri*, HKAT 1.2 [Göttingen: Vandenhoeck & Ruprecht, 1903], 43–44). Cf. Blum, *Studien*, 241n45.

38. See a few representatives of the Documentary Hypothesis such as Kuenen, *Historical-Critical Inquiry*; August Dillmann, *Die Bücher Numeri, Deuteronomium und Josua*, KeH 13, 2nd ed. (Leipzig: Hirzel, 1886), 634. In contrast to this, Wellhausen, *Composition des Hexateuchs*, 62, dismisses the question "at Q" as inappropriate; Baentsch, *Exodus*, 44, ignores the issue and sees 6:2, 3 as a "direct continuation of 2:25."

39. Graf, "Die s. g. Grundschrift des Pentateuchs," 472–73; more recently and trenchant, Cross, "Priestly Work," 317–18.

40 Erhard Blum

3. The Toledot Framework in the Ancestral History[40]

Turning now to the toledot elements, we have to discuss further the completeness and coherence of the narrative P texts. However, they also raise further-reaching questions of structure.

The toledot headings in the ancestral history (PN ת[ו]לד[ו]ת אלה) introduce three generational successions in the main line and two collateral lines. With the exception of Esau's toledot, whose lists include Edomite kings, each heading has its counterpart in the age and death notice of the patriarch whose name is given in the heading. The wording[41] used recurrently for them is found only in the ancestral history (with an echo in the fate of Aaron in Num 20:23–29). In the main line, the burial of the patriarch in the common family grave by their respective sons is mentioned as well. The fact that these elements are intended to build up a framework can be inferred from the matter itself: At the burial, the subject of the toledot, the progenitor and the descendants are gathered together once more and the generational succession is celebrated. But above all, the literary arrangement is clear: The death notice and, in some cases, the burial are followed each time (without interruption) by the next toledot heading (cf., e.g., Gen 25:9–10/12–17/19). In between, we find only a short note on the main line of the descendants of the deceased, namely, on their place of residence (25:11, 18), with a slight variation in the case of Jacob/Esau:

> After Isaac's death, Esau's Toledot gives at first his place of residence (which also subdivides the Toledot): first Canaan (36:5b), then (finally) the Seir mountains (36:8b). In a clear contrast to this, 37:1 declares, that Jacob stayed to live in the land of his father Isaac.... This clarifies the meaning of these details: they show clearly in each case, that the main heir stays in the land of promise, while the collateral lines take possession of other territories.[42]

From a structural point of view, the collateral lines (Ishmael and Esau) come before the corresponding main heirs. The heading is then followed by a list of descendants, as is to be expected for toledot, but the main line

---

40. On the following section, cf. Blum, *Die Komposition der Vätergeschichte*, 432–46.

41. Cf. the synoptic compilation in Blum, *Die Komposition der Vätergeschichte*, 436.

42. Blum, *Die Komposition der Vätergeschichte*, 437. Incidentally, a corresponding P note for Joseph also follows Jacob's burial in Gen 50:22a.

Once Again: The Literary-Historical Profile of the P Tradition 41

is different: in this case, the toledot set phrase constitutes a heading for *stories* about the descendants of the (logical) toledot subject!

This is also the case for the Isaac toledot in 25:19: verse 19b seems *prima facie* like a genealogical continuation, but the sentence אברהם הוליד את יצחק only repeats—against the logic of the heading—the information בן אברהם from verse 19a.[43] In the immediate context, it is followed by the birth story of the twins *Esau and Jacob* and their sibling rivalry. The evidence in Gen 37 is even more telling: the sentence אלה תלדות יעקב begins the great story of *Joseph* and his brothers.

What does this mean for the semantics of תלדות? The basic meaning "production, begetting" refers to the descendants in the genealogical lists, but in the main lines of the patriarchs, the term is metonymically expanded to mean the descendants *and* what they do or what happens to them, in short: the "story of the descendants." Furthermore, in accordance with the basic meaning of the term, it always refers to the "story" of the *descendants*, not of the subject of the toledot.

Finally, a further structural observation seems appropriate: the toledot frame does not enclose an epoch. Without exception, the progenitor, whose death and burial were told, lives on for some time during the following toledot story:[44] Terah died (according to MT) no sooner than sixty years after Abraham's departure from Haran.[45] Abraham saw the birth of his grandsons Jacob and Esau; and Isaac may still have been alive at the time when Joseph rose to become the pharaoh's deputy. This means that the transition from one toledot complex to the next implies no continuum on the timeline, in other words no narrative sequence, but rather serves to mark the boundaries of textual units. To put it in a nutshell: the toledot do not constitute epochs but chapters.[46] This is made possible by the use

---

43. See above.

44. On the relationship between the characters' ages and the plot in the P texts, see also Lohfink, "Die Priesterschrift und die Geschichte," 210–11.

45. According to the Samaritanus, Abraham left Haran in the year of Terah's death. It is not clear which of the *lectiones* is *facilior* in this case. See Walther Zimmerli, *1. Mose 12–25: Abraham*, ZBK 1.2 (Zürich: TVZ, 1976), 17, who prefers the reading of the Samaritanus.

46. For this reason, the distinction between "epochal toledot" and "generational toledot" drawn by Klaus Koch, "Die Toledot-Formeln als Strukturprinzip des Buches Genesis," in *Recht und Ethos im Alten Testament: Gestalt und Wirkung, FS H. Seebass*, ed. Stefan Beyerle et al. (Neukirchen-Vluyn: Neukirchner, 1999), 183–92 does not

42   Erhard Blum

of toledot formulae interrupting the narrative continuum at the discursive level and marking a new, independent beginning in every case.

With regard to the history of the literary formation of the texts, two observations concerning this structural shaping seem fundamental: First, the fact that the headings of the Isaac and (even more clearly) the Jacob toledot do not introduce P narratives but non-Priestly stories. If the toledot headings had belonged to an independent Priestly document, then Gen 37:2a would have introduced a Priestly Joseph story, but there is no such story, as shown above, and there most probably never was one. To put it in a positive manner: the simplest and most elegant explanation for our findings is that the toledot framework was *conceived* as a connecting element between the P and the non-P material (see significance criterion 2 above).

The second observation has a deeper impact at the structural level: the system we have shown in the basic structure of the toledot is breached repeatedly at the beginning of the ancestral history. The toledot heading for Terah is indeed followed as usual by genealogical information and a simple death notice. But then, the text continues with *Abraham*'s story, and this story ends with his death and burial by both sons. According to the logic usually followed, this burial should constitute the conclusion of Abraham's toledot. However, a toledot heading for Abraham is missing. Correspondingly, there is no separate Isaac story, because according to the pattern followed by the main toledot (Isaac's and Jacob's), the heading אלה תלדות אברהם would have to introduce an *Isaac* story.

Of course, exegetes have long been asking how come Abraham, of all people, should have no toledot heading. The suggestion from Bernardus D. Eerdmans, Karl Budde, and others to change "Terah" in 11:27 to "Abraham" basically ignores the toledot system described above; the same applies to Julius Wellhausen's assumption that the Abraham heading was lost somewhere before 12:4b.[47] However, the conspicuous asymmetry of the toledot framework in Abraham's case can be simply explained as the result of the special care the scribes took in following the Priestly

---

seem very helpful. In addition, this distinction neglects the toledot's connection with the death and burial notices.

47. Bernardus D. Eerdmans, *Die Komposition der Genesis*, vol. 1 of *Alttestamentliche Studien* (Gießen: Alfred Töpelmann, 1908), 22; this suggestion was considered by Gunkel, *Genesis*, 157; Karl Budde, "Ellä toledoth," *ZAW* 34 (1914): 249; Wellhausen, *Composition des Hexateuchs*, 15.

Once Again: The Literary-Historical Profile of the P Tradition 43

and pre-Priestly material. There was no Isaac story that could have been included as an Abraham toledot, mostly because the Isaac chapter, Gen 26, had already been integrated compositionally within the Jacob story. Accordingly, the episodes involving Abraham begin with Terah's toledot heading but end with Abraham's burial. The latter was necessary if only with regard to the Machpelah tradition.[48]

In short: the fundamental structuring device of the Priestly ancestral history, the toledot framework, was not written freely but is closely wrapped around the non-Priestly ancestral history. This strongly confirms the probabilistic conclusions from section 2.1.

We now turn to a final textual example of Priestly texts being related to a pre-Priestly context in a completely different manner.

4. Discontinuous Coherence: The Bethel Tradition in P[49]

The Priestly texts of promise in Gen 28 and 35 are unmistakably in competition with their pre-Priestly predecessors in Gen 27, 28, and 32. The literary treatment given to this competition in the P texts is very significant for their literary-historical explanation; this will be demonstrated in the following, with a focus on Gen 35:9–15.

There is a wide consensus that this passage belongs to P. Some question the original connection between verse 10 (with the change of name to "Israel") and verses 11–15, because God does not introduce himself until after the second introduction of speech in verse 11. Verse 14 is even more often excluded as non-P.[50]

Verses 35:11–15 prove to be a unique problem. It is not too much to claim that this passage and 28:11–19 constitute the only water-tight doublet in Genesis (see table 2 on page 61): one and the same figure, Jacob, has a divine vision with a promise speech at the exact same place (28:13–15 //

---

48. This sheds a new light on the sentence in Gen 25:19b, which seems displaced. In the context of the ancestral history, it reads like a reminiscence of an Abraham toledot that could not be realized: אברהם הוליד את יצחק.

49. See Blum, *Die Komposition der Vätergeschichte*, 265–70.

50. Most recently, Horst Seebass, *Genesis II: Vätergeschichte II (23,1–36,43)* (Neukirchen-Vluyn: Neukirchner, 1999), 444–47, rearranged the text source-critically with E as the basic story consisting of 35:1–5b, 14*(without the relative clause), 7a, 9b, 10 and P having 35:6, 9a, 11–13a. The reconstructed E thread, however, shows no coherence (cf. 5b/14* and 7a/9b!); it is also hard to imagine how the final text should have been put together from these sources. See more below, esp. section 5 (3.2).

44 Erhard Blum

35:11–12). As a result, he puts up a מצבה (28:18a // 35:14a), pours oil on it (28:18b // 35:14b), and gives the same name ("Bethel") to the place (28:19a // 35:15). At the same time, there is not even a trace of an attempt to harmonize both episodes.[51] How should we read them both within one context? The key lies in the conflicting messages of Gen 35: as a Hieros Logos, Gen 28 recounts Jacob's discovery of the holiness of the place and its consequences, which include consecrating the stone he used as a pillow as a cultic stone and naming the place Bethel. Genesis 35 takes up these same elements—using wording so similar that is comes close to plagiarism—but reverses the basic message: Bethel is not the place where God *dwells* anymore (cf. 28:16–17: "YHWH is in this place!"; "This is none other than the house of God!"), but rather "the place, where he (God) had talked with him" (המקום אשר דבר אתו שם), a wording used no less than three times to hammer the point home. This place cannot be more, because God ascended from there after he had talked with him: ויעל מעליו אלהים במקום אשר דבר אתו (v. 13).

Both supplementary elements in 35:14 must be interpreted against this background: the explanation of the pillar as מצבת אבן and the libation. Concerning the former, August Dillmann already remarked that מצבת אבן was "strange" ("merkwürdig"), "as though the sacred pillar should be characterized only as a stone monument."[52] The sentence ויסך עליה נסך fits in with this view, if it is understood as an epexegesis put in front of its referent ויצק עליה שמן. In this way, the anointing, that is, the consecration of the pillar, gets transformed into a spontaneous libation, which *per se* is not bound to a cultic place or even a cultic context at all.[53] In other words: the Priestly author transforms the ancient cultic etiology into an antietiology,

---

51. For instance, by explicitly referring back in 35:9–15 to 28:11–12 (even the word עוד in 35:9 is ambiguous in this regard, since it may refer to 32:23–33 or to 31:13 in the pre-P context) or by speaking of a "further pillar" or of a "confirmation of the name given to the place," etc.

52. August Dillmann, *Die Genesis*, KeH 11.6, 6th ed. (Leipzig: Hirzel, 1892), 378.

53. See David's water libation in 2 Sam 23:16. Wellhausen, who does not notice the correcting purpose, thinks otherwise: "Neither can 35:14 be attributed to Q.… The author of Q would have had to completely forget himself once—which may not be expected of him" (*Composition des Hexateuchs*, 322). Surely referring to the libation in v. 14, he claims here to know more than we do: the root נסך appears in P only occasionally in the sense of an accompanying offering (at the holy place). P texts reveal nothing on what their scribes thought of individual rites of piety outside of the holy place (without any sacrificial killing and burning), including spontaneous libations (in this exceptional case with oil). This silence may indicate an adiaphoron. If not, the

Once Again: The Literary-Historical Profile of the P Tradition   45

which negates the theology from Gen 28, according to which God dwells at this place. Admittedly, only a reader who knows about Gen 28 can see this connection. It is indeed possible that the author could assume on the part of his addressees some knowledge of the Bethel etiology. A purely inter-textual reference seems therefore possible at first sight. However, this is improbable for many reasons. First, genuine P texts avoid (with the significant exception of Gen 35) naming the location of God's apparitions or speeches when they occur outside of the Ohel Moed. In an independent Priestly work, there would have been no reason to break this rule for Jacob; silence would have been a more practical and safer way.[54]

Second, in a freely written work, we would expect the correction of Gen 28 to appear in its current place, that is, when Jacob leaves for Paddan Aram, especially since P generally follows the sequence of the plot from the pre-Priestly story. This would be almost impossible in an independent Priestly work, because this position is already occupied in P by Isaac's transmission of Abraham's blessing (28:1–5). The potential result of this can be seen in Hermann Gunkel's reconstruction, which moves the blessing from 35:6aα[!], 11–12, 13a[!], 15* as an etiology for Bethel (!) to the spot right after 28:1–9 and detaches 35:9–10 from 35:11–15, which causes further inconsistencies on closer inspection.[55]

---

question would remain why a redactor using P as his basis should have inserted v. 14 here (and whence this verse should have come).

54. After all, a massive reference to Bethel might have been unclear and counterproductive if the readers/listeners did not remember well enough the concrete textual references. *Si tacuisses …*

55. See Gunkel, *Genesis*, 386–88; Albert de Pury ("Der priesterschriftliche Umgang mit der Jakobsgeschichte," in *Schriftauslegung in der Schrift: FS O. H. Steck*, ed. R. G. Kratz et al., BZAW 300 [Berlin: De Gruyter, 2000], 33–60; de Pury, "The Jacob Story and the Beginning of the Formation of the Pentateuch," in *A Farewell to the Yahwist?*, ed. Thomas Dozeman and Konrad Schmid, SymS 34 [Atlanta: Society of Biblical Literature, 2006], 51–72) took up this suggestion again (though he included 35:14 in P[G] and considered that 28:3–4 are not original). The additional divine apparition thus created would be the only one in P before the erection of the Mishkan in which God would not introduce himself, and Jacob's renaming would remain—in contrast to Abraham and Sarah—without any explicit or implicit explanation. This is not a problem in the given context 35:9–11, where the name "Israel"—analogous to "Sarah" in 17:15–16—is explained with the hidden semantic pun between the element שׂר and the word מלך, which has a similar meaning, in the following promise of royal descendants; see Yair Zakovitch, "The Synonymous Word and Synonymous Name in Name-Midrashim" [Hebrew] *Shnaton* 2 (1977):

46   Erhard Blum

Third, the double communication (which is per se redundant) of the blessing to Jacob, which sets up narrative brackets before his departure to Laban and after his return, provides a structure which helps to join the Priestly elements together with the pre-Priestly material. This observation corresponds to what we found above in the Lot material, in the list of Jacob's sons and their mothers provided in retrospect (35:22–26) or in the structuring of the toledot: some formulations and the positioning of certain elements in these passages are as much in conflict with the logic of an independent Priestly work as they are suitable for a joining with the pre-Priestly material. In the case of the Priestly promises for Jacob, the purpose of the double blessing is not just to create a compositional bracket, but also to provide a narrative Priestly correction to the contextually associated pre-Priestly traditions.[56]

Such pointedly discontinuous and antagonistic Priestly references to pre-Priestly tradition appear not only in the Jacob story, but also just as prominently in further narrative and programmatic contexts such as Exod 6:2–8 with respect to Exod 3 and various pre-Priestly divine apparitions in Genesis or in the hard confrontation of the mutually exclusive holiness concepts for Israel as God's people in the Sinai pericope[57] and the marginalization of the prophetic Ohel Moed of Exod 33:7–11 et cetera through the interpretation of the Ohel Moed as a priestly sanctuary. The important conflicts concerning halakic or cultic law in the Pentateuch on such topics as the definition of the priesthood, profane slaughtering, tithing, debt bondage, et cetera also support this assessment of P's relationship to pre-Priestly material.

103–4, who finds numerous examples of this type of indirect name interpretation (including further instances with "Israel") in all parts of the Hebrew canon. On the sequence Gen 35:9–10, 11–15, see below in section 5 (3.2).

56. On the correcting *relecture* of the story in Gen 27 through the Priestly brackets 26:34–35 + 27:46–28:9, see Blum, *Die Komposition der Vätergeschichte*, 263–365.

57. On this topic, especially on the vain attempts to find mediating redactions, cf. Erhard Blum, "Esra, die Mosetora und die persische Politik," in *Religion und Religionskontakte im Zeitalter der Achämeniden*, ed. Reinhard G. Kratz, VGTh 22 (Gütersloh: Gütersloher, 2002), 231–56, esp. 235–46.

5. Consequences for the Literary-Historical Profile of P

The evidence presented above on the so-called P story in the ancestral history of Genesis (and Exodus) points in different, or even (at first sight) mutually exclusive, directions from a literary-historical point of view. In my opinion however, it allows us to draw clear conclusions that paint a complex picture of P's development with, nevertheless, clear components:

(1) The P texts in the textual sections discussed above *do not* constitute a redactional *expansion* of a basic textual layer. This follows firstly from their literary features: the doublets, the partly *dis*continuous joints with pre-Priestly material, and especially the continuous narrative or discursive threads within the extracted P pieces that are obvious in certain cases. Such threads are also visible in whole episodes or narrative units from other sections such as the flood story or the miracle at the Reed Sea. Second, the kerygmatic threads often become more sharply visible when the non-P connections are removed (so to speak), as Norbert Lohfink in particular has shown. At the same time, it is the contrasting and antagonistic references between Priestly and pre-Priestly traditions that, again, let P's conception stand out with particular sharpness. Both aspects constitute in a certain way two sides of the same coin.

By the way, P as a whole cannot be a redactional expansion layer if there never was the one pre-P basic layer from the Primeval History to Exodus and beyond, for which there are good reasons, in my opinion.

(2) Just as clearly, the P texts from the sections discussed above *cannot constitute an independent source.* Among the evidence which corroborates this are gaps in the narrative substance that cannot be explained in any plausible manner by redactional omissions, but especially structural characteristics which were clearly shaped to match the profile of the pre-Priestly story (toledot framework), and, not least, intentional discontinuous joints with their contrasting references to pre-P texts.

The picture may be different in the Primeval History with regards to its possible independence. Should we therefore reckon with the possibility that the basic character of the Priestly tradition could change from one textual section to another between being an independent source and being something else with another literary character? This would only be an illusory solution, because it would deprive not only the common term source/document of meaning, but also the very concept of an independent text.

(3) Instead, we should be looking for a comprehensive model that would allow us to integrate the divergent findings (if only in the ancestral

48 Erhard Blum

history) as well as possible differences between the textual sections of the Pentateuch without minimizing or even ignoring the importance of any aspect of the evidence.

A possible approach for such a comprehensive model would be, in my opinion, the *assumption of a multistage production history for P*. This assumption will be outlined as a series of theses in the following paragraphs 3.1–3.3; the evidence supporting them was already provided, for the most part, in the findings previously described. Aspects of the tradition history of the P layer in the Pentateuch that belong to the prerequisites of its formation but not to its literary production are expressly left aside. These include oral and written stories in particular, which the P scribes knew and inherited from their own Priestly tradition, as well as the knowledge of non-Priestly literary traditions from all parts of the later Pentateuch.

The literary genesis of P took place in a multistage process. For the sake of clarity, the *fundamental production phases* will be initially described as a process in two stages in sections 3.1 and 3.2, and finally, some necessary additional distinctions will be addressed in section 3.3.

3.1. The basic textual substance of P—at least in Genesis, Exodus, and Leviticus—was *conceived separately*, partly by using given Priestly material and partly by formulating new textual bits freely.[58]

In this phase, we are still dealing with a separate draft or drafts, because these sheets or partial scrolls were not conceived as independent works, but rather as preliminary sketches for a more comprehensive work in which external traditions that were not of Priestly origin would be integrated as well. This draft, which we may call P^0, was prepared with these external blueprints in mind but separately from them.

Obviously, the extent of textual preparation and of consideration of and orientation toward external texts varied. In Genesis, the textual evidence points to a far-reaching transition: from an almost complete draft in the sense of an autonomous writing ("source") in the Primeval History, through the shaping of a mostly continuous line in the Abraham story, to the shrinking of the narrative thread to some isolated markings in the Jacob and Joseph traditions. In any case, the draft did not have to

---

58. Candidates for preformulated material in Genesis are, e.g., a possible toledot book and similar lists (this can be inferred, for instance, from well-known contradictions internal to P such as the ones between Gen 26:34–35; 28:9, and 36:2–5). Candidates for newly formulated material are theological texts, in particular those which determine the programmatic "contour line" ("Höhenlinie").

Once Again: The Literary-Historical Profile of the P Tradition   49

be complete. That is why the transition from the end of Exod 2 to 6:2–5, for example, could have a seemingly smooth formulation on the one hand, while omitting the introduction of the main character Moses on the other hand, since this introduction was already provided in the external pre-Priestly material.

In the ancestral history and at the beginning of the exodus story, the writer(s) of P^0 not only clearly kept the sequence of the plot from the pre-Priestly traditions, but the narrative breadth of these traditions also allowed him/them to restrict in a reductionistic way their input from Gen 12 on to a few basic elements of the plot, as outlined in the analysis above. It is possible that these notes in P^0 mainly had the function of showing the progression of the plot with a few strokes and especially of marking[59] or preparing the place of its own main programmatic texts (Gen 17, etc.).

3.2. In a *next step*, the Priestly groundwork, that is, P^0, and the material from other sources, which were not of Priestly origin,[60] were *combined in a literary composition*. This work probably corresponded to the conventional source-critical view of a redaction, though with the important difference that the author(s) of the source-like draft was (were) the redactor(s) of the whole work at the same time.[61] Additionally, we should reckon from the start with the probability that this composition was not limited to some additive arrangement of the textual pieces at the disposal of the redactor(s) but could also involve some literary expansions as well.

---

59. This makes sense, for instance, in the P-elements of Gen 16 (including the remarks on the age of the protagonists) leading up to Gen 17. Afterwards, the loose mark at the end of the Sodom-Lot-episode was sufficient (cf. above), which Isaac's birth in Gen 21 could probably follow (on the "Abraham-Abimelech-story" in Gen 20 + 21:22–32 as a really late entry in this context, cf. Blum, *Die Komposition der Vätergeschichte*, 405–19).

60. According to my assessment explained elsewhere, these external materials consisted mainly of three independent literary units: a pre-Priestly Primeval History, a (late) exilic ancestral history, and the larger D composition (from the birth of Moses to his death, including the deuteronomistic Deuteronomy).

61. This is not meant to affirm that the author and the redactor were the same person. Not only does this question lie beyond our capacity to make a historical judgment, but we should also take the plural used above seriously and reckon with the possibility that a work such as KP—even if limited to some sort of first edition ("KP^G")—was not shaped by only one individual, but rather by a group (maybe a school linked to the temple?) as part of a process (with more than two stages) going through several generations of writers.

50   Erhard Blum

Since the Priestly scribes were, so to speak, their own authors and redactors, it would be advisable to adopt another overarching terminology for them; I would suggest using the terms "composition/compositor." This terminology seems especially fitting if the more ancient traditions concerning the Primeval History, the time of the patriarchs, and the Exodus/Sinai were put together for the first time in a literary context with and through their integration in the great Priestly work, a view that is currently gaining adherents in the exegetical community. I call this "second stage" of the production process of P correspondingly the "P-Composition" ("KP," "composition" being written with a "K" in German), both in terms of the process (*nomen actionis*) and in terms of the result (*nomen acti*).

The fact that elementary insights of the Documentary Hypothesis on P can be integrated in this composition model without any difficulty seems to me significant. This is especially valid for the picture described above, in which the P story was used as "the literary basis of the Pentateuchal narrative"[62] by the redaction. This assumption, which is based on many convincing observations, keeps its analytical validity within the hypothesis of a formation process in stages as well, inasmuch as the draft(s) P^0 is (are) assumed to play the same role within the P-Composition.

On the other hand, the higher complexity of the assumed formation makes it possible to address questions that had not been conceived before. For instance, it may be asked whether some difficult findings could eventually find a satisfying explanation in the distinction between P^0 and the compositional text formation in KP. For example, the unusual structure of the divine speech in Gen 35:10–13, with God introducing himself only in verse 11, might be attributed to a compositional Priestly expansion of the promise speech already present in P^0, adding Jacob's change of name in verse 10. The adoption of Joseph's sons in Gen 48:3–7 may also belong to this category, a passage whose reference quoting pre-P (Gen 35:16–20) is not quite usual within P (P^0?) texts, and whose strikingly close integration in the direct pre-P context has already been noted several times. In addition, with classical redactional phenomena such as the P elements in Gen 33:18 or 35:6, we have the option of linking them compositionally with KP instead of attributing them to a later hand. More examples of this sort would be easy to find; they all have in common the option given by

---

62. Noth, *History of Pentateuchal Traditions*, 11 (this sentence is emphasized through extra spaces between the letters in the original text and in italics in the English translation).

Once Again: The Literary-Historical Profile of the P Tradition 51

the basic model, according to which authorial and redactional aspects of the text formation are distinguished, but these do not correspond *per se* to different persons/hands.

3.3. This sketch of a process in two stages for the formation of KP was introduced explicitly as a *simplification*. This point will now be underlined with a few remarks on necessary distinctions and methodical implications (without claiming to be exhaustive).

Regarding the extent of the proto-Pentateuch molded by the Priestly school, the two-stage model turns quickly into a picture of various extensions, supplements, corrections, et cetera, which is not reducible to a simple outline. In other words: the phenomenon called P^S, which was postulated within the framework of the Documentary Hypothesis, fundamentally keeps its usual meaning as a kind of black box for the continuation of tradition literature shaped by generations of writers in the KP-model as well. As a complement, even the concept of a P^G can be incorporated into this model as long as it is detached from the independent Priestly Code and applied to the matter of a basic composition of P in Genesis, Exodus, and beyond. We should then naturally reckon not only with a certain time span for the formulation of this composition, but also with a considerable diversity of the compositional processes. For instance, the problem of P's redactional connection to non-P is evidently different in the case of texts concerning the shrine or even nonexistent in the case of the cultic and ethical/paraenetic material in Leviticus, whereas in parts of Numbers, the modification of drafts from P^0 might be diminished in comparison to a primarily transformative and compositional text formation.[63] On the whole, the complexity of the object of study requires a fundamental openness of the overall model in terms of the time perspective, text types, and text sections, as well as the model's structure.

In addition, there are questions of method in the framework outlined above that concern the prerequisites of the traditional definitions of a basic Priestly work (P^G, i.e., "P-Grundschrift" in German) in the Pentateuch, whose criteria are determined in the end by the idea of a single source author. Apart from the a priori commitment to the hypothesis of a narrative work,[64] these criteria have to do with matters of linguistic

---

63. See, e.g., Blum, *Studien zur Komposition des Pentateuch*, 271–78, on Num 20.

64. The loose argumentation in favor of this in the fundamental analysis of Noth (*History of Pentateuchal Traditions*, 8–10) is surprising; it leads too easily to the desired result: "In any case, they [i.e. the cultic and ritual material] should be totally

52   Erhard Blum

and conceptual consistency; even comparatively minor differences in the linguistic usage or in details of cultic law could have an impact on hypotheses of diachronic strata. Without addressing here more fundamental problems of the methodical relationship between textual incoherence and diachronic compositeness, the question remains whether the presupposed standard is appropriate for this kind of literature. As an alternative option to a text coming from a single author, we should reckon with the concept of a *work*, which would have been realized in a longer process by not just one person alone. How can we determine the boundaries and unity of such a work?[65] Not with literary-critical incoherence standards alone, in any case, but rather by looking at macro- and micro-structural signals and at certain aspects of the inherent compositional logic, as well as by building on observations concerning redactional techniques.[66]

Last, but not least, the outlined model of a P-composition has important consequences for the debate on the end of P, which has so far been waged without leading to any agreement on the result. On the one hand, this question cannot be handled within the composition hypothesis without determining the extent of the pre-Priestly tradition integrated into it: a KP that would extend to Exod 29 or 40 while the non-Priestly story would go further would be preposterous. On the other hand, once the claim of the literary independence of the Priestly work is dropped, Lothar Perlitt's effective denial of a P-ending in Deut 34 loses its most important prerequisite.[67]

---

disregarded in the consideration of the P narrative. Accordingly, the P narrative shows itself to be a *narrative* much more decisively and clearly than might appear from the customary use of the siglum P" (p. 10; emphasis original).

65. See, for example, the discussion on the relation of H to P in Erhard Blum, "Issues and Problems in the Contemporary Debate Regarding the Priestly Writings," in *The Strata of the Priestly Writings. Contemporary Debate and Future Directions*, ed. Sarah Shectman and Joel S. Baden, ATANT 95 (Zürich: TVZ, 2009), 33–39 with further references.

66. See, for instance, the supplements in Exod 30–31 following the *programmatic* finale at the end of Exod 29, in Lev 27 after the concluding summary in Lev 26:46, and in Numbers following the introduction of the *narrative* finale in Num 27:*12–23, which finds its conclusion in the last chapters of Deuteronomy (mediated through the resumptive repetition in Deut 32:48–52).

67. Lothar Perlitt, "Priesterschrift im Deuteronomium?," *ZAW* 100 (1988): 44–88.

Once Again: The Literary-Historical Profile of the P Tradition 53

Table 1. The so-called P story in Gen 11:27–50:13
according to Martin Noth

Texts that I would add to Noth's reconstruction appear in parentheses (), texts that I would remove appear in square brackets [], and texts whose inclusion seems questionable are marked with a question mark (?). The arrangement of lines usually follows the sentence structure, with some exceptions due to layout issues. In the case of Gen 23 and 36, only excerpts are presented due to the large size of these chapters.

וְאֵלֶּה תּוֹלְדֹת תֶּרַח	11:27
תֶּרַח הוֹלִיד אֶת־אַבְרָם אֶת־נָחוֹר וְאֶת־הָרָן	
וְהָרָן הוֹלִיד אֶת־לוֹט׃	
וַיָּמָת הָרָן עַל־פְּנֵי תֶּרַח אָבִיו בְּאֶרֶץ מוֹלַדְתּוֹ בְּאוּר כַּשְׂדִּים׃	11:28
וַיִּקַּח תֶּרַח אֶת־אַבְרָם בְּנוֹ וְאֶת־לוֹט בֶּן־הָרָן בֶּן־בְּנוֹ	11:31
וְאֵת שָׂרַי כַּלָּתוֹ אֵשֶׁת אַבְרָם בְּנוֹ	
וַיֵּצְאוּ אִתָּם מֵאוּר כַּשְׂדִּים לָלֶכֶת אַרְצָה כְּנַעַן	
וַיָּבֹאוּ עַד־חָרָן וַיֵּשְׁבוּ שָׁם׃	
וַיִּהְיוּ יְמֵי־תֶרַח חָמֵשׁ שָׁנִים וּמָאתַיִם שָׁנָה	11:32
וַיָּמָת תֶּרַח בְּחָרָן׃	
וְאַבְרָם בֶּן־חָמֵשׁ שָׁנִים וְשִׁבְעִים שָׁנָה בְּצֵאתוֹ מֵחָרָן׃	12:4b
וַיִּקַּח אַבְרָם אֶת־שָׂרַי אִשְׁתּוֹ וְאֶת־לוֹט בֶּן־אָחִיו וְאֶת־כָּל־רְכוּשָׁם	12:5
אֲשֶׁר רָכָשׁוּ	
וְאֶת־הַנֶּפֶשׁ אֲשֶׁר־עָשׂוּ בְחָרָן	
וַיֵּצְאוּ לָלֶכֶת אַרְצָה כְּנַעַן	
וַיָּבֹאוּ אַרְצָה כְּנָעַן׃	
וְלֹא־נָשָׂא אֹתָם הָאָרֶץ לָשֶׁבֶת יַחְדָּו	13:6
כִּי־הָיָה רְכוּשָׁם רָב וְלֹא יָכְלוּ לָשֶׁבֶת יַחְדָּו׃	
וַיִּפָּרְדוּ אִישׁ מֵעַל אָחִיו׃	13:11b (?)
אַבְרָם יָשַׁב בְּאֶרֶץ־כְּנָעַן	13:12a
וְלוֹט יָשַׁב בְּעָרֵי הַכִּכָּר	13:12bα
[–]	[19:29 (!)]
וְשָׂרַי אֵשֶׁת אַבְרָם לֹא יָלְדָה לוֹ	16:1a?
וַתִּקַּח שָׂרַי אֵשֶׁת־אַבְרָם אֶת־הָגָר הַמִּצְרִית שִׁפְחָתָהּ	16:3
מִקֵּץ עֶשֶׂר שָׁנִים לְשֶׁבֶת אַבְרָם בְּאֶרֶץ כְּנָעַן	

וַתִּתֵּן אֹתָהּ לְאַבְרָם אִישָׁהּ לוֹ לְאִשָּׁה:

16:15 וַתֵּלֶד הָגָר לְאַבְרָם בֵּן
וַיִּקְרָא אַבְרָם שֶׁם־בְּנוֹ אֲשֶׁר־יָלְדָה הָגָר יִשְׁמָעֵאל:

16:16 וְאַבְרָם בֶּן־שְׁמֹנִים שָׁנָה וְשֵׁשׁ שָׁנִים
בְּלֶדֶת־הָגָר אֶת־יִשְׁמָעֵאל לְאַבְרָם:

17:1 וַיְהִי אַבְרָם בֶּן־תִּשְׁעִים שָׁנָה וְתֵשַׁע שָׁנִים
וַיֵּרָא יְהוָה אֶל־אַבְרָם וַיֹּאמֶר אֵלָיו
אֲנִי־אֵל שַׁדַּי
הִתְהַלֵּךְ לְפָנַי וֶהְיֵה תָמִים:

17:2 וְאֶתְּנָה בְרִיתִי בֵּינִי וּבֵינֶךָ
וְאַרְבֶּה אוֹתְךָ בִּמְאֹד מְאֹד:

17:3 וַיִּפֹּל אַבְרָם עַל־פָּנָיו
וַיְדַבֵּר אִתּוֹ אֱלֹהִים לֵאמֹר:

17:4 אֲנִי הִנֵּה בְרִיתִי אִתָּךְ וְהָיִיתָ לְאַב הֲמוֹן גּוֹיִם:

17:5 וְלֹא־יִקָּרֵא עוֹד אֶת־שִׁמְךָ אַבְרָם וְהָיָה שִׁמְךָ אַבְרָהָם
כִּי אַב־הֲמוֹן גּוֹיִם נְתַתִּיךָ:

17:6 וְהִפְרֵתִי אֹתְךָ בִּמְאֹד מְאֹד וּנְתַתִּיךָ לְגוֹיִם וּמְלָכִים מִמְּךָ יֵצֵאוּ:

17:7 וַהֲקִמֹתִי אֶת־בְּרִיתִי בֵּינִי וּבֵינֶךָ וּבֵין זַרְעֲךָ אַחֲרֶיךָ לְדֹרֹתָם לִבְרִית עוֹלָם
לִהְיוֹת לְךָ לֵאלֹהִים וּלְזַרְעֲךָ אַחֲרֶיךָ:

17:8 וְנָתַתִּי לְךָ וּלְזַרְעֲךָ אַחֲרֶיךָ אֵת אֶרֶץ מְגֻרֶיךָ אֵת כָּל־אֶרֶץ כְּנַעַן לַאֲחֻזַּת עוֹלָם
וְהָיִיתִי לָהֶם לֵאלֹהִים:

17:9 וַיֹּאמֶר אֱלֹהִים אֶל־אַבְרָהָם
וְאַתָּה אֶת־בְּרִיתִי תִשְׁמֹר אַתָּה וְזַרְעֲךָ אַחֲרֶיךָ לְדֹרֹתָם:

17:10 זֹאת בְּרִיתִי אֲשֶׁר תִּשְׁמְרוּ בֵּינִי וּבֵינֵיכֶם וּבֵין זַרְעֲךָ אַחֲרֶיךָ

17:11 הִמּוֹל לָכֶם כָּל־זָכָר:
וְהָיָה לְאוֹת בְּרִית בֵּינִי וּבֵינֵיכֶם:

17:12 וּבֶן־שְׁמֹנַת יָמִים יִמּוֹל לָכֶם כָּל־זָכָר לְדֹרֹתֵיכֶם
יְלִיד בָּיִת וּמִקְנַת־כֶּסֶף מִכֹּל בֶּן־נֵכָר אֲשֶׁר לֹא מִזַּרְעֲךָ הוּא:

17:13 הִמּוֹל יִמּוֹל יְלִיד בֵּיתְךָ וּמִקְנַת כַּסְפֶּךָ
וְהָיְתָה בְרִיתִי בִּבְשַׂרְכֶם לִבְרִית עוֹלָם:

17:14 וְעָרֵל זָכָר אֲשֶׁר לֹא־יִמּוֹל אֶת־בְּשַׂר עָרְלָתוֹ
וְנִכְרְתָה הַנֶּפֶשׁ הַהִוא מֵעַמֶּיהָ אֶת־בְּרִיתִי הֵפַר:

17:15 וַיֹּאמֶר אֱלֹהִים אֶל־אַבְרָהָם
שָׂרַי אִשְׁתְּךָ לֹא־תִקְרָא אֶת־שְׁמָהּ שָׂרָי כִּי שָׂרָה שְׁמָהּ:

17:16 וּבֵרַכְתִּי אֹתָהּ

Once Again: The Literary-Historical Profile of the P Tradition   55

וְגַם נָתַתִּי מִמֶּנָּה לְךָ בֵּן

וּבֵרַכְתִּיהָ

וְהָיְתָה לְגוֹיִם

מַלְכֵי עַמִּים מִמֶּנָּה יִהְיוּ:

17:17   וַיִּפֹּל אַבְרָהָם עַל־פָּנָיו

וַיִּצְחָק וַיֹּאמֶר בְּלִבּוֹ

הַלְּבֶן מֵאָה־שָׁנָה יִוָּלֵד וְאִם־שָׂרָה הֲבַת־תִּשְׁעִים שָׁנָה תֵּלֵד:

17:18   וַיֹּאמֶר אַבְרָהָם אֶל־הָאֱלֹהִים

לוּ יִשְׁמָעֵאל יִחְיֶה לְפָנֶיךָ:

17:19   וַיֹּאמֶר אֱלֹהִים

אֲבָל שָׂרָה אִשְׁתְּךָ יֹלֶדֶת לְךָ בֵּן

וְקָרָאתָ אֶת־שְׁמוֹ יִצְחָק

וַהֲקִמֹתִי אֶת־בְּרִיתִי אִתּוֹ לִבְרִית עוֹלָם לְזַרְעוֹ אַחֲרָיו:

17:20   וּלְיִשְׁמָעֵאל שְׁמַעְתִּיךָ

הִנֵּה בֵּרַכְתִּי אֹתוֹ וְהִפְרֵיתִי אֹתוֹ וְהִרְבֵּיתִי אֹתוֹ בִּמְאֹד מְאֹד

שְׁנֵים־עָשָׂר נְשִׂיאִם יוֹלִיד וּנְתַתִּיו לְגוֹי גָּדוֹל:

17:21   וְאֶת־בְּרִיתִי אָקִים אֶת־יִצְחָק

אֲשֶׁר תֵּלֵד לְךָ שָׂרָה לַמּוֹעֵד הַזֶּה בַּשָּׁנָה הָאַחֶרֶת:

17:22   וַיְכַל לְדַבֵּר אִתּוֹ

וַיַּעַל אֱלֹהִים מֵעַל אַבְרָהָם:

17:23   וַיִּקַּח אַבְרָהָם אֶת־יִשְׁמָעֵאל בְּנוֹ וְאֵת כָּל־יְלִידֵי בֵיתוֹ

וְאֵת כָּל־מִקְנַת כַּסְפּוֹ כָּל־זָכָר בְּאַנְשֵׁי בֵּית אַבְרָהָם

וַיָּמָל אֶת־בְּשַׂר עָרְלָתָם בְּעֶצֶם הַיּוֹם הַזֶּה

כַּאֲשֶׁר דִּבֶּר אִתּוֹ אֱלֹהִים:

17:24   וְאַבְרָהָם בֶּן־תִּשְׁעִים וָתֵשַׁע שָׁנָה בְּהִמֹּלוֹ בְּשַׂר עָרְלָתוֹ:

17:25   וְיִשְׁמָעֵאל בְּנוֹ בֶּן־שְׁלֹשׁ עֶשְׂרֵה שָׁנָה בְּהִמֹּלוֹ אֵת בְּשַׂר עָרְלָתוֹ:

17:26   בְּעֶצֶם הַיּוֹם הַזֶּה נִמּוֹל אַבְרָהָם וְיִשְׁמָעֵאל בְּנוֹ:

17:27   וְכָל־אַנְשֵׁי בֵיתוֹ יְלִיד בָּיִת וּמִקְנַת־כֶּסֶף מֵאֵת בֶּן־נֵכָר נִמֹּלוּ אִתּוֹ:

...   ...

19:29 (!)   וַיְהִי בְּשַׁחֵת אֱלֹהִים אֶת־עָרֵי הַכִּכָּר

וַיִּזְכֹּר אֱלֹהִים אֶת־אַבְרָהָם

וַיְשַׁלַּח אֶת־לוֹט מִתּוֹךְ הַהֲפֵכָה

בַּהֲפֹךְ אֶת־הֶעָרִים אֲשֶׁר־יָשַׁב בָּהֵן לוֹט:

21:1b?   וַיַּעַשׂ יְהוָה לְשָׂרָה כַּאֲשֶׁר דִּבֵּר:

21:2   וַתַּהַר וַתֵּלֶד שָׂרָה לְאַבְרָהָם בֵּן לִזְקֻנָיו לַמּוֹעֵד

אֲשֶׁר־דִּבֶּר אֹתוֹ אֱלֹהִים:

Erhard Blum

21:3	וַיִּקְרָא אַבְרָהָם אֶת־שֶׁם־בְּנוֹ ... אֲשֶׁר־יָלְדָה־לּוֹ שָׂרָה יִצְחָק:
21:4	וַיָּמָל אַבְרָהָם אֶת־יִצְחָק בְּנוֹ בֶּן־שְׁמֹנַת יָמִים כַּאֲשֶׁר צִוָּה אֹתוֹ אֱלֹהִים:
21:5	וְאַבְרָהָם בֶּן־מְאַת שָׁנָה בְּהִוָּלֶד לוֹ אֵת יִצְחָק בְּנוֹ:
23:1	וַיִּהְיוּ חַיֵּי שָׂרָה מֵאָה שָׁנָה וְעֶשְׂרִים שָׁנָה וְשֶׁבַע שָׁנִים שְׁנֵי חַיֵּי שָׂרָה:
20 –	–
25:7	וְאֵלֶּה יְמֵי שְׁנֵי־חַיֵּי אַבְרָהָם אֲשֶׁר־חָי מְאַת שָׁנָה שִׁבְעִים שָׁנָה וְחָמֵשׁ שָׁנִים:
25:8	וַיִּגְוַע וַיָּמָת אַבְרָהָם בְּשֵׂיבָה טוֹבָה זָקֵן וְשָׂבֵעַ וַיֵּאָסֶף אֶל־עַמָּיו:
25:9	וַיִּקְבְּרוּ אֹתוֹ יִצְחָק וְיִשְׁמָעֵאל בָּנָיו אֶל־מְעָרַת הַמַּכְפֵּלָה אֶל־שְׂדֵה עֶפְרֹן בֶּן־צֹחַר הַחִתִּי אֲשֶׁר עַל־פְּנֵי מַמְרֵא:
25:10	הַשָּׂדֶה אֲשֶׁר־קָנָה אַבְרָהָם מֵאֵת בְּנֵי־חֵת שָׁמָּה קֻבַּר אַבְרָהָם וְשָׂרָה אִשְׁתּוֹ:
25:11a	וַיְהִי אַחֲרֵי מוֹת אַבְרָהָם וַיְבָרֶךְ אֱלֹהִים אֶת־יִצְחָק בְּנוֹ
(25:11b)	(וַיֵּשֶׁב יִצְחָק עִם־בְּאֵר לַחַי רֹאִי):
25:12	וְאֵלֶּה תֹּלְדֹת יִשְׁמָעֵאל בֶּן־אַבְרָהָם אֲשֶׁר יָלְדָה הָגָר הַמִּצְרִית שִׁפְחַת שָׂרָה לְאַבְרָהָם:
25:13	וְאֵלֶּה שְׁמוֹת בְּנֵי יִשְׁמָעֵאל בִּשְׁמֹתָם לְתוֹלְדֹתָם בְּכֹר יִשְׁמָעֵאל נְבָיֹת וְקֵדָר וְאַדְבְּאֵל וּמִבְשָׂם:
25:14–15	וּמִשְׁמָע וְדוּמָה וּמַשָּׂא: חֲדַד וְתֵימָא יְטוּר נָפִישׁ וָקֵדְמָה:
25:16	אֵלֶּה הֵם בְּנֵי יִשְׁמָעֵאל וְאֵלֶּה שְׁמֹתָם בְּחַצְרֵיהֶם וּבְטִירֹתָם שְׁנֵים־עָשָׂר נְשִׂיאִם לְאֻמֹּתָם:
25:17	וְאֵלֶּה שְׁנֵי חַיֵּי יִשְׁמָעֵאל מְאַת שָׁנָה וּשְׁלֹשִׁים שָׁנָה וְשֶׁבַע שָׁנִים וַיִּגְוַע וַיָּמָת וַיֵּאָסֶף אֶל־עַמָּיו:
(25:18*)	(וַיִּשְׁכְּנוּ מֵחֲוִילָה עַד־שׁוּר אֲשֶׁר עַל־פְּנֵי מִצְרַיִם בֹּאֲכָה אַשּׁוּרָה)
25:19	וְאֵלֶּה תּוֹלְדֹת יִצְחָק בֶּן־אַבְרָהָם אַבְרָהָם הוֹלִיד אֶת־יִצְחָק:
25:20	וַיְהִי יִצְחָק בֶּן־אַרְבָּעִים שָׁנָה בְּקַחְתּוֹ אֶת־רִבְקָה בַּת־בְּתוּאֵל הָאֲרַמִּי מִפַּדַּן אֲרָם אֲחוֹת לָבָן הָאֲרַמִּי לוֹ לְאִשָּׁה:
...	...
25:26b	וְיִצְחָק בֶּן־שִׁשִּׁים שָׁנָה בְּלֶדֶת אֹתָם:
26:34	וַיְהִי עֵשָׂו בֶּן־אַרְבָּעִים שָׁנָה

Once Again: The Literary-Historical Profile of the P Tradition   57

וַיִּקַּח אִשָּׁה אֶת־יְהוּדִית בַּת־בְּאֵרִי הַחִתִּי וְאֶת־בָּשְׂמַת	
הָיֶיןָ מֹרַת רוּחַ לְיִצְחָק וּלְרִבְקָה:	26:35
וַתֹּאמֶר רִבְקָה אֶל־יִצְחָק	27:46
קַצְתִּי בְחַיַּי מִפְּנֵי בְּנוֹת חֵת	
אִם־לֹקֵחַ יַעֲקֹב אִשָּׁה מִבְּנוֹת־חֵת כָּאֵלֶּה מִבְּנוֹת הָאָרֶץ	
לָמָּה לִי חַיִּים:	
וַיִּקְרָא יִצְחָק אֶל־יַעֲקֹב	28:1
וַיְבָרֶךְ אֹתוֹ	
וַיְצַוֵּהוּ וַיֹּאמֶר לוֹ	
לֹא־תִקַּח אִשָּׁה מִבְּנוֹת כְּנָעַן:	
קוּם לֵךְ פַּדֶּנָה אֲרָם בֵּיתָה בְתוּאֵל אֲבִי אִמֶּךָ	28:2
וְקַח־לְךָ מִשָּׁם אִשָּׁה מִבְּנוֹת לָבָן אֲחִי אִמֶּךָ:	
וְאֵל שַׁדַּי יְבָרֵךְ אֹתְךָ	28:3
וְיַפְרְךָ וְיַרְבֶּךָ וְהָיִיתָ לִקְהַל עַמִּים:	
וְיִתֶּן־לְךָ אֶת־בִּרְכַּת אַבְרָהָם לְךָ וּלְזַרְעֲךָ אִתָּךְ	28:4
לְרִשְׁתְּךָ אֶת־אֶרֶץ מְגֻרֶיךָ	
אֲשֶׁר־נָתַן אֱלֹהִים לְאַבְרָהָם:	
וַיִּשְׁלַח יִצְחָק אֶת־יַעֲקֹב	28:5
וַיֵּלֶךְ פַּדֶּנָה אֲרָם אֶל־לָבָן בֶּן־בְּתוּאֵל הָאֲרַמִּי אֲחִי רִבְקָה אֵם יַעֲקֹב וְעֵשָׂו:	
וַיַּרְא עֵשָׂו	28:6
כִּי־בֵרַךְ יִצְחָק אֶת־יַעֲקֹב	
וְשִׁלַּח אֹתוֹ פַּדֶּנָה אֲרָם לָקַחַת־לוֹ מִשָּׁם אִשָּׁה בְּבָרֲכוֹ אֹתוֹ	
וַיְצַו עָלָיו לֵאמֹר	
לֹא־תִקַּח אִשָּׁה מִבְּנוֹת כְּנָעַן:	
יִשְׁמַע יַעֲקֹב אֶל־אָבִיו וְאֶל־אִמּוֹ וַיֵּלֶךְ פַּדֶּנָה אֲרָם:	28:7
וַיַּרְא עֵשָׂו כִּי רָעוֹת בְּנוֹת כְּנָעַן בְּעֵינֵי יִצְחָק אָבִיו:	28:8
וַיֵּלֶךְ עֵשָׂו אֶל־יִשְׁמָעֵאל	28:9
וַיִּקַּח אֶת־מָחֲלַת בַּת־יִשְׁמָעֵאל בֶּן־אַבְרָהָם	
אֲחוֹת נְבָיוֹת עַל־נָשָׁיו לוֹ לְאִשָּׁה:	
...	...
(וַיָּקָם יַעֲקֹב וַיִּשָּׂא אֶת־בָּנָיו וְאֶת־נָשָׁיו עַל־הַגְּמַלִּים:)	(31:17)
(וַיִּנְהַג אֶת־כָּל־מִקְנֵהוּ וְאֶת־כָּל־רְכֻשׁוֹ אֲשֶׁר רָכָשׁ) מִקְנֵה קִנְיָנוֹ	31:18(*)
אֲשֶׁר רָכַשׁ בְּפַדַּן אֲרָם לָבוֹא אֶל־יִצְחָק אָבִיו אַרְצָה כְּנָעַן:	
[וַיָּבֹא יַעֲקֹב שָׁלֵם עִיר שְׁכֶם]	33:18a[*]
אֲשֶׁר בְּאֶרֶץ כְּנַעַן בְּבֹאוֹ מִפַּדַּן אֲרָם	

58 Erhard Blum

35:6[*]	[וַיָּבֹא יַעֲקֹב] לוּזָה אֲשֶׁר בְּאֶרֶץ כְּנַעַן [הוּא בֵּית־אֵל הוּא וְכָל־הָעָם אֲשֶׁר־עִמּוֹ]:
35:9	וַיֵּרָא אֱלֹהִים אֶל־יַעֲקֹב עוֹד בְּבֹאוֹ מִפַּדַּן אֲרָם וַיְבָרֶךְ אֹתוֹ:
35:10	וַיֹּאמֶר־לוֹ אֱלֹהִים שִׁמְךָ יַעֲקֹב לֹא־יִקָּרֵא שִׁמְךָ עוֹד יַעֲקֹב כִּי אִם־יִשְׂרָאֵל יִהְיֶה שְׁמֶךָ וַיִּקְרָא אֶת־שְׁמוֹ יִשְׂרָאֵל:
35:11	וַיֹּאמֶר לוֹ אֱלֹהִים אֲנִי אֵל שַׁדַּי פְּרֵה וּרְבֵה גּוֹי וּקְהַל גּוֹיִם יִהְיֶה מִמֶּךָּ וּמְלָכִים מֵחֲלָצֶיךָ יֵצֵאוּ:
35:12	וְאֶת־הָאָרֶץ אֲשֶׁר נָתַתִּי לְאַבְרָהָם וּלְיִצְחָק לְךָ אֶתְּנֶנָּה וּלְזַרְעֲךָ אַחֲרֶיךָ אֶתֵּן אֶת־הָאָרֶץ:
35:13	וַיַּעַל מֵעָלָיו אֱלֹהִים (בַּמָּקוֹם אֲשֶׁר־דִּבֶּר אִתּוֹ):
(35:14)	(וַיַּצֵּב יַעֲקֹב מַצֵּבָה בַּמָּקוֹם אֲשֶׁר־דִּבֶּר אִתּוֹ מַצֶּבֶת אָבֶן וַיַּסֵּךְ עָלֶיהָ נֶסֶךְ וַיִּצֹק עָלֶיהָ שָׁמֶן:)
35:15	וַיִּקְרָא יַעֲקֹב אֶת־שֵׁם הַמָּקוֹם אֲשֶׁר דִּבֶּר אִתּוֹ שָׁם אֱלֹהִים בֵּית־אֵל:
35:22b	וַיִּהְיוּ בְנֵי־יַעֲקֹב שְׁנֵים עָשָׂר:
35:23	בְּנֵי לֵאָה בְּכוֹר יַעֲקֹב רְאוּבֵן וְשִׁמְעוֹן וְלֵוִי וִיהוּדָה וְיִשָּׂשכָר וּזְבוּלֻן:
35:24	בְּנֵי רָחֵל יוֹסֵף וּבִנְיָמִן:
35:26	וּבְנֵי בִלְהָה שִׁפְחַת רָחֵל דָּן וְנַפְתָּלִי:
35:25	וּבְנֵי זִלְפָּה שִׁפְחַת לֵאָה גָּד וְאָשֵׁר אֵלֶּה בְּנֵי יַעֲקֹב אֲשֶׁר יֻלַּד־לוֹ בְּפַדַּן אֲרָם:
35:27	וַיָּבֹא יַעֲקֹב אֶל־יִצְחָק אָבִיו מַמְרֵא קִרְיַת הָאַרְבַּע הִוא חֶבְרוֹן אֲשֶׁר־גָּר־שָׁם אַבְרָהָם וְיִצְחָק:
35:28	וַיִּהְיוּ יְמֵי יִצְחָק מְאַת שָׁנָה וּשְׁמֹנִים שָׁנָה:
35:29	וַיִּגְוַע יִצְחָק וַיָּמָת וַיֵּאָסֶף אֶל־עַמָּיו זָקֵן וּשְׂבַע יָמִים וַיִּקְבְּרוּ אֹתוֹ עֵשָׂו וְיַעֲקֹב בָּנָיו: פ
36:1	וְאֵלֶּה תֹּלְדוֹת עֵשָׂו הוּא אֱדוֹם:
–	
36:5	אֵלֶּה בְּנֵי עֵשָׂו אֲשֶׁר יֻלְּדוּ־לוֹ בְּאֶרֶץ כְּנָעַן: ...
36:6	וַיִּקַּח עֵשָׂו אֶת־נָשָׁיו וְאֶת־בָּנָיו וְאֶת־בְּנֹתָיו וְאֶת־כָּל־נַפְשׁוֹת בֵּיתוֹ

Once Again: The Literary-Historical Profile of the P Tradition 59

וְאֶת־מִקְנֵהוּ וְאֶת־כָּל־בְּהֶמְתּוֹ וְאֵת כָּל־קִנְיָנוֹ
אֲשֶׁר רָכַשׁ בְּאֶרֶץ כְּנָעַן
וַיֵּלֶךְ אֶל־אֶרֶץ מִפְּנֵי יַעֲקֹב אָחִיו:

36:7	כִּי־הָיָה רְכוּשָׁם רָב מִשֶּׁבֶת יַחְדָּו
	וְלֹא יָכְלָה אֶרֶץ מְגוּרֵיהֶם לָשֵׂאת אֹתָם מִפְּנֵי מִקְנֵיהֶם:
36:8	וַיֵּשֶׁב עֵשָׂו בְּהַר שֵׂעִיר עֵשָׂו הוּא אֱדוֹם:
36:9	וְאֵלֶּה תֹּלְדוֹת עֵשָׂו אֲבִי אֱדוֹם בְּהַר שֵׂעִיר:
[–43]	–
37:1	וַיֵּשֶׁב יַעֲקֹב בְּאֶרֶץ מְגוּרֵי אָבִיו בְּאֶרֶץ כְּנָעַן:
37:2*	אֵלֶּה תֹּלְדוֹת יַעֲקֹב
(?)	[יוֹסֵף] בֶּן־שְׁבַע־עֶשְׂרֵה שָׁנָה [הָיָה רֹעֶה אֶת־אֶחָיו בַּצֹּאן]
…	…
41:46a	וְיוֹסֵף בֶּן־שְׁלֹשִׁים שָׁנָה בְּעָמְדוֹ לִפְנֵי פַּרְעֹה מֶלֶךְ־מִצְרָיִם
(41:46b)	(וַיֵּצֵא יוֹסֵף מִלִּפְנֵי פַרְעֹה וַיַּעֲבֹר בְּכָל־אֶרֶץ מִצְרָיִם:)
…	…
46:6	וַיִּקְחוּ אֶת־מִקְנֵיהֶם וְאֶת־רְכוּשָׁם אֲשֶׁר רָכְשׁוּ בְּאֶרֶץ כְּנַעַן
	וַיָּבֹאוּ מִצְרַיְמָה יַעֲקֹב וְכָל־זַרְעוֹ אִתּוֹ:
46:7	בָּנָיו וּבְנֵי בָנָיו אִתּוֹ בְּנֹתָיו … וְכָל־זַרְעוֹ הֵבִיא אִתּוֹ מִצְרָיְמָה:
[46:8–27]	
…	…
(47:8)	(וַיֹּאמֶר פַּרְעֹה אֶל־יַעֲקֹב
	כַּמָּה יְמֵי שְׁנֵי חַיֶּיךָ:
(47:9)	וַיֹּאמֶר יַעֲקֹב אֶל־פַּרְעֹה
	יְמֵי שְׁנֵי מְגוּרַי שְׁלֹשִׁים וּמְאַת שָׁנָה
	מְעַט וְרָעִים הָיוּ יְמֵי שְׁנֵי חַיַּי
	וְלֹא הִשִּׂיגוּ אֶת־יְמֵי שְׁנֵי חַיֵּי אֲבֹתַי בִּימֵי מְגוּרֵיהֶם:
(47:10)	וַיְבָרֶךְ יַעֲקֹב אֶת־פַּרְעֹה
	וַיֵּצֵא מִלִּפְנֵי פַרְעֹה:
…	…
(47:11*)	(וַיִּתֵּן לָהֶם אֲחֻזָּה בְּאֶרֶץ מִצְרַיִם …:)
47:27(*)	(וַיֵּשֶׁב יִשְׂרָאֵל בְּאֶרֶץ מִצְרַיִם בְּאֶרֶץ גֹּשֶׁן)
	וַיֵּאָחֲזוּ בָהּ וַיִּפְרוּ וַיִּרְבּוּ מְאֹד:
47:28	וַיְחִי יַעֲקֹב בְּאֶרֶץ מִצְרַיִם שְׁבַע עֶשְׂרֵה שָׁנָה
	וַיְהִי יְמֵי־יַעֲקֹב שְׁנֵי חַיָּיו שֶׁבַע שָׁנִים וְאַרְבָּעִים וּמְאַת שָׁנָה:
48:3	וַיֹּאמֶר יַעֲקֹב אֶל־יוֹסֵף

Erhard Blum

אֵל שַׁדַּי נִרְאָה־אֵלַי בְּלוּז בְּאֶרֶץ כְּנָעַן וַיְבָרֶךְ אֹתִי:

48:4 וַיֹּאמֶר אֵלַי
הִנְנִי מַפְרְךָ וְהִרְבִּיתִךָ וּנְתַתִּיךָ לִקְהַל עַמִּים
וְנָתַתִּי אֶת־הָאָרֶץ הַזֹּאת לְזַרְעֲךָ אַחֲרֶיךָ אֲחֻזַּת עוֹלָם:

48:5 וְעַתָּה שְׁנֵי־בָנֶיךָ הַנּוֹלָדִים לְךָ בְּאֶרֶץ מִצְרַיִם
עַד־בֹּאִי אֵלֶיךָ מִצְרַיְמָה לִי־הֵם
אֶפְרַיִם וּמְנַשֶּׁה כִּרְאוּבֵן וְשִׁמְעוֹן יִהְיוּ־לִי:

48:6 וּמוֹלַדְתְּךָ אֲשֶׁר־הוֹלַדְתָּ אַחֲרֵיהֶם לְךָ יִהְיוּ
עַל שֵׁם אֲחֵיהֶם יִקָּרְאוּ בְּנַחֲלָתָם:

(48:7) (וַאֲנִי בְּבֹאִי מִפַּדָּן מֵתָה עָלַי רָחֵל בְּאֶרֶץ כְּנַעַן בַּדֶּרֶךְ
בְּעוֹד כִּבְרַת־אֶרֶץ לָבֹא אֶפְרָתָה
וָאֶקְבְּרֶהָ שָּׁם בְּדֶרֶךְ אֶפְרָת הִוא בֵּית לָחֶם:)

[49:1a] [וַיִּקְרָא יַעֲקֹב אֶל־בָּנָיו]

49:29 וַיְצַו אוֹתָם וַיֹּאמֶר אֲלֵהֶם
אֲנִי נֶאֱסָף אֶל־עַמִּי
קִבְרוּ אֹתִי אֶל־אֲבֹתָי אֶל־הַמְּעָרָה אֲשֶׁר בִּשְׂדֵה עֶפְרוֹן הַחִתִּי:

49:30 בַּמְּעָרָה אֲשֶׁר בִּשְׂדֵה הַמַּכְפֵּלָה אֲשֶׁר עַל־פְּנֵי־מַמְרֵא בְּאֶרֶץ כְּנָעַן
אֲשֶׁר קָנָה אַבְרָהָם אֶת־הַשָּׂדֶה מֵאֵת עֶפְרֹן הַחִתִּי לַאֲחֻזַּת־קָבֶר:

49:31 שָׁמָּה קָבְרוּ אֶת־אַבְרָהָם וְאֵת שָׂרָה אִשְׁתּוֹ
שָׁמָּה קָבְרוּ אֶת־יִצְחָק וְאֵת רִבְקָה אִשְׁתּוֹ
וְשָׁמָּה קָבַרְתִּי אֶת־לֵאָה:

49:32 מִקְנֵה הַשָּׂדֶה וְהַמְּעָרָה אֲשֶׁר־בּוֹ מֵאֵת בְּנֵי־חֵת:

49:33* וַיְכַל יַעֲקֹב לְצַוֹּת אֶת־בָּנָיו

[ ] [וַיֶּאֱסֹף רַגְלָיו אֶל־הַמִּטָּה]
וַיִּגְוַע וַיֵּאָסֶף אֶל־עַמָּיו:

50:12 וַיַּעֲשׂוּ בָנָיו לוֹ כֵּן כַּאֲשֶׁר צִוָּם:

50:13 וַיִּשְׂאוּ אֹתוֹ בָנָיו אַרְצָה כְּנַעַן
וַיִּקְבְּרוּ אֹתוֹ בִּמְעָרַת שְׂדֵה הַמַּכְפֵּלָה
אֲשֶׁר קָנָה אַבְרָהָם אֶת־הַשָּׂדֶה לַאֲחֻזַּת־קֶבֶר ... :

(50:22a) (וַיֵּשֶׁב יוֹסֵף בְּמִצְרַיִם הוּא וּבֵית אָבִיו)

(—) Joseph's age

(50:26a*) (וימת יוסף)

Table 2. Synopsis of Gen 28 // 35

Gen 35		Gen 28	
וַיֵּרָא אֱלֹהִים אֶל־יַעֲקֹב עוֹד בְּבֹאוֹ מִפַּדַּן אֲרָם	9	וַיַּחֲלֹם ...	12
וַיְבָרֶךְ אֹתוֹ:		וְהִנֵּה יְהוָה נִצָּב עָלָיו	13
וַיֹּאמֶר־לוֹ אֱלֹהִים	10	וַיֹּאמַר	
שִׁמְךָ יַעֲקֹב		אֲנִי יְהוָה אֱלֹהֵי אַבְרָהָם אָבִיךָ וֵאלֹהֵי יִצְחָק	
לֹא־יִקָּרֵא שִׁמְךָ עוֹד יַעֲקֹב		הָאָרֶץ אֲשֶׁר אַתָּה שֹׁכֵב עָלֶיהָ לְךָ אֶתְּנֶנָּה וּלְזַרְעֶךָ:	
כִּי אִם־יִשְׂרָאֵל יִהְיֶה שְׁמֶךָ		וְהָיָה זַרְעֲךָ כַּעֲפַר הָאָרֶץ	14
וַיִּקְרָא אֶת־שְׁמוֹ יִשְׂרָאֵל:		וּפָרַצְתָּ יָמָּה וָקֵדְמָה וְצָפֹנָה וָנֶגְבָּה	
וַיֹּאמֶר לוֹ אֱלֹהִים	11	וְנִבְרְכוּ בְךָ כָּל־מִשְׁפְּחֹת הָאֲדָמָה וּבְזַרְעֶךָ:	
אֲנִי אֵל שַׁדַּי		וַיִּיקַץ יַעֲקֹב מִשְּׁנָתוֹ וַיֹּאמֶר	16
פְּרֵה וּרְבֵה		אָכֵן יֵשׁ יְהוָה בַּמָּקוֹם הַזֶּה	
גּוֹי וּקְהַל גּוֹיִם יִהְיֶה מִמֶּךָּ		וְאָנֹכִי לֹא יָדָעְתִּי:	
וּמְלָכִים מֵחֲלָצֶיךָ יֵצֵאוּ:		וַיִּירָא וַיֹּאמַר	17
וְאֶת־הָאָרֶץ לְךָ אֶתְּנֶנָּה	12	מַה־נּוֹרָא הַמָּקוֹם הַזֶּה	
אֲשֶׁר נָתַתִּי לְאַבְרָהָם וּלְיִצְחָק		אֵין זֶה כִּי אִם־בֵּית אֱלֹהִים	
וּלְזַרְעֲךָ אַחֲרֶיךָ אֶתֵּן אֶת־הָאָרֶץ:		וְזֶה שַׁעַר הַשָּׁמָיִם:	
וַיַּעַל מֵעָלָיו אֱלֹהִים בַּמָּקוֹם	13	וַיַּשְׁכֵּם יַעֲקֹב בַּבֹּקֶר	18
אֲשֶׁר־דִּבֶּר אִתּוֹ:		וַיִּקַּח אֶת־הָאֶבֶן אֲשֶׁר־שָׂם מְרַאֲשֹׁתָיו	
וַיַּצֵּב יַעֲקֹב מַצֵּבָה בַּמָּקוֹם מַצֶּבֶת אֶבֶן	14	וַיָּשֶׂם אֹתָהּ מַצֵּבָה	
אֲשֶׁר־דִּבֶּר אִתּוֹ			
וַיַּסֵּךְ עָלֶיהָ נֶסֶךְ			
וַיִּצֹק עָלֶיהָ שָׁמֶן:		וַיִּצֹק שֶׁמֶן עַל־רֹאשָׁהּ:	
וַיִּקְרָא יַעֲקֹב אֶת־שֵׁם הַמָּקוֹם בֵּית־אֵל	15	וַיִּקְרָא אֶת־שֵׁם־הַמָּקוֹם הַהוּא בֵּית־אֵל	19
אֲשֶׁר דִּבֶּר אִתּוֹ שָׁם אֱלֹהִים		וְאוּלָם לוּז שֵׁם־הָעִיר לָרִאשֹׁנָה:	

Genesis 5:
Priestly Redaction, Composition, or Source?

Jan Christian Gertz

1. Introduction

Studies of the origins and development of the Pentateuch consider that the difference between the Priestly and non-Priestly texts are a secure minimum result of a debate in scholarship that is characterized by large differences.[1] In fact, Theodor Nöldeke's almost 150-year-old delineation of what belongs to the Priestly texts in a broad sense enjoys general agreement, although much controversy remains in discussions over the

---

The (German edition of this) paper was prepared while I was part of the group "Convergence and Divergence in Pentateuchal Theory" at the Israel Institute for Advanced Studies in Jerusalem, whom I would like to thank for their generous support. For my analysis of the entire Primeval History, see now Jan Christian Gertz, *Das erste Buch Mose (Genesis): Die Urgeschichte Gen 1–11*, 2nd ed., ATD 1 (Göttingen: Vandenhoeck & Ruprecht, 2021).

1. See only the authors of the present volume: Erhard Blum, *Studien zur Komposition des Pentateuch*, BZAW 189 (Berlin: De Gruyter, 1990), 221; Christoph Levin, *Der Jahwist*, FRLANT 157 (Göttingen: Vandenhoeck & Ruprecht, 1993), 437 (with less emphasis); Jan Christian Gertz, *Tradition und Redaktion in der Exoduserzählung: Untersuchungen zur Endredaktion des Pentateuch*, FRLANT 186 (Göttingen: Vandenhoeck & Ruprecht, 2000), 9–10; Christophe Nihan, *From Priestly Torah to Pentateuch: A Study in the Composition of the Book of Leviticus*, FAT 2/25 (Tübingen: Mohr Siebeck, 2007), 20; Eckart Otto, "Forschungen zur Priesterschrift," *TRu* 62 (1997): 1–2; Thomas Römer, "The Exodus Narrative according to the Priestly Document," in *The Strata of the Priestly Writings: Contemporary Debate and Future Directions*, ed. Sarah Shectman and Joel S. Baden, ATANT 95 (Zürich: Theologischer Verlag, 2009), 157–58; rather casually in Christoph Berner, *Die Exoduserzählung*, FAT 7 (Tübingen: Mohr Siebeck, 2010), 2.

64 Jan Christian Gertz

problems' details.[2] Though the consensus over the basic delineation of the Priestly texts is widespread, the internal literary differentiations within the Priestly texts are all the more contested. There is, admittedly, a principle agreement over the fact that the Priestly texts do not come from one author and that they have a specific history of development. Nevertheless, the arguments for differentiation in individual cases are based less on linguistic or literary-critical arguments that can gain a consensus than on considerations of plausibility, which are based on overarching theses about the Priestly texts and the literary character of the Priestly *Kernbestand* (core collection). And this is where the consensus ends. The thesis that a more or less strongly reduced *Kernbestand* formed a previously independent Priestly literary work still appears to have the majority support among scholars.[3] However, the scholars who begin with an extensive *Kernbestand* including text passages that, without question, presuppose a connection with the non-Priestly texts—and then consider the Priestly texts from the start to be redactional- or compositional layers—are equally significant and persistent.[4]

In taking up the discussion anew here, it is to be affirmed from the outset that the thesis of an originally independent Priestly literary work has been remarkably stable. It has been maintained as a feature in various forms of the Documentary Hypotheses as well as in most forms of the Supplementary Hypothesis and various combination models—and thus

---

2. Theodor Nöldeke, "Die s. g. Grundschrift des Pentateuchs," in *Untersuchungen zur Kritik des Alten Testaments* (Kiel: Schwers'sche Buchhandlung, 1869), 1–144.

3. See from "the cloud of witnesses": Thomas Pola, *Die ursprüngliche Priesterschrift: Beobachtungen zur Literarkritik und Traditionsgeschichte von PG*, WMANT 70 (Neukirchen-Vlyun: Neukirchener Verlag, 1995); Reinhard Gregor Kratz, *Die Komposition der erzählenden Bücher des Alten Testaments: Grundwissen der Bibelkritik*, UTB 2157 (Göttingen: Vandenhoeck & Ruprecht, 2000), 224–48; Jan Christian Gertz, "Tora und Vordere Propheten," in *Grundinformation Altes Testament: Eine Einführung in Literatur, Religion, und Geschichte des Alten Testaments*, ed. Jan Christian Gertz et al., 6th ed., UTB 2745 (Göttingen: Vandenhoeck & Ruprecht, 2019), 237–48, Nihan, *From Priestly Torah to Pentateuch*.

4. To mention a few: Frank Moore Cross, *Canaanite Myth and Hebrew Epic: Essays in the History of the Religion of Israel* (Cambridge, MA: Harvard University Press, 1973), 293–25; John Van Seters, *Abraham in History and Tradition* (New Haven, 1975), 279–95; Rolf Rendtorff, *Das Überlieferungsgeschichtliche Problem des Pentateuch*, BZAW 147 (Berlin: De Gruyter, 1977), 112–42; Erhard Blum, *Die Komposition der Vätergeschichte*, WMANT 57 (Neukirchen-Vluyn: Neukirchener Verlag, 1984); Blum, *Studien zur Komposition des Pentateuch*; Berner, *Die Exoduserzählung*.

Genesis 5: Priestly Redaction, Composition, or Source?   65

in all models discussed in pentateuchal studies apart from in the Fragmentary Hypothesis, which is hardly consistently applied anyway. This goes without saying for the beginning of historical-critical research on the formation of the Pentateuch. This stage of research was characterized by the search for documents used by Moses or other biblical historians, and the material that later became known as the Priestly document or Priestly code, the "*Elohim* epic," belongs to the first results of this investigation. The thesis that the Priestly texts belong to an originally independent literary work has only been so broadly accepted because these texts were at the same time characterized as a *Grundschrift* of the Pentateuch. Already Wilhelm Martin Leberecht de Wette had described what later became known as the Priestly document as "a type of epic poem," which is supplemented by Jehowistic sections and which represented the "foundation" of Genesis and the beginning of Exodus.[5] As far as I know, it was characterized as the *Grundschrift* of the Hexateuch for the first time by Friedrich Tuch in his commentary on Genesis.[6] Tuch himself advocated for a Supplementary Hypothesis. The presentation of a *Grundschrift* corresponding to this model also survived through the emergence and prevailing of the New Documentary Hypothesis. It was reformulated redaction-critically, in that this Priestly document (*Priesterschrift*)—as it has been called since Abraham Kuenen—was seen to have served as the literary foundation for the redactor connecting the pentateuchal sources.[7] This widely accepted view, however, has not remained without opposition. So, for example, Christoph

---

5. Wilhelm Martin Leberecht de Wette, *Kritik der Mosaischen Geschichte*, vol. 2 of *Beiträge zur Einleitung in das Alte Testament* (Halle: Schimmelpfennig, 1807), 28–29.

6. Friedrich Tuch, *Kommentar über die Genesis* (Halle: Buchhandlung des Waisenhauses, 1838), LI, with reference to Wilhelm Martin Leberecht de Wette and Heinrich Ewald, states, "therefore we call it the *Grundschrift*—because the plan and organization (viz. of the Pentateuch) are conditioned on it, the legislative parts were taken from it, and in the historical parts the basic principles, and in larger parts also the whole realization, belong to it alone."

7. Abraham Kuenen, "Dina en Sichem," *TT* 14 (1880): 257–81, who was the first to use the siglum P. Hermann Hupfeld (*Die Quellen der Genesis und die Art ihrer Zusammensetzung* [Berlin: Wiegandt & Grieben, 1853]), in his division of the material into two *Elohistic* works, speaks of the "elohistic *Urschrift*," which is usually called the "Elohim document" or "*Grundschrift*" (43). See primarily Martin Noth, *Überlieferungsgeschichte des Pentateuch* (Stuttgart: W. Kohlhammer, 1948), 11, and already Julius Wellhausen, *Die Composition des Hexateuchs*, 4th ed. (Berlin: de Gruyter, 1963), 15; Wellhausen, *Prolegomena zur Geschichte Israels*, 6th ed. (Berlin: Reimer, 1905), 330, "it is as if P were the red thread on which the pearls of JE are strung."

66 Jan Christian Gertz

Levin assesses the situation as follows, with view to the structure of the present form of the patriarchal narratives: "In the conceptualization of the Priestly document as a '*Grundschrift*,' the New Documentary Hypothesis carried over a relic from the older Documentary Hypothesis, which is out of place due to the late dating of the Priestly document."[8] Can the same be argued for the presumption of a previously independent Priestly literary work? The early positions on the late dating of the Priestly texts, among which also Karl Heinrich Graf's assessment belongs, show that this question is not far-fetched: "the so-called *Grundschrift* of the Pentateuch is not the foundation of the narrative of the Pentateuch, but it rather consists of additions added later to the 'Jahwistic' work."[9]

2. Arguments against an Originally Independent Priestly
Literary Work Based on the Example of Genesis 1–11

We will utilize a text from the biblical Primeval History to test Graf's thesis of a Priestly redactional layer that would have had considerable redactional portions of its own. Therein the discussion returns to a certain extent back to its beginnings.[10] In this section of text, the notoriously difficult but significant question of internal differentiation of layers within the Priestly texts, which has important consequences for the overall model, only plays a subordinate role. Since the thesis of a previously independent Priestly literary work is surprisingly persistent, so also do the arguments for and against this thesis persevere across different models. I will therefore begin with an extensive criticism of the Supplementary Hypothesis as advocated by Tuch:

---

8. Levin, *Der Jahwist*, 438 n. 12. In return, Levin however establishes his Jahwist as a new *Grundschrift* (cf. 151 [for Gen 12–50], 315 [for Gen 50–Exod 6], 436 and 438 [for the overall outline]).

9. Karl Heinrich Graf, "Die s. g. Grundschrift des Pentateuchs," in *Archiv für wissenschaftliche Erforschung des Alten Testamentes*, ed. Adalbert Merx, vol. 1 (Halle: Buchhandlung des Waisenhauses, 1869), 474.

10. According to Eckart Otto, a deficiency in pentateuchal research results from the fact that it always begins from Genesis, but the starting points of research need not be played off against one another—provided that it is remembered that the results in the individual books of the Pentateuch are quite different; cf. Eckart Otto, *Das Deuteronomium im Pentateuch und Hexateuch: Studien zur Literaturgeschichte von Pentateuch und Hexateuch im Lichte des Deuteronomiumrahmens*, FAT 30 (Tübingen: Mohr Siebeck, 2000), VII.

Genesis 5: Priestly Redaction, Composition, or Source? 67

If one compares however the texts assigned to the *Grundschrift*, then after the removal of the texts derived from a supplementer, the "original plan and coherence" [viz. as proposed by Tuch] is often completely missed. It is an erroneous assertion (by Tuch) to say that only the supplementer goes back partially to his own document, and partially to the *Grundschrift*, and presupposes its existence, whereas the *Grundschrift* only refers back to itself. On the contrary, also the narratives of the *Grundschrift* frequently refer back to sections of the supplementer, necessarily presupposing them to be understood themselves; without them the book would have gaps, would be without a plan, and would be disjointed and incomprehensible. The critics have not succeeded in proving that the *Grundschrift* is a coherent connected whole, despite the abundant and hackneyed palliative medicine like the assumptions of interpolations and later editing of certain passages.[11]

The quote comes from an *Introduction to the Old Testament* by Karl Friedrich Keil that is concerned with proving the "unity and authenticity" of the Old Testament writings. For Keil, Tuch's Supplementary Hypothesis epitomized rationalistic biblical criticism. As for the "gaps" of the reconstructed *Grundschrift* in the area of the Primeval History, he accounts for the first gap with the seamless transition from Gen 2:3 to the toledot of Adam in Gen 5 as follows:

without the fall the corruption of all flesh and the whole world (Gen 6:11, 13) would be a mystery, because God had created everything good and very good (1:9, 12, 18, 21, 25, 31), and even the origins of the Theocracy would be incomprehensible.[12]

---

11. Carl Friedrich Keil, *Lehrbuch der historisch-kritischen Einleitung in die kanonischen und apokryphischen Schriften des Alten Testaments*, 2nd ed. (Frankfurt: Heyder & Zimmer, 1859), 64, my translation (with reference to the quotation from Tuch's commentary on Genesis noted above and a chart listing the differences between the *Grundschrift* and the supplementary layer according to Tuch's commentary). In the third edition of the book Keil refrains from a detailed examination of Tuch's Supplementary Hypothesis. Instead, he addresses in more detail the New Documentary Hypothesis and the emerging of a late dating of the Priestly texts by Vatke and Graf. Keil concludes his overview of the history of research with the remark that the "much praised historical critique failed ... to prove the post-Mosaic origin of the Pentateuch." See Keil, *Lehrbuch der historisch-kritischen Einleitung in die kanonischen und apokryphischen Schriften des Alten Testaments*, 3rd ed. (Frankfurt: Heyder & Zimmer, 1873), 72–94. Unless otherwise noted, subsequent references are to the second edition.

12. Keil, *Lehrbuch*, 64, with reference to Benedikt Welte, *Nachmosaisches im Pentateuch* (Karlsruhe: Herder'sche Verlagshandlung, 1841), 157–60, and Johann Heinrich

68 Jan Christian Gertz

This indicates that for Keil the important Christian doctrine of the fall belongs to the indispensable base form of the *Grundschrift* and thus to the blueprint of the Pentateuch. The absence of the preparation for the flood narrative within the Priestly narrative that is constantly brought up in present discussions only has a subordinate role. It comes into view only in light of a further gap between Gen 5:32 and 6:9, insofar as "without 6:1–8, the universality of the corruption (also of the line of Seth) and thus the universality of the flood, are without rationale."[13] Keil identified references from the *Grundschrift* to sections of the Jehowistic supplementer in Gen 5:29 and Gen 5:3. The reference to the cursing of the soil at the naming of Noah in Gen 5:29 alludes to the pronouncement of punishment against Adam in Gen 3:17, and the notice regarding Adam's son Seth presupposes the birth notice in Gen 4:25.[14]

The argument regarding the gaps within the *Grundschrift*, or what became the Priestly narrative thread, and the approach of a critical examination of the results of reconstructions in the mode of literary-critical crosschecking have formed a precedent. Since Graf's late dating of the *Grundschrift* and its new characterization as a "Priestly redactional layer"[15] of the Pentateuch, references to the conceptual inconsistency of the reconstructed sources are also found in works which were by no means concerned with the "origins, unity, authenticity, and trustworthiness" of the Pentateuch in the sense of Keil's work.[16] Only a few observations need

---

Kurtz, *Beiträge zur Vertheidigung und Begründung der Einheit des Pentateuchs*, Nachweis der Einheit von Genesis I–IV (Königsberg: Gräfe & Unzer, 1844), 69–73.

13. Keil, *Lehrbuch*, 64, with reference to Johann Heinrich Kurtz, *Die Einheit der Genesis: Ein Beitrag zur Kritik und Exegese der Genesis* (Berlin: Justus Albert Wohlgemuth, 1846), 35–36.

14. Keil, *Lehrbuch*, 66, with reference to Kurtz, *Beiträge*, 129–30, 132.

15. The expression is not found exactly stated in Graf, but is present in content (cf. Graf, "Die s. g. Grundschrift des Pentateuchs," 475–77).

16. Graf, "Die s. g. Grundschrift des Pentateuchs," preface. On the argument regarding the missing rationale for the flood within an isolated Priestly writing, see Cross, *Canaanite Myth and Hebrew Epic*, 306–7; Rolf Rendtorff, "L'histoire biblique des origines (Gen 1–11) dans le contexte de la redaction 'sacerdotale' du Pentateuque," in *Le Pentateuque en question: Les origines et la composition des cinq premiers livres de la Bible à la lumière des recherches récentes*, ed. Albert de Pury and Thomas Römer, MdB 19 (Geneva: Labor et Fides, 1989), 83–94, 91; Blum, *Studien zur Komposition des Pentateuch*, 280. On the assessment of the Priestly writing in Gen 1–11 as insufficient in form and content, see also Carmino Joseph de Catanzaro, *A Literary Analysis of Genesis I–XI* (MA thesis; University of Toronto, 1957). Usually the argument is made

Genesis 5: Priestly Redaction, Composition, or Source? 69

to be added: Already Graf recognized a doublet in the immediate sequence of the toledot formulae in Gen 2:4a and 5:1–3 and argued for a redaction-critical solution, according to which a link was formed from Gen 5 back to the Priestly creation account after the interruption by the non-Priestly sections using the technique of *Wiederaufnahme*.[17] According to Erhard Blum, the situation is comparable to the mention of the age of Noah and the births of his three sons at the end of the genealogy of Adam in Gen 5:32, and the repetition of this information at the beginning of the genealogy of Noah in Gen 6:10, as well as the mention of Noah's age at the time of the beginning of the flood in Gen 7:6 and 7:11.[18] These verses would have followed more or less immediately after one another in an independent Priestly document. References from the Priestly texts to non-Priestly passages are recognized by Blum also in the mentions of the walking of Enoch and Noah before God in Gen 5:22, 24, insofar as these notices draw associations to the concepts of the garden of Eden narrative and the walking of Yahweh-Elohim in the garden (each with הלך in the *hithpael*).[19] Also the Priestly promise of a ברית עולם in Gen 9:1–17 corresponds with the divine promise at the end of the non-Priestly composition of the flood narrative in Gen 8:21–22.[20] Finally, already Graf noted a point that was further developed by Sven Tengström in the sense of supporting the view of a Priestly redactional layer: the toledot formula is always used as a heading to introduce material, and therefore in Gen 2:4a it is compiled for the opening of the non-Priestly garden of Eden narrative in Gen 2:4b–7.[21]

However, this latter argument has recently been used as evidence for the thesis that the non-Priestly passages of the Primeval history represent a supplement to the Priestly *Grundschrift*.[22] A comparable ambiguity in

---

from the example of the dispersed Priestly passages in the Patriarchal narratives. On this, see below.

17. Graf, "Die s. g. Grundschrift des Pentateuchs," 470. See also Blum, *Studien zur Komposition des Pentateuch*, 280.

18. Blum, *Studien zur Komposition des Pentateuch*, 280–81.

19. Blum, *Studien zur Komposition des Pentateuch*, 291.

20. Rendtorff, *L'histoire*, 91; cf. also Blum, *Studien zur Komposition des Pentateuch*, 289–90, 293.

21. Graf, "Die s. g. Grundschrift des Pentateuchs," 470–71; Sven Tengström, *Die Toledotformel und die literarische Struktur der priesterlichen Erweiterungsschicht im Pentateuch*, ConBOT 17 (Lund: CWK Gleerup, 1981).

22. See, for example, Eckart Otto, "Die Paradieserzählung Genesis 2–3: Eine nachpriesterschriftliche Lehrerzählung in ihrem religionshistorischen Kontext," in

70 Jan Christian Gertz

the evaluation of the observations on textual details—shared by all models of the formation of the Pentateuch—is also to be noticed with regard to the function of the Priestly structural markers in their present contexts and the obvious tensions in the juxtaposition of Priestly and non-Priestly sections. I consider these two points only briefly here, because they do not have an important role in the discussion of Gen 5.

Already August Klostermann concluded in his foundational critique of the New Documentary Hypothesis that the Priestly texts "were composed from the outset like a frame around the underlying older texts."[23] This assumption was based on the structure of the final form of the Pentateuch and the function of the isolated Priestly texts within it. He understood the Priestly redactor to be aligning the earlier traditions "with pious harmonizing, into the framework of a genealogical-chronological and itinerary-calendrical structure."[24] Many followed him in this assessment or brought forward similar arguments.[25] However, Klostermann himself confessed that the evidence could also be explained from the perspective of the New Documentary Hypothesis that he was contesting, that is, in the sense of a redactional process of connecting the Priestly with the Jahwistic document. He added: "Whether these two theories are in so severe incongruity, that based on common recognition no crossing over from one to the other is possible in the favor of my view, must be judged by readers themselves."[26] In any case, one must ask whether the starting observation is coherent.

Jedes Ding hat seine Zeit...': Studien zur israelitischen und altorientalischen Weisheit: Festschrift für Diethelm Michel zum 65. Geburtstag, ed. Anja A. Diesel et al., BZAW 241 (Berlin: De Gruyter, 1996), 167–92.

23. August Klostermann, *Der Pentateuch: Beiträge zu seinem Verständnis und zu seiner Entstehungsgeschichte* (Leipzig: Deichert, 1893), 59.

24. Klostermann, *Der Pentateuch*, 185–84 with regard to the author of the "pre-Josianic Pentateuch" in Gen 1–Num 36; Deut 31:14–34:9; Josh 1–24.

25. See de Catanzaro, *Literary Analysis of Genesis I–XI*, 25–74, 244 (with regard to the flood narrative, which according to de Catanzaro differs from the Priestly creation account in that the Priestly supplementer formulated an independent text in Gen 1:1–2:4a and placed it before the garden of Eden narrative, while in the flood narrative he worked as a supplementer); Rendtorff, *L'Histoire*, 89; Jacques Vermeylen, *La formation du Pentateuque: Bref historique de la recherche et essai de solution cohérente*, pro manu scripto (Brüssel: CETP, 1990), 99–100.

26. Klostermann, *Der Pentateuch*, 59. In view of Klostermann's tone of voice, which is usually offended, this statement seems surprisingly irenic. It is certainly based on a quite imprecise rendering of the picture of the redactional process drawn by Wellhausen.

Genesis 5: Priestly Redaction, Composition, or Source?   71

As in the reconstructed Priestly document, the creation account in Gen 1:1–2:3 in its current position does indeed serve as a prologue before a history of humanity introduced with the toledot formula (Gen 2:4a resp. 5:1), whose most notable characteristic is this toledot formula (cf. Gen 6:9; 10:1, 33; 11:10, 27); however, deviations from the Priestly structure are also noted. In the flood narrative, framed by a twofold prologue and epilogue (Gen 6:5–8; 8:20–22 [non-P] and 6:9–22; 9:1–17 [P]), a non-Priestly section forms the prelude, while the beginning of the toledot of Noah in Gen 6:9 only marks a new section within the flood narrative. This deviates from the usual use of the toledot formula, and it does not correspond with the other genealogical notices about Noah and his sons, with which the Priestly document marks the flood as the central event within the toledot of Noah (cf. Gen 7:6; 9:28; 10:1, 32; 11:10). On the other hand, the flood narrative ends with a Priestly section, while the non-Priestly finale in Gen 8:20–22 marks an important internal cesura. It appears that in the flood narrative, two versions with different structuring principles were combined. This finding is not favorable for the view of a classic Supplemental or *Fortschreibung* Hypothesis—regardless of whether the Priestly or non-Priestly materials are understood to have the primary position.[27]

With regard to the tensions in the juxtaposition of obviously parallel traditions, these have always been the strongest arguments for the thesis of a redactional combination of originally independent literary works. This applies particularly for the Primeval history, since here the "non-Priestly

---

27. For a detailed statement, see Jan Christian Gertz, "Beobachtungen zum literarischen Charakter und zum geistesgeschichtlichen Ort der nichtpriesterschriftlichen Sintfluterzählung," in *Auf dem Weg zur Endgestalt von Genesis bis II Regum: Festschrift Hans-Christoph Schmitt*, ed. Martin Beck and Ulrike Schorn, BZAW 370 (Berlin: De Gruyter, 2006), 41–57, in dispute with the thesis that the non-Priestly texts of the flood narrative are a redactional supplement to the Priestly account. On the renewed interest in the thesis first advanced by Tuch (*Kommentar über die Genesis*, LXVII, 137–95), cf. Jean Louis Ska, "The Story of the Flood: A Priestly Writer and Some Later Editorial Fragments," in *The Exegesis of the Pentateuch: Exegetical Studies and Basic Questions*, FAT 66 (Tübingen: Mohr Siebeck, 2009), 1–22; Erich Bosshard-Nepustil, *Vor uns die Sintflut: Studien zu Text, Kontexten und Rezeption der Fluterzählung Genesis 6–9*, BWANT 165 (Stuttgart: Kohlhammer, 2005); Andreas Schüle, *Der Prolog der hebräischen Bibel: Der literar- und theologiegeschichtliche Diskurs der Urgeschichte (Gen 1–11)*, ATANT 86 (Zürich: Theologischer Verlag, 2006), 247–301; Martin Arneth, *'Durch Adams Fall ist ganz verderbt ...': Studien zur Entstehung der alttestamentlichen Urgeschichte*, FRLANT 217 (Göttingen: Vandenhoeck & Ruprecht, 2007), 169–200.

72   Jan Christian Gertz

and Priestly traditions [evince] comparable content."[28] In the context of the Documentary Hypothesis, the "discontinous composition" (*diskontinuierliche Fügung*, Blum) and remaining tensions can be explained usually by proposing that the redaction was conservative in the preservation of material. Also, one must strongly distinguish between the critical view of an analysis oriented at the history of origins and development and the understanding of the text that begins with the concept of redaction and is practiced over centuries. Such a redaction, which perceives the texts in a complementary and harmonizing way, can combine them into a new unity.

It is likely that a pure redactional layer would have had more freedom for literary design and correspondingly would leave behind less tensions in the text in comparison to a process of redactional combination of preceding texts, but this view can also be contested. Thus Paul Volz, in his refutation of the thesis of an originally independent Priestly document, considered the proposal as problematic that two versions of the flood narrative have been combined, because too many contradictions were left standing in the text.[29] Volz explains the literary record with a theory of a redaction of the non-Priestly flood narrative in the spirit of Gen 1 for a "liturgical usage in New Year's liturgy." Genesis 1 and the flood narrative, which had been edited for this purpose, were read together at the New Year's festival. This redaction led to three changes: the flood became a "cosmic event, the destruction of the world … a return to chaos"; chronological data was added, which was connected with the liturgical sequence; and the number of animals was corrected, with a view to the pending cultic legislation. Volz does not present a detailed analysis of the text. Instead, he confesses:

> The manner of redaction and the way it was carried out is no longer apparent to us in all its details. One can ask for example, why the redactor did not carry out the tendential corrections (time length, number of animals) so consistently that the original data (40 days, 7 and 2 etc.) was completely removed. However, one may presume that the original wording was fixed at the time of the redactor, and that he was not able to completely abandon it. Such questions of detail are not the decisive issue, but rather the thesis that an independent P Flood narrative did not

---

28. Blum, *Studien zur Komposition des Pentateuch*, 279, who correctly notes in this context also the "unique position of the Primeval history in the history of research" (278).

29. Paul Volz, "Anhang: P ist kein Erzähler," in *Der Elohist als Erzähler: Ein Irrweg der Pentateuchkritik an der Genesis erläutert*, ed. Paul Volz and William Rudolph, BZAW 64 (Gießen: Töpelmann, 1933), 140–41 (the following citations also from there).

Genesis 5: Priestly Redaction, Composition, or Source?

exist; there was only the original single [non-Priestly] narrative that was edited over [by P].

Thus, according to Volz, a redaction that edits a *Vorlage* would have much greater tolerance for the tensions that come to be in the present context of the text than a redaction that connects two previously independent literary works. This premise is not persuasive. If the thesis of an originally independent Priestly literary work is to be rejected, in any case the view that the Priestly redaction would also have incorporated its own traditional material in the flood narrative with its redaction of the non-Priestly tradition[30] is more plausible than the claim of a pure Supplementary Hypothesis.

3. Evaluation of the Arguments with regard to Genesis 5

Some of the arguments presented here have already been considered in passing. In the following we will consider the textual details of Gen 5 and their evaluation. The reference to the association from the walking of Enoch and Noah before God to the scenery of the garden of Eden has a rather dec-

---

30. A corresponding approach which seeks to combine the insights of the Documentary and the Supplementary Hypothesis has been proposed by Blum with his thesis of a "Priestly Compositional layer." On this, see Blum, *Studien zur Komposition des Pentateuch*, 281–85 (on the flood) and 333–60 (on the model and its anchoring in the history of institutions). Blum speaks of the Pentateuch as a "singular composition-structure" (cf. the critical objections by Konrad Schmid, "Der Abschluss der Tora als exegetisches und historisches Problem," in *Schriftgelehrte Traditionsliteratur*, FAT 77 [Tübingen: Mohr Siebeck, 2011], 177–78), which is solely to be explained as the result of external influences, namely, the pressure to form an inner-Judean consensus imposed by the Persian government. See Blum, *Studien zur Komposition des Pentateuch*, 358, 360; Blum, "Esra, die Mosetora und die persische Politik," in *Religion und Religionskontakte im Zeitalter der Achämeniden*, ed. Reinard G. Kratz, VGTh 22 (Gütersloh: Gütersloher Verlagshaus, 2001), 235–46. In accordance with Blum, hypotheses on the formation of the Pentateuch, which assume the compilation of highly profiled literary works or even just blocks of compositions, must determine the historical circumstances of this redactional process, which differs clearly from the scholarly activity of scribes—regardless the discussion about the so-called imperial authorization of the Torah (see on this, the contributions in James W. Watts, ed., *Persia and the Torah: The Theory of the Imperial Authorization of the Pentateuch*, SymS 17 [Atlanta: Society of Biblical Literature Press, 2001]; as well as Konrad Schmid, "Persische Reichsauthorisation und Tora," *TRu* 71 [2006]: 494–506; and most recently, Kyong-Jin Lee, *The Authority and Authorization of Torah in the Persian Period*, CBET 64 [Leuven: Peeters, 2011]).

74 Jan Christian Gertz

orative character. The phrase הלך *hithpael* + NN + את האלהים that occurs only in Gen 5:22, 24; 6:9 can be derived also from the Priestly occurrences of the phrase הלך *hithpael* + (אלהים/יהוה) לפני (Gen 17:1; cf. 1 Sam 2:30), whereas the formulation with את האלהים in Gen 5 and 6 expresses a special nearness to God in the time before the flood.[31] A derivation of Gen 5:22, 24; 6:9 from Gen 3:8 is thus not necessary. More important, however, are the observations on doublets within the isolated Priestly texts and the question of a rationale for the flood and the return to chaos.

3.1. On the Text Sequence of Genesis 2:3–4a and 5:1–3

I begin with the issue of the toledot of Adam in Gen 5 following directly after the Priestly creation account that is considered problematic. Much depends on the redaction-critical assessment of the toledot formula in Gen 2:4a. Up to the printed image of the Biblia Hebraica Stuttgartensia, which differs from the Codex Leningradensis on this point,[32] it has become customary to see Gen 2:4a as a subscript of the Priestly creation account. In favor of this view of division of the text, it is noted following initial indications by Wilhelm Friedrich Hezel and Werner Carl Ludwig Ziegler that the toledot formula belongs to the characteristic markers of P and that it clearly relates to the preceding text, while the subsequent text is clearly of post-Priestly origins.[33] The immediate sequence of the two toledot formulae, as a concluding notice (Gen 2:4a) and a heading (Gen 5:1–3), could be understood within an originally independent Priestly literary work as a structuring marker,[34] which would hardly satisfy the aesthetic sense of the

---

31. See most recently Nihan, *From Priestly Torah to Pentateuch*, 62–63, with reference to Gerhard von Rad, *Die Priesterschrift im Hexateuch untersucht und theologisch bewertet*, BWANT 65 (Stuttgart: Kohlhammer, 1934), 171 n. 6; Erich Zenger, *Gottes Bogen in den Wolken*, SBS 112, 2nd ed. (Stuttgart: Kohlhammer, 1987), 107 n. 17; Blum, *Studien zur Komposition des Pentateuch*, 293.

32. The Leningrad Codex leaves an empty line between Gen 2:3 and Gen 2:4. Cf. also the Biblia Hebraica Quinta, which no longer suggests a separation within Gen 2:4.

33. Wilhelm Friedrich Hezel, *Ueber die Quellen der Mosaischen Urgeschichte* (Lemgo: Meyer, 1780), 25; Werner Carl Ludwig Ziegler, "Kritik über den Artikel von der Schöpfung nach unserer gewöhnlichen Dogmatik," *Magazin für Religionsphilosophie, Exegese und Kirchengeschichte*, ed. Heinrich Philipp Conrad Henke, vol. 2 (Helmstedt: Fleckeisen, 1794), 13, 50.

34. See Noth, *Überlieferungsgeschichte des Pentateuch*, 17 (with n. 41); Claus Westermann, *Genesis 1–11* (Darmstadt: Wissenschaftliche Buchgesellschaft, 1972), 22;

critics of this thesis. The observation that the toledot formula is elsewhere exclusively found as a heading is more significant.[35] Moreover, the Priestly creation account has its own summary in Gen 2:3 that corresponds with Gen 1:1. The toledot formula in Gen 2:4a is therefore to be considered as the heading to the following garden of Eden narrative.[36] As such, it forms a bridge between the Priestly creation account and the garden of Eden narrative by taking up the content and formulations of the preceding text section and at the same time anticipating what is to follow.[37]

But how are the details to be interpreted from a redaction-historical perspective?

There is a widespread presumption that Gen 2:4a originally stood before Gen 1:1 in an independent Priestly Primeval History and was only secondarily placed in its current location as a connection between the creation account and the garden of Eden narrative as a redactional transition and heading.[38] Yet this is hardly plausible, because Gen 1:1 already constitutes a full heading, and by suggesting that there was an additional heading before it one would create a new problem. It is likely, therefore, that Gen 2:4a was already composed as a redactional transition to the garden of Eden narrative. We will not look further at the redaction-historical conditions within the prelude of the garden of Eden narrative in Gen 2:4–7 at this point.[39] In any case, it is certain that the toledot formulae in Gen 2:4a and 5:1 never followed one another within a previously independent

---

Odil Hannes Steck, *Der Schöpfungsbericht der Priesterschrift*, FRLANT 115, 2nd ed. (Göttingen: Vandenhoeck & Ruprecht, 1981), 242–43; Zenger, *Gottes Bogen in den Wolken*, 143; Peter Weimar, "Die Toledotformel in der priesterschriftlichen Geschichtsdarstellung," in *Studien zur Priesterschrift*, FAT 56 (Tübingen: Mohr Siebeck, 2008), 163–64, n. 43; Pola, *Die ursprüngliche Priesterschrift*, 82 n. 134, 343 n. 144; Kratz, *Komposition*, 230, 233–35; Arneth, *Fall*, 24–27.

35. Gen 5:1; 6:9; 10:1; 11:10, 27; 25:12, 19; 36:1, 9; 37:2. Cf. David Carr, "Βίβλος γενέσεως Revisited: A Synchronic Analysis of Patterns in Genesis as Part of the Torah," *ZAW* 110 (1998): 164–65.

36. See above.

37. See Wellhausen, *Die Composition des Hexateuchs*, 320.

38. So most recently Markus Witte, *Die biblische Urgeschichte: Redaktions- und theologiegeschichtliche Beobachtungen zu Genesis 1,1–11,26*, BZAW 265 (Berlin: De Gruyter, 1998), 55 (with n. 14, with additional references).

39. See Jan Christian Gertz, "The Formation of the Primeval History," in *The Book of Genesis: Composition, Reception, and Interpretation*, ed. Craig A. Evans, Joel N. Lohr, and David L. Petersen, VTSup 152 (Leiden: Brill, 2012), 115–18.

76   Jan Christian Gertz

Priestly literary work. Additionally, there are strong indications that both notices are not from the same author. The unique mention of the "Book of the Toledot" in Gen 5:1 suggests that the series of toledot originally began with Adam. The LXX already recognized a problem here and therefore inserted the ἡ βίβλος from Gen 5:1 into 2:4a. Also, it should not be overlooked that the toledot formula in a Priestly context otherwise never portrays the origins account of something mentioned in the genitive construct but always treats the subsequent family history of a certain person. In short, the toledot formula in Gen 2:4a is redactional, and it never was part of a previously independent literary work.

By excluding Gen 2:4a, the complaints of an ill-fitting text-sequence within an independent Priestly document are not fully invalidated, insofar as Gen 5:1–3 immediately following on Gen 1:1–2:3 would repeat "awkwardly that which was developed broadly a few lines before."[40] Some advocates of a previously independent Priestly literary work share this assessment and assign the allegedly disruptive repetitions from Gen 1:27–28 in 5:1b–2 to the final redaction of the Pentateuch or at least post-Priestly glosses.[41] The literary-critical differentiation is then grounded in the observation that in Gen 5:1a, 3 אדם is used as a proper name and thus in a way that corresponds to the scheme of the subsequent genealogy. By contrast, 5:1b–2 uses the term as a species label for "humanity," which would contradict the other schema and could result from the *Wiederaufnahme* of Gen 1:27–28. However, the consideration of either Gen 5:1b–2 or 5:1–3 as a *Wiederaufnahme*, depending on which model is chosen, overlooks the compositional function of the verses, which lead from the creation of the species of humans as the image of God (Gen 5:1b; cf. 1:26a, 27a), their sexual differentiation (Gen 5:2b; cf. 1:27b), and creator's blessing (Gen 5:2b; cf. 1:28) to the history of individual humans (Gen 5:1a) in whom the blessing is realized (Gen 5:3). The text describes the process

---

40. Blum, *Studien zur Komposition des Pentateuch*, 280.

41. Heinrich Holzinger, *Genesis*, KHC 1 (Freiburg: Mohr, 1898), 58–59; Weimar, *Toledotformel*, 165–71; Levin, *Der Jahwist*, 99–100; Horst Seebass, *Genesis I: Urgeschichte (1:1–11:26)* (Neukirchen-Vluyn: Neukirchener Verlag, 1996), 180. Considerations according to which P has taken up an earlier toledot book and integrated it into his work (Gen 5:1–32*; 10:1–32*; 11:10; 26:27–32*) are on a different redaction- and tradition-historical level. See among others Noth, *Überlieferungsgeschichte des Pentateuch*, 17 (with n.41); Steck, *Der Schöpfungsbericht der Priesterschrift*, 145; David Carr, *Reading the Fractures of Genesis: Historical and Literary Approaches* (Louisville: John Knox, 1996), 71–73.

Genesis 5: Priestly Redaction, Composition, or Source? 77

of individuation, which is essential for the development of humanity, in which the naming of the species by God (Gen 5:2b) corresponds to the naming of Seth by Adam (Gen 5:3b). Likewise, the remark that deviates from the schema, that Adam fathered Seth "in his likeness, according to this image" (ויולד בדמותו כצלמו; Gen 5:3a), points beyond Gen 5:1b to the creation of humanity in Gen 1:26–27. In a significant way the concept of fathering and giving birth takes the place of divine creation from this point on, realizing the blessing promised in Gen 1:28. The transition from the creation of humanity to the sequence of generations is carried out in the naming of the first descendant and—logically preceding that—in the birth of the subsequent generations. As part of this chain, these subsequent generations have a share in the divine image of the first human as part of the human species. At first glance, the section may give the impression of redundancy; however, in its connection with Gen 1:1–2:3 the thorough construction of the verses is obvious.[42] As a redactional *Wiederaufnahme*

---

42. See also Witte, *Die biblische Urgeschichte*, 123–26. It is often claimed, that the use of ביום + inf. cstr. in Gen 5:1a links back to the non-Priestly text of Gen 2:4b (cf. among others Weimar, *Toledotformel*, 168 n. 56). However, the phrase is not necessarily dependent on the non-Priestly context (cf. the Priestly materials in Lev 6:13; 7:16, 36, 38; Num 6:13; 7:10; 9:15, etc.), especially since in Gen 5:1 ביום means a particular day, while in Gen 2:4b the term is simply used as a temporal determination for "when." Moreover, Gen 2:4b uses the verb עשה for creation instead of ברא, which also speaks against an intentional backreference. Recently Benjamin Ziemer has argued differently in "Erklärung der Zahlen von Gen 5 aus ihrem kompositionellen Zusammenhang," *ZAW* 121 (2009): 1–18. According to Ziemer, the end-compositional Priestly text of Gen 5:1 dates the events of Gen 3:5, 22 to the day of Gen 1:26. With reference to Ps 90:4, Ziemer understands Gen 1:26 along with the other six days of creation as "divine days" lasting thousand years each. If Gen 2:17 announces death to the one who transgresses the prohibition to eat from the tree of knowledge, then in the end-compositional context this is to be referred to the (sixth) day as a "divine day." According to Ziemer this explanation solves the problem that Adam survives the day of transgressing the prohibition (according to human-astronomical time calculations). The events in the garden and with Cain and Abel as well as the remaining lifetime of Adam all occurred during the day of the creation of humanity that lasts one-thousand years, with Adam dying toward the end of the day at the age of 930. This harmonizing reading is found already in the early Jewish literature (cf. Jub. 4.30; Ber. Rab. 22:1). However, it does hardly correspond to the original intentions of the end-compositional text of Gen 1–5 and its *Vorlagen*: The formulation of Ps 90:4 does not develop a concept of a "divine day," but mentions the shortest (a "night watch") and longest ("thousand years") conceivable periods of time, to describe God's external perspective on the course of created time. Likewise, Gen 1 is not calculating time with "divine

78   Jan Christian Gertz

after Gen 2–4, Gen 5:1–3 or 5:1b–2 would be clearly underestimated. This
is particularly the case because within a redactional passage formulated in
light of the non-Priestly texts the transition to Adam and his descendants
would come too late. After all, Adam already appeared as a personal name
(Gen 4:25), and events involving him and his descendants have already
been described.[43] Furthermore, within a classic *Wiederaufnahme*, the
thread would typically resume at the point where it had left off due to the
insertion, which, in our case, would be the notice on the completion of
creation with the sanctification of the seventh day.

3.2. On the Text Sequence Genesis 5:32 and 6:9–10

The toledot of Adam concludes in Gen 5:32 with the age of its last member
Noah, and a remark on the begetting of his sons including their names.
In the isolated Priestly document this would immediately be followed by
the toledot of Noah (Gen 6:9–10), which after the heading again notes the
births of the three sons Shem, Ham, and Japheth. For critics of the thesis
of an originally independent Priestly literary work, this is considered a
"blatant doublet ... which no source critic would tolerate in the transmitted text."[44] Together with a few suspicious formulations, this assessment
has led Christoph Levin to remove the remark about the birth of Noah's
sons in Gen 5:32 from the Priestly text.[45] The literary-critical reasons used

---

days," which is seen from the fact that the establishment of the categories of time on
the first day of creation results from the distinction between light/day and darkness/
night. Only the combination of both biblical texts that is not indicated anywhere in
the Priestly creation account leads to the conception of a "divine day" that has been
read into the text of Gen 1–5 since early Jewish interpretation. See already Hermann
Gunkel, *Genesis*, HKAT 1.1, 9th ed. (Göttingen: Vandenhoeck & Ruprecht, 1977), 106.

43. Compare also Witte, *Die biblische Urgeschichte*, 125–26; Blum, *Die Komposition der Vätergeschichte*, 451–52 also notes this but explains it with the view that the
"Priestly Composition" links back to a preceding toledot book. However, in that case it
remains unexplained, why after the use of אדם as a proper name in Gen 4:25, in 5:1b–2
אדם is used again as an appellative, especially since precisely these verses have hardly
belonged to the preceding toledot book.

44. Blum, *Studien zur Komposition des Pentateuch*, 280.

45. So Levin, *Der Jahwist*, 100. See for a critical discussion of this view extensively
Witte, *Die biblische Urgeschichte*, 114–16 as well as Jan Christian Gertz, "Hams Sündenfall und Kanaans Erbfluch: Anmerkungen zur kompositionsgeschichtlichen Stellung von Gen 9:18–29," in *'Gerechtigkeit und Recht zu üben' (Gen 18:19): Studien zur
altorientalischen und biblischen Rechtsgeschichte, zur Religionsgeschichte Israels und zur*

Genesis 5: Priestly Redaction, Composition, or Source? 79

for this are interesting for our question, because an analysis shows that the sequence of the aforementioned notices in an isolated Priestly document is by no means objectionable. The starting point for the removal of Gen 5:32a from P is the deviation from the usual genealogical schema of the Priestly writing, while for Gen 5:32b an "unwarranted ... repetition of the subject נח"[46] is cited as a reason. Both observations are explained by the assumption that the redaction connects the Priestly thread from Gen 5:31 with a scattered fragment of a (pre-)Jahwistic genealogy in 5:32b. It is beyond debate, that the formulation ויהי + PN + בן + XY שנה varies the genealogical schema that is usually formed without בן (mostly: ויהי + PN + XY שנה). There are, however, parallels (Gen 25:20) and similarly designed formulations (Gen 7:6; 11:10; 37:2) within Priestly literature. It is hardly a coincidence that the mention of Noah's age in the Priestly flood narrative (Gen 7:6) is among these parallels. The picture becomes clear when Gen 5:32 is seen in connection with the toledot of Noah in Gen 6:9–10, the next text assigned to P. The example of a concluding formulation of one toledot that already points to the following toledot is seen in Gen 11:26 and 11:27. In view of the extensive elaboration of the toledot of Noah by the flood narrative, such an anticipation is not unusual and is even to be expected. Seen in connection with the fourfold mention of Noah in Gen 6:9–10, the repetition of his name in Gen 5:32b is no longer surprising. In any case, it is more important for the understanding of the supposed doublet that here at its particular place in the toledot the necessary segmenting of the genealogy of Noah carries forth in three lines with a view to the coming events.[47] Accordingly, after the birth of his firstborn, Noah's remaining lifespan is not mentioned. This is given only at the conclusion of the toledot of Noah in Gen 9:28–29. In summary, the sequence of the toledot of Adam and Noah is deliberate, the prima facie redundant style

---

Religionssoziologie; Festschrift für Eckart Otto zum 65. Geburtstag, ed. Rinhard Achenbach and Martin Arneth, BZAR 13 (Wiesbaden: Harrassowitz, 2009), 86–90.

46. Levin, *Der Jahwist*, 100.

47. See Thomas Hieke, *Die Genealogien der Genesis*, HBS 39 (Freiburg: Herder, 2004), 76. Also in this regard we can point to Gen 11:26–27, where the conclusion of the genealogy refers to the three sons of Terah (Gen 11:26), while they are mentioned again in the immediately following toledot of Terah (Gen 11:27). As with Noah, after the birth of the firstborn, reference to the births of the further sons and daughters as well as the dates for the remainder of the years of his live is missing. This latter information is added, as with Noah, at the end of the toledot as an indication over the whole lifetime (Gen 11:32).

80 Jan Christian Gertz

can also be observed elsewhere, as in Gen 11:26–27 where two toledot stand in a connecting position, and the deviations from the schema can be explained by the expansion of the toledot of Noah by the flood narrative.[48]

3.3. On the Question of the Transition from the Good Creation to the Corrupt World within an Isolated Priestly Document

Within an isolated Priestly thread, the creation account would be followed by the toledot of Adam and then Noah, including the flood narrative. This was seen already by Keil and his companions as an intolerable gap. It appears to me that his view is motivated by unease about a *Grundschrift* of the Pentateuch that would not contain the texts about the fall that are important for Christian doctrine. For sure, modern critics of the thesis of an originally independent Priestly work do not share this concern. Yet behind the statement that "in an isolated 'P-thread' the corruption of the good creation by violence (חמס) is stated (6:11–13) but is not narratively developed,"[49] there is an unstated assumption that the Priestly thread must be exactly like the non-Priestly text in its narrative sequence in order to be considered an independent literary work. However, already Erich Zenger considered this presupposition as unproven and unlikely, particularly because it is assumed that the Priestly document does not have independent narrative interests.[50] According to Zenger, the Priestly texts characterize the sin as a "structural disruption of the creation- and life-order." That the sin understood in this way triggers God's judgment, is one of the most prominent themes of the Priestly document. As such, P would not necessarily describe processes but would rather focus on a definition-like statement of the violence as the expression of the disruption brought about by sin (cf. Gen 6:11, 13; Exod 1:13–14). Markus Witte has taken up this thought and pointed to the fact that the prelude of the Priestly

---

48. In the flood narrative, the sequence of the age data of Noah in Gen 7:6 and 7:11 is discussed as a further doublet within the isolated Priestly document (cf. Blum, *Studien zur Komposition des Pentateuch*, 280). For the sake of completeness, this should at least be dealt with briefly: Gen 7:6 marks a new beginning, referring back to Gen 5:32 (the age of Noah) and Gen 6:17 (the announcement of the flood), whereas Gen 7:11a mentions the precise date of the beginning of the flood and is connected with the dating in Gen 8:4, 5, 13, 14. See Witte, *Die biblische Urgeschichte*, 135–36.

49. Blum, *Studien zur Komposition des Pentateuch*, 280, following Cross, *Canaanite Myth and Hebrew Epic*, 302.

50. See Zenger, *Gottes Bogen in den Wolken*, 33.

flood narrative in Gen 6:9–13 "attempts to form a contrasting image to the sevenfold טוב כי of the first creation account by juxtaposing the righteous Noah and the corrupt world, the fourfold use of the term שחת (vv. 11–13), the repeated emphasis on the fact that the whole earth is filled with violence (חמס, vv. 11–13), as well as with the twofold repetition of the statement that 'all flesh' (כל בשר) is corrupt in vv. 12, 13."[51]

Regarding the textual evidence Witte concludes: "The section of 6:9–13 is sufficient to function as an introduction to the flood narrative based on the repeated emphasis of the universal corruption of the earth and on the direct references to 1:1–2:3*; it is not reliant on a preceding narrative of a fall."[52] If, on the other hand, the section were understood as a redactional link to Gen 1:1–2:3 that intends to integrate a narrative that is necessary to understand the theme of the corruption of the good creation, then in light of the effusive and redundant style the question would remain as to why allusions to Gen 2:4–4:26 and 6:1–4 are missing. Critics of the thesis of an originally independent Priestly literary work must, however, insist on a narrative introduction. For their part, they might respond to the objection that there are no allusions to the non-Priestly narratives in Gen 6:9–13, a section that is considered redactional by them, by pointing to an associative connection of Noah's "walking with God" and the basic mood and scenery from Gen 2–3. But then again, this proposal will hardly convince opponents of the view of a Priestly redaction.

4. Text-Historical Evidence for a Flood Narrative without a Narrative Introduction?

By mutually contesting what is indispensable for an originally independent literary work or for a redactional layer as well as what is not compatible with the respective thesis, the debate boils down to plausibility judgements that are more or less convincing. The significant role given to historically-grounded expectations for a literary work in the reconstruction of the historical development of a text, especially of traditional literature, is common in historical studies and is not to be objected to. Given the condition of the source material, only in a few cases one can attain more certainty through text-historical evidence. In the final part of this contri-

---

51. Witte, *Die biblische Urgeschichte*, 131.
52. Witte, *Die biblische Urgeschichte*, 131.

82   Jan Christian Gertz

bution, I want to consider whether this is the case in Gen 5 by discussing a thesis of Karl Budde.[53]

The widely accepted proposal that the genealogical notes in Gen 4 and the toledot of Adam in Gen 5 are two compositions based on one common genealogy was made for the first time by Philipp Buttmann.[54] Though the non-Priestly notes in Gen 4 distinguish between a Cain- and Seth-line and regardless of small deviations in the spelling and some changes in the order, all members in both lines with the exception of the descendants of Lamech are also found in the Priestly text of Gen 5. Before evaluating this finding in terms of redaction-history, the present context must first be dealt with. The toledot formula in Gen 2:4 introduces a section that extends to 4:26. It reports the fate of both the first human couple and the first generation of their descendants. Actually, the children and grandchildren of the first human couple already belong to the toledot of Adam, which only follows in Gen 5:1. The slight anachronism, however, does not hinder a coherent reading of the present text sequence.[55] If one reads the toledot formula in 5:1 as a heading that links back with its variable elements to the immediately preceding events, then on the level of the present text the subsequent notices about Seth in Gen 5:3 and the conception of Enoch in Gen 5:6 are to be understood as references back to the concluding section of Gen 4 (compare Gen 5:3 with Gen 4:25 and Gen 5:6 with Gen 4:26). The toledot of Adam that extends to Noah in Gen 5 thus provides a direct link to the line of descendants: Adam–Seth–Enoch. For the present form of the text, the following overall model results: due to the fratricide of Cain and the violent outbreaks of Lamech, the Cainites are characterized negatively. Their genealogical line in Gen 4:17–24 is not carried forward in the present text. Instead, a new genealogical line begins in Gen 4:25 with Seth, who replaces the murdered Abel and is the third

---

53. Karl Budde, *Die Biblische Urgeschichte (Gen 1–12,5)* (Gießen: Ricker, 1883), 89–116. I have presented the following considerations already previously, however with different intentions and in a slightly different form, in Gertz, *Formation of the Primeval History*, 118–24. See also Martin Rösel, *Übersetzung als Vollendung der Auslegung: Studien zur Genesis-Septuaginta*, BZAW 223 (Berlin: De Gruyter, 1994); Seebass, *Genesis I*, 177–82. See there also for the following.

54. Phillip Buttmann, *Mythologus oder gesammelte Abhandlungen über die Sagen des Alterthums*, vol. 1 (Berlin: Mylius, 1828), 171.

55. Hieke, *Die Genealogien der Genesis*, 80–90.

Genesis 5: Priestly Redaction, Composition, or Source? 83

son of the first human couple. He is characterized positively in contrast to the Cainites. If the toledot of Adam in Gen 5 is added into the line of descendants of Adam–Seth–Enoch in Gen 4:25–26, it presents a genealogy that no longer includes the Cainites, notwithstanding the overlaps between Gen 5 and Gen 4:17–24. Consequently, Noah as the hero of the flood narrative is not a descendant of Cain but rather stands in the line of descendants of Seth, who had taken the place of Abel, whose offering YHWH had accepted (Gen 4:4), and Enosh, during whose lifetime the worshiping of YHWH begins (Gen 4:26).[56]

Additionally, Noah's family tree of the righteous is characterized by the fact that the line from Seth and Enosh to Noah leads through a series of ancestors, who all enjoyed a truly biblical lifespan and passed away peacefully before the flood. Two exceptions emphasize this. Enoch walks with God and is taken up at the age of 365, and, although Methuselah dies in the year of the flood, he nevertheless had the longest lifespan among the ancestors.

This, however, only applies for the ages given in the Masoretic Text (MT) and not for those in the Samaritan Pentateuch (SamPent). The notices on the age of the ancestors in the MT and the SamPent agree for the first five generations from Adam to Mahalalel. But not only does the age data in these two textual traditions clearly differ from one another in the following five generations from Jared to Noah, but so also does the year of the flood calculated from the data.[57] The MT dates the beginning of the flood to the year 1656, but the SamPent to 1307. We will not discuss

---

56. This is also the reason for the fact that with the combination of the Priestly and non-Priestly texts, the birth notice for Noah from the non-Priestly primeval history is omitted, since there Noah is seen as a son of Lamech and thus as a descendant of Cain.

57. A synopsis is presented by Rösel, *Übersetzung als Vollendung der Auslegung*, 131. See there also on the following as well as for the chronology of the Septuagint, which according to Rösel presents an intentional new calculation which is oriented toward the year 5000 of the history of the world as the date of the consecration of the Second Temple. On the question of how the chronology of the Septuagint can contribute to the reconstruction of the original chronology, see below. The different dates found in the book of Jubilees and Josephus can be left out of consideration for our purposes. With view to the book of Jubilees, which coincides with deviations of up to three years with the SamPent, we can still affirm that the conception of the premature deaths of the impious patriarchs is less important, because the dates of the deaths remain unmentioned with the exception of Adam.

84 Jan Christian Gertz

the overarching chronological concepts that govern each text here.[58] For our question it is only of interest that different fates and evaluations of the ancestors can be derived from the differences in the chronologies. The SamPent in Gen 5 clearly distinguishes between the first five generations and the following five generations; this differs from the Masoretic design. While the death dates for the first five generations are clearly before the year of the flood, Methuselah, who is significantly younger in the Sam-Pent, perishes in the year of the flood along with Jared and Lamech. Aside from Noah, of all the ancestors of the second half of the genealogy, only Enoch survives, who is taken up in the year 887 (SamPent). The conception of the SamPent is clear. With the exception of Enoch and Noah, the lives of the ancestors of the sixth to tenth generations end in the year of the flood. Because the genealogy has a general life expectancy of about 900 years, the deaths of Jared at 847 years, Methuselah at 720, and Lamech at 653 each occur prematurely. As such, they are characterized as sinners compared to their two younger contemporaries Enoch and Noah; their righteousness, however, is mentioned explicitly, and they do not fall victim to the flood. The comparison is also apparent with the ancestors of the first to the fifth generations, who peacefully passed away at an old age. The case of Enoch is especially interesting. He would have only lived to be 780 when the deadly flood struck. However, since he walked with God, he was preserved from death and was, according to the tradition, taken away by God. The significance of Enoch's special fate is further emphasized by the fact that, according to the SamPent, all the ancestors were witnesses of him being taken up. In contrast, according to the MT, Adam had already died (930 MT) by the time that Enoch was taken up (987 MT) and Noah had not yet been born (1056 MT). Since, according to the SamPent, the lifespans of the ancestors who died in the year of the flood gradually decreased,

---

58. The point of orientation for the longer chronology of the MT is most likely the rededication of the Second Temple by the Maccabees in the 4000th year of the history of the world. See on this, Rösel, *Übersetzung als Vollendung der Auslegung*, 135, with reference to A. E. Murtonen, "On the Chronology of the Old Testament," *ST* 8 (1954): 133–37; Klaus Koch, "Sabbatstruktur der Geschichte: Die sogenannte Zehn-Wochen-Apokalypse (I Hen 93,1–10; 91,11–17) und das Ringen um die alttestamentlichen Chronologien im späten Israelitentum," *ZAW* 95 (1983): 403–30, as well as similar considerations in Jeremy Hughes, *Secrets of the Times: Myth and History in Biblical Chronology*, JSOTSup 66 (Sheffield: Sheffield Academic, 1990), 237–38. The SamPent however is oriented to the establishment of the sanctuary on Mount Gerizim, dated to year 2800 of the world. Cf. Alfred Jepsen, "Zur Chronologie des Priesterkodex," *ZAW* 47 (1929): 253.

Genesis 5: Priestly Redaction, Composition, or Source? 85

the reverse conclusion is likely: sin increased from generation to generation up to the contemporaries of Noah (cf. Gen 6:9). Thus the genealogies evince a clear trajectory leading to the divine judgment over the wickedness of all flesh (cf. 6:12). In this way, the SamPent does not present a *narrative* development of the theme of the corruption of the good creation but does so in *genealogical* form. On the other hand, the data of the MT agrees with the overall conception of the present text, according to which the genealogy of the Cainites did not survive the flood, whereas the line of Seth is regarded positively.

Should this result be considered an indication of the fact that the briefer chronology of the SamPent preserves the older form of a previously independent Priestly document, while the MT has used the details of the present sequence of texts in the interpretation of its longer chronology?[59] Naturally, this form of external evidence for the existence of an originally unbroken sequence of the Priestly texts in Gen 1:1–2:3 and 5:1–32* is burdened with considerable uncertainties; these uncertainties increase when further textual witnesses and the toledot of Shem in Gen 11:10–26 are also considered. In any case, a few details support the priority of the Samaritan chronology in Gen 5. For example, the MT significantly raises the ages for the conception of the first son from Jared onward. While the SamPent and MT begin with an average age of 92 years at procreation for the first five ancestors, the procreative age for Jared, Methuselah, and Lamech increases to 177 according to the chronology of the MT in contrast to an average age of 61 in the SamPent. This in turn fits well with the information on Enoch in both the SamPent and the MT (Gen 5:21: 65 years MT and SamPent) and also corresponds to the ages in the MT seen throughout Gen 11.[60] Furthermore, the personal acquaintance of Noah with Enoch, which would be possible according to the SamPent, accords with the intentions of the text. Additionally, the names of the ancestors Jared ("descent") and Methuselah ("man of the spear") suggest violent connotations. Like the violence (traditionally?) associated with Lamech, this would accord well with their deaths in the year of the flood per the Samaritan chronology.[61]

---

59. The SamPent takes up the necessary adjustments for its chronological conception in Gen 11, whereas the MT in Gen 11 has preserved the older chronology.

60. See Rösel, *Übersetzung*, 130. The exception in Gen 11:10–26 (MT) is Shem, who is mentioned first. As in the SamPent and the LXX, he is one hundred years old at the time of procreation.

61. See Budde, *Urgeschichte*, 96, 99–100.

Ronald S. Hendel has proposed another solution.[62] He advances the thesis that the chronological data of the MT and the SamPent, as well that of the Hebrew *Vorlage* of the LXX are a later correction of the so called "Genesis archetype." The correction was necessary, because according to the Genesis archetype the three ancestors Jared, Methuselah, and Lamech would have lived long after the date of the beginning of the flood, which is incompatible with the flood narrative. The starting point for this thesis are the details of the LXX, according to whose chronology Methuselah continued to live fourteen years after the flood. The chronological disagreements within the Genesis archetype came about because the dates of the ancestors come from a previously independently transmitted Book of the Generations of Adam (Gen 5:1–31*), which was only secondarily connected with the flood narrative: "When the P writer or redactor integrated this work into the narrative context, he may not have perceived (or may have been unconcerned with) the implicit chronological conflicts. It remained for later scribes to detect the problems and to incorporate their textual solutions."[63]

Hendel's reconstruction of the chronology of the Genesis archetype is based on the LXX and a scheme developed from the comparison of MT and SamPent with the example of the first five ancestors and Enoch, with which the Hebrew *Vorlage* of the LXX had edited the Genesis archetype.[64] The LXX raised the age of each of the ancestors at the time of their first son's conception by one hundred years in contrast to the Genesis archetype and correspondingly reduced their remaining lifespans by one hundred years, so that the timespan before the flood is significantly extended. On the other hand, both the MT and SamPent have preserved the chronology of the Genesis archetype for the first five ancestors as well as for Enoch. For the reconstruction of the chronology of the Genesis archetype with regard to Jared, Methuselah, and Lamech, Hendel uses the data of the LXX as his foundation. In the case of these three ancestors he proceeds from

---

62. See Ronald S. Hendel, *The Text of Genesis 1–11: Textual Studies and Critical Edition* (Oxford: Oxford University Press, 1998), following Ralph W. Klein, "Archaic Chronologies and the Textual History of the Old Testament," *HTR* 67 (1974): 255–63; Hughes, *Secrets of the Times*; Donald V. Etz, "The Numbers of Genesis V:3–31: A Suggested Conversion and Its Implications," *VT* 43 (1993): 171–89.

63. Hendel, *Text of Genesis 1–11*, 63.

64. The schema was already recognized by Budde and is not itself a matter of debate. See Budde, *Urgeschichte*, 112–13.

Genesis 5: Priestly Redaction, Composition, or Source? 87

corresponding changes in the data of the first son's conception and the remaining lifespan thereafter. This results in a brief chronology for the Genesis archetype by which in connection with Gen 7:6 the flood can be calculated to begin in the year 1342 (MT 1656; SamPent 1307; LXX 2242). Interestingly, the reconstructed dates of the Genesis archetype are partially confirmed by the SamPent or MT. The dating for the conception of the first son by Jared and Methuselah agrees with the SamPent, and the lifespans of Jared and Methuselah agree with the MT. The congruencies and deviations between the MT and SamPent, on the one hand, and the LXX, on the other, as well as the absence of congruence between the MT and SamPent over against the LXX (disregarding the schematic changes) can be explained according to the proposed model in which the LXX has preserved the Genesis archetype (except for its systematic changes), while the MT and SamPent deviate occasionally.

Although this solution seems obvious on a first glance, the difficulties are in the details and in the basic assumptions necessary for this reconstruction. First, regarding the details: the deviations between the MT and SamPent pertain to the ancestors Jared, Methuselah, and Lamech. For Jared and Methuselah, the reconstruction of a Genesis archetype according to the described manner seems possible; the data from the LXX would be confirmed partially by the MT and partially by the SamPent. The case of Lamech is completely different. Here the reconstructions do not lead to a persuasive result, because the reconstructed dates are not supported by the MT or SamPent. In particular, the thirty-five-year difference regarding the date of Lamech's first procreation between the SamPent (53rd year) and that of the Genesis archetype reconstructed from the LXX (88th year = 188th year according to the LXX minus one hundred years), remains inexplicable, because the SamPent otherwise basically presents the data of "LXX minus 100 years." It is also notable that the MT raises the date of the first procreation of Jared, with the LXX and against the SamPent, by one hundred years; then, compared to the reconstructed Genesis archetype, decreases the remaining lifespan by one hundred years. The same can be observed in the case of Methuselah, save that it is 120 years there. Should LXX and MT have come up with the same idea completely independently of one another in handling the underlying Genesis archetype? Usually, a shared deviation from the text that is recognized as original is considered to be an indication for a common textual foundation shared by the deviating texts. Furthermore, Jared's remaining years of life after his first procreation differ between the MT and LXX (800 years) and SamPent (785

88   Jan Christian Gertz

years), and his whole age differs correspondingly by fifteen years. Hendel explains this by suggesting that the SamPent wanted to avoid the idea that Jared survived the flood, unlike the postulated Genesis archetype.[65] If, however, one takes as a foundation Hendel's reconstruction of the Genesis archetype (the text of the LXX without its schematic changes), then the SamPent would not have needed to intervene with Jared. A correction of the data regarding the life of Methuselah and the date of Noah's conception would have been quite sufficient.

The explanation of the differences in the case of Jared in the Sam-Pent, on the one hand, and the MT and LXX, on the other hand, as a secondary adjustment of the preflood chronology to the flood narrative by the SamPent also draws attention to Hendel's problematic premises: the observation that, according to the LXX, Methuselah survives the flood, leads to the conclusion of the existence of a toledot book. This toledot book then had been connected secondarily with the Priestly flood narrative, but its chronology was incompatible with that of the Priestly writing. However, the assumption of an originally independent toledot book must, after long discussion, be considered uncertain.[66] But if such a book is to be considered, then a revision by the Priestly writing with the integration of this book is to be assumed. This is seen from the cross-references in the toledot of Adam to passages of the Priestly text which clearly could not have belonged to the toledot book (cf. Gen 5:1b, 2, 3 with Gen 1:26–28; Gen 5:22 with Gen 6:9). In the context of such a reworking, it seems that at least the chronology of Noah's age at the procreation of his three sons (in one year!), which deviates strongly from the other patriarchs, and the

---

65. See Hendel, *Text of Genesis 1–11*, 64. Hughes, *Secrets of the Times*, 12–14; Hendel, *Text of Genesis*, 66, brought forward a similar proposal for the MT in the case of Methuselah, where in comparison with the LXX the age of the conception of the first son is raised by 120 years instead of 100 years in relation to the SamPent. Thereby, the beginning of the flood were postponed with the result that all patriarchs die before the flood. This is in principle seen correctly, but the calculation operations of the MT are caused by other requirements. For this, see the following.

66. The thesis of a toledot book developed prominently by von Rad (see *Priesterschrift*, 33–40), has been recently taken up, with a clearly reduced extent of this source, among others by Blum, *Studien zur Komposition des Pentateuch*, 279–81; Carr, "Βίβλος γενέσεως Revisited," 169–70; and Schüle, *Der Prolog der hebräischen Bibel*, 44–46. The agreements with the genealogical data in Gen 4 speak in fact for the view that the Priestly document in these points cites from a preceding text and does not just refer to a fictional source (so also Seebass, *Genesis I*, 185–86)—more can hardly be said.

Genesis 5: Priestly Redaction, Composition, or Source? 89

chronology of the flood narrative (Noah was 600 years old at the beginning of the flood; cf. Gen 7:6), and the toledot of Shem (Shem was 100 years old in the second year after the flood; cf. Gen 11:10) have been adjusted. Hendel's supposition, that the author of the Priestly document, who is otherwise very interested in such questions, had overlooked that the lifespans of three ancestors extended far beyond the flood (Jared 80 years; Methuselah 214 years; Lamech 65 years), while it was noticed by the scribes of the MT, the SamPent, and the *Vorlage* of the LXX only later and independently of one another (?), seems unlikely. The burden of proof for this proposal is on the assumption that the error assumed for P has been preserved in the LXX, although the latter has changed the chronology in order to avoid precisely this issue. Hendel's explanation for this observation states: "This mishap may be an unintended consequence of a systematic application of the revision. For Methuselah to have died at or before the flood, a scribe would have had to alter the system, and this may have seemed too radical for a systematizing scribe."[67] Such a proposal seems to be an ad hoc thesis. Moreover, the principle faithfulness of the LXX to the transmitted dates in the case of Lamech cannot be substantiated.

A possible alternative with fewer presuppositions emerges: the SamPent has preserved the Priestly chronology of the toledot of Adam associated with the flood narrative. The question of the existence of an originally independent Book of the Toledot of Adam and some kind of editing of this book with its integration into the Priestly document can be left out of the reconstruction of the textual history. It must be explained separately.

Unlike the SamPent, the MT and the Hebrew *Vorlage* of the LXX are based upon a multistaged adjustment of the Priestly chronology in the process of an initially shared but later largely independent textual history. Based on its overall chronology, the MT has extended the time before the flood by raising the conception dates of the firstborn by 100 years for Jared, 120 years for Methuselah, and 129 years for Lamech. At the same time the MT has prolonged the lifespans of these ancestors by the years thus gained in the interests of a longer chronology. The Hebrew *Vorlage* of the LXX has widely followed it.[68] But then the Hebrew *Vorlage* (or the translator) has also adjusted the data of conception of the first son for all

---

67. Hendel, *Text of Genesis 1–11*, 64.

68. For Gen 11, the case is different. Since here the SamPent and the LXX agree in all data for the ages of the births of the firstborn sons against the (more original) chronology of the MT, "the presumption of a common source text is inevitable" (Rösel,

90   Jan Christian Gertz

patriarchs to the higher ages of Jared and Methuselah in the interests of an even longer overall chronology. In these cases, it also reduced their remaining lifespans.

It remains to be explained why Methuselah's age at the conception of his first son differs by twenty years between the MT and the LXX even though there is agreement over against the SamPent regarding his whole lifespan. It is conceivable that, after the separation of the Hebrew *Vorlage* of the LXX from the common text-tradition, which would later become the MT, the age of Methuselah at the conception of Lamech in the MT was increased twenty years (without impacting the overall lifespan). According to the MT, through this change Lamech reached the age of 777 years before the beginning of the flood, as an allusion to Gen 4:24.[69] Following from this, another explanation can be considered carefully: the MT might have simply deducted twenty years from the age of Lamech's conception of Noah in order to preserve the absolute chronology and the flood date of 1656. In this case, one could use the LXX for the reconstruction of a common precursor (V* from the German *Vorstufe*) of the MT and the Hebrew *Vorlage* of the LXX for all the dates of Methuselah. As for Lamech, at least the data on the remaining years after the conception of Noah could be transferred from the LXX.

Therefore, the chronology of the common precursor (V*) of the MT and the Hebrew *Vorlage* of the LXX and its developments can be reconstructed with necessary caution as follows: On the level of the common precursor (V*), the ages of Jared and Methuselah at their first procreation is raised by one hundred years in comparison with the original chronology found in the SamPent. After the branching of the textual history of the MT and the Hebrew *Vorlage* of the LXX, the MT raised the age of Methuselah at the first procreation by twenty years and correspondingly reduced his remaining lifespan. In agreement with the LXX, for the common precursor (V*) we can consider an age of 167 years for the first procreation. As with Jared, this corresponds to raising the data of the SamPent by one hundred years, which preserves the original chronology. If the MT simply removed twenty years from the age of Lamech at his procreation of Noah in order to preserve the absolute chronology and the date of the flood in 1656 in the precursor (V*), then this results in a calculated age of 202 years

---

Übersetzung, 224), which does not however rule out the possibility of later redactions in each textual history.

69. See Wellhausen, *Prolegomena to the History of Ancient Israel*, 309.

Genesis 5: Priestly Redaction, Composition, or Source? 91

for Lamech at the procreation of Noah within V*. This means an increase of 149 years in comparison to the original data of the SamPent, which has fifty-three years. This increase was necessary, because the chronology for the beginning of the flood threatened to become inconsistent due to the prolonged ages for Jared and Methuselah.[70] The raising of Lamech's age at the procreation of his first son by 149 years could have been oriented to the number seven, which is connected closely with Lamech, insofar as the increase by forty-nine years in comparison to the one hundred years of Jared (MT; LXX; V*) and Methuselah (LXX; V*) is the result of seven times seven (cf. likewise Gen 4:24). Such considerations may even have been in the background for the 188 years that the LXX gives as the age of Lamech at the procreation of Noah. Beginning from the fifty-three years, which the SamPent has for the age at the conception of the first son, the 188 years result from the usual raise by one hundred years and an additional thirty-five years. In this case, the multiplier of five has been the decisive factor for the scribe.[71] Regarding the chronological data on Lamech, there is a large uncertainty, because here the MT, SamPent, and LXX each have different data. It appears to be plausible that the SamPent has preserved the original age concerning the firstborn's procreation for Lamech, as well as for the other ancestors,[72] and that the MT is guided by Gen 4:24 in its calculation of Lamech's age.

In any case, the contradictory data on Lamech is a clear indication that the original chronology experienced a multi-staged development.[73] And it is also a clear indication that this process must have developed differently and was directed by different premises in different textual traditions.

5. Summary

Regardless of whether or not the differences between the MT and the SamPent in Gen 5 can bear the burden of proof placed upon them, the

---

70. Also according to the *Vorstufe* (V*), none of the patriarchs survived the flood.

71. The considerations on the derivation of the 100 + 49 years (*Vorstufe* [V*]) and 100 + 35 years (LXX) from the connection of Lamech with the number seven are from a conversation with Martin Rösel.

72. With Hughes, *Secrets of the Times*, 19–20.

73. The harmonization of a series of Greek textual witnesses with the MT regarding Methuselah's age at the conception of Lamech (see the apparatus of the Göttingen LXX) is along these same lines.

92   Jan Christian Gertz

reexamination of well-known arguments speaks in favor of the existence
of an independent Priestly thread in the Primeval History. Its conceptual
connection with Priestly texts outside the Primeval History is beyond
question for me. For the Exodus narrative, I essentially adhere to a two-
source model. The arguments brought forth most recently against the
existence of P as an independent source in Exod 1–15 have not convinced
me. The situation is different, however, with the Priestly texts in the patriarchal narratives, not to mention those in the Joseph narratives. Perhaps
the findings from each individual textual unit should be evaluated differently. It may well be that Blum's proposal that P is neither exclusively a
source nor a redaction but rather a compositional layer, which integrates
its own textual units and has these first and foremost in view in the overall
composition, is fitting for the major thematic blocks. I can, however, only
repeat my old opinion in this regard:

> Due to the sparse Priestly texts in Gen 12ff., it remains to be considered
> whether in this area P has already integrated the non-Priestly texts. P
> would in this case have to be understood for Gen 12ff as a redactional
> layer. Following an independently formulated Priestly Primeval History,
> this redactional layer would have integrated the patriarchal and Joseph
> narratives, and then would have continued with an again independent
> presentation of the origins of Israel in Egypt and the time of Moses.[74]

6. Appendix: Charts on the Chronology in Genesis 5

The chart on the facing page illustrates (1) the common textual history of
the MT and the Hebrew *Vorlage* of the LXX after the separation from the
SamPent, as it results from the reconstruction we have described above,
and (2) the continuation of the separated textual history of the MT and the
LXX. Additionally listed are (3) the dates according to the SamPent, which
preserved the original chronology. The dates for the ancestors from Adam
to Mahalalel are listed for comprehensiveness. They agree wholly in the
MT and the SamPent; here, the LXX dates the conception of the first sons
one hundred years later for each and reduces the remaining lifespan by one

---

74. Gertz, *Tradition und Redaktion in der Exoduserzählung*, 389. See now Jakob
Wöhrle, *Fremdlinge im eigenen Land: Zur Entstehung und Intention der priesterlichen Passagen der Vätergechichte*, FRLANT 246 (Göttingen: Vandenhoeck & Ruprecht, 2012).

	Anno mundi	Age at the birth of the firstborn son			Remaining lifespan			Total age		
	V*/MT*	V*/MT	LXX	SP	V*/MT	LXX	SP	V*/MT	LXX	SP
Adam	1–930	130	230	130	800	700	800	930	930	930
Seth	130–1042	105	205	105	807	707	807	912	912	912
Enosh	235–1140	90	190	90	815	715	815	905	905	905
Kenan	325–1235	70	170	70	840	740	840	910	910	910
Mahalalel	395–1290	65	165	65	830	730	830	895	895	895
Jared	460–1422	162	162	62	800	800	785	962	962	847
Enoch	622–987	65	165	65	300	200	300	365	365	365
Methuselah MT	687–1656	187	167	67	782	802	653	969	969	720
Methuselah V*	687–1656	167	167	67	802	802	653	969	969	720
Lamech MT	874–1651	182	188	53	595	565	600	777	753	653
Lamech V*	854–1621	202	188	53	565	565	600	767	753	653
Flood MT/V*	1656 (six hundredth year of Noah)									

* The dates of the common *Vorstufe* [precursor] (V*) of the MT and the Hebrew *Vorlage* of the LXX agree up to Methuselah and Lamech and are listed for reasons of space in one column. Deviations of the MT compared with the (reconstructed) *Vorstufe* (V*) are especially noted.

hundred years, so that the ages of the ancestors remain unchanged, but the absolute chronology is extended by four hundred years. It remains to be noted that also according to the chronology of the reconstructed common precursor (V*) of the MT and the Hebrew *Vorlage* of the LXX, none of the ancestors survives the flood. This problem appears to have already been solved in the Priestly document. It is only in the LXX that Methuselah dies fourteen years after the flood, which has erroneously occurred because of the repeated changes. The information on Lamech in V* cannot be supported by the corroborating witnesses and is thus uncertain.

The second chart shows the lifespans of the ancestors according to the calculated absolute chronology for the MT, SamPent, LXX, and V*. Usually it is presumed in the calculations that the year of the conception falls together with the year of the birth of the respective ancestor. If on the basis of Gen 18:14, a rounded-out year for the time between conception and birth is calculated, the absolute chronology would be correspondingly extended.[75]

	MT	SP	LXX	V*
Adam	1–930	1–930	1–930	1–930
Seth	130–1042	130–1042	230–1142	130–1042
Enosh	235–1140	235–1140	435–1340	235–1140
Kenan	325–1235	325–1235	625–1535	325–1235
Mahalalel	395–1290	395–1290	795–1690	395–1290
Jared	460–1422	460–1307	960–1922	460–1422
Enoch	622–987	522–877	1122–1487	622–987
Methuselah	687–1656	587–1307	1287–2256	687–1656
Lamech	874–1651	654–1307	1454–2207	854–1621
Beginning of the flood	1656	1307	2242	1656

---

75. See Ziemer, "Erklärung," 2–4.

The Literary Character of the Priestly Portions of the Exodus Narrative (Exod 1–14)

Christoph Berner

1. Introduction

Do the Priestly portions of Exod 1–14 form an originally independent source, a redactional layer, or a combination of both? The question has been heavily debated in the past decades, and all the options mentioned have found advocates.[1] The majority of scholars probably favor a source model as before,[2] and there are understandable reasons for this. Unlike the

---

The original German version of this essay was completed in 2012 and concluded with a cautious sketch of a redactional model. Today, after additional years of continuous research in the Pentateuch and on the book of Exodus, I have further refined this model and reworked the English translation of this essay accordingly. The model, which will be presented in greater detail in the first volume of my forthcoming commentary on the book of Exodus for the German series Das Alte Testament Deutsch (ATD), distinguishes five successive stages in the development of the book: pre-Priestly (pre-P), early Priestly (P 1), late Deuteronomistic (D), late Priestly (P 2), and proto-Chronistic (C). In what follows, I will use the above sigla to clarify which particular stage of the text I am referring to.

1. On the history of research, see the contribution by Christoph Levin in this volume, as well as Eckart Otto, "Forschungen zur Priesterschrift," *TRu* 62 (1997): 1–50. A glance at the current discussion is given in the contributions in Sarah Shectman and Joel S. Baden, eds., *The Strata of the Priestly Writings*, AThANT 95 (Zürich: TVZ, 2008); Thomas B. Dozeman, Konrad Schmid, and Baruch J. Schwartz, eds., *The Pentateuch: International Perspectives on Current Research*, FAT 78 (Tübingen: Mohr Siebeck, 2011), esp. 243–432.

2. Among the prominent opponents of this majority opinion are Frank Moore Cross, *Canaanite Myth and Hebrew Epic: Essays in the History of the Religion of Israel* (Cambridge, MA: Harvard University Press, 1973), 293–325; Rolf Rendtorff, *Das überlieferungsgeschichtliche Problem des Pentateuch*, BZAW 147 (Berlin: De Gruyter,

situation in the patriarchal narratives and the Joseph story (Gen 12–50), in Exod 1–14 the thread of a continuous Priestly source can be reconstructed over wide swaths. Moreover, this reconstructed text repeatedly stands in clear tension with the non-Priestly passages. The juxtaposition of the two revelation scenes in Exod 6 (P) and Exod 3 and the rather forced intertwining of two different representations of the miracle at the sea (Exod 14) are already sufficient grounds for many scholars to exclude the possibility that the Priestly texts in Exod 1–14 are supplements to the non-Priestly material. Rather, it is assumed that some sort of final redaction must have formed the present connection between the Priestly and non-Priestly texts.

However, for several reasons this view needs to be critically reevaluated. For one thing, there is a growing number of scholars who point out that the Priestly text has striking narrative gaps and is sometimes so closely intertwined with the non-Priestly text that it should better be interpreted as an editorial layer.[3] Moreover, the overall landscape of pentateuchal criticism in Europe has changed significantly. Although the texts under consideration have remained the same, the presuppositions concerning their interpretation have been strongly challenged by the results of recent redaction-critical scholarship. So, for example, non-Priestly texts can no longer automatically be considered pre-Priestly, as many of these texts often seem to have been composed in reference to the P-texts and so are post-Priestly (D or C).[4] Additionally, there is an increasing tendency

---

1976); Helmut Utzschneider, *Das Heiligtum und das Gesetz*, OBO 77 (Göttingen: Vandenhoeck & Ruprecht, 1988); Erhard Blum, *Studien zur Komposition des Pentateuch*, BZAW 189 (Berlin: De Gruyter, 1990); John Van Seters, *The Life of Moses*, CBET 10 (Kampen: Kok, 1994); Jean Louis Ska, "Quelques remarques sur P^g et la dernière rédaction du Pentateuque," in *Le Pentateuque en question: Les origines et la composition des cinq premiers livres de la Bible à la lumière des recherches récentes*, ed. Albert de Pury and Thomas Römer, MdB 19, 3rd ed. (Geneva: Labor et Fides, 2002), 95–125; Rainer Albertz, "Die Josephsgeschichte im Pentateuch," in *Diasynchron: Beiträge zur Exegese, Theologie und Rezeption der hebräischen Bibel; Walter Dietrich zum 65. Geburtstag*, ed. Thomas Naumann and Regine Hunziker-Rodewald (Stuttgart: Kohlhammer, 2009), 11–37; Albertz, *Ex 1–18*, vol. 1 of *Exodus*, ZBK.AT 2.1 (Zürich: TVZ, 2012); Helmut Utzschneider and Wolfgang Oswald, *Exodus 1–15*, IEKAT (Stuttgart: Kohlhammer, 2013).

3. See the authors mentioned in the previous note.

4. See foundationally Reinhard Gregor Kratz, *Die Komposition der erzählenden Bücher des Alten Testaments: Grundwissen der Bibelkritik*, UTB 2157 (Göttingen: Vandenhoeck & Ruprecht, 2000), 249–304.

The Literary Character of the Priestly Portions of the Exodus Narrative   97

toward distinguishing various levels within the Priestly texts of the Pentateuch, with passages that were traditionally identified as integral portions of the P-source (P 1) being now instead explained as late redactions of non-Priestly texts (P 2 or C).[5] While for advocates of the Documentary Hypothesis the literary-historical relationship between the individual textual strata appeared to be essentially clear, now even certain basic lines have become blurred.

Therefore, it is useful to consider anew the question of the literary character of the Priestly texts in Exod 1–14. This will be carried out in what follows by a step-by-step treatment of the relevant textual units (sections 2–6). First, the literary evidence of each section of text will be presented, followed by an evaluation of the plausibility of both methodological approaches, the Documentary Hypothesis and Supplementary Hypothesis. A brief results section summarizes the findings of each subsection and prepares for a short redaction-critical synthesis at the end of the article (section 7).

2. The Situation of the Israelites in Egypt (Exod 1:1–7*, 13–14; 2:23aβ–25)

2.1. The Literary Evidence

It is generally recognized that Exod 1:13–14; 2:23aβ–25 belong to the earliest Priestly text (P 1).[6] Both groups of verses are closely related to one another, insofar as 1:13–14 first describe how Israel came to be under forced labor, and 2:23aβ–25 then narrate the crying out of the enslaved followed by the reaction of YHWH. This prepares for the revelation scene in 6:2–7:7*, which likewise must be assigned to the P 1 stratum. However, both 1:13–14 and 2:23aβ–25 show traces of editorial reworking.[7] In 1:14,

---

5. This applies especially to the Priestly sections of Numbers; see, for example, Reinhard Achenbach, *Die Vollendung der Tora*, BZAR 3 (Wiesbaden: Harrassowitz, 2003); Thomas Römer, "Israel's Sojourn in the Wilderness and the Construction of the Book of Numbers," in *Reflection and Refraction: Studies in Biblical Historiography in Honour of A. Graeme Auld*, ed. Robert Rezetko, VTSup 113 (Brill: Leiden, 2007), 419–45. For recent discussion on the book of Leviticus, see Christophe Nihan, *From Priestly Torah to Pentateuch*, FAT 2/25 (Tübingen: Mohr Siebeck, 2007).

6. Cf. Werner H. Schmidt, *Exodus*, BK 2.1 (Neukirchen-Vluyn: Neukirchner, 1988), 89–90.

7. See already Peter Weimar, *Untersuchungen zur priesterschriftlichen Exoduserzählung*, FB 9 (Würzburg: Echter-Verlag, 1973), 70.

98   Christoph Berner

the details of the Israelites' servitude are perhaps secondary, since they do not play any role in the following P 1 passages and are rather reminiscent of other non-Priestly passages, that is, the Tower of Babel story in Gen 11 and the plague of hail in Exod 9.[8] Even more important, however, is the observation that the motif of the Egyptians enslaving the Israelites "with rigor" (בפרך) stands out as a later addition which was introduced at the end of 1:13 and emphasized through the rather redundant resumptive repetition in 1:14b ("all their labors which they rigorously imposed on them").

As for the scene in Exod 2:23aβ–25, there is strong evidence that the final verses 2:23b, 25 are secondary. Regardless of whether one follows the LXX or the MT reading of 2:25,[9] it is striking that the motifs of YHWH seeing the Israelites and knowing (MT) or revealing himself (LXX) are completely absent from the Priestly story of the call of Moses. Rather, Exod 6:5 (P 1) contains a verbatim repetition of 2:24 (P 1), namely, of YHWH hearing the groaning of the Israelites. Therefore, it stands to reason that 2:25 is a later redactional harmonization with the non-Priestly revelation scene at the burning bush where the motif(s) of YHWH seeing (and knowing) take(s) center stage (3:7). Basically, the same also applies to the idea that the Israelites' cry rose up to God (2:23b). The phrase is redundant in its immediate context, and its wording is not taken up in the Priestly revelation scene (Exod 6:2–7:7*, P 1). Instead, the imagery of the *ascending* cry of the enslaved is best explained against the background of the non-Priestly text in 3:8, which states that YHWH has *descended* to end the Israelites' misery. Thus, 2:23b should be regarded as a further redactional harmonization with the non-Priestly revelation scene in Exod 3.

While Exod 1:13*, 14a; 2:23aβ, 24 can be assigned to P 1, it is questionable whether the same also applies to 1:1–7. Traditionally, this section has been, at least in its substance, assigned to P 1,[10] but important challenges to this perspective have been raised recently. The list of the sons of Jacob who came to Egypt (1:1–5) presupposes both the list of the twelve

---

8. Cf. Christoph Berner, *Die Exoduserzählung: Das literarische Werden einer Ursprungslegende Israels*, FAT 73 (Tübingen: Mohr Siebeck, 2010), 35–37.

9. See, e.g., Martin Noth, *Das Zweite Buch Mose: Exodus*, ATD 5 (Göttingen: Vandenhoeck & Ruprecht, 1958), 17, who opts for the priority of the LXX reading.

10. See, among others, Noth, *Das Zweite Buch Mose*, 10 (1:1–4, 5b, 7); Brevard S. Childs, *The Book of Exodus*, OTL (London: Westminster John Knox, 1974), 2 (1:1–5, 7); Schmidt, *Exodus*, 26–31 (1:1a, 2–4, 5b, 7*); Blum, *Studien zur Komposition des Pentateuch*, 241 (1:1–5, 7).

The Literary Character of the Priestly Portions of the Exodus Narrative   99

sons of Jacob from Gen 35:22b–26, which is Priestly at the earliest, as well as the detailed post-Priestly list of Jacob's descendants who came to Egypt from Gen 46:8–27. As a result, Exod 1:1–5 should likewise be excluded from P 1. It is a later addition in the Priestly tradition (C) and is associated with the separation of the books of the Pentateuch.[11]

This also applies to the multiplication notice in 1:7, which repeats Gen 47:27 P but, in contrast to its *Vorlage*, also relates to the non-Priestly multiplication vocabulary from the subsequent context (1:8, 12, 20) and presupposes the preceding context 1:1–5(6) in content and syntax.[12] The verse should therefore be considered a late post-Priestly expansion from the same hand as 1:1–5 (C).[13] As a result, the text remaining for the earliest Priestly layer (P 1) in Exod 1–2 is limited to 1:13*, 14a; 2:23aβ, 24*.

2.2. The Interpretation of the Literary Evidence in the Context of the Documentary Hypothesis

The observation that the early Priestly references to the forced labor of the Israelites (Exod 1:13*, 14a; 2:23aβ, 24) not only build on one another in content but can also be combined into a seamless textual connection is a strong argument for the view of a Priestly source-thread in Exod 1–2. The text would have read:[14]

---

11. See Christoph Levin, *Der Jahwist*, FRLANT 157 (Göttingen: Vandenhoeck & Ruprecht, 1993), 315; Kratz, *Komposition*, 243; Jans Christian Gertz, *Tradition und Redaktion in der Exoduserzählung: Untersuchungen zur Endredaktion des Pentateuch*, FRLANT 186 (Göttingen: Vandenhoeck & Ruprecht, 2000), 352–57; Berner, *Die Exoduserzählung*, 38–41. On the book transition in Gen 50 and Exod 1, see the recent discussion in Christoph Berner and Harald Samuel, eds., *Book-Seams in the Hexateuch I*, FAT 120 (Tübingen: Mohr Siebeck, 2018).

12. The construction of Exod 1:7 as an inverted verbal sentence yields a meaningful continuation of the verse within the directly preceding context only to 1:5a (so Erhard Blum, "Die literarische Verbindung von Erzvätern und Exodus," in *Textgestalt und Komposition*, Erhard Blum, FAT 69 [Tübingen: Mohr Siebeck, 2010], 115), or to 1:6 (so Berner, *Die Exoduserzählung*, 47). In contrast, the transition from Gen 50:22 to Exod 1:7 postulated by Gertz, *Tradition und Redaktion in der Exoduserzählung*, 357, is not impossible but would be unusual; this gap leads to Gertz presuming that an introduction of Moses is missing.

13. See Levin, *Der Jahwist*, 315; Kratz, *Komposition*, 243; Berner, *Die Exoduserzählung*, 38–41.

14. Here and in what follows the Priestly texts are highlighted in italics.

100   Christoph Berner

1:13* And the Egyptians compelled the Israelites to labor 14a and made their lives bitter with hard labor [in mortar and brick and in every kind of field labor.] 2:23aβ And the Israelites groaned under the labor and cried out. 24 And God heard their groaning, and God remembered his covenant with Abraham, Isaac, and Jacob.

There are no issues with the connection of these texts. The problem lies in other places, because the narrative introduction of the forced labor in 1:13 is missing a suitable anchor in the earlier context of the Priestly material. Without the multiplication notice in 1:7, the potential preceding Priestly texts are limited to the notices about Joseph's age (Gen 50:22) or the death of Jacob (Gen 49:33).[15] Though the connection of Exod 1:13 to one of these verses is syntactically possible, it remains unsatisfactory in terms of content.[16] The difficulties sketched here lead to a more basic problem, because the reconstruction of a continuous Priestly source in the Joseph narrative is practically impossible.[17] The Documentary Hypothesis can explain the Priestly texts in Exod 1:13*, 14a; 2:23aβ, 24* no better than it can explain the literary evidence in Gen 37–50. Those who favor a source model must presume that the final redaction has suppressed parts of the P text in favor of its non-Priestly parallels with regard to the preceding context of 1:13–14.[18]

2.3. The Interpretation of the Literary Evidence in the Context of the Supplementary Hypothesis

The only possible way to avoid the incoherence that results from applying the Documentary Hypothesis to the Joseph story is to interpret its Priestly portions as a redaction of an earlier narrative. Such a model leads

---

15. So for example Levin, *Der Jahwist*, 315; Kratz, *Komposition*, 243.

16. Gen 50:22 is missing an explicit reference to the death of Joseph, as is testified twice in the non-Priestly text (Gen 50:26; Exod 1:6). A narrative break, which would make the transition to the oppression of the Israelites narratively plausible, is not found. The same applies for Gen 49:33, insofar as the death of the patriarch Jacob (what about Joseph?) hardly suffices as a sufficient reason for the oppression of his descendants.

17. See Blum, *Studien zur Komposition des Pentateuch*, 434; Albertz, "Die Josephsgeschichte im Pentateuch," 16–19.

18. See Levin, *Der Jahwist*, 271.

The Literary Character of the Priestly Portions of the Exodus Narrative   101

to coherent results in Gen 37–50,[19] so that it is justified to test its ability to explain the opening chapters of the book of Exodus as well. Two variant models can be considered: either the Priestly text is likewise a redaction of an older text in Exod 1 and so presupposes a pre-Priestly transition between the Joseph story and the exodus narrative, or it has established this connection for the first time itself as a redaction that links both of the older narrative works.[20] Among others, Erhard Blum has argued strongly for this second option. In a modification of his KD/KP hypothesis, he now considers Gen 50:22–23; Exod 1:1–5a, 7 to be a Priestly hinge text that bridges the end of the Joseph story (Gen 50:21) with the beginning of the exodus narrative in Exod 1:9. In addition, he presumes that Exod 1:9 was preceded in a pre-Priestly context by an introduction that can no longer be reconstructed.[21] This model, however, fails, since it considers Exod 1:1–5a, 7 part of the earliest Priestly material (P 1); yet, as argued above in section 2.1, these verses must be evaluated as later additions (C).

The alternative is to assume that there was a pre-Priestly transition from the Joseph narrative to the exodus narrative, in which the author introduces a new Pharaoh, who appears after Joseph's death (Exod 1:6aα) and begins to oppress the Israelites (1:8–9, 10ab*, 11–12, 22).[22] In this hinge text, the Priestly verses 1:13*, 14a would have been inserted after the pre-Priestly oppression notice in 1:11–12, and the redactor would have intentionally created the present text connection as follows:

---

19. See Berner, *Die Exoduserzählung*, 11–17. On this particular issue and the redaction history of the Joseph story as a whole see also the recent study of Franziska Ede, *Die Josefsgeschichte: Literarkritische und redaktionsgeschichtliche Untersuchungen zur Entstehung von Gen 37–50*, BZAW 485 (Berlin: De Gruyter, 2016).

20. A third option, which leads again to the realm of the Documentary Hypothesis, consists in taking P in the patriarchal and Joseph narratives as a redaction, which then in the realm of the book of Exodus continued as literarily independent source; see Gertz, *Tradition und Redaktion in der Exoduserzählung*, 391; Jakob Wöhrle, *Fremdlinge im eigenen Land: Zur Entstehung und Intention der priesterlichen Passagen der Vätergeschichte*, FRLANT 246 (Göttingen: Vandenhoeck & Ruprecht, 2012), 163–64. This, of course, depends on whether a Priestly source can be identified in Exod 1–14.

21. See Blum, "Die literarische Verbindung," 110–17.

22. See my proposal formulated in following the classical text-transition of the Yahwist in Berner, *Die Exoduserzählung*, 17–26. See also Ludwig Schmidt, "Die vorpriesterliche Verbindung von Erzvätern und Exodus durch die Josefsgeschichte (Gen 37; 39–50*) und Exodus 1," *ZAW* 124 (2012): 19–37. See also the recent contribution of Stephen Germany, "The Literary Relationship between Genesis 50–Exodus 1 and Joshua 24–Judges 2," in Berner and Samuel, *Book-Seams in the Hexateuch I*, 387–89.

102   Christoph Berner

1:11 Then they set taskmasters over them, to oppress them with hard labor. [and they built the storage cities for Pharaoh, Pithom and Ramses]. 12 The more they oppressed them, the more they multiplied and grew, so that they were horrified of the Israelites.
13* *Then the Egyptians compelled the Israelites to labor* 14a *and made their lives bitter with hard labor* [*in mortar and brick and in every kind of field labor.*]

From a syntactic point of view, Exod 1:13–14* fits seamlessly to its preceding context in 1:11–12. The question is whether this can also be said in terms of content. According to Blum, the P 1 passage was deliberately added at its present position to establish a "narrative climax"[23]: The fear which the Egyptians experience at the relentless multiplication of the Israelites (1:12b non-P) leads them to oppress the Israelites and force them to labor (1:13a* P 1). However, this assumption is weakened if one takes into consideration that those parts of 1:13–14* that mainly support a climactic reading (i.e., the reference to the oppression "with rigor" at the end of 1:13 and the corresponding section 1:14b) only originate from a redactional reworking of the P 1 text. Without them, the P 1 text in 1:13–14* reads more or less like a repetition of the two preceding non-Priestly verses, and it appears that the climactic reworking of 1:13–14* might have taken place precisely to avoid this impression. As a result, there certainly remains the possibility that the early Priestly section in Exod 1:13*, 14a was placed after its preceding, pre-Priestly counterpart (1:11–12) from the outset, but there is no positive evidence to support this claim.

If one interprets Exod 1:13–14* as an extension of the pre-Priestly text in 1:11–12, further difficulties arise with respect to the continuation of the narrative. In this model, it is impossible that 1:13*, 14a P 1 were followed directly by the section in 2:23aβ, 24 (P 1). According to a broad scholarly consensus, one would have to assume various pre-Priestly texts in between these two Priestly passages, namely, at least Pharaoh's command to kill the infants (1:22) and the infancy narrative of Moses (2:1–10*) along with the text about Moses's stay in Midian (2:15bβ–22) as well as its narrative preparation in 2:11–15abα. Since the reference to the death of the king of Egypt (2:23aα) is often interpreted as a narrative prelude to the return of Moses, which would have initially followed directly in 4:19–20 and would have only been separated later from 2:23aα through the addition of

---

23. Blum, *Studien zur Komposition des Pentateuch*, 240 ("erzählerischen Klimax").

The Literary Character of the Priestly Portions of the Exodus Narrative   103

the burning bush scene (3:1–4:18),[24] one could read the P 1 text (2:23aβ, 24) as an intentional insertion into this key position of the pre-Priestly composition: It would have either been placed before the burning bush scene (between 2:23aα and 3:1), or it would have found its original place immediately before the return of Moses (between 2:23aα and 4:19), if the burning bush scene as a whole should be post-Priestly.[25]

However, the assumption that Exod 2:23aβ, 24 (P 1) was initially composed to fit between 2:23aα and 3:1 or 4:19 appears plausible only at first glance, and closer consideration suggests that this hypothesis should be abandoned. The problem is that the transition postulated in the pre-Priestly text is jarring, if not impossible, both in content and syntax.[26] Exodus 4:19 presupposes that several of Moses's opponents have perished, not only Pharaoh, so that this verse could hardly have constituted the original continuation from 2:23aα. Moreover, the new narrative beginning in 3:1 connects seamlessly to 2:22 (non-P) or 2:24 (P 1), but not to 2:23aα, because 2:23aα seems to be designed for precisely the narrative continuation it finds in the following P 1 text (2:23aβ, 24).

> 23 And it came to pass during those many days that the king of Egypt died. *And the Israelites groaned under the labor and cried out.* 24 *And God heard their groaning, and God remembered his covenant with Abraham, Isaac, and Jacob.*

The time designation "during those many days" is of decisive importance for determining the literary-historical place of Exod 2:23aα. It does not state that the king of Egypt died *at the end* of Moses's long stay in Midian, but rather emphasizes that the event occurred *during* the stay, but Moses's stay in Midian still continued thereafter. This, however, ultimately leads to the conclusion that 2:23aα was formulated from the outset with the intention of linking the Priestly description of the situation in Egypt (2:23aβ,

---

24. So, for example, Martin Noth, *Überlieferungsgeschichte des Pentateuch*, 2nd ed. (Stuttgart: Kohlhammer, 1960), 31–32, as well as more recently Blum, *Studien zur Komposition des Pentateuch*, 20; Gertz, *Tradition und Redaktion in der Exoduserzählung*, 255–56; Konrad Schmid, *Erzväter und Exodus*, WMANT 81 (Neukirchen-Vluyn: Neukirchener, 1999), 189.

25. On this proposal, see, e.g., Eckart Otto, "Die nachpriesterschriftliche Pentateuchredakton im Buch Exodus," in *Studies in the Book of Exodus*, ed. Marc Vervenne, BETL 126 (Leuven: Peeters, 1996), 101–11; Schmid, *Erzväter und Exodus*, 197–209.

26. See Kratz, *Komposition*, 293.

104 Christoph Berner

24, P 1) with the non-Priestly description of Moses's stay in Midian. Since 2:23aα does not come from P 1 itself,[27] only two possibilities remain: either this part of the verse is from the final redaction, or it belongs to a post-Priestly editorial layer of Exod 2 and serves to establish a link with the earlier P 1 text in 2:23aβ, 24.

If one seeks to explain the literary development of Exod 2 based on the Supplementary Hypothesis alone, then naturally only the second option is possible. In this case, at least the scene at the well in Midian would have to be considered a post-Priestly addition (2:15bβ$_2$-22), the author of which would also have composed 2:23aα as a transition to the earlier P 1 text (2:23aβ, 24).[28] In turn, this P 1 text would have been added directly after the notice that Moses settled in Midian (2:15abαβ$_1$), which would result in the following transition in the text:

2:15* And Pharaoh heard of this incident and sought then to kill Moses. And Moses fled before Pharaoh and settled in the land of Midian.
2:23aβ *And the Israelites groaned under the labor and cried out.*

This textual sequence is not entirely impossible but also not very likely, since the change in setting from Midian to Egypt occurs rather abruptly. To avoid this problem one could speculate whether there might have been an even earlier textual sequence which did not yet mention Moses's flight to Midian. In this model, the Priestly verses 2:23aβ, 24 would have directly followed 2:11a:

2:11a And it happened one day, when Moses was grown, that he went to his brothers. And he saw that they were burdened by labor.
2:23aβb *And the Israelites groaned under the labor and cried out.*

---

27. Against Van Seters, *Life of Moses*, 66–67.

28. A post-Priestly origin of the well scene is also likely from the perspective of content: With the mistaken statement of the daughter (2:19: "*An Egyptian* has *saved* us from the shepherds") it alludes to the use of central exodus vocabulary from the burning bush scene (3:8) and prepares for the confession of Jethro in 18:10 ("May YHWH be praised, who has saved us from the hand of the Egyptians and the hand of Pharaoh"). Additionally, the whole scene in 2:16–22 is rooted in content in the Patriarchal traditions (cf. Gen 24; 29) and appears to ascribe the traits of the patriarchs to the figure of Moses. Its counterpart is found in Gen 12:10–20, where Abraham experiences an exodus. Both texts point to a comparable post-Priestly horizon (D).

The Literary Character of the Priestly Portions of the Exodus Narrative   105

This hypothetical transition in the text has its advantages, since it avoids the abrupt change in setting that persists in the alternative models discussed above. Moreover, it would provide a parallel to the potential development of Exod 1:

In both chapters, the Priestly editor would have created the same sequence of non-Priestly (1:11–12; 2:11a: סבלות) and Priestly vocabulary (1:13*, 14a; 2:23aβ: עבדה). Despite all this, however, the model appears rather forced since, ultimately, there is insufficient literary-critical evidence to assume that the pre-Priestly stratum of Exod 2 originally ended with 2:11a and did not continue with Moses's flight to Midian (2:11b, 12, 15abαβ₁). All things considered, an interpretation of the early Priestly portions of Exod 1–2 (i.e., Exod 1:13*, 14a; 2:23aβ, 24) in the context of the Supplementary Hypothesis may not be impossible, but it is hardly compelling.

2.4 Results

When placed together, the early Priestly passages in Exod 1:13*, 14a; 2:23aβ, 24 form a seamless narrative thread, which continues in 6:2–7:7* (P 1). Until today, advocates of the Documentary Hypothesis have used this reconstructed sequence to argue that P 1 was an originally independent source, and one cannot deny the impact of this argument, at least with respect to the chapters under consideration. Its weakness lies in the fact that the original preceding context of 1:13* (P 1) cannot be identified with any certainty and that the P 1 thread lacks a narrative introduction of Moses. In theory, both problems could be solved by interpreting the P 1 passages as a supplementary layer placed in the context of the pre-Priestly portions of Exod 1–2. However, there is ultimately no positive evidence to support this model. While the literary transition between 1:11–12 (non-P) and 1:13*, 14a (P 1) reads like a doublet, it seems virtually impossible to find a plausible pre-Priestly passage to which 2:23aβ, 24 (P 1) might have originally connected. Even more importantly, there are elements in 1:13–14; 2:23–25 that do link the two Priestly passages with their non-Priestly contexts, but those elements (i.e., 1:14b; 2:23aαb, 25) prove to be later additions throughout. Thus, later editors obviously saw the need to enhance the level of integration of the Priestly portions within their non-Priestly contexts, which strongly corroborates the observation that they were not written for those contexts in the first place. As a result, although the source model has its own shortcomings, it nevertheless offers the more convincing paradigm to account for the Priestly portions of Exod 1–2.

106   Christoph Berner

3. The Call of Moses and Aaron (Exod 6:2–7:7; 7:8–13) and Its Literary Relationship to the Plague Cycle

3.1. The Literary Evidence

It is generally recognized that Exod 6:2–7:7* form an integral part of the earliest Priestly text stratum (P 1). In contrast, the genealogical list in 6:12bβ–30 appears to be a later Priestly addition (P 2).[29] Furthermore, at least in 7:3, 5aβb, there are occasional non-Priestly supplements.[30] The remaining text in 6:2–5, [6–8,] 9–12aα; 7:1–2, 4–5aα, 6 can be considered largely a unity.[31] It is divided into a call narrative (6:2–8), the failed transmission of the promise of salvation to the Israelites, which causes Moses to doubt the chances of the success of his commission to Pharaoh (6:9–12aα), as well as the subsequent installation of Aaron as the speaker on behalf of Moses as a reaction to Moses's doubts (7:1–6*). The intricate sequence of events is therefore designed from the start with a view to the plague cycle, and more specifically to the appearance of Aaron as the speaker of the demand of departure (7:1–2, 4, 6).

It is interesting to note that the continuation of the Priestly text does not narrate specifically what is outlined in 7:1–6*. Rather, what follows in Exod 7:8–13 is a miracle that serves to legitimize Aaron as YHWH's spokesman at the Egyptian court but in the end fails to convince Pharaoh. Exodus 7:8–13 thus concludes the call of Aaron.[32] At the same time, the scene also serves as the first of five episodes in the Priestly "contest of wonders."[33] However, there are two strong indicators that Aaron's miracle in Exod 7:8–13 did not originally prepare for a contest of wonders consist-

---

29. On the redaction-critical assessment of the addition, see section 7 below.

30. See Berner, *Die Exoduserzählung*, 163.

31. On Exod 6:6–8, see section 3.2 below. Contrary to a widespread view, the reference to the age of Moses and Aaron in Exod 7:7 is not part of the early Priestly text (P 1). Like similar notes scattered throughout the Pentateuch, it belongs to a very late editorial stage (C) which evinces a previously undocumented interest in chronological systematization. In the specific case of 7:7, the late origin of the verse is also proven by the fact that it is influenced by the genealogical list from 6:12bβ–30 (P 2) when declaring Aaron the older brother of Moses and claiming that both of them—not only Aaron—spoke to Pharaoh (cf. 6:27 [P 2] against 7:2 [P 1]).

32. See Utzschneider and Oswald, *Exodus 1–15*, 183.

33. See 4.1 below.

The Literary Character of the Priestly Portions of the Exodus Narrative   107

ing of more than one episode. First, when Aaron's staff swallows the staffs of the Egyptian magicians in 7:12, he already proves his superiority, and there is no need for a further contest. Second, it is striking that the designation of the Egyptian magicians that is used throughout the following episodes of the contest of wonders, namely, חרטמי מצרים, is only introduced in an rather awkward apposition in 7:11b, while the magicians are initially referred to as חכמים and מכשפים in 7:11a. This striking terminological shift is best explained by assuming that the apposition mentioning the חרטמי מצרים in 7:11b is a later addition, which was introduced to prepare for the continuation of the contest of wonders. In other words, this continuation in the following episodes must be regarded as secondary compared to the scene in 7:8–13* (P 1).

3.2. The Interpretation of the Literary Evidence in the Context of the Documentary Hypothesis

If P 1 is considered a formerly independent source, then the beginning of the revelation scene in Exod 6:2–7:7* must have followed immediately after 2:24.

> 2:24 *And God heard their groaning, and God remembered his covenant with Abraham, Isaac, and Jacob.*
> 6:2 *And God spoke to Moses and said to him: I am YHWH …*

As argued above in section 2.2, Exod 6:2 connects smoothly to 2:24. The only problem that is frequently addressed is the missing narrative introduction of Moses. This is indeed noticeable—especially since the author handles the case of Aaron differently in 7:1!—and is therefore one of the main objections against the literary independence of P 1.[34] Some advocates of the Documentary Hypothesis have resorted to the auxiliary assumption that the final redaction has suppressed the Priestly introduction of Moses in favor of the non-Priestly text in 2:1–10,[35] which is certainly a possibility but can hardly be proven. Moreover, one has to notice that the final redactor would have apparently not been troubled by narrative doublets and contradictions in

---

34. See Blum, *Studien zur Komposition des Pentateuch*, 240–41; differently for example Kratz, *Komposition*, 244.

35. See Gertz, *Tradition und Redaktion in der Exoduserzählung*, 250–51.

108 Christoph Berner

other texts.[36] Ultimately, therefore, the missing narrative introduction of Moses remains unresolved.

A further difficulty pertains to the wording of Exod 6:6, because the verse employs characterizations for the Egyptian oppression which have their origins in non-Priestly texts. The term סבלות used emphatically at the beginning of the verse is encountered only once more in the material generally ascribed to P, namely, in the following verse (6:7). In contrast, the second term (עבדה) is found in 1:13–14*; 2:23aβ–24* (P 1) and is thus not only widely attested but is introduced in the respective texts, which first and foremost creates the presupposition for the fact that YHWH can refer back to the Israelites' labor (עבדה) in 6:6. An introduction of the servitude (סבלות), however, is missing in the P 1 text, but it is found in 1:11–12, in the immediately preceding pre-Priestly context of 1:13–14*. Thus, 6:6 is phrased according to the combined pre-Priestly and Priestly text in 1:11–14*, which cannot be dismissed as accidental, nor explained by mere awareness of pre-Priestly terminology; it rather indicates that the combined form of 1:11–14* is presupposed.[37]

Since it is impossible to reconstruct an earlier stage of the text in Exod 6:6–7, which would use only the genuinely Priestly oppression terminology, the present form of the text cannot be ascribed to an independent Priestly source. Therefore, it must be either ascribed to the redaction that combined the two sources, which would have suppressed the original wording, or—and this seems to be the more likely alternative—the entire text must be interpreted as a redactional expansion. For instance, Eckart Otto has proposed that 6:6–8 as a whole is an addition from a post-Priestly redaction, because the language and theological concepts of the three verses are on the whole atypical of P.[38] One could add that there are already several shifts in terminology and meaning if one compares 6:6–8 with the immediately preceding beginning of the divine speech in 6:2–5 (P 1). While all this clearly supports the proposal made by Otto, others have at the same time correctly claimed that 6:6–8 show clear references

---

36. Consider for example the double burial of Jacob (Gen 50:7–11, 14; 50:12–13 [P]), the juxtaposition of the two revelation scenes (Exod 3; 6 [P]), or the interweaving of the two narrative threads in the miracle at the sea (Exod 14).

37. So with Blum, *Studien zur Komposition des Pentateuch*, 233, against Ludwig Schmidt, *Studien zur Priesterschrift*, BZAW 214 (Berlin: De Gruyter, 1993), 6–7.

38. See Otto, "Forschungen zur Priesterschrift," 10 n. 45.

The Literary Character of the Priestly Portions of the Exodus Narrative   109

to the following context in 6:9 and that 6:2–8 overall evinces a planned structure.[39] The diachronic placement of 6:6–8 thus remains debatable, and it is thus not advisable to establish comprehensive redactional models based on these verses. It is merely to be noted that the present form of the verses is incomprehensible from the perspective of a literarily independent Priestly source.

Finally, under the premises of the source model it also needs to be explained why Exod 6:9–12a; 7:1–6* (P 1) provide a lengthy introduction of Aaron as a messenger to demand the Israelites' departure, but in the following Priestly passages there is no mention of such an action by Aaron. Rather, the call story concludes with the scene in 7:8–13*, where Aaron proves his legitimacy as YHWH's messenger by transforming his staff into a snake which then swallows the transformed staffs of the Egyptian sorcerers. By concluding the scene with the remark that Pharaoh did not listen "as YHWH had said" (7:13, P 1) the author apparently refers back to the divine announcement from 7:2, 4 (P 1), yet it is nevertheless striking that the motif of Aaron demanding the exodus is not elaborated here or in what follows. In an independent Priestly source, 7:13 would need to continue directly to the beginning of the Passover ordinances in 12:1 (P 1).

3.3. The interpretation of the Literary Evidence in the Context of the Supplementary Hypothesis

The main objection that is constantly brought up against an interpretation of Exod 6:2–7:7* as a redaction of a pre-Priestly exodus narrative rightly argues that the text is formulated as an initial revelation, and therefore it is conceived as an alternative to the burning bush scene in Exod 3, not as an extension of it.[40] Above all, the proclamation of the name of YHWH in 6:2, 8 occurs after the use of the same name in 3:15, 16, 18 and thus appears clearly out of place—assuming that the latter verses are pre-Priestly. Otto and Gertz have shown, however, that this is not the case. The respective

---

39. See Christian Frevel, *Mit Blick auf das Land die Schöpfung erinnern*, HBS 23 (Freiburg: Herder, 2000), 115–16; Gertz, *Tradition und Redaktion in der Exoduserzählung*, 245–50; Thomas Römer, "The Exodus Narrative according to the Priestly Document," in Shectman and Baden, *Strata of the Priestly Writings*, 161.

40. See Klaus Koch, "P—kein Redaktor! Erinnerung an zwei Eckdaten der Quellenscheidung," *VT* 37 (1987): 462–67.

110   Christoph Berner

passages of Exod 3 contain statements throughout that were composed already in light of Exod 6 and are thus post-Priestly.[41]

However, the pre-Priestly kernel of Exod 3 that is embedded in 3:1–10* did not yet contain a revelation of the name of YHWH but was limited to the announcement of the exodus and the sending of Moses to Pharaoh. The P 1 text in 6:2–7:7* can thus be read as a recapitulation of 3:1–10* that develops a particular theology of revelation. One could consider that the revelation scene in 6:2–7:7* (P 1) was added directly after Moses's return (4:18*, 20aβ) and his first appearance before Pharaoh (5:1–2*).[42] However, since 5:1–2 can only be preserved as a pre-Priestly text with questionable literary-critical interventions, and additionally, since Pharaoh's lack of recognition of YHWH presents a motif which is attested elsewhere only in (post-)Priestly passages (see, among others, Exod 6:7; 7:5; 14:4, 18; 29:46), it appears more likely that 5:1–2 belong to a post-Priestly stage of development of the exodus narrative (C).[43] As a result, Exod 6:2–7:7* would have originally followed directly after the return notice in 4:20aβ.

> 4:20aβ And he returned to the land of Egypt.
> 6:2 *And God spoke to Moses and said to him: I am YHWH …*

The suggested transition between the pre-Priestly text (4:20aβ) and the beginning of the Priestly call story in Exod 6:2–12*, 7:1–13* is easily conceivable both in terms of content and syntax. As for the transition to the following non-Priestly texts, no further discussion is needed, since the sequence between Aaron's wonder in 7:8–13* (P 1) and the Nile plague (7:14–25 non-P) is the one we find in the present text. An interpretation of

---

41. See Otto, "Die nachpriesterschriftliche Pentateuchredakton," 109; Gertz, *Tradition und Redaktion in der Exoduserzählung*, 294–98.

42. The composer would thus have responded to the questioning of YHWH by Pharaoh in 5:1–2 (who is YHWH?) with the revelation of the name in 6:2–7:7* (I am YHWH, and I…). So Berner, *Die Exoduserzählung*, 155, following an observation from Ska, "Quelques Remarques," 97–107.

43. Differently still in Berner, *Die Exoduserzählung*, 137–52, where Exod 5:1–2 is assigned to the pre-Priestly tradition, following Gertz, *Tradition und Redaktion in der Exoduserzählung*, 336. To assign 5:1–2 as pre-P, one must assume, for example, that Exod 5:1a was originally formulated in the singular and prepared for an appearance of Moses.

The Literary Character of the Priestly Portions of the Exodus Narrative   111

the Priestly call story as an editorial insertion between 4:20aβ; 7:14 (non-P) is thus easily conceivable.

However, the question remains if this interpretation offers any advantages as compared with a source model. The strongest potential evidence would certainly be the scene in 6:6–8 with its conflation of Priestly and non-Priestly terminology. Yet, since the verses in question cannot be ascribed to P 1 with certainty and show clear traces of a later redactional supplement, they fail to carry any burden of proof. What can be said in favor of a supplementary model, however, is that it closes the narrative gaps in the P 1 stratum: if one assumes that the call story in 6:2–7:13* (P 1) was placed between 2:1–4:20* and 7:14ff., the pre-Priestly context would have provided the otherwise missing introduction of Moses. Moreover, the continuation of the Priestly call story with the pre-Priestly plagues would offer an explanation why P 1 contains a lengthy introduction of Aaron as YHWH's messenger but does not develop this motif. In the context of the Supplementary Hypothesis, one could assume that P 1 merely wanted to establish a new interpretive perspective for the earlier, pre-Priestly plague narrative where Moses appears as the one who presents the demand of departure. Exodus 7:1–6* (P 1) claims this function for Aaron, and the formulation in 7:6 "they did just as YHWH commanded" leaves no doubt that in what follows it was Aaron who brought the word before Pharaoh.

3.4. Results

If one considers only the Priestly call story in Exod 6:2–7:13* (P 1), both the Documentary and the Supplementary Hypothesis provide plausible results. In the first case, the scene would have been embedded in the context of a Priestly narrative between 2:24 and 12:1 (P 1), while in the second case it would have been placed between the non-Priestly notice mentioning Moses's return to Egypt (4:20aβ) and the beginning of the plague cycle (7:14). There is a certain advantage of the Supplementary Hypothesis in that it provides the otherwise missing introduction of Moses (via 2:1–10*, pre-P) and a narrative explication of Aaron's role as divine messenger (via 7:14ff., pre-P). However, this advantage is relativized by the fact that with respect to the preceding context it proved difficult to interpret the P 1 portions in 1:13*, 14a; 2:23aβ, 24 as redactional expansions of the pre-Priestly text (see section 2 above).

112   Christoph Berner

4. The Priestly Contest of Wonders (Exod 7:8–11:10)

4.1. The Literary Evidence

It is generally assumed that the Priestly portions of Exod 7:8–9:12 form a sequence of five wonders "in which YHWH and Pharaoh compete with each other through their representatives."[44] Three of the wonders (7:8–13; 8:12–15; 9:8–12) stand on their own, and in two further cases—the Nile pestilence and the plague of frogs (7:14–8:11)—the Priestly text is interwoven with the non-Priestly text. Also the summary notice in 11:10 is usually considered Priestly.

Upon closer investigation, however, it becomes apparent that the literary evidence is more complex. As argued above in section 3.1, only Aaron's first wonder in Exod 7:8–13 belongs to the earliest version of the Priestly text (P 1), while the continuation of the contest of wonders in the following episodes must be regarded as secondary compared to 7:8–13*. Considering these secondary episodes of the contest of wonders, that is, the Priestly portions interwoven in the description of the plague on the Nile and the plague of frogs in 7:14–8:11* as well as the two independent scenes in 8:12–15 and 9:8–12, one must observe that, strictly speaking, the contest of wonders in its redactionally extended form reaches its climax with the Egyptian magicians failing to turn dust into gnats and acknowledging their defeat (8:12–15).

From a narrative perspective, the subsequent episode in 9:8–12 is rather surprising, since it adds another even more dramatic defeat of the magicians, who fall victim to the plague of boils, and since it significantly changes the plot of the contest of wonders. Now, both Moses and Aaron appear before Pharaoh to perform the miracle, but, strangely enough, it is only Moses who does so in the end. All things considered, the final episode of the contest of wonders in 9:8–12 is best explained as an even later redactional passage[45] which was devised to create a transition between

---

44. Julius Wellhausen, *Die Composition des Hexateuchs*, 3rd ed. (Berlin: de Gruyter, 1963), 62; cf. Werner H. Schmidt, *Exodus*, BKAT 2 (repr. Neukirchen-Vlyun: Neukirchner, 1995), 352–56.

45. Similarly already Peter Weimar, "'Nicht konnten die Magier vor Mose hintreten' (Exod 9:11)," in *Berühungspunkte: Studien zur Sozial- und Religionsgeschichte Israels und seiner Umwelt*, ed. Ingo Kottsieper et al., AOAT 350 (Münster: Ugarit Verlag, 2008), 97–117.

The Literary Character of the Priestly Portions of the Exodus Narrative 113

the first part of the plague cycle dominated by the actions of Aaron as a miracle worker and the second part in 9:13–11:10*, where Moses claims this role. Apparently, the retrospect that concludes the second part of the plague cycle in 11:10 and shares the motif of YHWH hardening Pharaoh's heart (חזק *piel*; cf. 9:12) comes from the hand of the same editor.

As a result, the five episodes of the Priestly contest of wonders can be shown to consist of three distinct redactional stages: an initial miracle concluding the call story of Aaron (7:8–13, P 1) was later supplemented with three more episodes (7:14–8:11*; 8:12–15, P 2), which describe the gradual triumph of Aaron over the חרטמי מצרים; finally, the scene in 9:8–12 and the concluding statement in 11:10 were supplemented as a redactional framework of the second part of the plague cycle (C).

Moreover, there is an apparent influence of the Priestly narrative scheme on the execution reports of the non-Priestly hail-, locust, and darkness plagues, insofar as in these Moses is presented as a wonder-worker at divine behest, who brings about the occurrence of the plagues together with YHWH (9:22–25; 10:12–15) or alone (10:21–23). The Priestly influence on these three plagues is seen also in the use of the hardening expression with חזק, which originates in 7:4 (P 1) (cf. 9:35; 10:20, 27, non-P). Since there is no evidence to argue for a Priestly source thread in the respective plague triad,[46] their Priestly elements call for a different explanation. Various options have been considered. Either a pre-Priestly form of the plague-triad was extended with P elements by a Priestly editor or the final redaction and thus aligned with the Priestly conception, or the three plagues are to be considered from the outset as a literarily unified composition by the final redaction or to be identified respectively as post-Priestly additions that already presuppose the connection of the pre-P and P 1 materials.[47] As I have argued elsewhere in great detail, an interpretation of Exod 9:13–10:27 as a post-Priestly redactional layer comprising several stages provides the most suitable

---

46. Against Noth, *Das Zweite Buch Mose*, 52–53.

47. An extension of a pre-Priestly triad by a P editor: Blum, *Studien zur Komposition des Pentateuch*, 245–50. An extension of a pre-Priestly triad during a final redaction: Fujiko Kohata, *Jahwist und Priesterschrift in Exodus 3–14*, BZAW 166 (Berlin: De Gruyter, 1986), 99–100. Considered a unified literary unit by the final redaction: Gertz, *Tradition und Redaktion in der Exoduserzählung*, 132–88. Post-Priestly additions: Levin, *Der Jahwist*, 337.

114 Christoph Berner

explanation for the literary history of the passage.[48] Since Exod 9:13–10:27 thus contain no genuine Priestly elements (P 1 or P 2), the passage will not be discussed in what follows.

4.2. The Interpretation of the Literary Evidence within the Context of the Documentary Hypothesis

If one considers initially the findings in the first part of the plague cycle (Exod 7:14–9:12), at first glance the evidence appears to speak for the combination of two previously independent sources. The fact that the (late) Priestly wonders and the non-Priestly plagues are sometimes intertwined and sometimes stand side by side can be explained by the proposal that the final redaction has formed a composite text in places where the keywords of the plagues are identical (7:14–8:11: Nile pestilence and frogs) and otherwise has been content with the sequential arrangement of the different episodes (8:12–15: gnats; cf. the secondary passage in 9:8–12: boils). While the reconstruction of the supposed sources in the second group of texts naturally does not cause problems, disentangling 7:14–8:11 in detail is quite a complicated undertaking. This applies already for the Nile plague, where the assignments of the text in the decisive section 7:17–23 can be represented as follows:

> 7:17* Thus says YHWH: See, [with the staff that is in my hand] I will strike the water that is in the Nile. [And it will turn to blood.]
> 18 The fish in the Nile will die, and the Nile will stink, so that the Egyptians will be disgusted to drink water from the Nile.
> 19* *And YHWH said to Moses: say to Aaron: take your staff and stretch your hand over the waters of Egypt, over the streams, branches of the Nile, and rivers, and all its water sources. They are to become blood. In all of Egypt it will be blood. 20 And Moses and Aaron did, as YHWH had commanded.*
> In the sight of Pharaoh and of his officials he lifted up the staff and struck the water in the river, and all the water in the river was turned into blood
> And he [lifted up the staff and] struck the waters of the Nile [in the sight of Pharaoh and of his officials and all the water of the Nile changed into blood] 21 and the fish in the Nile perished, and the Nile stank and the Egyptians could no longer drink the water from the Nile.
> *And the blood was in all Egypt.*

---

48. See Berner, *Die Exoduserzählung*, 215–41.

The Literary Character of the Priestly Portions of the Exodus Narrative   115

22 *The magician priests of Egypt however did the same with their magic, and the heart of Pharaoh remained hard, and he did not listen, as YHWH had said.*
23 And Pharaoh turned away and went to his house, and he did not take even this to heart.

Basically, one must recognize that it is possible to read and comprehend both narrative threads on their own. A slight syntactic ambiguity can be observed within the non-Priestly text in 7:20, insofar as here the subject of the verb of striking is not made explicit. This ambiguity is due to an editorial reworking. In its original form, the non-Priestly plague account referred to YHWH striking the river (pre-P), while a later editor (D) added the motifs of the staff and the transformation of the water into blood to transform the plague to a sign worked by Moses.[49] If one considers now the Priestly stratum, it is notable that the execution report in 7:20aα*, 21b is quite brief in comparison to the preceding announcement in 7:19*. This is unique in the context of the Priestly contest of wonders,[50] but, as with the syntactic ambiguity in 7:20 noted above, it does not exclude the possibility that both representations initially existed independently of one another.

While the present text of the Nile plague can be explained based on the Documentary Hypothesis, the application of this methodological paradigm to the plague of frogs inevitably results in problems. A complete Priestly narrative thread cannot be reconstructed here, because in 8:11aγb only the second part of the hardening statements typical for P are preserved. This statement would not be meaningfully readable without its non-Priestly preparation.

11aα*β When, however, the Pharaoh saw this, he hardened his heart,
11aγb *and he did not listen, as YHWH had said.*

Exodus 8:2b presents further problems; this non-Priestly phrase is firmly integrated into the Priestly context in 8:1, 2a, 3 (P 2) and describes the consequences of Aaron's gesture with the staff.

---

49. See already Berner, *Die Exoduserzählung*, 209–10. In the above translation, the secondary passages have been placed in brackets and underlined.
50. See Exod 7:10, 12a; 8:2–3, 13; 9:10.

116   Christoph Berner

> 8:1 *And YHWH spoke to Moses: Say to Aaron: stretch out your hand with your staff over the waters, the Nile, the streams, and bring up frogs over the land of Egypt.* 2 *And Aaron stretched out his hand over the waters of Egypt.* Then the frog came up and covered the land of Egypt.
> 3 *The magicians, however, did the same with their magic and brought up frogs over the land of Egypt.*

If 8:2b is assigned to P,[51] then the non-Priestly text would be lacking a report on the outbreak of the plague of frogs. But if the half-verse is identified with the non-Priestly plague report, which seems possible considering that the formulations in 8:2b differ significantly from 8:2a, 3b,[52] then P inevitably loses a part of the execution report, and this results in a further gap in the Priestly text. In any case, one is forced to assume that in the compilation of the two source threads, elements from (at least) the Priestly text were suppressed by the final redaction, which for inexplicable reasons would have used a completely different redactional technique here than it has in the immediately preceding Nile plague.

4.3. The Interpretation of the Literary Evidence in the Context of the Supplementary Hypothesis

Especially with the plague of frogs, the advantages of the Supplementary Hypothesis are immediately apparent. The text in Exod 8:1–3, 11, which in the context of the Documentary Hypothesis requires numerous problematic assumptions, can be explained without these difficulties by stating that a non-Priestly plague description was reworked by a Priestly editor. The editor framed the non-Priestly report found in 8:2b (the arrival of the frogs) with the statements in 8:1, 2a, 3 (P 2), thus transforming it into a description of the consequences of Aaron's action, and integrating it skillfully into the presentation of the wonder contest. Finally, he extended the non-Priestly hardening notice in 8:11aαβ with 8:11aγb (P 2), thus giving it its present shape.

---

51. See Noth, *Das Zweite Buch Mose*, 57; Kohata, *Jahwist und Priesterschrift*, 152; Gertz, *Tradition und Redaktion in der Exoduserzählung*, 123.

52. See Van Seters, *Life of Moses*, 107. The collective singular formulation (lit., "the frog") differs from the plural announcement in Exod 7:27, 28a, but finds a parallel in the use of the collective singular in the pre-Priestly description of the Nile plague (7:18, 21).

The Literary Character of the Priestly Portions of the Exodus Narrative   117

While the Priestly fragments of the plague of frogs strongly favor an interpretation as redactional additions, the question is less clear with the plague on the Nile. As shown above, the literary evidence here *can* be explained within a source model. Still, however, the origins of the text are also conceivable in the context of the Supplementary Hypothesis. As in the plague of frogs, also here we would have to assume that an earlier pre-Priestly plague report (7:17*, 18, 20*, 23) was integrated into the wonder contest through Priestly additions in 7:19abα, 20aα*, 21b, 22. In this scenario, the Priestly editor would have imagined the change of all the waters in Egypt into blood (7:19abα, P 2) as a process initiated with the pollution of the Nile (7:20*, non-P), to which Aaron so to speak gives the sign.

If the non-Priestly plague report was integrated into the Priestly presentation of the Nile pestilence from the outset, this could also possibly explain why P 2 here does not report in detail of the execution of what is commanded and the beginning of what is announced as is usual but rather is limited in 7:20aα*, 21b to mentioning the framing information. Also the fact that 7:21b (P 2) differs from 7:19bα (P 2) in stating that "*the blood*" (definite) was in all Egypt could indicate that 7:21b was formulated with respect to the preceding non-Priestly verse 7:20b (D) ("and all the water of the Nile was changed into blood"). However, regardless of whether one interprets these slight irregularities within the Priestly text as an expression of its literary character as an editorial layer dependent on the non-Priestly text or not, it seems most likely that the Priestly form of the blood motif with *all possible bodies of water* in Egypt being transformed into blood reflects a deliberate climax of the non-Priestly form of the same motif where *only the water of the Nile* is affected.[53] This climax is proof that the Priestly text was in any case devised as a reaction to—if not as a redaction of—its earlier non-Priestly *Vorlage*.

While it is easily possible to interpret the Priestly portions of the Nile plague as an editorial layer and it seems even imperative to do so with respect to the following plague of frogs, the situation changes when it comes to the final episode of the (late) Priestly wonder contest, the plague of gnats in 8:12–15 (P 2). Here, no intertwining of Priestly and non-Priestly elements can be identified, and the scene can be attributed entirely to the (late) Priestly text. Technically, this is also explicable in the context of the

---

53. See Ludwig Schmidt, *Beobachtungen zu der Plagenerzählung in Exodus VII 14–XI 10*, StudBib 4 (Leiden: Brill, 1990), 80.

118   Christoph Berner

Supplementary Hypothesis, but it raises the question why the editor would have differed from his usual approach in 7:14–8:11 and did not rework the existing report of the following non-Priestly plague of flies in 8:16–28. The simplest answer to this is that the P 2 editor chose to create his own concluding scene for the contest of wonders, since by then the plague of flies had already gained such a narrative complexity[54] that it would have been difficult to rewrite it accordingly. Instead, the editor decided to add the episode in 8:12–15 (gnats), which draws on the imagery from the following non-Priestly plague of flies and is entirely focused on the Egyptian magicians admitting their defeat, thereby providing a fitting conclusion for the entire wonder contest.

4.4. Results

Regardless of the preferred methodological paradigm, the following basic observations can be made: The passages usually attributed to the Priestly text of the plague cycle belong to three different literary layers. While the initial wonder in Exod 7:8–13 concludes the call story of Aaron in the early Priestly text (P 1),[55] a late Priestly editor (P 2) created a contest of wonders by supplementing three more episodes, namely, the Priestly portions of the Nile pestilence and the frogs plague in Exod 7:14–8:11* and the scene in 8:12–15 (gnats). The final episode in 9:8–12, together with the concluding note in 11:10, belongs to an even later editorial stage (C) that definitely presupposes an advanced stage of the plague cycle including both its non-Priestly and Priestly parts and that can, therefore, only be explained in the framework of the Supplementary Hypothesis.

As for the relationship of the late Priestly episodes of the contest of wonders to the non-Priestly plagues, everything speaks for the fact that P 2 presupposes at least an awareness of them and has conceptually developed their underlying presentation-principle. It is hardly a coincidence that the second and third wonders in 7:14–8:11* (water to blood, frogs) correspond to the first two non-Priestly plagues,[56] and their dependence on these plague accounts is demonstrated by the fact that they still contain

---

54. See Berner, *Die Exoduserzählung*, 194–209.

55. See section 3 above.

56. On the correspondences between the further Priestly and non- or post-Priestly plagues, see Moshe Greenberg, *Understanding Exodus* (New York: Behrman, 1969), 151–82.

The Literary Character of the Priestly Portions of the Exodus Narrative   119

features of a plague, which would not make sense if they had been conceived for the context of a contest of wonders necessitating the repetition of the wonder by the Egyptian magicians in the first place. Significantly, this imbalance in motifs is seen clearly in the two wonders which are interwoven with the non-Priestly plague descriptions in 7:14–8:11, whereas the episode formulated freely by P 2 (that is, without taking up the keywords from the non-Priestly plague texts; 8:12–15, P 2) is largely unremarkable in this regard.[57] This is not a compelling proof but a strong indication for the fact that the Priestly reformulation of the pre-Priestly plague cycle into a contest of wonders could have taken place from the outset as a redactional transformation of the pre-Priestly plagues.

Ultimately, however, the question of which methodological paradigm is more suitable to explain the Priestly passages in the Exod 7:14–8:15 is not decided based on thematic considerations but on the concrete literary evidence. While the Nile plague can generally be explained by both paradigms—with a slight preference for the Supplementary Hypothesis—the literary relationships in the plague of frogs must be given decisive importance. Here, the Documentary Hypothesis proves to be ineffective, because it yields a fragmented Priestly source and has to allow for inexplicable omissions by the final redaction, which would be uncharacteristic of how this redaction would have otherwise operated in the plague on the Nile. The Supplementary Hypothesis, however, can explain the findings without any problem as a Priestly redaction (P 2) of the non-Priestly plague description, and thus is preferable to the source model.

5. The Passover, the Killing of the Firstborn, and the Conclusion of the Egyptian Sojourn (Exod 12)

5.1. The Literary Evidence

It is a broad scholarly consensus that in Exod 12 Priestly texts are interwoven with non-Priestly texts, and there is also widespread agreement over the fundamental literary-critical demarcations. The regulations for the Passover and Maṣṣot festival in 12:1–20, 28 (42), 43–50 are ascribed to P, as well as additionally the notices on the length of the stay in Egypt at the

---

57. The last two wonders in Exod 8:12–15 and 9:8–12 also have plague-like features, but these do not cause comparable disturbances in the narrative coherence, since the Egyptian magician priests are no longer in the position to repeat the wonder.

120   Christoph Berner

points of departure in 12:40–41 and 12:51. In contrast, the Passover ordinances in 12:21–27, the report on the killing of the firstborn (12:29–33), and the subsequent remarks on the detailed conditions of the departure (12:34–39) are regarded as non-Priestly.[58] There is also consensus that both the Priestly and the non-Priestly texts have undergone literary growth. We can in any case assign the Passover etiology in 12:1–13*, 28 to the earliest Priestly text (P 1); all prescriptions which pertain to the festival of Maṣṣot (cf. 12:14–20) or regulating allowance to the Passover (12:43–50) should in contrast be considered late Priestly additions (P 2).

Basically, the same also applies to the notice of the Israelites' departure after a 430-year sojourn in Egypt (Exod 12:40–41), which is often wrongly ascribed to the earliest layer of the Priestly text (P 1). However, the designation of the Israelites as YHWH's hosts echoes the concept of the Israelite camp in Num 1–4 (P 2), which already points to a late Priestly context. This observation is corroborated by the fact that the wording in 12:41b is almost identical with the late Priestly announcement from 12:17; both verses should thus be assigned to the same late Priestly horizon (P 2). This, however, does not apply to the reference to the 430 years in 12:40, 41a. This passage is an even later addition (C), which can already be seen from the clumsy redactional transition in 12:41a reiterating 12:40 to bring the new perspective of the 430 years in line with the following P 2 notice mentioning the departure "on that very day." Moreover, one has to observe that the literary *Wiederaufnahme* in 12:51, which seeks to integrate the stipulations on the admission to Passover in 12:43–50 (a secondary passage within P 2) still shows no awareness of the 430 years but echoes 12:41b alone. As a result, it becomes apparent that Exod 12:40–41 consist of two different literary layers, an earlier one in 12:41b (P 2) and a later one in 12:40, 41a (C). Conversely, no part of the two verses can be claimed for P 1.

With regard to the non-Priestly texts, at least the kernel of the report on the killing of the firstborn (12:29–33*) can be considered original; more precisely, it can be considered as the goal and climax of the pre-Priestly plague cycle. In contrast to this agreement, there is disagreement as to whether parts of the Passover ordinances in 12:21–27 are also original or whether these are rather to be considered a post-Priestly development as

---

58. On this and what follows, see the foundational discussion in Gertz, *Tradition und Redaktion in der Exoduserzählung*, 31–50.

The Literary Character of the Priestly Portions of the Exodus Narrative 121

a whole. In consideration of the clear references of the section to the P 1 context preceding it, the latter can be considered likely.[59]

5.2. The Interpretation of the Literary Evidence in the Context of the Documentary Hypothesis

While Martin Noth divided the text in Exod 12 almost completely into two independent sources, Gertz has suggested grounds for considering that at least parts of the chapter should be assigned to the final redaction, which combined the sources and mediated between them.[60] However, the basic outlines of Noth's model of development are not impacted by this. As before, there is the assumption of an original text-transition between the alleged end of the Priestly contest of wonders in 11:10, the Passover ordinances in 12:1–13*, and their accompanying execution notice in 12:28. According to the traditional view, the latter verse would then have been followed immediately by the mention of the time of departure of the Israelites in 12:40–41.[61]

> 12:28 *And the Israelites went and did, just as YHWH had commanded Moses and Aaron, so they did.*
> 12:40 *The time, however, that the Israelites sojourned in Egypt, was 430 years. 41 And it happened after the course of these 430 years, and it happened on that very day, that all the hosts of YHWH departed from the land of Egypt.*

Although the postulated transition between 12:28 and 12:40 is syntactically possible, it has a serious deficit in terms of content. Thus, the Priestly text would have reported that the Israelites observed the Passover as instructed (12:28, P 1), but with no mention of the killing of the firstborn, although this had emphatically been announced earlier (12:12–13, P 1).

---

59. See Berner, *Die Exoduserzählung*, 278–93. For an alternative explanation, see Shimon Gesundheit, *Three Times a Year*, FAT 82 (Tübingen: Mohr Siebeck, 2012), 89–95.

60. See Noth, *Das Zweite Buch Mose*, 71–73. Noth distinguishes between a pre-Priestly (Yahwistic) text (12:21–23, 27b, 29–39) with Deuteronomistic additions (12:24–27a), on the one hand, and Priestly texts, on the other (P^G: 12:1–20*, 40–41; P^S: 12:42, 43–51). See also Gertz, *Tradition und Redaktion in der Exoduserzählung*, 396.

61. See Noth, *Das Zweite Buch Mose*, 72; Levin, *Der Jahwist*, 339.

122   Christoph Berner

The narrative gap is so striking that it can hardly be explained by proposing some narrative strategy of the author.[62] The only remaining alternative is to assume that the final redaction has suppressed the Priestly report of the killing of the firstborn in favor of its non-Priestly counterpart.[63] This would, however, be a unique procedure, considering the fact that elsewhere the narrative doublets between the Priestly and non-Priestly texts are retained.[64]

Already the noted lack of an execution report on the killing of the firstborn poses a serious problem for any attempt to interpret the earliest form of the Priestly Passover ordinances in Exod 12:1–13*, 28 (P 1) in the context of the Documentary Hypothesis. However, further problems arise if one considers that neither the concluding notice in 11:10 nor the reference to the Israelites' departure after 430 years in 12:40–41 are likely to have belonged to the P 1 layer. As argued above,[65] Exod 11:10 together with 9:8–12 reflects a very late editorial layer within the plague cycle (C). As a result, the Priestly Passover ordinances in Exod 12:1–13*, 28 must have followed directly after Aaron's wonder in Exod 7:8–13 if one adheres to the source model.

While a transition between 7:8–13 and 12:1–13*, 28 (P 1) is conceivable, the loss of Exod 12:40–41 again results in a severe narrative gap. Without the two verses, P 1 lacks a reference to the Israelites' departure from Egypt and a plausible connection for the Priestly account of the miracle at the sea in Exod 14. It is precisely to avoid this deficit that the two verses 12:40–41 are traditionally ascribed to the earliest Priestly text, but this assumption is not based on the literary evidence. Rather, it merely follows the constraints of the Documentary Hypothesis and must there-

---

62. According to Schmidt, *Studien zur Priesterschrift*, 30, the killing of the firstborn is presupposed in Exod 12:41 (P) but is not introduced in the narrative, because "for P, in contrast to the pre-Priestly presentation in 12:29ff.*, after the killing of the firstborn there was no further dialogue between Pharaoh and Moses." This is certainly true, but it does not explain why the author does not report the occurrence of that which is announced in 12:12–13 at least with a brief notice as seen with the pattern of 12:28. The true observation, "that the installation of the Passover according to P is oriented completely toward the Israelite cultic practice" (Gertz, *Tradition und Redaktion in der Exoduserzählung*, 88), does not change this issue.

63. So, for example, Adolf Jülicher, "Die Quellen von Exodus I–VII,7," *JPTh* 8 (1882): 101.

64. See esp. sections 2 and 6.

65. See section 4.1.

The Literary Character of the Priestly Portions of the Exodus Narrative   123

fore be judged as the result of circular reasoning. If the earliest Priestly text in Exod 12 is interpreted in a source model, one has to admit that this alleged Priestly thread lacks both an account of the killing of the firstborn and of the departure of the Israelites and thus does not form a coherent narrative.

5.3. The Interpretation of the Literary Evidence in the Context of the Supplementary Hypothesis

The absence of a Priestly description of the killing of the firstborn does not pose a problem if one considers the Passover ordinances in Exod 12:1–13*, 28 (P 1) to be a redactional extension, which was conceived from the outset to supplement the pre-Priestly plague report in 12:29–33*.[66] In this model, the pre-Priestly description of the killing of the firstborn (12:29a) fills the narrative gap of the P material. The literary connection between the Priestly Passover ordinances and the pre-Priestly plague report would have looked as follows:[67]

> 1* And YHWH spoke to Moses and Aaron: 3aα* Speak to the whole community of Israel, 3b they are to take a lamb for each household, a lamb per house. And they shall slaughter it in the evening 7aα and take its blood 7aβ* and bring it on the houses 7b in which they are eating. 8a And they shall eat the flesh in this night, 8ba* roasted in fire 8bβ and with bitter herbs. 11bβ It is a Passover for YHWH.
>
> 12aα In that night, however, I will pass through the land of Egypt and strike all the firstborn in the land of Egypt. 13 Then the blood shall be as a sign on the houses in which you dwell. When I see the blood, I will "pass over" you, and there will be no mortal blow against you when I strike the land of Egypt.
>
> 28 And the Israelites went and did as YHWH commanded Moses and Aaron, so they did.
>
> 29a And it happened in the middle of the night that YHWH struck all firstborn in the land of Egypt, from the firstborn of Pharaoh, who sits on his throne, to the firstborn of the prisoner in the dungeon.

---

66. So, for example, Van Seters, *Life of Moses*, 108–9.

67. For the reconstruction of the Priestly form of the Passover ordinance that is presupposed here, see Berner, *Die Exoduserzählung*, 278–93.

124   Christoph Berner

A comparison between the Priestly announcement of the killing of the firstborn (Exod 12:12aα) and the pre-Priestly plague report (12:29aα) indicates that both passages correspond closely not only in content but even in exact wording. In both cases, there is mention of YHWH striking all the firstborn in Egypt (12:12aα: והכתי כל בכור בארץ מצרים ;12:29aα: ויהוה הכה כל הבכור בארץ מצרים), which occurs in the night. Only the specific time designation "in the middle of the night" (בחצי הלילה) from 12:29aα (pre-P) is replaced with a more general "in this night" (בלילה הזה) in 12:12aα (P 1); in so doing, the Priestly author takes into account the ritual ordinance, which describes the nighttime eating of the Passover offering in 12:8a with the same words (בלילה הזה). In light of the linguistic evidence as well as the general structure of the chapter, it is most plausible to interpret Exod 12:1–13*, 28 (P 1) as an extension of a pre-Priestly plague report, which was supplemented with an etiology of the Passover festival by the Priestly author. The execution report in 12:28 covers those parts of the Passover ritual in 12:1–13* to which the pre-Priestly report has no parallels, while the announcement of the killing of the firstborn in 12:12aα anticipates the older narrative strand in 12:29–33* (pre-P).

5.4. Results

Considering the literary evidence in Exod 12, the interpretation of the early Priestly portions of the chapter, that is, 12:1–13*, 28 (P 1), as context-conditioned *Fortschreibungen* appears not just to be a possibility but indeed required. Only with the inclusion of the pre-Priestly report of the killing of the firstborn (12:29aα), which is anticipated verbatim in 12:12aα, does the Priestly presentation attain narrative coherence. In the context of the Documentary Hypothesis, the only possible solution would be that either a Priestly report of the killing of the firstborn never existed, or that it has been suppressed in the editing of the text. Both proposals would appear to be makeshift solutions which do not result from the specifics of the text but from the necessity to maintain the hypothesis.

The failure of the Documentary Hypothesis to account for the earliest portions of the Priestly Passover ordinances in Exod 12:1–13*, 28 has important implications for the interpretation of the P 1 text as a whole. If one presumes that the P 1 text throughout represents a formerly independent source and that it has been preserved in its entirety, one would consequently have to claim that the Passover ordinances did not belong to the respective source and were only introduced by the so-called final

The Literary Character of the Priestly Portions of the Exodus Narrative   125

redaction (i.e., the redaction combining P with non-P) or an even later editorial stage.[68] This, however, is problematic for two reasons: first, the killing of the firstborn appears to be presupposed elsewhere in the Priestly narrative conception, most clearly in 7:4 (P 1), where there is mention of a leading out of Egypt with "great judgments."[69] Without the pre-Priestly text in Exod 12:29–33*, this announcement from 7:4 is not fulfilled. Second, the overall redaction-critical evidence in Exod 12–13 needs to be considered. The early Priestly Passover ordinances in 12:1–13*, 28 (P 1) stand at the beginning of the complex developmental history of the regulations assembled in both chapters. In a second developmental phase, the prescriptions characterized by Dtr language for the Passover (12:21–27), Maṣṣot (13:3–10), and firstborn offerings (13:11–16) follow, before the literary development concludes with a series of late Priestly extensions, among others 12:14–20, 42–51, as well as additions to 12:1–13* (P 2).[70] The early Priestly Passover ordinances in 12:1–13*, 28 thus in any case represent a relatively early developmental stage, and it appears highly questionable as to how these findings could be compatible with the idea that already the basic layer in 12:1–13*, 28 (P 1) should be allocated to the final redaction or an even later editorial stage.

6. The Miracle at the Sea (Exod 14)

6.1. The Literary Evidence

Presently it is considered uncontested that two differently accentuated accounts of the miracle at the sea are combined in Exod 14, one of which belongs to P.[71] The Priestly text, to which usually Exod 14:1–4, 8–10*, 15–18, 21aα$_1$b, 22–23, 26, 27aα$_1$, 28–29 are assigned,[72] describes how the Israelites passed through the divided sea on dry ground and were pur-

---

68. See Jean Louis Ska, "Les plaies d'Egypte dans le recit sacerdotal," *Bib* 60 (1979): 23–35; Kratz, *Komposition*, 245 n. 25.

69. See the foundational discussion by Gertz, *Tradition und Redaktion in der Exoduserzählung*, 87–88.

70. See more extensively Berner, *Die Exoduserzählung*, 276–342.

71. See fundamentally Levin, "Source Criticism: The Miracle at the Sea," in *Method Matters: Essays on the Interpretation of the Hebrew Bible in Honor of David L. Petersen*, ed. Joel M. LeMon and Kent Harold Richards, RBS 56 (Atlanta, GA: Society of Biblical Literature, 2009), 39–61.

72. So, for example, Noth, *Das Zweite Buch Mose*, 83; and similarly Gertz, *Tradi-*

126 Christoph Berner

sued by the Egyptian army, which in turn then perished in the waters that overcame them. While in P Moses is characterized as a wonderworker who brings about the division of the sea at divine command with a hand signal, and with the same gesture also undoes it, in the non-Priestly text he appears as a prophetic mediator who announces the intervention of YHWH to save the people (14:13–14). Consequently, in the non-Priestly account it is YHWH himself who brings about the destruction of the Egyptian army. He comes between the Israelites and their Egyptian pursuers in the form of a pillar of cloud and fire (14:19–20) and pushes back the sea during the night with a strong wind ($14:21a\alpha_2\beta$). This results in the Egyptians panicking in the morning, which causes them to flee into the sea that is then crashing back in on them (14:24–25, $27a\alpha_2\beta$); finally, YHWH throws them into the sea (14:27b).

In the present text, both presentations are interwoven in such a way that the non-Priestly passages specify more closely how the individual events of the Priestly account occurred.[73] This is especially clear in Exod 14:21: Moses brings about the division of the sea ($14:21a\alpha_1b$, P), such that YHWH acts in response to his sign and pushes back the water ($14:21a\alpha_2\beta$, non-P).

> *And Moses stretched his hand over the sea.*
> Then YHWH drove back the sea with a strong east wind through the night.
> *And the waters were split.*

It is obvious that the tension in the two depictions results from redactional processes; it remains to be explained, however, which redactional model is the most plausible explanation. As usual, also here the Documentary and Supplementary Hypotheses are the basic alternatives.

6.2. The Interpretation of the Literary Evidence in the Context of the Documentary Hypothesis

The most apparent interpretation of the two manners of presentation of the miracle at the sea is as a combination of two independent sources; to

---

tion und Redaktion in der Exoduserzählung, 195–206; Levin, "Source Criticism," 52. The reconstruction of the Priestly narrative is especially contested in 14:8–10.

73. See Peter Weimar, *Die Meerwundererzählung*, ÄAT 9 (Wiesbaden: Harrassowitz, 1985), 239–40.

The Literary Character of the Priestly Portions of the Exodus Narrative   127

this day, this view is advocated by the majority of interpreters of the text. From this perspective, the non-Priestly text is considered to be an integral part of a pre-Priestly exodus narrative, which had not yet conceived of the miracle at the sea as a sea crossing. Rather, it is presupposed that the Israelites at no point left their camp on the shore of the sea, while YHWH protected them by hindering the approaching Egyptians and arranging for their destruction. In contrast to this pre-Priestly YHWH-war narrative, it is assumed that P conceived of the miracle at the sea as a sea crossing and linked it to the wonders of Moses. The connection of the two sources is considered ultimately as the work of a compiler, who used the Priestly version as a base text and sought to integrate the pre-Priestly version as well as possible into this text.[74]

While the older advocates of the Documentary Hypothesis considered the compilation of the sources to be a simple mechanical process,[75] in more recent times there have increasingly been advocates who assign certain parts of the present text of Exod 14 to the redactor of the two earlier versions. Especially Gertz, following Walter Groß and Thomas Krüger, has been concerned with finding materials that stem from the compilation of the pre-Priestly and Priestly versions of the miracle at the sea and seek to mediate between the two versions.[76] To this redactional phase he assigns, for example, the information on the location given in 14:2bβ, 8b, 9*, which mediates between the different locations of the events, as well as the dual form of the pillar of cloud and fire. According to Gertz, the pre-Priestly text had only mentioned the presence of a pillar of cloud; the final redaction, however, was confronted with the problem of how the Israelites could have accomplished the passing through the divided sea (P) in the night (pre-P). To resolve the problem, the pillar of fire was conceived as a nocturnal source of light, and anchored in the presentation in 13:21–22*, 14:24*.

---

74. See Weimar, *Meerwundererzählung*, 61–67; Levin, "Source Criticism," 47–51.

75. See, for example, Otto Eißfeldt, *Hexateuch-Synopse: Die Erzählung der fünf Bücher Mose und des Buches Josua mit dem Anfange des Richterbuches* (Leipzig: Hinrichs, 1922), 133*–37*, and in the same spirit, more recently, Joel S. Baden, *J, E, and the Redaction of the Pentateuch*, FAT 68 (Tübingen: Mohr Siebeck, 2009).

76. See Walter Groß, "Die Wolkensäule in Ex 13 + 14," in *Biblische Theologie und Gesellschaft im Wandel*, ed. Georg Braulik, Seán McEvenue, and Norbert Lohfink (Freiburg: Herder, 1993), 142–65; Thomas Krüger, "Erwägung zur Redaktion der Meerwundererzählung (Exodus 13,17–14, 31)," *ZAW* 108 (1996): 519–33; Gertz, *Tradition und Redaktion in der Exoduserzählung*, 206–32.

128   Christoph Berner

The examples mentioned show that parts of the non-Priestly text are clearly influenced by the Priestly conception of the miracle at the sea. This could suggest that it is the work of a final redaction that has compiled sources, but it could also be explained with the presumption of post-Priestly *Fortschreibungen*. A stronger argument for the impact of the final redaction is presented by the scattering of non-Priestly texts among the Priestly text. So, for example, 14:8 mentions "Pharaoh, the king of Egypt," although otherwise P only speaks of Pharaoh. The apposition "king of Egypt" alludes to the non-Priestly language from 14:5 and suggests that its occurrence in 14:8 originates in an adaptation of the Priestly wording to the preceding non-Priestly context. Such punctual interventions can be explained as the harmonizing work of a final redaction, and the same can be said for the notoriously contested literary assignment of the formulations in 14:10a, 15aβ, which are found precisely in an interface between Priestly and non-Priestly texts.[77] The literary evidence thus clearly appears to support the Documentary Hypothesis.

6.3. The Interpretation of the Literary Evidence in the Context of the Supplementary Hypothesis

The miracle at the sea is certainly the part of the exodus narrative where the explanation of the Priestly text as a redaction of the pre-Priestly text is least favorable. Unlike with the plagues, for example, P would not have simply undertaken a newly-accentuated narration of a sequence of events that has been basically retained but would rather have drastically edited it and produced a series of blatant tensions. Such a model is theoretically conceivable, but it is not necessarily compelled by the evidence of the text. It is therefore not surprising that those who advocate for the redactional character of the Priestly writings in Exod 14 do this primarily based on the observations in other areas of the Priestly text, in which P can more clearly be interpreted as a supplementary layer. To maintain this explanatory model, one claims that the corresponding theory also applies to the Priestly portions in Exod 14.

It would, however, be an oversimplification to claim that those who interpret the Priestly narrative of the miracle at the sea as a supplementary layer do so simply out of external considerations. Rather, the content of Exod 14 itself is also considered in support of this interpreta-

---

77. See Levin, "Source Criticism," 51.

The Literary Character of the Priestly Portions of the Exodus Narrative   129

tion. Thus, for example, Marc Vervenne correctly notes that YHWH's demand that the Israelites are to turn back in order to give Pharaoh the impression that they are lost *in the wilderness* (14:2–3) presupposes the pre-Priestly itinerary notice in 13:20, where Etam is mentioned as a campsite on the border of the wilderness.[78] This argument, however, is invalid, because the demand that is considered (14:2a [only וישבו], 2b, 3) is not an original part of P 1 but comes from a post-Priestly redaction.[79] Vervenne's second argument faces a similar objection. Although it is correct that YHWH's question directed to Moses, "why do you cry to me" (14:15aβ: מה תצעק אלי), has a reference point in the non-Priestly text, namely, the cry of the Israelites in 14:10bβ and Moses's announcement of salvation from 14:13–14 ("YHWH will fight for you"), this does not prove that P 1 refers to the non-Priestly text. Rather, the question in 14:15aβ can be interpreted more adequately as a later harmonization by a post-Priestly redaction.[80]

Finally, attempts to propose that narrative gaps in the Priestly text disprove its independence are not compelling for similar reasons. To begin with, it is certainly correct that YHWH's announcement that he will be glorified over Pharaoh and all his hosts (14:4, 17) is only partly resolved in P when YHWH hardens the Egyptians' hearts and they advance to the prepared death trap. However, P makes no reference to a direct divine intervention that would allow for the Egyptians to recognize that it is YHWH who glorifies himself by destroying them. It is only in the non-Priestly verses 14:24–25, 27b that the announcement of the Egyptians recognizing YHWH's glory is fulfilled. At first glance, the observation of this narrative gap in the Priestly text could be interpreted to support the conclusion that P was designed as a reworking of the pre-Priestly text.[81] However, although the observation is correct, the conclusion drawn from it is not, since the motifs of hardening and glorification are again no original part of the P 1 text, but belong to a later editorial stage.[82]

---

78. See Marc Vervenne, "The 'P' Tradition in the Pentateuch," in *Pentateuchal and Deuteronomistic Studies*, ed. Christian Brekelmans and Johan Lust, BETL 94 (Leuven: Leuven University Press, 1990), 86–87.

79. See Berner, *Die Exoduserzählung*, 368–70.

80. See Weimar, *Meerwundererzählung*, 272; Levin, "Source Criticism," 51.

81. See Berner, *Die Exoduserzählung*, 363–64.

82. See Levin, "Source Criticism," 51–54.

130 Christoph Berner

To sum up, it can be shown that there are passages within the Priestly text that do refer to the non-Priestly portions of Exod 14, but the respective passages are later editorial additions throughout and did not belong to the P 1 account. In contrast, it is all the more significant that P 1, when read without those later harmonizations, appears to ignore the basic outline of the non-Priestly account. We would certainly expect different results if P 1 were a redaction of an older account than what we actually find in 14:21 and 14:27–28.

Rather, the Priestly portions of Exod 14 can be combined into a seamless narrative that appears to be ignorant of the non-Priestly statements and is even disrupted by them. Thus, there is no convincing literary evidence to argue that that the P 1 account of the miracle at the sea was conceived as an editorial layer of an earlier, pre-Priestly account.[83] On the contrary, it is compelling to conclude that the respective account of P 1 was conceived independently and only connected with the non-Priestly portions of Exod 14 at a later stage.

In the original German version of this essay I arrived at the same conclusion but tried to argue that the entire non-Priestly text of Exod 14 represents a successive editorial reworking of P 1.[84] Although I am still convinced that considerable parts of the non-Priestly text do in fact postdate P 1,[85] I must admit that there is also clear evidence for a brief pre-Priestly account of the miracle at the sea (12:37a; 14:5a, 6, 10b, 13aα, 14b, 21aα₂β, 24aαβb, 25b, 27aα₂, 30). The latter text was neither composed as an editorial layer of P 1 nor was it reworked by a P 1 editor. Rather, it appears that the two accounts existed independently from each other.

---

83. These problems are also noted by Erhard Blum, who tries to solve them with the additional assumption that we have to consider Exod 14 as containing the editing of a preformulated narrative text by P tradents; cf. Blum, *Studien zur Komposition des Pentateuch*, 256–62. However, postulating a procedure that comes close to the work of the final redaction as assumed in the context of the Documentary Hypothesis is only a makeshift solution.

84. See also Christoph Berner, "Gab es einen vorpriesterlichen Meerwunderbericht?," *Bib* 95 (2014): 1–25; see also the response of Hans-Christoph Schmitt, "Wie deuteronomistisch ist der nichtpriesterliche Meerwunderbericht von Ex 13,17–14,31?," *Bib* 95 (2014): 26–48.

85. See already Hans-Christoph Schmitt, "'Priesterliches' und 'prophetisches' Geschichtsverständnis in der Meerwundererzählung Ex 13,17–14,31," in *Theologie in Prophetie und Pentateuch*, BZAW 310 (Berlin: De Gruyter, 2001), 203–19.

The Literary Character of the Priestly Portions of the Exodus Narrative   131

6.4. Results

The literary analysis of Exod 14 clearly suggests that the present text of the chapter is based on the redactional combination of two previously independent sources, a pre-Priestly (12:37a; 14:5a, 6, 10b, 13aα, 14b, 21aα₂β, 24aαβb, 25b, 27aα₂, 30) and an early Priestly one (14:1, 2a*, 4b, 9aα, 15aαb, 16aβb, 21aα₁b, 22, 23aαb, 26, 27aα₁, 28a). In other words, the Documentary Hypothesis provides the only appropriate paradigm to account for the *origins* of the chapter, including the P 1 version embedded therein.

At the same time, much of the present text in Exod 14 must be explained against the background of the Supplementary Hypothesis. The passages in question contain successive redactional additions and harmonizations that seek to integrate the two originally separate accounts (pre-P / P 1) into one more or less coherent narrative. Part of this redactional material is also a late editorial layer in 14:2b–4a, 8a, 9aβb, 10a, 15aβ, 16aα, 17–18, 23aβ, 29 (C), which introduces the hardening theme and the motif of YHWH's glorification as a new narrative principle and theological perspective for the entire account. The redactional verses in question are mainly placed within the P 1 portions of the chapter since the latter govern the narrative structure of the combined account. This editorial placement of the redactional verses led to the traditional misconception that the verses were an integral part of P 1; since, moreover, these verses feature explicit literary connections with the non-Priestly portions of Exod 14, some exegetes wrongly concluded that the P 1 account in Exod 14 was conceived as an editorial layer—despite its massive tensions with the non-Priestly text. Only a thorough redaction-historical analysis of the Priestly passages can illuminate the contradictory literary evidence. It shows that while the secondary material (C) was indeed devised with both Priestly and non-Priestly passages in view, the original P 1 account was not.

7. Redaction-Critical Synthesis

The above analysis of the Priestly portions of the exodus narrative has produced a complex picture. However, before summarizing the results I wish to start with a basic observation. It appears that much of the confusion and misunderstanding in the present debate on the literary character of P is due to a lack of redaction-critical differentiation within what is traditionally assumed to be the Priestly text. If the Priestly portions are treated as a more or less unified block of material, this inevitably leads to the dilemma that in some instances the text looks like a formerly independent source while in others it appears to be an editorial layer. However, this literary conundrum cannot be solved by claiming a consistent nature for the Priestly text as a whole—in the words of Blum, it is "neither source nor redaction"—but first and foremost calls for a literary stratification of P. In other words, it is essential to clarify whether the somewhat diffuse character of P oscillating between a source and a redaction might be due to the fact that the different strata of the Priestly text have different literary characteristics.

The in-depth analysis of Exod 14 offered in this article has confirmed that this suggestion is correct. To begin with, it could be shown that several passages which are traditionally attributed to the earliest layer of the Priestly text do in fact belong to the latest editorial stage, which I label proto-Chronistic (C). The C passages in question (e.g., Exod 1:1–5, 7; 9:8–12; 11:10; 12:40, 41a; 14:2b–4a, 8a, 9aβb, 10a, 15aβ, 16aα, 17–18, 23aβ, 29) have been placed in the context of both Priestly (P 1, P 2) and non-Priestly texts (pre-P, D), often at major turning points of the narrative, and they show the clear tendency to mediate between the often conflicting literary strata (D as opposed to P 1 and P 2) and to establish a clearer narrative and conceptual structure for the larger units of the exodus narrative. The C passages thus show characteristics of what is traditionally called the final redaction. However, it is crucial to point out that C did not *create* the combined text of P and non-P but rather *reworks* a text where this combination had already been made.

Like C, the late Priestly portions of the exodus narrative (P 2) prove to be a redactional layer. However, P 2 shows no harmonizing tendency but provides an often polemical response to the preceding late Deuteronomistic stage (D).[86] Although most of the P 2 text has been placed in the context of earlier P 1 passages (e.g., Exod 6:13–30; 12:14–20, 43–51), the editorial layer was not added to an independent Priestly source. Rather, the literary evidence of the plague of frogs where P 2 proves to be a reworking of the non-Priestly text shows that the late Priestly editor already worked with a combined text including pre-P, P 1, and D.[87]

---

86. See in more detail Christoph Berner, "*Moses vs. Aaron: The Clash of Prophetic and Priestly Concepts of Leadership in the Pentateuch*," in *Debating Authority: Concepts of Leadership in the Pentateuch and the Former Prophets*, ed. Katharina Pyschny and Sarah Schulz, BZAW 507 (Berlin: 2018), 31–44.

87. Additional evidence can be found in Exod 16, where P 2 has also reworked an

The Literary Character of the Priestly Portions of the Exodus Narrative   133

Turning to the P 1 text, things become more difficult. To begin with, there are passages where the only sensible conclusion seems to be that P 1 represents a formerly independent source. This is most clearly the case in Exod 14, where two complete source threads can be reconstructed (pre-P and P 1). Likewise, the assumption of a continuous P 1 thread in 1:13*, 14a; 2:23aβ, 24; 6:2–7:13* still provides the more convincing theory when compared with a supplementary approach, which ultimately fails to explain the place of 1:13*, 14a; 2:23aβ, 24 in their respective pre-Priestly contexts. However, when it comes to the early Priestly Passover ordinances in 12:1–13*, 28 (P 1), the situation suddenly changes, since the passage in question is best explained as a redactional prefix to the pre-Priestly account of the killing of the Egyptian firstborn and the departure of the Israelites (12:29–33*). Without the latter verses, P 1 would lack a report of execution for the announcement of the final plague (12:13) and would not have mentioned that the Israelites left Egypt in the first place. Furthermore, this would result in the P 1 account of the miracle at the sea having no point of connection in the preceding narrative.

Although the P 1 text cannot be explained as a redactional layer in its entirety, the situation in Exod 12 raises the possibility that P 1 might have incorporated certain passages from the pre-Priestly narrative when creating its own independent account.[88] In particular, one could think of the pre-Priestly plague narrative in Exod 7:14–8:28*; 12:29–33*. This assumption would not only solve the issues with the P 1 text in Exod 12, but it might also explain why Aaron's role as a divine messenger and deliverer of the demand to set the Israelites free claims such a prominent place in Exod 7:1–6* (P 1) even though this particular motif is not elaborated by P 1. Read as a prefix to the pre-Priestly plagues, Exod 7:1–6* would simply have introduced a new perspective for the following account. Of course, the assumption that in Exod 1–14 P 1 represents a source incorporating some of the pre-Priestly material is more speculative than the explanations provided for the successive redactional stages. This is also due to the fact that in a heavily edited document such as the book of Exodus, the level of

---

earlier D text; see Christoph Berner, "Der Sabbat in der Mannaerzählung Ex 16 und in den priesterlichen Partien des Pentateuch," *ZAW* 128 (2016): 562–78.

88. The earliest redactional integration of P 1 one pre-P most likely occurred on the level of D. This model would provide a more refined version of the basic idea, that in the Patriarchal narratives and the Joseph story, P 1 is an editorial layer, while in the exodus narrative it represents an independent source. See above.

uncertainty naturally rises the earlier the layers become. Still, the received literary evidence must be explained, and it can sensibly be explained in the proposed manner. As an alternative, one would have to assume that several parts of P 1 have been suppressed in the editorial process. This assumption is certainly possible, yet it is also anything but free from speculation.

From the Call of Moses to the Parting of the Sea: Reflections on the Priestly Version of the Exodus Narrative

Thomas Römer

1. Research History as Reflected in Contemporary Debates about the Pentateuch

1.1. The End of the Documentary Hypothesis?

To nonspecialists, contemporary discourse regarding research on the Pentateuch can only be explained and simplified up to a certain extent. The impression of chaos in scholarship—caused by differing premises, methods, and literary-historical reconstructions that constantly clash—arises promptly, and any hopes to arrive at a scholarly consensus are quickly dashed.

With the classical Documentary Hypothesis being questioned from various sides in the mid-1970s, the late 1980s gave the impression that it would be possible to survive by adhering to a hypothesis based on two documents to explain the origin of the Pentateuch: a rejuvenated Yahwist or rather Deuteronomist (or a D-composition) and the Priestly source (or rather the P-composition).

However, the attitude in research changed radically in the following decades as doubts arose whether there actually was a contiguous pre-Priestly

---

This is a revised version of an essay in German: "Von Moses Berufung zur Spaltung des Meers: Überlegungen zur priesterschriftlichen Version der Exoduserzählung." An English translation of the original German text was published in *The Book of Exodus: Composition, Reception, and Interpretation*, ed. Thomas Dozeman, Craig A. Evans, and Joel N. Lohr, VTSup 164 (Leiden: Brill, 2014), 121–50.

136 Thomas Römer

line of narration in the Torah that recounted events from the creation of the world to Moses's death or the conquest the of land. This discussion arose mainly due to questions about the literary transition from the patriarchal narrative to the exodus story, but also because of the thesis of an independent Primeval History, as well as the later insertion of the Sinai-pericope. When combined, these matters would lead scholars to a return to the Fragmentary Hypothesis. Additionally, the extent of the so-called Priestly *Grundschrift* (P^G) was widely discussed (we will return to this discussion below). If neither P^G nor a pre-Priestly source or composition included the whole narrative arc of the Pentateuch, respectively the Hexateuch, the question of the origin of the Torah arises anew. Is the Torah the product of extensive post-Priestly redactions or some kind of mere coincidental writings that developed from a huge number of successive expansions?

If, however, one postulates "the complete abandonment of the Documentary Hypothesis, which has simply outlived its usefulness as a paradigm inherited from a nineteenth-century ideology,"[1] this assertion is not statistically correct. The rejection of the traditional source theory can be found primarily in pentateuchal research of German-speaking Protestants. In Anglo-Saxon—especially North American—exegesis, the Documentary Hypothesis is still being utilized and objections to it are raised by a minority of scholars (e.g., Thomas Dozeman or David Carr).[2] In the United States, students of Baruch Schwartz (Joel Baden, Jeffrey Stackert) started a strong dogmatic defense of the New Documentary Hypothesis as a reaction to objections against the model based on Julius Wellhausen.[3] Going beyond Wellhausen, they assume that the three or four sources in all of the narrative texts of the Pentateuch (including the

---

1. Christoph Berner, *Die Exoduserzählung: Das literarische Werden einer Ursprungslegende Israels*, FAT 73 (Tübingen: Mohr Siebeck, 2010), 49.

2. Thomas B. Dozeman, *Exodus*, ECC (Grand Rapids: Eerdmans, 2009); David Carr, *The Formation of the Hebrew Bible: A New Reconstruction* (New York: Oxford University Press, 2011).

3. See, e.g., Baruch J. Schwartz, "How the Compiler of the Pentateuch Worked: The Composition of Genesis 37," in *The Book of Genesis: Composition, Reception, and Interpretation*, ed. Craig A. Evans, Joel N. Lohr, and David L. Petersen, VTSup 152 (Leiden: Brill, 2012), 263–78; Joel S. Baden, *The Composition of the Pentateuch: Renewing the Documentary Hypothesis*, AYBRL (New Haven: Yale University Press, 2012); and Jeffrey Stackert, *A Prophet Like Moses: Prophecy, Law, and Israelite Religion* (Oxford: Oxford University Press, 2014); Joel S. Baden and Jeffrey Stackert, eds., *The Oxford Handbook of the Pentateuch* (Oxford: Oxford University Press, 2021), esp.

From the Call of Moses to the Parting of the Sea 137

story of Joseph) can be reconstructed almost in their entirety. These were simply compiled mechanically without any redactor(s) adding any substantial amount of their own writing. This is probably not the mainstream (yet) in North American scholarship. However, most North American textbooks still present the traditional Documentary Hypothesis as the best way to explain the formation of the Pentateuch.

Thus, scholarship on the Hebrew Bible is currently in the unfortunate situation that certain discussions and approaches are confined to specific schools that are sometimes restricted to a small group of researchers and their students. This situation makes the development of a new, widely accepted model quite difficult.

However, a few points can be enumerated in which a consensus may be possible:

- In the middle of the Persian Period, around 400–350 BCE, the Pentateuch existed as a concept; this does not exclude later additions and revisions.
- In the Pentateuch, Priestly and non-Priestly texts can be differentiated; non-Priestly does not necessarily mean pre-Priestly.

1.2. Discussion on the Priestly Texts

Almost no one doubts the existence of Priestly texts in the Pentateuch. Georg Fischer, who opposes the existence of a P-source or redaction, is one of the few exceptions. He accepts that there are indeed linguistically specific P-texts; he argues, however, that these texts cannot be divorced from their context and should therefore be ascribed to one and the same "pentateuchal narrator" together with non-Priestly, Dtr, and other texts.[4] For Fischer "the attempt to reconstruct the historical genesis of these texts today is questionable. It presupposes that those texts were written down and edited over a long period of time, for which we really lack appropriate comparative examples from the ancient world."[5] In this way, Fischer makes a virtue out of necessity and seeks to postulate a single narrator or compiler, who would have

---

1–22. For a critical examination of their presupposition, see Konrad Schmid, "The Neo-Documentarian Manifesto: A Critical Reading," *JBL* 140 (2021): 461–79.

4. Georg Fischer, "Keine Priesterschrift in Ex 1–15?," *ZKT* 117 (1995): 203–11.

5. Georg Fischer, "Zur Lage der Pentateuchforschung," *ZAW* 115 (2003): 612.

138   Thomas Römer

been responsible for the origin and development of the Pentateuch (as Robert Whybray had similarly argued before).[6]

It is difficult, however, to explain the linguistic deviations, tensions, and contradictions found in the Hebrew Bible without postulating literary growth and a plurality of authors; to this end, the differentiation of P and non-P remains a valid starting point.

To a great extent there is agreement that P was not composed in its entirety at one time; rather, Wellhausen's differentiation of P^G and P^S is still appropriate. A consensus in terms of the end of the original Priestly source does not exist, however.

Recently, theories that assume a vastly shorter P^G have been added to the traditional theory (i.e., that P actually included the complete narrative arc of the Hexateuch or the Pentateuch). The assumption of an original Hexateuch, which would also be the extent of P, is promoted by researchers who identify Josh 19:51 (Joseph Blenkinsopp, Norbert Lohfink) or 18:1 (Ernst Axel Knauf, Horst Seebass) as the conclusion of the Priestly source.[7] The framing character of 18:1 is a commonly used as an argument in favor of the thesis. The words "then the whole congregation of the Israelites assembled at Shiloh, and set up the tent of meeting there. The land lay subdued before them" (Josh 18:1 NRSV) should be seen as an *inclusio* with the Priestly command at creation in Gen 1:28 (according to which humankind should subject the world to its rule). However, Gen 1:28 refers to the task of humankind as a whole and does not refer to the gift of a specific land to Israel. Apart from that, in Gen 9:1–7*, after the flood, the order of Gen 1:28 is revised in the context of the Priestly source, since the submission of the earth is no longer mentioned. Beyond that a continuous Priestly line of narration cannot be identified in the book of Joshua.[8]

---

6. Robert N. Whybray, *The Making of the Pentateuch: A Methodological Study*, JSOTSup 53 (Sheffield: Sheffield Academic, 1987).

7. Joseph Blenkinsopp, "The Structure of P," *CBQ* 38 (1976): 275–92; Norbert Lohfink, "Die Priesterschrift und die Geschichte," in *Congress Volume: Göttingen 1977*, ed. J. A. Emerton, VTSup 29 (Leiden: Brill, 1978), 189–225; Horst Seebass, "Josua," *BN* 28 (1985): 53–65; Ernst Axel Knauf, "Die Priesterschrift und die Geschichten der Deuteronomisten," in *The Future of the Deuteronomistic History*, ed. Thomas Römer, BETL 147 (Leuven: Peeters, 2000), 101–18. In his *Josua*, ZBKAT 6 (Zürich: Theologischer Verlag, 2008), 29, Knauf adds as a possibility verse 24:29b.

8. According to Knauf, *Josua*, 29, P comprises in Joshua only 4:19a; 5:10–12, 18:1, (24:29b).

From the Call of Moses to the Parting of the Sea   139

Probably the most popular opinion identifies the conclusion of P in Deut 34:7–9 at the end of the Pentateuch (it is postulated that the actual Priestly account of Moses's death was displaced by the fusion of P and the older sources). This idea presumably goes back to Martin Noth, who saw the narrative outline of the Pentateuch in P^G, and was recently defended by Ludwig Schmidt and Christian Frevel.[9] Both (correctly) argue that the conquest of the land does not represent one of P's primary concerns. It is however questionable whether the note of Joshua being appointed as Moses's successor in Deut 34:7–9 represents an adequate ending. Deuteronomy 34:9 is only understandable with a continuation in Josh 1. Frevel recognized this problem and suggested that Deut 34:8 (when the Israelites stop grieving about Moses's death) should be understood as the conclusion of P^G. Nonetheless, this solution is not convincing either, because it also awakens expectations for a narrative continuation.

Lothar Perlitt tried to prove, based on linguistic reasons and in terms of contents, that the Priestly verses in Deut 34 cannot be attributed to P^G: they require secondary Priestly texts such as Num 27:12–23 and stand out due to a style that mixes Priestly and Deuteronomic elements that is characteristic of late texts.[10] Consequently, the end of P can be found neither in Deut 34, nor in Num 27, as recently suggested (by Jean-Louis Ska, Félix García López).[11]

As no satisfying end for P^G can be found in the books of Numbers, Deuteronomy, or Joshua, it is not very surprising that the conclusion of P has recently been increasingly sought in the Sinai pericope. Thomas Pola's thesis, in which he claims that P^G finished his work in Exod 40 with the erection of the shrine in the desert, marks the beginning of this tendency.[12] According to Pola, the Priestly texts in Numbers clearly differ from P^G (in

---

9. Ludwig Schmidt, *Studien zur Priesterschrift*, BZAW 214 (Berlin: de Gruyter, 1993); Christian Frevel, *Mit dem Blick auf das Land die Schöpfung erinnern*, HBS 23 (Freiburg: Herder, 2000).

10. Lothar Perlitt, "Priesterschrift im Deuteronomium?," *ZAW* 100 (1988): 65–88.

11. Jean Louis Ska, "Le récit sacerdotal: Une 'histoire sans fin'?," in *The Books of Leviticus and Numbers*, ed. Thomas Römer, BETL 215 (Leuven: Peeters, 2008), 631–53; Félix García López, *El Pentateuco: Introducción a la lectura de los cinco primeros libros de la Biblia*, Introducción al estudio de la Biblia 3a (Estella: Verbo Divino, 2003), 332–33.

12. Thomas Pola, *Die ursprüngliche Priesterschrift: Beobachtungen zur Literarkritik und Traditionsgeschichte von P^g*, WMANT 70 (Neukirchen-Vluyn: Neukirchener, 1995), esp. 224–98.

140   Thomas Römer

the Priestly texts of Numbers, Israel is constructed as an "ecclesia militans," and the division into twelve tribes plays an important role in contrast to the books of Genesis–Leviticus). The close interplay between P[G] and Ezek 20 are another of Pola's arguments. According to Ezek 20:40, the goal of the intervention of YHWH for Israel is service on Mount Zion. From this, Pola concludes that the shrine on Sinai was not originally designed to be transportable but was a kind of projection of Zion into the desert. Consequently, Pola categorizes all of the verses that presume the mobility of the shrine as secondary and reconstructs the end of P[G] in the following texts: Exod 19:1; 24:15b, 16–17, 18a; 25:1, 8a, 9; 29:45–46; 40:16, 17a, 33b.

This reconstruction offers a readable text; however, the question remains whether such a short hand somewhat lapidary text (about two percent of Exod 19–40) really can be seen as a plausible conclusion of P[G]; the problem is that Pola considers most of the verses that refer back to Gen 1 as secondary (cf. also Eckart Otto, who identifies the end of the original Priestly source in Exod 29:42b–46 since the descriptions of the construction do not match the commandments).[13] The parallelization of the creation of the world and the erection of the tabernacle (which, we might add, can be found in parallels from the ancient Near East like the Enuma Elish and the Ugaritic Baal-mythos), something already observed by the rabbis, constitutes an important argument in favor of the theory according to which the Priestly narration finds its appropriate end with the construction of the tabernacle.[14] Is it possible that P[G] only narrated the erection of the shrine and without recounting the installation of the Aaronide priesthood and the establishment of the sacrificial cult? Therefore, would not Lev 9 be a more plausible end to the Priestly source (Erich Zenger)?[15] It recounts the consecration of Aaron and his sons (however, with some deviations from Exod 29). A conclusion at Lev 9 also permits the assumption that P[G] already included some basic ritual regulations in Lev 1–7*. This would preclude the presumption that has often been made that P[G] consisted exclusively of narrative material. Another option would be to allow the original Priestly source to continue until the so-called Holiness

---

13. Eckhart Otto, "Forschungen zur Priesterschrift," *TRu* 62 (1997): 1–50.

14. Moshe Weinfeld, "Sabbath, Temple and the Enthronement of the Lord: The Problem of the Sitz im Leben of Genesis 1:1–2:3," in *Mélanges bibliques et orientaux en l'honneur de M. Henri Cazelles*, ed. André Caquot and Mathias Delcor, AOAT 212 (Neukirchen-Vluyn: Neukirchener, 1981), 501–12.

15. Erich Zenger, "Priesterschrift," *TRE* 27 (1997): 435–46.

From the Call of Moses to the Parting of the Sea   141

Code, at the Yom Kippur in Lev 16, which emphasizes God's forgiveness and the never-ending opportunity to purify the shrine and the community. This too seems to be a plausible climax and conclusion to the Priestly source (Matthias Köckert, Christophe Nihan).[16] In contrast to that, one could agree with Reinhard Kratz and others that P[G] initially concluded with Exod 40 and that Lev 1–16 (on another scroll) presented "additions within the framework of the still independent Priestly Writing," with the result that P[G] consisted of two scrolls: one narrative (Genesis–Exodus*) and one ritual (Lev 1–16*).[17] But such an abbreviated P raises the question of how to understand the promises regarding the land included in P texts.

The question of whether to understand P as an originally autonomous document or as a redaction of older, non-Priestly sources remains controversial. The idea of P as a redactor, promoted primarily by Frank Moore Cross, Rolf Rendtorff, and John Van Seters, finds advocates in Rainer Albertz and Christoph Berner in more recent discussions.[18] This thesis is based on the observation that, despite many attempts, no one has succeeded in completely reconstructing the P source. The story of Jacob in particular demonstrates many lacunae; furthermore, Moses appears abruptly and without any introduction in the Priestly exodus narrative (should one read the P texts in Exod 2:23aβ–25 and 6:2–8 successively), and, the search for a contiguous Priestly narrative fails completely in the book of Numbers. However, the assumption that the different source documents survived the process of compilation in their entirety is based on the spurious presupposition that the redactors actually sought to keep the sources as complete as possible. Examples from Mesopotamia, espe-

---

16. Matthias Köckert, "Leben in Gottes Gegenwart. Zum Verständnis des Gesetzes in der priesterschriftlichen Literatur," *JBT* 4 (1989): 29–61; Christophe Nihan, *From Priestly Torah to Pentateuch: A Study in the Composition of the Book of Leviticus*, FAT 2/25 (Tübingen: Mohr Siebeck, 2007), 150–98.

17. Reinhard G. Kratz, *The Composition of the Narrative Books of the Old Testament*, trans. John Bowden (London: T&T Clark, 2005), 114.

18. Frank Moore Cross, *From Epic to Canon: History and Literature in Ancient Israel* (Baltimore: Johns Hopkins University Press, 1998); Rolf Rendtorff, *Das überlieferungsgeschichtliche Problem des Pentateuch*, BZAW 147 (Berlin: De Gruyter, 1976); John Van Seters, The Pentateuch. A Social-Science Commentary, Trajectories 1 (Sheffield: Sheffield Academic, 1999); Rainer Albertz, *Ex 1–18*, vol. 1 of *Exodus*, ZBK.AT 2.1 (Zürich: TVZ, 2012); Berner, *Die Exoduserzählung*. See also Jakob Wöhrle, *Fremdlinge im eigenen Land: Zur Entstehung und Intention der priesterlichen Passagen der Vätergeschichte*, FRLANT 246 (Göttingen: Vandenhoeck & Ruprecht, 2012).

142   Thomas Römer

cially the Epic of Gilgamesh, attest to the loose handling of old documents, which in the course of a new edition can be shortened, left out, or rewritten (Jeffrey Tigay).[19] Erhard Blum tried to solve the problem of whether P was initially a source or was always a redaction by suggesting that we should understand the Priestly composition neither as a source nor as a redaction.[20] According to him, some Priestly texts were initially planned to exist on their own before being used as part of the editorial work that the same Priestly circles undertook on older non-Priestly traditions. This basically leads to the identification of one or more Priestly documents and one or more Priestly redactions.

In what follows, this discussion shall be addressed in the context of an analysis of the main texts of the Priestly Exodus narrative.

2. The Priestly Depiction of Moses's Commission and the Revelation of the Name YHWH in Exod 6

2.1. Structure and Diachrony

God's speech in Exod 6:2–8 is always classified as Priestly. It is clearly distinguished from the preceding speech of YHWH via a narrative reintroduction. The end is marked by a change of subjects in verse 9. The text is precisely structured by a series of refrains and frames:

---

19. Jeffrey H. Tigay, *The Evolution of the Gilgamesh Epic* (Philadelphia: University of Pennsylvania Press, 1982).

20. Erhard Blum, *Studien zur Komposition des Pentateuch*, BZAW 189 (Berlin: de Gruyter, 1990), 229–86.

From the Call of Moses to the Parting of the Sea 143

אני יהוה 6:2
6:3 וארא אל אברהם אל יצחק ואל יעקב
6:4 הקמתי את בריתי אתם לתת להם את ארץ כנען
6:5 נאקת בני ישראל אשר מצרים מעבדים אתם
ואזכר את בריתי
אני יהוה 6:6
והוצאתי אתכם מתחת סבלת מצרים

וגאלתי אתכם
6:7 ולקחתי אתכם לי לעם
והייתי לכם לאלהים
אני יהוה
המוציא אתכם מתחת סבלת מצרים
6:8 והבאתי אתכם אל הארץ אשר
נשאתי את ידי לתת אתה לאברהם ליצחק וליעקב ונתתי אתה לכם מורשה
אני יהוה

The main motif of the speech is definitely the formula of self-introduction, which appears four times and makes clear that these parts have to do with the introduction, or rather the identity, of the God YHWH. The formula frames the entire speech in verse 2 and verse 8. Its further appearance in verse 6 opens the prophetic oration[21] that Moses should transmit to the Israelites and that is subdivided in verse 7 by the phrase אני יהוה. From verse 6 onward, the Israelites are directly addressed in the second-person plural. Thereafter, the first part of the discourse directed to the Israelites contains the announcement of the exodus from Egypt and the promise that the Israelites will become YHWH's people. The promise of the land, which appears in verses 3–4 and verse 8 in connection with the three patriarchs Abraham, Isaac, and Jacob, provides another frame for the whole speech. Here, the following displacement can be seen:

Verse 4 references giving the land to the patriarchs, which YHWH ratifies with his ברית, whereby the land is referred to as "Canaan" and "land where they were foreigners." In verse 8, raising the hand (for an oath) equals the covenant. YHWH now wants to give the Israelites the land he promised the patriarchs as מורשה.

YHWH's sophistically constructed speech appears brief and succinct. In contrast to the text of Gen 17, which this speech presupposes, neither

---

21. This introduction is often and mainly used in Ezekiel, when the prophet is commanded to deliver a speech: Ezek 11:16–17; 12:23, 28; 20:30; 33:25; 36:22.

144   Thomas Römer

YHWH's theophany and ascension nor Moses's reaction to the theophany he witnessed is reported.

The divine speech in Exod 6 hardly presents an occasion for literary-critical operations. Verse 8 has occasionally been attributed to a later redactor because it is said to contradict the Priestly conception of the land as a gift[22] as expressed in verse 4. The question of the Priestly concept of land still has to be discussed.

In verse 6b the phrase "with an outstretched arm" stands before the phrase "mighty acts of judgment," which some scholars regard as a later retouching because it reflects Deuteronomic language and the non-Priestly 6:1 mentions the "mighty hand."[23] This observation raises the question of whether Priestly texts can have knowledge of and incorporate Deuteronomic phraseology.

There is a broad consensus regarding the fact that verses 9–12 belong to the same literary layer as 6:2–8. Moses fulfills the divine mandate of 6:6 immediately and without contradiction; however, he fails due to the Israelites' not hearing. Therefore, another divine speech follows in which YHWH sends Moses to the pharaoh. Moses at this point anticipates the probability of a renewed failure. Due to the *Wiederaufnahme* in verses 28–30, the following genealogy of Moses and Aaron can be identified as a later insertion. Consequently, the strand beginning in 6:2–12* continues in 7:1–7. That Exod 2:23aβ–25 prepares the reader for 6:2–12 is obvious as well, but it is questionable how one should judge this connection. To this end, the relationship between Exod 6:2–12 and the non-Priestly account of Moses's call in Exod 3:1–4:18 must be analyzed first. In contrast to the traditional assumption, according to which Exod 3–4 consists of various layers and presents a generally older text around which a redactor draped the originally related P-text 2:23–25; 6:1–8, different analyses have been increasing recently: for some Exod 3:1–4:18 is generally a post-Priestly textual unity; for others the P-fragments in 2:23–25 and 6:2–12 must be understood as a Priestly redaction of the older narration of Moses's calling.

---

22. See Fujiko Kohata, *Jahwist und Priesterschrift in Exodus 3–14*, BZAW 166 (Berlin: de Gruyter, 1986), 29–31; Bernard Gosse, "Le livre d'Ezéchiel et Ex 6,2–8 dans le cadre du Pentateuque," *BN* 104 (2000): 20–25.

23. See Kohata, *Jahwist und Priesterschrift*, 28–29; Jan Christian Gertz, *Tradition und Redaktion in der Exoduserzählung: Untersuchungen zur Endredaktion des Pentateuch*, FRLANT 186 (Göttingen: Vandenhoeck & Ruprecht, 1999), 243, and recently Berner, *Die Exoduserzählung*, 158.

From the Call of Moses to the Parting of the Sea   145

2.2. The Relationship between Exodus 3:1–4:18 and 6:1–12

Otto and Konrad Schmid have both argued for the post-Priestly dating of Exod 3–4; Schmid presents the most substantial explanations.[24] Otto and Schmid postulate that a "substantial literary unity" (Schmid) must be assumed for Exod 3:1–4:18, which already presupposes Exod 6*. To support his thesis, Schmid refers to the relationships that are "generally excluded, in the exegetical literature of this century," between Exod 3:1–4:18 and the preceding Priestly passages in Exod 2:23aβ–25.[25] Indeed, both texts actually refer to the Israelites' crying out (צעקה in Exod 3:7–9; ויזעקו in Exod 2:23), as well as YHWH's seeing, hearing, and knowing (Exod 3:7; 2:23–25), and finally the patriarchal triad.

From this, contrary to Schmid, it does not follow that Exod 3–4 was composed a priori as a sequel to Exod 2:23aβ–25.[26] It is also possible that the author of Exod 2:23aβ–25 was familiar with Exod 3–4*. The Israelites' crying out in Exod 3:7 can be understood without reference to 2:23 (note the different orthography) because it is rooted in the so-called Dtr Credo (Deut 26:7). God's knowing (וידע אלהים), used in Exod 2:25 (MT), is syntactically difficult because it has no object. If Exod 3:1ff. had been conceptualized as a sequel of Exod 2:25, a better link could have been established. It is by far easier to understand the form of the verb in Exod 2:25 as originally being a *niphal* as attested by LXX.[27] Consequently, the

---

24. Eckart Otto, "Die nachpriesterliche Pentateuchredaktion im Buch Exodus," in *Studies in the Book of Exodus*, ed. Marc Vervenne, BETL 126 (Leuven: Peeters, 1996), 61–111; Konrad Schmid, *Erzväter und Exodus*, WMANT 81 (Neukirchen-Vluyn: Neukirchener, 1999); see further Jürgen Kegler, "Die Berufung des Mose als Befreier Israels: Zur Einheitlichkeit des Berufungsberichts in Exodus 3–4," in *Freiheit und Recht: Festschrift für Frank Crüsemann zum 65. Geburtstag*, ed. Christof Hardmeier, Rainer Kessler, and Andreas Ruwe (Gütersloh: Gütersloher Verlagshaus, 2003), 162–88.

25. Schmid, *Erzväter und Exodus*, 193. For the following arguments, see 193–209.

26. See also the criticism of Schmid's thesis in Erhard Blum, "Die literarische Verbindung von Erzvätern und Exodus," in *Abschied vom Jahwisten: Die Komposition des Hexateuch in der jüngsten Diskussion*, ed. Jan Christian Gertz, Konrad Schmid, and Markus Witte, BZAW 315 (Berlin: De Gruyter, 2002), 124–27.

27. Berner, *Die Exoduserzählung*, 64–65, recently argued against this solution, which has been presented by Werner H. Schmidt, *Exodus*, BKAT 2 (Neukirchen-Vluyn: Neukirchener, 1974), 79; Alain Le Boulluec and Pierre Sandevoir, *L'Exode*, BA 2 (Paris: Cerf, 1989), 87 among many others. His argument of the lectio difficilior is, however, untenable since the consonantal text does not distinguish between *qal* and

146   Thomas Römer

end of Exod 2:25 does not lead to 3:1 but to 6:2 ("God revealed himself and spoke to Moses"). The criterion of the mutual attestation of the three patriarchs is not satisfactory either. Even if one does not consider the fact—which Schmid does not discuss—that in Exod 3–4 the triad of the patriarchs often appears in contexts which make literary criticism necessary, it is hardly conceivable that an author familiar with Exod 2:23–25 would have omitted a reference to the patriarchal ברית mentioned in 2:24 when introducing the land. In fact, the land is reintroduced in Exod 3 without any reference to God's promises to Abraham, Isaac, and Jacob, but rather with phrases known primarily from Deuteronomy and not from Genesis.

The other noted observation cannot prove the post-Priestly dating of Exod 3–4 in its entirety either. Schmid indicates that Exod 3–4 already alludes to the Priestly plague narratives and the later text of Num 12 (this narrative, which is often mentioned as parallel to Moses's leprous hand, is, however, not the most plausible textual referent.[28] We can more likely identify in its background a reflection of the tradition of Moses as the leader of a group of lepers, as found in Manetho in the third century BCE).[29] These arguments refer to the episode of Exod 4:1–17, which actually can readily be considered post-Priestly *Fortschreibung* but not to Exod 3*.[30]

Is it therefore more reasonable to interpret Exod 2:23–25 and 6:2–12 as a Priestly redaction of the older narration of Moses's commissioning in Exod 3? As evidence, one could note the inclusion of non-Priestly expressions in those texts. This is, however, only convincing if one presumes that an independent Priestly source had been written without any knowledge of the Priestly Exodus narrative. But the idea of various completely autonomous milieus for the production of protobiblical literature seems unlikely in terms of literary-sociology. Furthermore, assuming that every part of

---

niphal. The *niphal* form is more logical if Exod 2:23–25 had preceded Exod 6:2–8, as 6:3 refers to the YHWH's revelation to the patriarchs. The *niphal* form can be found more often in P-texts as in Exod 25:22; 29:42; 30:6, 36. The Masoretic vocalization can explained by the fact that "through the separation of 6:2 the reference point was lost and a statement about God's revelation before 3:1 comes too early" (Schmidt, *Exodus*, 79). Therefore the Masoretes opted for a *qal* and did not understand the end of 2:25 as a transition but as a conclusion.

28. Schmid, *Erzväter und Exodus*, 203–6.

29. Thomas Römer, "Tracking Some 'Censored' Moses Traditions Inside and Outside the Hebrew Bible," *HeBAI* 1 (2012): 64–76.

30. See also Gertz, *Tradition und Redaktion in der Exoduserzählung*, 305–26.

From the Call of Moses to the Parting of the Sea   147

P has a redactional function, it remains generally inexplicable that the assertions that differ from, or advance beyond, Exod 3 were not directly incorporated into the text.

Franck Michaeli, Käre Berge, Schmid, and others have observed that Exod 6 and Exod 3 agree in their perceptions that the revelation of YHWH's name to Moses is the reason for Israel's knowledge of God's name.[31] According to biblical and nonbiblical authors, the fact that the knowledge of YHWH's name is connected with Moses or rather the Exodus is a solid date in terms of tradition criticism and tradition history. Had the author of P been working as a redactor from the outset, he could have inserted his theory of the revelation into the scene of Moses's calling in Exod 3 without any difficulties. The idea in Exod 6:3 that the name YHWH was not known to the patriarchs is more difficult to explain as a redactional concept than it would be if the Genesis texts that are traditionally ascribed to P[G] were considered separately.

Furthermore, the transition from 6:1 to 6:2, which bears difficulties in terms of style and contents and which some textual witnesses have already tried to smooth, is difficult to explain assuming a redactor's work in 6:2–8. If the author of 6:2–8 had already seen and read 6:1 on a scroll, he could have spared himself the writing of an introduction to the speech or could have characterized this one as a continuation by using a עוֹד (as in, e.g., Exod 3:15).

Therefore, the comparison of Exod 3 and Exod 6 more likely leads to the conclusion that Exod 1:13–14; 2:23aβ–25; 6:2–8 should be read in a continuous and coherent context.[32] The fact that Moses is not introduced separately can be explained by the supposition that the author of this

---

31. Franck Michaeli, *Le livre de l'Exode*, CAT 2 (Neuchâtel: Delachaux et Niestlé, 1974), 65; Käre Berge, *Reading Sources in a Text: Coherence and Literary Criticism in the Call of Moses*, ATAT 54 (Saint Ottilien: EOS Verlag, 1997), 116; Schmid, *Erzväter und Exodus*, 206.

32. Thus: [1:13] The Egyptians became ruthless in imposing tasks on the Israelites, [1:14] and made their lives bitter with hard service in mortar and brick and in every kind of field labor. They were ruthless in all the tasks that they imposed on them. [2:23*] The Israelites groaned under their slavery, and cried out. Out of the slavery their cry for help rose up to God. [2:24] God heard their groaning, and God remembered his covenant with Abraham, Isaac, and Jacob. [2:25] God looked upon the Israelites, and God took notice of them. [6:2] God also spoke to Moses and said to him: "I am YHWH. [6:3] I appeared to Abraham, Isaac, and Jacob as El Shaddai, but by my name YHWH I did not make myself known to them" (adapted from NRSV).

148   Thomas Römer

context presumed the knowledge about Moses or a familiarity with some Moses narrative.[33]

2.3. Exodus 6 and the Patriarchs

It is obvious that Exod 6:3–4 ("I appeared to Abraham, Isaac, and Jacob as El Shaddai, but by my name YHWH I did not make myself known to them. I also established my covenant with them, to give them the land of Canaan, the land in which they resided as aliens" [adapted from NRSV]) refers to the patriarchal narratives, especially to Gen 17. According to the title of Lohfink's famous essay, the author's intention in Exod 6 was a "Priestly devaluation of the tradition of the revelation of YHWH's name to Moses," to the benefit of the patriarchs.[34] However, a depreciation cannot be seen here; it is about connecting the time of the patriarchs with the time of Moses theologically. The covenant with the patriarchs,[35] mentioned in Exod 2:24 and 6:4, actually becomes the main reason for YHWH's intervention; the revelation of YHWH's name is, however, left to the time of Moses. The apparent three-stage theology of the revelation of P (God reveals himself to humankind as Elohim in Gen 1, to Abraham and his descendants as El Shaddai in Gen 17, and to the Israelites via Moses as YHWH in Exod 6[36]) works better if the P-texts in Genesis and Exodus are separated from the non-Priestly texts. Besides the theological concern of P, which can be called "inclusive monotheism" and which according to Albert de Pury contains an ecumenical perspective, Exod 6 literally emphasizes the connection between the patriarchs and the exodus.[37]

---

33. For a detailed refutation of the arguments in favor of a post-P setting of Exod 3–4, see Jaeyoung Jeon, *The Call of Moses and the Exodus Story: A Redactional-Critical Study in Exodus 3–4 and 5–13*, FAT 2/60 (Tübingen: Mohr Siebeck, 2013), 188–206.

34. Norbert Lohfink, "Die priesterschriftliche Abwertung der Tradition von der Offenbarung des Jahwenamens an Mose," *Bib* 49 (1968): 1–8.

35. The P-texts of Genesis only explicitly recount a ברית for Abraham. Genesis 17:19–21 presumes that a covenant will be made with Isaac, but it is not mentioned. Is this a stylistic device or maybe a sign that some P-texts were not incorporated in the process of the compilation of the Pentateuch? For Jacob, one could think of Gen 35:10–13, where Gen 17 is played upon, although it does not attest the keyword *covenant*.

36. Michaeli, *Le livre de l'Exode*, 67.

37. Albert de Pury, "Pg as the Absolute Beginning," in *Les dernières rédactions du Pentateuque, de l'Hexateuque et de l'Ennéateuque*, ed. Thomas Römer and Konrad Schmid, BETL 203 (Leuven: Peeters, 2007), 99–128.

From the Call of Moses to the Parting of the Sea 149

Recent research has increasingly interpreted the connection between Gen 17 and Exod 6 in the following way: the literary link of patriarchs and exodus was created by P. Consequently, P would be responsible for the theological and literarily associative joining of two originally autonomous traditions about Israel's origin. If this thesis were correct, it would also explain why an autonomous Priestly source sometimes appears brief and apparently truncated. This would require its addressees being familiar with the pre-Priestly patriarchal and Moses narratives. Among other things, this narrative connection would have had to have been dedicated to demonstrating that the patriarchal and the Exodus traditions belong together theologically and literarily. However, the thesis identifying P as the creator of the literary connection of Genesis and Exodus is vehemently doubted, too. For some, this connection is the work of an exilic (John Van Seters, Christoph Levin) or an older (Schmidt) Yahwist, an Elohistic composition from the seventh century BCE (Hans-Christoph Schmitt), or generally of a pre-Priestly (exilic) link in Gen 50:21, Exod 1:6aα1, 8–10* (Kratz, Carr, Berner).[38] This assumption clearly requires the existence of a pre-Priestly Joseph narrative, a matter which, however, will not be discussed here.[39] Even if a literary connection between Genesis and Exodus had been created before P, it would remain extremely short and vague in literary terms. Only texts like Gen 17 and Exod 6 provide this connection with any theological depth.

---

38. John Van Seters, "The Patriarchs and the Exodus: Bridging the Gap between Two Origin Traditions," in *The Interpretation of Exodus: Studies in Honour of Cornelis Houtman*, ed. Riemer Roukema, CBET 44 (Leuven: Peeters, 2006), 1–15; Christoph Levin, "The Yahwist and the Redactional Link Between Genesis and Exodus," in *A Farewell to the Yahwist? The Composition of the Pentateuch in Recent European Interpretation*, ed. Thomas B. Dozeman and Konrad Schmid, SymS 34 (Atlanta: Society of Biblical Literature, 2006), 131–41; Ludwig Schmidt, "Die vorpriesterliche Verbindung von Erzväter und Exodus durch die Josefsgeschichte (Gen 37; 39–50*) und Exodus 1," *ZAW* 124 (2012): 19–37; Hans-Christoph Schmitt, "Erzvätergeschichte und Exodusgeschichte als konkurrierende Ursprungslegenden Israels—Ein Irrweg der Pentateuchforschung," in *Die Erzväter in der biblischen Tradition: Festschrift für Matthias Köckert*, ed. Anselm C. Hagedorn and Henrik Pfeiffer, BZAW 400 (Berlin: de Gruyter, 2009), 241–66; David M. Carr, "What Is Required to Identify Pre-Priestly Narrative Connections between Genesis and Exodus? Some General Reflections and Specific Cases," in Dozeman and Schmid, *Farewell to the Yahwist?*, 175; Berner, *Die Exoduserzählung*, 20–26.

39. See my discussion in "Deux repas 'en miroir' dans l'histoire de Joseph (Gn 37–50)," *RHPR* 93 (2013): 15–27, esp. 17–21.

150 Thomas Römer

2.4. The Meaning of the Land in Exodus 6:2–8 and in the Priestly-Source

Exodus 6:2–8 contains two explicit references to YHWH's promising the gift of the land.

6:4 וגם הקמתי את־בריתי אתם לתת להם את־ארץ כנען את ארץ מגריהם אשר־גרו בה

6:8 והבאתי אתכם אל־הארץ אשר נשאתי את־ידי לתת אתה לאברהם ליצחק וליעקב
ונתתי אתה לכם מורשה

The relevance of the land for P has been interpreted differently within exegetical discourse. For one group, the theme of the land only plays a marginal role (Noth, Rudolf Smend); for others the land represents a primary concern of the Priestly source (Karl Elliger, Ralph Klein).[40] The promise of the land also touches on the aforementioned discussion about the end of P. Carr, for example, assumes that P is "specifically *hexateuchal* in scope."[41] Must P therefore have ended with a narrative describing the conquest of the land?

The first mention of the land in Exod 6:4 clearly refers to Gen 17:

Gen 17:7–8

והקמתי את־בריתי ביני ובינך ובין זרעך אחריך
ונתתי לך ולזרעך אחריך
את ארץ מגריך את כל־ארץ כנען לאחזת עולם

Exod 6:4

וגם הקמתי את־בריתי אתם
לתת להם
את־ארץ כנען את ארץ מגריהם אשר־גרו בה

---

40. Martin Noth, *Überlieferungsgeschichte des Pentateuch* (Stuttgart: Kohlhammer 1948), 16; Rudolf Smend, *Die Entstehung des Alten Testaments*, 4th ed. (Stuttgart: Kohlhammer, 1989), 58; Karl Elliger, "Sinn und Ursprung der priesterlichen Geschichtserzählung," *ZTK* 49 (1952): 121–43; Ralph W. Klein, "The Message of P," in *Die Botschaft und die Boten: Festschrift für Hans Walter Wolff zum 70. Geburtstag*, ed. Jörg Jeremias and Lothar Perlitt (Neukirchen-Vluyn: Neukirchener, 1981), 57–66.

41. David M. Carr, "The Moses Story: Literary-Historical Reflections," *HeBAI* 1 (2012): 27.

From the Call of Moses to the Parting of the Sea   151

P considered the promise of the land to Abraham, Isaac, and Jacob as fulfilled, something Köckert correctly emphasized[42] and the ונתתי in Gen 17
and לתת להם in Exod 6:4 prove. According to this, the expression "the
land in which they resided as aliens" does not mean that the land granted
to the patriarchs was something temporary. Should one agree with Köckert, Michaela Bauks, and others that the term אחזה in Gen 17:8 can be
understood as "privilege of use" (*Nutzungsrecht*),[43] the expression explains
itself against the backdrop of Lev 25:23–24: "the land is mine; with me you
are but aliens and tenants" (NRSV). YHWH alone owns the land, but he
allows his people to use it in perpetuity. In contrast to Dtr theology, the
Priestly understanding of the land-grant does not contain the expulsion of
other peoples and does not depend on obedience to the law.

When the land is mentioned for the second time in 6:8, אחזה is sub-
stituted by the expression מורשה. Does this mean that Exod 6:8 represents
a different perspective than 6:4 and that therefore this verse should be
assigned to a younger author as sometimes thought? First, it can be seen
that verse 8 changes the message of verse 4 in two ways. Instead of the conclusion of a covenant, it is mentioned that YHWH raises his hand, which
can probably be best understood as a gesture demonstrating the swearing
of an oath. This gesture expresses YHWH's committing himself to support
the patriarchs, just as the ברית in verse 4 had. Accordingly, it should be considered whether מורשה can be understood as a parallel expression of אחזה.

In contrast to what has been previously claimed, no tension exists
between verse 4 and verse 8, because in verse 8 the land had been given
to the patriarchs too. The phrasing as an oath can possibly be understood
as Priestly reception of the Dtr promise of land to the ancestors. Passages
like Deut 10:11; 11:9, 21, and 31:7 presume that the addressed generation
should take possession of the land that YHWH had already sworn to give

---

42. Matthias Köckert, "'Land' als theologisches Thema im Alten Testament," in
*Ex oriente Lux: Studien zur Theologie des Alten Testaments: Festschrift für Rüdiger Lux
zum 65. Geburstag*, ed. Angelika Berlejung and Raik Heckl, abg 39 (Leipzig: Evange-
lische Verlagsanstalt, 2012), 503–22. See also Jakob Wöhrle, "The Un-empty Land:
The Concept of Exile and Land in P," in *The Concept of Exile in Ancient Israel and Its
Historical Contexts*, ed. Ehud Ben Zvi and Christoph Levin, BZAW 404 (Berlin: de
Gruyter, 2010), 196–97, who points out that the P-texts Gen 28:4 and 35:12 presuppose that YHWH renews the land grant for each individual patriarch.

43. Michaela Bauks, "Die Begriffe מוֹרָשָׁה und אֲחֻזָּה in P^g: Überlegungen zur Landkonzeption in der Priestergrundschrift," *ZAW* 116 (2004): 171–88; Nihan, *Torah*, 66–68.

152 Thomas Römer

to their ancestors (אשר נשבע יהוה לאבתיכם).[44] The closest literal matches with Exod 6:8 can, however, be found in Ezek 20:42, which also uses the expression "to raise one's hand."[45]

Ezek 20:42

וידעתם כי־ <u>אני יהוה</u>
בהביאי אתכם אל־אדמת ישראל
אל־הארץ אשר נשאתי את־ידי לתת אותה
לאבותיכם

Exod 6:8

והבאתי אתכם
אל־הארץ אשר נשאתי את־ידי לתת אתה
לאברהם ליצחק וליעקב
ונתתי אתה לכם מורשה
<u>אני יהוה</u>

In this way, P would have transferred the promise of land to the ancestors in Egypt, as recorded in Deuteronomy and Ezekiel, to the patriarchs. This transfer would have presumably been undertaken in order to emphasize the connection of the two traditions of Israel's origin (as it is also done in Deut 1:8; 30:20 and other verses assigned to the Pentateuch redaction).[46]

The combination of the motif of the promise of the land to the ancestors in Egypt and to the patriarchs is unique to the conception of P in Exodus. The Priestly texts in Numbers present a different conception of the land. Jaeyoung Jeon analyzes the accounts of the scouts (Num 13–14), of Moses's death outside the land (Num 20; 27), and of the distribution of the land (Num 32–36) and shows that no connection is made with the patriarchs narrative in which the land was an unconditional promise.[47] On

---

44. Deuteronomy 11:19 adds "their seed"; see also the tables in Thomas Römer, *Israels Väter: Untersuchungen zur Väterthematik im Deuteronomiumundin der deuteronomistischen Tradition*, OBO 99 (Göttingen: Vandenhoeck & Ruprecht, 1990), 13.

45. נשא יד to describe a gesture of swearing can be seen mostly in Ezekiel; see Römer, *Israels Väter*, 504–6, and Johan Lust, *Traditie, redactie en kerygma bij Ezechiel: Een analyse van Ez., xx, 1–26* (Brussel: Paleis der Academiën, 1969), 218–22.

46. The identification of the אבות with the patriarchs in the book of Deuteronomy is the work of a pentateuchal redaction.

47. Jaeyoung Jeon, "The Promise of the Land and the Extent of P," *ZAW* 130 (2018): 513–28.

From the Call of Moses to the Parting of the Sea   153

the contrary, the land is presented in Numbers as conditional on compliance with the covenant, as in the Dtr texts. According to Jeon, the focus shifts to the exiles who are reluctant to return to the land. In texts of the book of Ezekiel, Babylonia is indeed seen as a desert (cf. Ezek 19:13) so that the exodus would become a metaphor for the political situation of the Persian era (cf. also Ezek 20). Following the same metaphor, it is possible that the motif of Egypt nostalgia, which is also found in Numbers, could serve the same purpose.[48]

The lexeme מורשה in Exod 6:8, which is not often attested in the Hebrew Bible and mostly in the book of Ezekiel,[49] refers to Ezek 33:24, in which Abraham, having previously possessed the land, is correlated with the claim to the land of the population of Judah that was not deported:

אחד היה אברהם ויירש את־הארץ ואנחנו רבים לנו נתנה הארץ למורשה

If the statement found in Ezek 33:24 represents a kind of proverbial demand of the people who remained in the land, it is possible that this demand must also be seen behind Exod 6:8.[50] In the context of an early Persian Priestly source, the promise to lead Israel into the land seems to be an update of the gift of the land to the patriarchs. Now, did P report the fulfilling of this promise? For Pola, Exod 19:1 presents the fulfillment of Exod 6:8: "The arrival of the people from the exodus to Mount Sinai, which is understood in Exod 19:1 as Zion, signifies in this short verse the entire depiction of the 'conquest of the land.'"[51] Whether this allegory was obvious for the addressees of Exod 19:1 is unclear. Pola's reference to Exod 29:45–46 is interesting, however. According to Exod 6:7 the prevailing aim of exodus is the acceptance of Israel as YHWH's people and Israel's realization that YHWH is their God. YHWH's speech in Exod 29:45–46, which summarizes the meaning of the sacrificial cult, corresponds to this: "I will dwell among the Israelites, and I will be their God. And they shall know

---

48. On Egypt nostalgia, see Thomas Römer, "Egypt Nostalgia in Exodus 14–Numbers 21," in *Torah and the Book of Numbers*, ed. Christian Frevel, Thomas Pola, and Aaron Schart, FAT 62 (Tübingen: Mohr Siebeck, 2013), 66–86.

49. Exodus 6:8; Deut 33:4; Ezek 11:5; 25:4, 10; 33:24; 36:2, 5; see also מורש in Isa 14:23; Obad 17; Job 17:11.

50. Gosse understands Exod 6:8 to be an answer to Ezek 33:24; see Bernard Gosse, "Exode 6,8 comme réponse à Ezéchiel 33,24," *RHPR* 74 (1994): 241–47.

51. Pola, *Die ursprüngliche Priesterschrift*, 348.

154 Thomas Römer

that I am YHWH their God, who brought them out of the land of Egypt that I might dwell among them; I am YHWH their God" (adapted from NRSV). This would mean that in contrast to the Deuteronomic perception, the land has neither geopolitical or geotheological meaning for P, but it rather provides the frame in which the true cult of God can be realized. The transposition of the tabernacle in the desert provides no reason to date P^G before the consecration of the second temple in Jerusalem. P's intention is rather to embed all of the important elements of the worship of YHWH (Sabbath, circumcision, Pesach, cult) into the prehistory of the world and into the origin of the people of Israel. Whoever likes to speculate can raise the question of whether the transposition of the tabernacle into the desert, so to speak in a no man's land, does not indeed represent a certain neutral attitude regarding the localization of the shrine: is this a discrete acceptance of the fact that a sacrificial cult to YHWH existed not only in Jerusalem but also on Mount Garizim? Accordingly, it is possible that the original Priestly source ended in the Sinai pericope and did not recount the conquest of the land, as—we might add—was also presumed in traditional delineations (Gen 1–Deut 34*). However, this does not mean that P ignored any knowledge of such a tradition; rather, P presumed its addressees familiarity with such a tradition. Thus, the question of Priestly texts in the book of Joshua should be reopened in this context. Do these belong to a consistent Hexateuch redaction that sought to emphasize that the book of Joshua belongs to the Torah, or are they—as Albertz has suggested[52]—an attempt to adapt the book of Joshua into the canon?

2.5. Exodus 6:1–12 and Ezekiel

The similarity of Exod 6:8 and Ezekiel was mentioned above, and it has often been observed that Exod 6:1–12 generally contains many links to Ezekiel. These will not be discussed in detail here.[53]

It is certain that P and Ezek 20 share the opinion that YHWH's self-revelation to his people took place in Egypt for the first time (cf. ידע *niphal*

---

52. Rainer Albertz, "The Canonical Alignment of the Book of Joshua," in *Judah and the Judeans in the Fourth Century B.C.E.*, ed. Oded Lipschits, Gary N. Knoppers, and Rainer Albertz (Winona Lake, IN: Eisenbrauns, 2007), 287–303.

53. Peter Weimar, *Untersuchungen zur priesterschriftlichen Exodusgeschichte*, FB 9 (Würzburg: Echter, 1973); Schmidt, *Exodus*, 280–85; Gertz, *Tradition und Redaktion in der Exoduserzählung*, 245–48, and especially Lust, *Traditie*.

From the Call of Moses to the Parting of the Sea   155

in Exod 2:25 [LXX]; 6:3 and Ezek 20:5; as well as the almost identical opening of the speech: אני יהוה in Exod 6:2 and אני יהוה אלהיכם in Exod 20:5; furthermore the continuation of the YHWH speech with the promise of the exodus from Egypt [יצא, *hiphil*] in Exod 6:6–7 and Ezek 20:5). The Israelites' not hearing also appears in both texts: לא שמע in Exod 6:9 and לא אבו לשמע in Ezek 20:8. However, the historical retrospect in Ezek 20 has its own profile. The link between the patriarchs and the exodus claimed in P appears neither in Ezek 20 nor in any other texts of the book of Ezekiel. Ezekiel 20:5 references the "seed of the house of Jacob" that was in Egypt, which apparently presupposes the tradition of Jacob's immigration to Egypt; the three patriarchs, however, never appear together in Ezekiel. Abraham is mentioned in Ezek 33:24; Jacob appears as YHWH's servant and the recipient of the land in Ezek 28:25 and 37:25, as well as in 39:25.[54] Apparently the redactors of Ezekiel did not possess the same interests in the patriarchs as did P.

These observed parallels and differences between Ezekiel and Exod 6 (and other P texts) raise the question of the socioliterary classification of the tradents of P and Ezekiel. Is it possible to stand by Jan Christian Gertz's assumption that, "in addition to formulations from the 'Ezekiel tradition,' P itself was also able to fall back on those from the non-Priestly accounts,"[55] or should P be considered to have been written and edited by writers who were in contact with some group of people who were commissioned to edit the Ezekiel scroll? This question must remain unanswered here. It compels us to undertake a more intense analysis of the material and the specific situations behind the formation of the protobiblical scrolls.

3. The Priestly Competition with the Magicians in Exodus 7–9

Following the Priestly introduction of the quarrel between the pharaoh, Moses, and Aaron in Exod 7:1–7, which presumes and advances the narrative in 6:1–12 (cf. the "mighty acts of judgment" in 6:6 and 7:4), a broad consensus exists regarding the extent of the Priestly narration preserved in Exod 7–9. Priestly material can be identified in 7:8–13, 19–20a, 21b, 22; 8:1–3, 11aγb, 12–15; 9:8–12, which most likely comes to an end in 11:10. This verse sums up once more the wonders of Moses and Aaron,

---

54. For this, see Römer, *Israels Väter*, 506–17.
55. Gertz, *Tradition und Redaktion in der Exoduserzählung*, 249.

156 Thomas Römer

as well as the obstinacy of the pharaoh, which also fulfills the prediction in 7:4.

According to Kratz, these narratives do not belong to the original Priestly exodus narrative because of the breadth of their presentation and their "concurrency" with the narration of the parting of the sea.[56] A certain randomness adheres to this argumentation; it is not obvious to me that the narrative material about the confrontation with the king of Egypt contradicts the narrative of the parting of the sea in Exod 14*. Rather, they can best be understood as transition to this story.

Recently, Jeon has developed the idea that the Priestly competition with the magicians might, like Exod 6:1–12, depend on traditions in Ezekiel, especially Ezek 29–32.[57] Thus, the "serpent" or "dragon" תנין of Exod 7:9–10 is also found in Ezek 29:2–6a and 32:1–8 associated with Egypt, darkness, and blood in a cosmic mythological scenario (water, earth, sky). In addition, the hardening of the heart is expressed differently in P-texts and Ezekiel by the rare expressions קשה (Exod 7:3; Ezek 2:7) or חזק (Exod 7:13, 22; 8:15; 9:12, 35; 10:20, 27; 11:10; Ezek 3:7) + לב than in non-P texts כבד (Exod 7:14; 8:11, 28; 9:7, 34; 10:1) + לב.

The five scenes, of which the first four can more readily be characterized as "evidentiary miracles" (*Erweiswunder*) than as plagues, are constructed in a parallel way and contain a clearly recognizable line of narration:[58] the Egyptian magicians, who can generally keep up with Moses and Aaron,[59] finally have to admit that the god whom they do not know is stronger than their arts and powers. The elimination of the Egyptian magical-priests from the core of the narrative, as has been occasionally suggested, would render this story superfluous because, as Gertz has correctly commented,

---

56. Kratz, *Composition*, 244–46.

57. Jaeyoung Jeon, "A Source of P? The Priestly Exodus Account and the Book of Ezekiel," *Sem* 58 (2016): 77–92.

58. John Van Seters, "A Contest of Magicians? The Plague Stories in P," in *Pomegranates and Golden Bells: Studies in Biblical, Jewish, and Near Eastern Ritual, Law, and Literature in Honor of Jacob Milgrom*, ed. David P. Wright, David Noel Freedman, and Avi Hurvitz (Winona Lake, IN: Eisenbrauns, 1995), 569–80; Thomas Römer, "Competing Magicians in Exodus 7–9: Interpreting Magic in Priestly Theology," in *Magic in the Biblical World: From the Rod of Aaron to the Ring of Solomon*, ed. Todd E. Klutz, JSNTSup 245 (London: T&T Clark, 2003), 12–22.

59. Thus, one should consider (with Berner, *Die Exoduserzählung*, 184) whether the statement in 7:12b that emphasizes the superiority of Aaron's staff should be understood as a gloss.

"the priestly account of the plagues lives only from the competition with the magicians."[60]

The five scenes are constructed in a parallel way and can be read as a single narrative without any problems:

	Snakes	Blood	Frogs	Gnats	Boils
YHWH said:					
"Speak to Aaron"	7:9	7:19	8:1	8:12	
"Take your staff"	7:9	7:19	8:1[61]	8:12	
"Stretch out your hand"		7:19	8:1		
Miracle to be executed	7:9	7:19	8:1	8:12	9:8–9
Execution and	7:10	7:20	8:2	8:13	9:10
results		7:21b	8:2	8:13	9:10
Actions of the Egyptian	7:11	7:22	8:3	8:14	
magicians and results	7:12a		8:3	8:14–15	9:11
Hardening of Pharaoh's	7:13	7:22		8:15	9:12
heart and his not listening	7:13	7:22	8:11b[62]	8:15	9:12

7:1 YHWH said to Moses, "See, I have made you like God to Pharaoh, and your brother Aaron shall be your prophet. 2 You shall speak all that I command you, and your brother Aaron shall tell Pharaoh to let the Israelites go out of his land. 3 But I will harden Pharaoh's heart, and I will multiply my signs and wonders in the land of Egypt. 4 When Pharaoh does not listen to you, I will lay my hand upon Egypt and bring my people the Israelites, company by company, out of the land of Egypt by great acts of judgment. 5 The Egyptians shall know that I am YHWH, when I stretch out my hand against Egypt and bring the Israelites out from among them." 6 Moses and Aaron did so; they did just as YHWH commanded them. 7 Moses was eighty years old and Aaron eighty-three when they spoke to Pharaoh.

a. 8 YHWH said to Moses and Aaron, 9 "When Pharaoh says to you, 'Perform a wonder,' then you shall say to Aaron, 'Take your staff and throw it down before Pharaoh, and it will become a snake.'" 10 So Moses

---

60. Gertz, *Tradition und Redaktion in der Exoduserzählung*, 82 n. 24. For the elimination of the Egyptian priests, see e.g., Christoph Levin, *Der Jahwist*, FRLANT 157 (Göttingen: Vandenhoeck & Ruprecht, 1993), 336.

61. "Stretch out you hand with your staff."

62. The note about the hardening of pharaoh's heart is missing, probably due to the connection with the non-Priestly v. 11a*.

and Aaron went to Pharaoh and did as YHWH had commanded; Aaron threw down his staff before Pharaoh and his officials, and it became a snake. 11 Then Pharaoh summoned the wise men and the sorcerers; and they also, the magicians of Egypt, did the same by their secret arts. 12 Each one threw down his staff, and they became snakes; [but Aaron's staff swallowed up theirs]. 13 Still Pharaoh's heart was hardened, and he would not listen to them, as YHWH had said.

b. 19 YHWH said to Moses, "Say to Aaron, 'Take your staff and stretch out your hand over the waters of Egypt—over its rivers, its canals, and its ponds, and all its pools of water—so that they may become blood; and there shall be blood throughout the whole land of Egypt, even in vessels of wood and in vessels of stone.'" 20* Moses and Aaron did just as YHWH commanded. 21* And there was blood throughout the whole land of Egypt. 22 But the magicians of Egypt did the same by their secret arts; so Pharaoh's heart remained hardened, and he would not listen to them; as YHWH had said.

c. 8:1 And YHWH said to Moses, "Say to Aaron, 'Stretch out your hand with your staff over the rivers, the canals, and the pools, and make frogs come up on the land of Egypt.'" 6 So Aaron stretched out his hand over the waters of Egypt; and the frogs came up and covered the land of Egypt. 7 But the magicians did the same by their secret arts, and brought frogs up on the land of Egypt. 11* Pharaoh did not listen to them, just as YHWH had said.

d. 12 Then YHWH said to Moses, "Say to Aaron, 'Stretch out your staff and strike the dust of the earth, so that it may become gnats throughout the whole land of Egypt.'" 13 And they did so; Aaron stretched out his hand with his staff and struck the dust of the earth, and gnats came on humans and animals alike; all the dust of the earth turned into gnats throughout the whole land of Egypt. 14 The magicians tried to produce gnats by their secret arts, but they could not. There were gnats on both humans and animals. 15 And the magicians said to Pharaoh, "This is the finger of a god!" But Pharaoh's heart was hardened, and he would not listen to them, just as YHWH had said.

e. 9:8 Then YHWH said to Moses and Aaron, "Take handfuls of soot from the kiln, and let Moses throw it in the air in the sight of Pharaoh. 9 It shall become fine dust all over the land of Egypt, and shall cause festering boils on humans and animals throughout the whole land of Egypt." 10 So they took soot from the kiln, and stood before Pharaoh, and Moses threw it in the air, and it caused festering boils on humans and animals. 11 The magicians could not stand before Moses because of the boils, for the boils afflicted the magicians as well as all the Egyptians. 12 But YHWH hardened the heart of Pharaoh, and he would not listen to them, just as YHWH had spoken to Moses.

From the Call of Moses to the Parting of the Sea   159

11:10 Moses and Aaron performed all these wonders before Pharaoh; but YHWH hardened Pharaoh's heart, and he did not let the people of Israel go out of his land.

Christoph Berner also notes this methodical and elaborate structure. He concludes, however, that this does not permit the exegete to identify an author's compositional will, "but rather the case proves that editing processes, no matter how small, are anything but arbitrary."[63] Here, the methodological question arises as to whether it is more plausible to attribute a narrative to five or more selectively acting redactors, who were able to arrive at a surprisingly cogent narrative, rather than to ascribe a coherent and tension-free story to a single author.

The aforementioned episodes about the quarrel with the Egyptian magical-priests can be understood as a single narration without any problem.[64] In my opinion, its intention and objective become more obvious if you read these scenes in succession, which would contradict the supposition that these passages can be ascribed to one (Van Seters) or several (Berner) Priestly redactions.[65] It is indeed quite astounding that redactors editing an older text would do this in such a way that their insertions into the text produce an independently sensible context. When considering the Dtr redactions in the Former Prophets, we can see that this is not correct. The narrations about the dispute suitably match the Priestly context in terms of contents and theology.

In Exod 7:1 YHWH appoints Moses as אלהים, in contradistinction to the divine pharaoh, and Aaron as his prophet, who therefore equals the Egyptian magical-priests. This matches the constellation of the narrative about the dispute. After the Egyptian magicians fail to keep up in the fourth round, Aaron also takes a step back in the final scene;[66] now it is Moses who uses soot from a kiln to produce abscesses that affect all of

---

63. Berner, *Die Exoduserzählung*, 168 n. 2.

64. In 8:11 the P-note about the hardening of pharaoh's heart is missing, which can be explained by the connection to the non-Priestly narration (cf., Gertz, *Tradition und Redaktion in der Exoduserzählung*, 87). One might also consider whether the authors submitted themselves to some rigid system of conformity.

65. Van Seters, "Contest of Magicians?," 569–80; as well as the criticism of Gertz, *Tradition und Redaktion in der Exoduserzählung*, 85–89. See also Berner, *Die Exoduserzählung*.

66. See also Michaela Bauks, "Das Dämonische im Menschen: Einige Anmerkungen zur priesterschriftlichen Theologie (Ex 7–14)," in *Die Dämonen—Demons: Die Dämonologie der israelitisch-jüdischenundfrühchristlichen Literatur im Kontextihrer*

160 Thomas Römer

the Egyptians, even the magicians, as explicitly stated. If it were true that the plague of the killing of the first-born (Exod 12) was not recounted in P[G],[67] one might identify the end of the original Priestly cycle of plagues in 9:8–12. Then the mighty acts of judgment announced in 7:4 would refer to this scene. This question shall however remain unanswered at this point. The explicit declaration in 9:12 that YHWH can harden pharaoh's heart can be understood as the fulfillment of Exod 7:3 and transition to 11:10 and 14:4, 8.

In the fourth scene the magician-priests admit their inefficacy with the statement: "this is the finger of (a) God" (8:15). This widely-discussed expression[68] probably refers primarily to Aaron's staff; it might, however, also be explained in the Priestly context as an allusion to Moses's elohim-role in Exod 7:1. The exclamation of the Egyptian magicians should also be understood in the context of the Priestly revelation-theology, according to which YHWH is only available as elohim to the all peoples who cannot claim Abraham as their ancestor.

The Priestly narrative in Exod 7–9* therefore fits the context of Exod 6–7* and 14*, but also has a certain characteristic profile. Consequently, one might ask whether P possessed a written *Vorlage* or knew oral tradition, a question that is not broadly discussed in contemporary research. Such a *Vorlage* is sometimes believed to have existed for the Priestly account of creation in Gen 1.[69] For Exod 7–9, Blum recalled Joseph Reindl's thesis that, in this case, we find a narrative from the Egyptian diaspora that sought to depict YHWH's and his servants' superiority vis-à-vis the Egyptian magicians.[70] The parallels with Egyptian magical fairy-tales and also the expression חרטמים, which appears in the fifth scene (7:22; 8:3, 14–15;

Umwelt, ed. Armin Lange, Hermann Lichtenberger, and K. F. Diethard Römheld (Tübingen: Mohr Siebeck, 2003), 244–45.

67. See Jean-Louis Ska, "La sortie d'Egypte (Ex 7–14) dans le récit sacerdotal et la tradition prophétique," *Bib* 60 (1979): 191–215.

68. Bernard Couroyer, "Le 'doigt de Dieu' (Exode, VIII, 15)," *RB* 63 (1956): 481–95.

69. See on this question also Jürg Hutzli, "Tradition and Interpretation in Gen 1:1–2:4a," *JHS* 10/12 (2010): 1–22.

70. Blum, *Studien zur Komposition des Pentateuch*, 252; Joseph Reindl, "Der Finger Gottes und die Macht der Götter: Ein Problem des ägyptischen Diasporajudentums und sein literarischer Niederschlag," in *Dienst der Vermittlung: Festschrift Priesterseminar Erfurt*, ed. Wilhelm Ernst, Konrad Feiereis, and Fritz Hoffmann, Erfurter Theologische Studien 37 (Leipzig: St. Benno Verlag, 1977), 49–60.

From the Call of Moses to the Parting of the Sea   161

9:22) and apparently is an Egyptian loanword which only appears in the Hebrew Bible in contexts of the diaspora (Gen 41:8, 24, and Dan 1:20; 2:2), could speak in favor of such a hypothesis. It remains questionable, however, to what extent such a *Vorlage* could be literarily reconstructed if Exod 7–9* P requires the context of Exod 1–15. Nevertheless, the question of possible sources or *Vorlagen* for P should not be neglected.

4. The Priestly Depiction of the Parting of the Sea in Exodus 14

The Priestly version of the parting of the sea in Exod 14 confirms the examination of Exod 7–9*. The analysis of this text, which has traditionally been regarded as an exemplary text for source criticism, has achieved a broad consensus regarding the determination of the Priestly elements, just as in Exod 7–9*. The question as to what extent traces of *Fortschreibungen* can be identified within the P portions[71] will not be discussed here. It is, however, notable that the parts that had been identified as P (here, I am relying roughly on Levin's reconstruction) fit into a coherent narrative:

14:1 Then YHWH said to Moses: 2* Tell the Israelites to turn back and camp in front of Pi-hahiroth, between Migdol and the sea, in front of Baal-zephon. 3 Pharaoh will say of the Israelites, "They are wandering aimlessly in the land; the wilderness has closed in on them." 4 I will harden Pharaoh's heart, and he will pursue them, so that I will gain glory for myself over Pharaoh and all his army; and the Egyptians shall know that I am YHWH. And they did so. 8 YHWH hardened the heart of Pharaoh king of Egypt and he pursued the Israelites, who went out with hands raised. 9 The Egyptians pursued them, all Pharaoh's horses and chariots, his chariot drivers and his army; they overtook them camped by the sea, by Pi-hahiroth, in front of Baal-zephon. 10a As Pharaoh drew near, the Israelites looked back, and there were the Egyptians advancing on them. 15* Then YHWH said to Moses, "Tell the Israelites to go forward. 16* But you stretch out your hand over the sea and divide it, that the Israelites may go into the sea on dry ground. 17 Then I will harden the hearts of the Egyptians so that they will go in after them; and so I will gain glory for myself over Pharaoh and all his army, his chariots, and his chariot drivers. 18 And the Egyptians shall know that I am YHWH, when I have gained glory for myself over Pharaoh, his chariots, and his chariot drivers." 21a* Then Moses stretched out his hand over the sea.

---

71. See, e.g., Levin, *Der Jahwist*, 345.

162   Thomas Römer

21b And the waters were divided. 22 The Israelites went into the sea on dry ground, the waters forming a wall for them on their right and on their left. 23 The Egyptians pursued, and went into the sea after them, all of Pharaoh's horses, chariots, and chariot drivers.
26 Then YHWH said to Moses, "Stretch out your hand over the sea, so that the water may come back upon the Egyptians, upon their chariots and chariot drivers." 27a So Moses stretched out his hand over the sea. 28 The waters returned and covered the chariots and the chariot drivers, the entire army of Pharaoh that had followed them into the sea; not one of them remained. 29 But the Israelites walked on dry ground through the sea, the waters forming a wall for them on their right and on their left.

The repetitions within the Priestly narrative that have sometimes been criticized do not necessarily have to be categorized into various layers; a similar redundancy can also be found in Gen 17. Furthermore, Thomas Krüger commented correctly that three scenes can be differentiated in the Priestly narration of Exod 14: "With the repeated announcement and execution in 14:1–10,* 15–23, and 26–29* [P] demonstrates YHWH's sovereign control of events."[72] In contrast to the non-Priestly version—traditionally considered as a pre-Priestly version (J or D) but according to Berner a post-Priestly D redaction[73]—the Priestly depiction of the parting of the sea is deliberately constructed as a myth. Knauf correctly states that "for P the passage through the sea is not historical but a prehistoric, mythical fact. In it the creation of Israel ... comes to a conclusion."[74] At this point a literary observation also becomes relevant. In the same way that Exod 6 deliberately refers back to Gen 17, Exod 14 P obviously casts a line back to Gen 1 (and also to Gen 7–8 P), and thereby draws a parallel between the creation of the world and the creation of Israel:[75] in this way היבשה appears in Exod

---

72. Thomas Krüger, "Erwägungen zur Redaktion der Meerwundererzählung (Exodus 13,17– 14,31)," *ZAW* 108 (1996): 521.

73. Berner points out a link between Exod 14:13, 19a, 30, and Deut 20:1–4. According to him, the non-P texts would presuppose the P stratum. Thus, the function of the cloud in the mobile armies in 14:19b, 20, 24a is a comment on 14:10a; 14:9aα repeats the formula of 14:8aβ; and finally 14:25b would build on 14:4, 18. Christoph Berner, "Gab es einen vorpriesterlichen Meerwunderbericht?," *Bib* 95 (2014): 1–25.

74. Ernst Axel Knauf, "Der Exodus zwischen Mythos und Geschichte: Zur priesterschriftlichen Rezeption der Schilfmeer-Geschichte in Ex 14," in *Schriftauslegung in der Schrift: Festschrift für Odil Hannes Steck zu seinem 65. Geburtstag*, ed. Reinhard G. Kratz, Thomas Krüger, and Konrad Schmid (Berlin: de Gruyter, 2000), 77.

75. This is clearly shown by Jean-Louis Ska, *Le passage de la mer: Etude sur la*

From the Call of Moses to the Parting of the Sea   163

14:16, 22, and 29 and in Gen 1:9–10, where the dry land builds the necessary basis for the life-forms about to be created. Also the expression בתוך הים in Exod 14:16, 22–23, 27,[76] and 29 reminds the reader of בתוך המים in Gen 1:6 where the firmament appears in the middle of the water. The parting of the sea (בקע) in Exod 14:21 reminds the reader of the parting of the deep in Gen 1:6 (there however with בדל); the root appears in Gen 7:11 where the wells of the deep open up. As in Gen 1, in which God's word is the primary agent of creation, YHWH's word in Exod 14 P is the reason for Israel's being able to march through the parted sea. In this way, with the help of Exod 14, P accomplishes a theological and literary *inclusio* with Gen 1. The textual hinges of Gen 1:17; Exod 6; and 14 underscore the connection of the protohistory, the patriarchs, and the exodus. The creation of the world fulfills a double objective for P: the "birth" of Israel as YHWH's people in Exod 14, and the erection of the tabernacle in the desert as a place of encounter between YHWH and Israel in Exod 25–31* and 35–40* (in these chapters the allusions to Gen 1:1–2:3 are obvious as well).

5. Conclusion

This analysis of Exod 6:7–9 and 14 demonstrated that these texts belonged to what was originally an independent Priestly source. By clearly referring back to Gen 1 and Gen 17, they create a strong connection to the traditions of the book of Genesis and thereby design a protohistory consisting of three parts. Exodus 6 can be more readily understood as an independent version of Moses's calling in Exod 3 than as its redaction. Exodus 7–9 and 14 P can be read and understood more easily when connected to each other than in their current literary context; this datum also favors the assumption of an originally independent document. Proponents of redaction-historical hypotheses, however, are right when they say that P's narrative strand cannot be reconstructed in its entirety. This means that in all likelihood not all texts were kept when the Priestly source was edited. The idea that literary criticism can reconstruct every source and older tradition word for word is based on the anachronistic assumption that these texts possessed a kind of canonical status from the time of

---

construction du style et de la symbolique d'Ex 14,1–31, AnBib 109 (Rome: Pontifical Institute, 1986).

76. This part of this verse does not belong to P. The expression is used here to describe YHWH's destruction of the Egyptians in the sea.

164 Thomas Römer

their initial composition. The fact that the authors of P were familiar with the non-P traditions and even sometimes inserted something or reinterpreted does not necessarily prove redaction-critically oriented models; as Knauf informally, but correctly, noted: "In the small circle of the Jerusalem elite, from which both versions originated, people knew each other, were kin and related by marriage."[77] Ehud Ben Zvi goes even further with his postulation of a group of literati in the temple of Jerusalem in the Persian period that undertook the maintenance and editing of most of the protobiblical writing and that was capable of imitating and mixing various styles and ideas.[78] This assumption does not do justice to the complex structure of the texts, though it can be understood as a warning not to multiply the redactors and tradents ad infinitum. It is, for example, probable that the tradents of P were also involved in the process of editing the Ezekiel scroll and were familiar with other non-riestly scrolls. The compilation and promulgation of the Pentateuch is possibly the best example for the close collaboration of the presumably small, intellectual groups that consisted of priests and other members of the Judean (and Samaritan) elite.

---

77. Knauf, "Der Exodus zwischen Mythos und Geschichte," 83.

78. Ehud Ben Zvi, "Observations on Prophetic Characters, Prophetic Texts, Priests of Old, Persian Period Priests and Literati," in *The Priests in the Prophets: The Portrayal of Priests, Prophets and Other Religious Specialists in the Latter Prophets*, ed. Lester L. Grabbe and Alice Ogden Bellis, JSOTSup 408 (London: T&T Clark, 2004), 19–30.

The Priestly Writing and Deuteronomy in the Book of Leviticus: On the Integration of Deuteronomy in the Pentateuch

Eckart Otto

European pentateuchal scholarship that has developed particularly in the German-speaking world since the Newer Documentary Hypothesis of the nineteenth century and its revisions by redating texts (mostly late dates of a Yahwist) in the twentieth century has been recently lamented by Bernard M. Levinson and Jeffrey Stackert as a hindrance rather than progress in pentateuchal research. Though they accept that Deuteronomy has a key role in the reconstruction of the literary history of the Pentateuch, Levinson and Stackert believe that

> within recent academic discussion, the prominence afforded Deuteronomy in literary reconstructions of the Pentateuch has been accompanied by and even has motivated in part a significant challenge to the classical Documentary Hypothesis. Especially in Europe, some scholars have sought to offer new explanations for the compositional history of the Pentateuch that represent a sharp break from previous Documentary approaches. Yet these new theories have not produced the robust discussion across the 'geography' of biblical scholarship necessary to move the field forward. With few notable exceptions, scholars of the English-speaking world have not responded to the European critiques lodged against Documentary models and have even moved away from pentateuchal studies.[1]

---

1. So Bernard M. Levinson and Jeffrey Stackert, "Between the Covenant Code and Esarhaddon's Succession Treaty: Deuteronomy 13 and the Composition of Deuteronomy," *JAJ* 3 (2012): 123–24. A glance at positive reactions from various English speaking scholars to introductions to the literary history of the Hebrew Bible—Jean Louis Ska, *Introduction à la lecture du Pentateuque: Clés pour l'interprétation des*

166   Eckart Otto

I share the conviction with these authors that Deuteronomy and its relationship to the Tetrateuch has a key function in pentateuchal research;
this is also recognized by the advocates of the New Documentary Hypothesis. So, for example, for Joel S. Baden, the reception of the sources of the
Yahwist and especially the Elohist independently of one another in Deuteronomy supports the thesis that there was no Jehovist who combined these
sources before their reception in Deuteronomy, as was advocated by Julius
Wellhausen and numerous other proponents of the Newer Documentary
Hypothesis.[2] According to Baden, the purpose of Deuteronomy was to
replace the Elohist source to which the Book of the Covenant belonged.
However, against the proposals of Levinson and Stackert, the law code of
Deuteronomy in Deut 12–26* did not have the function of repealing and
suppressing the Book of the Covenant.[3] Rather, the Book of the Covenant
was not repealed but was interpreted with Deuteronomy as a hermeneutical key and supplemented especially by family laws.[4]

If it can already be demonstrated that it is unlikely that there is a relationship of abrogation between the legal portions of Deuteronomy and

---

cinque premiers livres de la Bible (Brüssel: Lessius, 2000), 188–34; Félix Garçía López,
El Pentateuco: Introducción a la lectura de los cincos primeros libros de la Biblia, Introducción al estudio de la Biblia 3a (Estella: Verbo Divino, 2003), 50–56; Jan Christian Gertz, Angelika Berlejung, Konrad Schmid, and Markus Witte, eds., *T&T Clark
Handbook of the Old Testament: An Introduction to the Literature, Religion and History
of the Old Testament* (London: T&T Clark, 2012), 237–50; and Konrad Schmid, *Literaturgeschichte des Alten Testaments: Eine Einführung* (Darmstadt: Wissenschaftliche
Buchgesellschaft, 2008), esp. 101–8, 137–39, 172–76—shows that this characterization
of the state of the discussion is rather one-sided and stands to serve as an advance-
ment of the New Documentary Hypothesis as an alternative to European pentateuchal
scholarship. The New Documentary Hypothesis, however, is viewed overwhelmingly
critically by European scholars.

2. See Joel S. Baden, *J, E, and the Redaction of the Pentateuch*, FAT 68 (Tübingen:
Mohr Siebeck, 2009), 99–195.

3. Eckart Otto, "*Ersetzen* oder *Ergänzen* von Gesetzen in der Rechtshermeneutik
des Pentateuch," in *Die Tora: Studien zum Pentateuch; Gesammelte Aufsätze*, BZAR 9
(Wiesbaden: Harrassowitz, 2009), 248–56. See Bernard M. Levinson, *Deuteronomy
and the Hermeneutics of Legal Innovation* (Oxford: Oxford University Press, 1997),
144–59; see Jeffrey Stackert, *Rewriting the Torah: Literary Revision in Deuteronomy
and the Holiness Legislation*, FAT 52 (Tübingen: Mohr Siebeck, 2007), 208–25.

4. See Eckart Otto, *Deuteronomium 12,1–23,15*, HKAT (Freiburg: Herder, 2016),
1082–107; Otto, *Das Deuteronomium: Politische Theologie und Rechtsreform in Juda
und Assyrien*, BZAW 284 (Berlin: De Gruyter, 1999), 236–351.

The Priestly Writing and Deuteronomy in the Book of Leviticus   167

the Sinai pericope[5]—which, in any case, would not have been effective because the Book of the Covenant, the Holiness Code, and Deuteronomy all now stand alongside one another combined in the same Pentateuch—then the same applies all the more for an Elohist source, because no text can be presented that intends to abolish the Elohist. This is not surprising, however, as even the existence of such a source remains more than doubtful.[6] In contrast to Deuteronomy, the Priestly writing was completely independent of the other sources, which further emphasizes the importance that Deuteronomy has for the advocates of the New Documentary Hypothesis. In fact, this hypothesis is right to correct the neglect of Deuteronomy in attempts in the late twentieth century to overcome the Wellhausen-Kuenen four-source hypothesis in that it continues to follow Martin Noth's thesis of a Deuteronomistic History.[7] It accepts the isolation of the literary history of Deuteronomy from that of the Tetrateuch, a view already incipient with Wellhausen's source hypothesis and which came to a high point with Noth. Therein a Deuteronomistic and Priestly composition of the Tetrateuch are each seen as an extended prologue to the Deuteronomistic History.[8] Already with Noth's thesis, according to which

---

5. See John Collins, "Changing Scripture," in *Changes in Scripture: Rewriting and Interpreting Authoritative Traditions in the Second Temple Period*, ed. Hanne von Weissenberg, Juha Pakkala, and Marko Martilla, BZAW 419 (Berlin: De Gruyter, 2011), 24–28, who confirms an interpretation of the relationship between Deuteronomy and the Book of the Covenant, following Hindy Najman, *Seconding Sinai. The Development of Mosaic Discourse in Second Temple Judaism*, JSJSup 77 (Leiden: Brill, 2003), 22–29, which I had advocated at the Annual Meeting of the Society of Biblical Literature in Washington, DC in 1993, and which I published in 1996; see Eckart Otto, "The Pre-exilic Deuteronomy as a Revision of the Covenant Code," in *Kontinuum und Proprium: Studien zur Sozial- und Rechtsgeschichte im Alten Orient und im Alten*, Orientalia Biblica et Christiana 8 (Wiesbaden: Harrassowitz, 1996), 112–22.

6. On this, see my review of *J, E, and the Redaction of the Pentateuch*, by Joel Baden, *ZAR* 15 (2009): 451–55.

7. See the research history, which is traced in Eckart Otto, *Deuteronomium 1,1–11,32*, HKAT (Freiburg: Herder, 2012), 33–230 and, most recently, Erhard Blum, "Das exilische deuteronomistische Geschichtswerk," in *Das deuteronomistische Geschichtswerk*, ed. Hermann-Josef Stipp, ÖBS 39 (Frankfurt am Main: Lang, 2011), 269–94; in contrast, among others, see Christian Frevel, "Die Wiederkehr der Hexateuchperspektive: Eine Her- ausforderung für die These vom deuteronomistischen Geschichtswerk," in Stipp, *Das deuteronomistische Geschichtswerk*, 13–53.

8. See Erhard Blum, *Studien zur Komposition des Pentateuch*, BZAW 189 (Berlin: De Gruyter, 1990), 101–207. See also Eckart Otto, "Kritik der Pentateuchkomposition,"

168 Eckart Otto

not even four verses link the Priestly writing to Deuteronomy, the question of how the Tetrateuch and Deuteronomy were brought together into one Pentateuch remained without a satisfactory answer.[9] Recent investigations of the Hexateuch and Enneateuch seek to avoid the problem with the assumption that the Pentateuch did not have an actual literary existence as a separately transmitted textual corpus; it is merely an expression of the phenomenon of reception or interpretation within the literary context of the Hexateuch or Enneateuch.[10] Nor is the response to the question of the literary relationship of Deuteronomy to the Tetrateuch found in the proposal that Deuteronomy suppresses an Elohist source. Rather, we should investigate the relationship of the Priestly writings and Deuteronomy and their shared functions for the composition of the postexilic Pentateuch.

In the book of Leviticus, postexilic *Fortschreibungen* of the Priestly writing and receptions of the postexilic *Fortschreibung* of Deuteronomy encounter one another. As a result, we must inquire about the encounter of these two literary works of the Priestly writing and Deuteronomy and their contribution to the postexilic composition of the Pentateuch through the integration of Deuteronomy in the Tetrateuch. Additionally, we will initially investigate the Priestly writing in the book of Leviticus and its conclusion in this book.

TRu 60 (1995): 163–91; with reference to the Priestly writings, still convincingly Klaus Koch, "P—kein Redaktor! Erinnerung an zwei Eckdaten der Quellenscheidung," *VT* 37 (1987): 446–67.

9. See Martin Noth, *Überlieferungsgeschichte des Pentateuch* (Stuttgart: Kohlhammer, 1948), 7–19.

10. So Frevel, "Die Wiederkehr der Hexateuchperspektive," 43–44, following Blum, *Studien zur Komposition des Pentateuch*, 84. However, the view that the torah references in Deuteronomy are "self-referential" is simply false; on this see recently Jean-Pierre Sonnet, "The Fifth Book of the Pentateuch. Deuteronomy in Its Narrative Dynamic," *JAJ* 3 (2012): 202 n. 12; against Erhard Blum, "Pentateuch-Hexateuch-Enneateuch? Or: How Can One Recognize a Literary Work in the Hebrew Bible?," in *Pentateuch, Hexateuch, or Enneateuch? Identifying Literary Works in Genesis through Kings*, ed. Thomas B. Dozeman, Thomas Römer, and Konrad Schmid, AIL 8 (Atlanta: Society of Biblical Literature, 2011), 43–72. Giving up on a literary identification of a Pentateuch in favor of a Hexateuch or Enneateuch is a surrender of pentateuchal scholarship before the task of explaining the literary development of the Pentateuch as a literary unity; on this, see Eckart Otto, "The Pivotal Meaning of Pentateuch Research for a History of Israelite and Judean Religion and Society," in *South African Perspectives on the Pentateuch between Synchrony and Diachrony*, ed. Jurie Le Roux and Eckart Otto, LHBOTS 463 (New York: T&T Clark, 2007), 29–54.

The Priestly Writing and Deuteronomy in the Book of Leviticus 169

1. *Fortschreibungen* of the Priestly Writing in the Book of Leviticus

If we are to consider the Priestly writing in the book of Leviticus, we must first investigate the ending of the *Grundschrift* of the Priestly writing (P^G). This requires a differentiation between the late-exilic *Grundschrift* of the Priestly writing and its postexilic extensions (P^S). The *Grundschrift* of the Priestly writing (P^G) ends in the Sinai pericope, as Thomas Pola has convincingly demonstrated.[11] He proposes that the end of P^G is found in Exod 40:16–17*, 33b as an *inclusio* with Gen 2:1. This proposal, however, comes at the cost of radically eliminating YHWH's instructions for building the tent of meeting following Exod 25:8–9*, as well as the execution of the instructions in Exod 35–39 from P^G, in order to assimilate the Priestly writing to the form of the non-Priestly sources as a purely narrative work. Most notably, Exod 29:42–46 is removed as literarily secondary from the *Grundschrift* of the Priestly writing, although it is precisely here that the theological concerns of the Priestly writing's Sinai pericope are developed, as noted by Bernd Janowski and many others.[12] The surrounding context of Exod 29:42–46 is indissolubly attached to it; this includes Exod 29:1–42a, as well as Exod 27:1–19*; 28:1–41, and even the building instructions in Exod 26. Exodus 29:42–46 cannot function without Exod 26:7–11.[13] In the section on instructions for the tabernacle, the *Grundschrift* of the Priestly

---

11. See Thomas Pola, *Die ursprüngliche Priesterschrift: Beobachtungen zur Literarkritik und Traditionsgeschichte von Pg*, WMANT 70 (Neukirchen-Vluyn: Neukirchener Verlag, 1995), 51–108; see also Eckart Otto, "Forschungen zur Priesterschrift," *TRu* 62 (1997): 20–27. Lothar Perlitt, "Priesterschrift im Deuteronomium?," *ZAW* 100 (1988): 65–88, has persuasively shown that the Priestly writing has no portions in Deuteronomy.

12. See Bernd Janowski, *Sühne als Heilsgeschehen: Studien zur Sühnetheologie der Priester- schrift und zur Wurzel KPR im Alten Orient und im Alten Testament*, WMANT 55 (Neukirchen-Vluyn: Neukirchener Verlag, 1982), 317ff.; see also Georg Steins, "Sie sollen mir ein Heiligtum machen": Zur Struktur und Entstehung von Ex 24,12–31,18," in *Vom Sinai zum Horeb: Stationen alttestamentlicher Glaubensgeschichte*, ed. Frank-Lothar Hossfeld (Würzburg: Echter, 1989), 161.

13. The differentiation between an אהל text in Exod 26:7–11(14) and a משכן text is linked by 26:12—following Klaus Koch, *Die Priesterschrift von Exodus 25 bis Leviticus 16: Eine überlieferungsgeschichtliche und literarkritische Untersuchung*, FRLANT 53 (Göttingen: Vandenhoeck & Ruprecht, 1959), 13–18; Janowski, *Sühne als Heilsgeschehen*, 335–36—is not needed. Rather, the Grundschrift has mediated between different sanctuary traditions, as seen in the juxtaposition of the terms מקדש, אהל מועד, and משכן used for the sanctuary in Exod 29:42–46.

170 Eckart Otto

writing is thus comprised of Exod 24:15b–18*; 25:8–9; 26:1–27:19*; 28:1–29:46.* The ultimate aim of P^G—beginning at creation and culminating with the tent of meeting in the wilderness—is the event of the indwelling of God in this world in the midst of his people and, relatedly, the installation of the Aaronic priesthood at the altar. The problem of the conclusion of P^G in the book of Exodus is that of the incongruence between the instructions for building the tent of meeting in Exod 25–31 and the execution of the instructions in Exod 35–39. This problem cannot be solved by the near complete removal of the section in which these instructions are carried out from the *Grundschrift* up to Exod 40:16, 17, 33b, as proposed by Volkmar Fritz and also accepted by Pola.[14] The execution section in Exod 35–39 has a more consistent structure than the command section in Exod 25–31. Exodus 29:42–46 is followed in Exod 30 by instructions added to Exod 29 for the production of incense altars, basins, anointing oils and aromas, which are integrated into Exod 35–39 in a cohesive structure with a tight sequence of the narrative for the execution of the instructions for building and setting up the tent and its inventory. According to Wellhausen, Exod 35–39 is literarily secondary compared with Exod 30–31.[15] But Exod 30–31 is also literarily secondary in relation to Exod 25–29*. These two chapters are an appendix, which became necessary when Exod 25–29 was supplemented with Exod 35–40*, because the section in which the instructions are given required the inclusion of elements from Exod 35–39 that were missing from the *Grundschrift* in Exod 25–29. These elements of the vessels for the sanctuary were added after Exod 29 but not inserted into Exod 25–29. Exodus 29:42–46, then, is not simply the theological summary and high point of the Priestly Sinai pericope. It is also the conclusion of both the Sinai pericope as well as the *Grundschrift* of the Priestly writing (P^G).[16] Composed in the exilic period as a counter statement to the Babylonian Enuma Elish, the Priestly *Grundschrift* narrates the history of the constitution of Israel from the creation of the world to the promise of the establishment of the sanctuary for the indwelling of God among the Israelites and the service of the Aaronides in this sanctuary. With its open

---

14. See Volkmar Fritz, *Tempel und Zelt: Studien zum Tempelbau in Israel und zu dem Zelthei- ligtum der Priesterschrift*, WMANT 47 (Neukirchen-Vluyn: Neukirchener Verlag, 1977), 113; Pola, *Die ursprüngliche Priesterschrift*, 51–108.

15. See Julius Wellhausen, *Die Composition des Hexateuchs*, 4th ed. (Berlin: de Gruyter, 1963), 142.

16. See Otto, "Forschungen zur Priesterschrift," 20–36.

The Priestly Writing and Deuteronomy in the Book of Leviticus   171

conclusion it is able to address concerns beyond the narrative; with the promise of the temple it points beyond the narrated Mosaic era to the time of the exilic addressees of the Priestly writing.

The literary history of the Priestly writing did not end there, as seen already in the postexilic *Fortschreibung* in Exod 30–31; 35–40. It then becomes a matter of relating the promises of the tent of meeting in the *Grundschrift* of the Priestly writing to the revival of the temple cult in Jerusalem. This same intention occurs also in the continuation of the *Fortschreibungen* of the Priestly writing in the book of Leviticus. The extent of two block-like *Fortschreibungen* of the P^S Priestly literature ends with Lev 16.[17] Wellhausen and Abraham Kuenen already assigned Lev 8 to P^S, a supplement that is literarily secondary to the *Grundschrift* of the Priestly writing P^G.[18] They connected this with the thesis that Lev 8 has replaced an original execution report for Exod 29 from P^G. But this view is unnecessary, if it is recognized that the *Grundschrift* P^G ends with the promises in Exod 29:42–46. On the other hand, Noth removed Exod 29 from the *Grundschrift* P^G in favor of Lev 8, and Karl Elliger has argued that Lev 8 is older than Exod 29.[19] The difficulty of balancing Exod 29 and Lev 8 within the horizon of P^G without resorting to a hypothesis that an execution report for Exod 29 that is no longer extant has not been replaced by Lev 8 can be resolved if it is recognized that that the *Grundschrift* of the Priestly writing (P^G) ends with Exod 29:42–46 and that continuations of it in Exod 30–31; 35–40*; Lev 8 are secondary additions from the postexilic era.

Leviticus 9 is connected with Lev 8 as an indissoluble unity and is to be considered part of the same *Fortschreibung* of the Priestly writing.[20] The

---

17. On this, see Eckart Otto, "Das Buch Levitikus zwischen Priesterschrift und Pentateuch," in *Die Tora*, 112–28.

18. See Wellhausen, *Die Composition des Hexateuchs*, 143–44; Abraham Kuenen, *Historisch-kritische Einleitung in die Bücher des Alten Testaments*, 2 vols. (Leipzig: Schulze, 1885), 1:70–78.

19. See Martin Noth, *Das zweite Buch Mose: Exodus*, ATD 5 (Göttingen: Vandenhoeck & Ruprecht, 1959), 186–91; See Karl Elliger, *Leviticus*, HAT 1.4 (Tübingen: Mohr Siebeck, 1966), 104–20.

20. See Christophe Nihan, *From Priestly Torah to Pentateuch: A Study in the Composition of the Book of Leviticus*, FAT 2/25 (Tübingen: Mohr Siebeck, 2007), 111–50. Nihan's attempt to place Lev 8 on the same literary level with Exod 29 by ascribing the divergences between these chapters to an editing of both is problematic. What kind of editor would not have smoothed out the tensions in the texts that were being reworked

172   Eckart Otto

fact that Lev 9 does not belong to the *Grundschrift* of the Priestly writing in
the book of Exodus is demonstrated by the unusual usage of the term עם,
which is used for the first time in Lev 9 in a way that departs from the typical
formulation in the *Grundschrift*.[21] Finally, Lev 8–9 also presuppose the sacrifice תרת from Lev 1–8, which can hardly be assigned to the *Grundschrift*.
Leviticus 1–3 presuppose the establishment of the tent of meeting in Exod
40:16–33(, 34), which is not to be assigned to the *Grundschrift*. As Israel
Knohl, among others, has shown, it is literarily secondary.[22] Even early literary critics since Heinrich Ewald saw that Lev 1–7 is literarily secondary
compared to the Priestly *Grundschrift*; this has been confirmed again by
Jacob Milgrom.[23] Within Lev 1–7 we can also make further literary distinctions. Leviticus 1–3 forms a literary connection with Lev 8–9 as part of a
first *Fortschreibung* of the *Grundschrift* of the Priestly writing together with
the *Fortschreibung* of the *Grundschrift* in Exod 30–31; 35–40.*[24]

Leviticus 10* begins a new literary stage within the *Fortschreibung*
of the Priestly writing. Reinhard Achenbach has presented important

---

and would rather have introduced contradictions into a text that was smooth, without connecting any apparent statements about its intentions? On this, see the following. After Nihan applies literary criticism to remove tensions, which in itself leads
to circular argumentation, and after he attempts to explain divergences that cannot
be removed with literary criticism as conditioned by the context, Nihan's attempt at
mediation still contains inconsistencies which contradict the thesis that Exod 29 and
Lev 8 are to be assigned to the same literary layer; so, for example, the tension between
Exod 29:5 and Lev 8:7 with regards to Priestly clothing, the absence of the Urim and
Thummim from Exod 29:5, and the introduction of the term עדה in Lev 8 instead of
the בני ישראל seen in Exod 29. Lev 8:9 mediates Exod 28:36–37 with Exod 29:6, which
points to the fact that Lev 8:9 presupposes Lev 28 [*sic* = Exod 28] as a whole. On the
arguments in detail, see Otto, "Das Buch Levitikus," 107–42.

21. See Lev 9:7, 15, 18, 22–24; see on this Pola, *Die ursprüngliche Priesterschrift*,
172–74, 221.

22. See Israel Knohl, *The Sanctuary of Silence: The Priestly Torah and the Holiness
School* (Winona Lake, IN: Eisenbrauns, 1995), 66–68. On this study, see Otto, "Forschungen zur Priesterschrift," 46–50.

23. See Heinrich Ewald, *Geschichte des Volkes Israels bis Christus*, 3rd ed. (Göt-
tingen: Dieterich, 1864), 141; Wellhausen, *Die Composition des Hexateuchs*, 135;
Kuenen, *Historisch-kritische Einleitung*, 78; See Jacob Milgrom, *Leviticus 1–16: A
Translation with Introduction and Commentary*, AB 3 (New Haven: Yale University
Press, 1991), 543.

24. Lev 1:1 is related to Exod 40:35 (P[S]), because Moses cannot enter the holy of
holies before Aaron has been consecrated to office and can accompany him (Lev 9:23).

The Priestly Writing and Deuteronomy in the Book of Leviticus   173

evidence for a post-Priestly literary position of Lev 10; Christoph Nihan widely agrees with him.[25] The character of Lev 10 as literarily later than Lev 8–9 is apparent in its opposition to Lev 8:10–11 in that all priests—not only the high priest—are to be anointed. This means that mourning for their brothers is prohibited even for the sons of Aaron. In this way, Lev 10 goes beyond the requirements of the Holiness Code in Lev 21:11, which only pertain to the high priest. This shows that Lev 10:1–7 is a late addition that also presupposes the post-Priestly Holiness Code. However, to go beyond Achenbach and Nihan, who regard Lev 10 as late but unified post-Priestly material, it is necessary to make further literary differentiations within this text.[26] Leviticus 10:1–7, 16–20 is a postpentateuchal redaction frame of a "theocratic redaction" in the book of Leviticus. Not only do these verses develop Lev 4–7 and the Priestly legislation of the Holiness Code, but they also presupposes the Aaronide-Zadokite genealogy in Exod 6,[27] which comes from a postpentateuchal redaction. Both Lev 10:1–7 and Lev 10:16–20 pertain to the question of the authority of the Aaronides in view of the catastrophe. In this situation, Aaron, as the father of Itamar and Eleazar and thus of the Aaronides in Zadokite garb, is granted the authority to interpret the sacrificial תרת.[28] Leviticus 10:8–15, by contrast, belongs in the context of the inauguration of the Aaronic priesthood on the eighth day in Lev 9. Leviticus 10:8–15 is, as demonstrated by the appended position of these verses after the conclusion of Lev 9 with the appearance of God's glory and the Priestly blessing in Lev 9:22–24, a supplemental *Fortschreibung* to Lev 8–9. It adds a further conclusion to Lev 9:22–24 and serves to mediate between Lev 4–7 and Lev 8–9. In addition to integrating Lev 4–7 into the horizon of the Priestly *Fortschreibungen*, Lev 10:8–15 also integrates Lev 1–3; 8–9 in this horizon. Leviticus 10:10–11 introduces the purity תרת of Lev 11–15 as part of the regulations for which the Aaronides are installed to teach the

---

25. See Reinhard Achenbach, *Die Vollendung der Tora*, BZAR 3 (Wiesbaden: Harrassowitz, 2003), 93–110; Nihan, *From Priestly Torah to Pentateuch*, 148–50.

26. See Otto, *Das Buch Levitikus*, 117–20.

27. On this, see Achenbach, *Die Vollendung der Tora*, 110–24.

28. The Zadokite theocratic redaction inserted Lev 10:1–7 as a hermeneutical key right before Lev 10:8–10, which embodies most clearly an Aaronide self-assertion with its direct address [by God] to Aaron that is unmediated by Moses. Lev 10 is a key text for the legal hermeneutics of a synchronically read Pentateuch; see Eckart Otto, *Das Gesetz des Mose: Die Literatur- und Rechtsgeschichte der Mose- bücher* (Darmstadt: Wissenschaftliche Buchgesellschaft, 2007), 64–65.

174   Eckart Otto

distinctions between clean and unclean and also forms a frame around
the purity תרת with Lev 15:31.[29] In Lev 20:25, the authors of the Holiness Code draw Lev 10:10 and Lev 11 together, which indicates that Lev
10:8–15 was known to the Holiness Code. Therefore, Lev 10:8–15 along
with Lev 11–15 belong in the context of the Priestly *Fortschreibung*.[30] The
list of clean and unclean animals of Lev 11 is taken up in a post-Priestly
and postexilic *Fortschreibung* of Deuteronomy in Deut 14, where it incorporated into the context of Deuteronomy as the interpretation of the Sinai
torah (Deut 1:1–5).[31] The assignment of Lev 11–15 to the literary horizon
of the *Fortschreibung* of the Priestly literature in Lev 10:8–12; 11:43–45;
15:31 excludes the possibility of assigning Lev 11–15 to the *Grundschrift*
of P[G].

The reception of Lev 11 in Deut 14 by the post-Priestly *Fortschreibungen* in Deuteronomy and the reference to Lev 13–14 in Deut 24:8 also
excludes the thesis that Lev 11–15 was only included in its position after
a pentateuchal redaction.[32] Rather, the *Grundschrift* of the Priestly writing from Exodus was extended in Leviticus with a first step in Lev 1–3;
8–9, and this *Fortschreibung* was carried forward with Lev 4–7; 10:8–15;
11–15 in a second stage of supplementation. This second *Fortschreibung*
is completed with Lev 16 as the conclusion of the sacrificial תרת in Lev
1–10, including the תרת concerning sin offerings in Lev 4–7.[33] The *Grundschrift* of the Priestly writing is, therefore, not found in Leviticus, though

---

29. See Milgrom, *Leviticus 1–16*, 616, 947.

30. Differently Nihan, who considers Lev 11–15 part of the Priestly *Grundschrift*,
while he considers Lev 10 as a whole to be a post-Priestly addition to P. This shows
that the differentiation between Priestly/post-Priestly, which disregards internal differentiations within the Priestly literature, is insufficient to account for the book of
Leviticus; on this, see my review of Nihan in Eckart Otto, "Das Buch Levitikus im
Pentateuch," *TRu* 74 (2009): 470–79.

31. See Otto, *Deuteronomium 1,1–11,32*, 298–330; Otto, *Deuteronomium 12,1–
23,15*, 1287–96. The thesis of Nihan (*Torah*, 283–99), that Lev 11 and Deut 14 go back
to the same *Vorlage* independently of one another, is unnecessary. For Lev 11 and Deut
14, see also Reinhard Achenbach, "Zur Systematik der Speisegebote in Lev 11 und in
Deuteronomium 14," *ZAR* 17 (2011): 161–210.

32. On Deut 14, see Otto, *Deuteronomium 1,1–11,32*, 248–57. For Deut 24:8, see
Otto, *Deuteronomium 23,16–34,12*, HKAT (Freiburg: Herder, 2017), 1836–38.

33. On the literarily structured form of Lev 16, see Roy E. Gane, *Cult and Character: Purification Offerings, Day of Atonement, and Theodicy* (Winona Lake, IN: Eisenbrauns, 2005), 217–48. On Lev 1–10, see Theodor Seidel, "Levitikus 16: 'Schlussstein'
des priesterlichen Systems der Sündenvergebung," in *Levitikus als Buch*, ed. Heinz-Josef

The Priestly Writing and Deuteronomy in the Book of Leviticus   175

there are two *Fortschreibungen* of the *Grundschrift*. The first of these two *Fortschreibungen* in Lev 1–3; 8–9 is concluded with Aaron's blessing and sacrifices, as well as the appearance of the divine כבד. The second *Fortschreibung* links Lev 10:8–11 to the first stage with Aaron's commission by YHWH to distinguish between what is clean and unclean. In Lev 11–15, this *Fortschreibung* presents the תרת necessary for this task and extends the sacrificial תרת of Lev 1–3 through Lev 4–7, while regulating the sacrifice-portions of the priests as a mediation to Lev 8–9 and developing the system of atonement and purification offerings in Lev 4–7 and Lev 16. This concludes the *Fortschreibungen* (P^S) of the *Grundschrift* and so also the Priestly writing.

2. The Post-Priestly Integration of Deuteronomy into the Pentateuch in Lev 17–26

Following the conclusion of the Priestly writing and its two *Fortschreibungen* (P^S) in Lev 1–3; 8–9 and Lev 4–7; 10:8–15; 11–16, the Holiness Code in Lev 17–26 begins a new stage of literary activity. It is also considered post-Priestly, insofar as it presupposes the *Grundschrift* and *Fortschreibungen* of the Priestly writing, as well as the Deuteronomistic Deuteronomy, and so belongs in the context of the formation of the Pentateuch.[34] With its extensive links to Deuteronomy, Lev 17–26 is distinguished categorically from the preceding chapters of Lev 1–15, which are only related to the horizon of the Priestly writing.[35] In the way that

---

Fabry and Hans-Wilfried Jüngling, BBB 119 (Berlin: Philo, 1999), 219–48. On Lev 4–7, see Otto, "Das Buch Levitikus zwischen Priesterschrift," 122–25.

34. See most recently Reinhard Achenbach, "Das Heiligkeitsgesetz und die sakralen Ordnungen des Numeribuches im Horizont der Pentateuchredaktion," in *The Books of Leviticus and Numbers*, ed. Thomas Römer, BETL 215 (Leuven: Peeters, 2008), 145–75. We can speak of post-Priestly and post-Deuteronomic literature of the Pentateuch in texts which have received both the Priestly writing and its *Fortschreibungen*, as well as Deuteronomy which has been edited Deuteronomistically.

35. For detailed arguments, I refer to my study on the post-Priestly Holiness Code, which shows Lev 17–26 to be laws that revise both the Priestly literature as well as the Deuteronomistically edited Deuteronomy. See Eckart Otto, "Innerbiblische Exegese im Heiligkeitsgesetz Levitikus 17–26," in Fabry and Jüngling, *Levitikus als Buch*, 125–96; see similarly, also, Nihan, *From Priestly Torah to Pentateuch*, 395–579; Achenbach, *Das Heiligkeitsgesetz*, 145–75. Attempts to consider the Holiness Code as part of the Priestly writing, such as the proposals by Blum, *Studien zur Komposition*

176   Eckart Otto

the law code of Deuteronomy is based on the structure of the Book of
the Covenant and carries out a revision of it, so also the Holiness Code
takes up the structure of the laws of Deuteronomy in Deut 12–26; 28.[36]
For example, the centralization law in Deut 12 links to the altar law of
the Book of the Covenant and revises it as the hermeneutical key for
interpreting the Book of the Covenant.[37] Leviticus 17 then links to Deut
12 and revises it.[38] The same applies also for the relationship of Lev 26
to Deut 28.[39] Additionally, there are the connections in Lev 19 to the
Decalogue in Deut 5 and Exod 20, the festival ordinances in Lev 23 connect to Deut 16, and Lev 25 to the legal theology of the *Privilegrecht* and
social legislation of Deuteronomy.[40] Above all, the parenetic framework

---

des Pentateuch, 318–29, and Andreas Ruwe, *"Heiligkeitsgesetz" und "Priesterschrift"*:
Literaturgeschichtliche und rechtssystematische Untersuchungen zu Levitikus 17–26,
FAT 26 (Tübingen: Mohr Siebeck, 1999), 39–52, fail due to the reception of Deuter-
onomy in Lev 17–26. Ruwe in any case excludes an analysis of Lev 26. On this, see
Eckart Otto, "Das Heiligkeitsgesetz zwischen Priesterschrift und Deuteronomium,"
ZAR 6 (2000): 330–40. Since the work of Elliger, *Leviticus*, 14–20; Alfred Cholewiński,
Heiligkeitsgesetz und Deuteronomium: Eine vergleichende Studie, AnBib 66 (Rome:
Pontifical Biblical Institute, 1976), 16–141; and Knohl, *Sanctuary of Silence*, 111–41,
it can be considered a consensus of scholarship that the chapters of Lev 17–26 never
existed independent of its literary context, but rather they were supplemented to Lev
1–15. This holds, despite the unpersuasive arguments of Klaus Grünwaldt, *Das Heiligkeitsgesetz Leviticus 17–26: Ursprüngliche Gestalt, Tradition und Theologie*, BZAW 271
(Berlin: de Gruyter, 1999), 121–30, who wants to renew the older thesis of an originally independent Holiness Code; against this view, see Nihan, *From Priestly Torah to
Pentateuch*, 398–401; Reinhard Achenbach, "Das Heiligkeitsgesetz im nachpriesterschriftlichen Pentateuch: Zu einem Buch von Klaus Grünwaldt," *ZAR* 6 (2000): 341–
50, as well as my review of *Die Heiligkeitsgesetz Leviticus 17–26: Ursprüngliche Gestalt,
Tradition und Theologie*, by Klaus Grünwaldt, *Bib* 82 (2001): 418–22.

36. See Eckart Otto, "Vom Bundesbuch zum Deuteronomium: Die deuteronomische Redaktion in Dtn 12–26," in *Biblische Theologie und Gesellschaft im Wandel*,
ed. Georg Braulik, Seán McEvenue, and Norbert Lohfink (Freiburg: Herder, 1993),
260–78; Otto, *Deuteronomium 12,1–23,15*, 1093–1107. The revision of the Book of
the Covenant carried out thus does not only relate to individual laws such as the altar
law, but above all also to the structuring of the laws. See also Achenbach, "Das Heiligkeitsgesetz und die sakralen Ordnungen," 146.

37. See Eckart Otto, "Rechtshermeneutik in der Hebräischen Bibel: Die innerbiblischen Ursprünge halachischer Bibelauslegung," *ZAR* 5 (1999): 75–98.

38. On Lev 17, see also the following discussion.

39. On Lev 26, see also the following discussion.

40. On the literary relationship between Lev 19 and the Decalogue, see Otto,

The Priestly Writing and Deuteronomy in the Book of Leviticus   177

of the Holiness Code in Lev 18:1–5, 24–30; 19:1–4; 20:7–8, 22–27; 22:8, 31–33; 25:18–19, 38, 42a, 55; 26:1–2 is designed by the compilers of the Holiness Code in relationship to Deuteronomy and the Priestly writing.[41] The frame for the family laws of Lev 18:6–23 in Lev 18:1–5 is developed from Deut 12:29–31 and Deut 18:9–14[42] and connected with the Priestly motif of contamination. The combination of "observe" (שמר) and "do" (עשה) with "commandments" (מצות) that is found in Lev 22:31a alludes to Deuteronomy. The theological starting point for the Holiness parenesis, however, is the theology of the indwelling of God in the sanctuary as the culminating goal of the *Grundschrift* of the Priestly writing in Exod 29:42–46, which in the Holiness Code is shifted into the horizon of the theology of Deuteronomy. Leviticus 25:18–19, 35–38, which is the command to help the economically disadvantaged, combines Deut 15:4–6 with its update in Deut 15:7–11,[43] the prohibition of taking interest from the Book of the Covenant in Exod 22:24, and the differentiation between loans of money and produce from Deut 23:20. The perspective of Deut 12:10–11, which assumes that secure dwelling in the land is a presupposition for obedience to the commandments, is corrected in Lev 25:18 so that obedience now becomes a condition for secure dwelling in the land. With the connection of the covenant and exodus formulas from Deuteronomy, a reference to Lev 26:45 is also constructed and through its connection with the declaration formula with Lev 26:13, on the one hand, and Lev 19:36, on the other. The legislation on personal liability in Lev 25:39–55 follows; this material is a dense revision of Deut 15:12–18. Lev 25:42a, 55 connects to Deut 15:15. The parenetic frame in Lev 25:23–

"Das Heiligkeitsgesetz," 146–52. On Lev 23 and Deut 16, see Otto, "Das Heiligkeitsgesetz," 153–61; Christophe Nihan, "Israel's Festival Calendars in Leviticus 23, Numbers 28–29 and the Formation of 'Priestly' Literature," in Römer, *Books of Leviticus and Numbers*, 212–21. On the literary history of Deut 16, see Otto, *Deuteronomium 12,1–23,15*, 1374–1416. On Lev 25 and Deuteronomy, see Otto, "Das Heiligkeitsgesetz," 161–72.

41. See Otto, "Das Heiligkeitsgesetz," 172–76.

42. See Cholewiński, *Heiligkeitsgesetz und Deuteronomium*, 253–55.

43. On the interpretation of Deut 15:4–6 in the context of Deuteronomy, see Otto, *Deuteronomium 12,1–23,15*, 1353–55; see also Otto, "Wie 'synchron' wurde in der Antike der Pentateuch gelesen?," in *"Das Manna fällt auch heute noch": Beiträge zur Geschichte und Theologie des Alten Testaments/Ersten Testaments*, ed. Frank-Lothar Hossfeld and Ludger Schwienhorst-Schönberger, HBS 44 (Freiburg: Herder, 2004), 420–85.

178   Eckart Otto

24, 38, 42, 55 corrects the view of the Priestly writing on the promise of the land possession in Gen 23:4(; Exod 6:4) by establishing a connection to Deuteronomy. In addition to Deuteronomy and the Priestly writing, Lev 17–26 also revises the Book of the Covenant.[44] This fact, like the reception of Deuteronomy in the Holiness Code, speaks against a unilinear assignment of Lev 17–26 to the Priestly writing. The *Privilege*-law frame of the Book of the Covenant in Exod 21:2–11 and Exod 23:10–12, which is revised in Deut 15, becomes the hermeneutical key in Lev 25:2–7 for the revision of Deut 15 in Lev 25.[45] The Book of the Covenant has precisely this function in the interpretation of Deut 14:21 in Lev 17. The compilation of the laws of Lev 17 is oriented toward Deut 12. Leviticus 17:11, 14 takes up Deut 12:23. The hermeneutical key for the revision in this instance is the interpretation of the Priestly writing in Gen 9:4, in that Lev 17:22–27 corrects the permission to slaughter from Deut 12. The rearrangement of the laws in Lev 17 is connected with the revision of Deut 12.[46] If the centralization of the sacrificial system as a revision of the altar law of the Book of the Covenant stands in the foreground and so prior to the granting of permission to perform profane slaughter, then Lev 17 shifts the critical revision of the sacrificial allowance to the central and primary position. The allusions to Deut 14:21 in Lev 17:15 follow after Lev 17:3–14 as a revision of Deuteronomy and the Priestly writing, wherein the Book of the Covenant serves as the key for interpretation with Exod 22:30.[47] Deutereonomy 14:21 and Exod 22:30 are important texts for the redaction of Lev 17–26, because the Book of the Covenant and Deuteronomy connect the motif of holiness with the prohibition of

---

44. On this, see also Stackert, *Rewriting the Torah*, 113–28.

45. On Exod 21 and 23, see Otto, *Deuteronomium 12,1–23,15*, 1092–93. On the revision in Lev 25, see Otto, "Das Heiligkeitsgesetz," 164–72. This hermeneutical relationship of the Book of the Covenant and Deuteronomy as sources of the Holiness Code speaks against the thesis of Stackert, *Rewriting the Torah*, 209–25, that the Holiness Code was a "super law" that was intended to replace both the Book of the Covenant and Deuteronomy. See the critical discussion of this thesis in Eckert Otto, "*Ersetzen* oder *Ergänzen* von Gesetzen in der Rechtshermeneutik des Pentateuch: Zu einem Buch von Jeffrey Stackert," *ZAR* 14 (2008): 434–42.

46. A similar process of rearranging is seen also in the revision of the Book of the Covenant in Deut 12–26.

47. See Otto, "Das Heiligkeitsgesetz," 142–43. Exod 22:30 is a postexilic addition to the Book of the Covenant; see Otto, *Theologische Ethik des Alten Testaments*, Theologische Wissenschaft 3.2 (Stuttgart: Kohlhammer, 1994), 231–33.

The Priestly Writing and Deuteronomy in the Book of Leviticus   179

eating torn animals or carcasses. Because the redactor of the Holiness Code does not take up this motif in the allusions to Deut 14:21 and Exod 22:30 in Lev 17, he leaves a gap here in the primary law for Lev 18–26, which calls for fulfillment beyond this chapter and so points beyond Lev 17. If the holiness statements form a central motif of the framework of the Holiness Code beginning with Lev 18, then this motif is understood as the overall fulfillment of the holiness statements given by Exod 22:30 and Deut 14:21. This motif sets Lev 17 apart as the introductory law to Lev 18–26 and at the same time connects these chapters.[48] The framework of the Holiness Code follows with Lev 18:2–5 directly after Lev 17 and interprets the postexilic *Fortschreibungen* of the centralization legislation of Deuteronomy in Deut 12:29–31. Leviticus 18:21 interprets the prohibition in Deut 12:31, which is developed further in Lev 20:2–5. In Lev 20:6, the Molech motif is connected with the prohibition of divination from Deut 18:10. Thus, the context of the interpreted text has an influence on the interpretation. The Molech motif that connects Lev 18:21 and Deut 12:29 also results in the connection of the Molech theme with divination in the Holiness Code, through the influence of Deut 18:9–13 and the law about prophets that follows it in Deuteronomy.[49] Here, the direction of influence goes from Deuteronomy to the post-Priestly Holiness Code.

The complexity of the two-sided allusions and influences between the Holiness Code and Deuteronomy in their post-Priestly and post-

---

48. See Otto, "Das Heiligkeitsgesetz," 143–44, with whom Nihan agrees (Nihan, *From Priestly Torah to Pentateuch*, 428–29). Only an interpretation that ignores the reception of the Book of the Covenant and Deuteronomy in the Holiness Code could come to the conclusion that Lev 17–26 has a marked conclusion in Lev 26 but not a beginning with Lev 17, since this chapter lacks a statement about holiness; so Rolf Rendtorff, *Leviticus 1–10*, BKAT 3.1 (Neukirchen-Vluyn: Neukirchener Verlag, 1985), 29, followed by Blum, *Studien zur Komposition des Pentateuch*, 320. Similarly already David Hoffmann, *Leviticus*, 2 vols. (Berlin: Poppelauer, 1905), 1:469, and Gordon J. Wenham, *The Book of Leviticus*, NICOT (London: Hodder, 1979), 7.

49. On the law about prophets in Deuteronomy, see Otto, *Deuteronomium 12,1–23,15*, 1417–1510; see also Otto, "'Das Deuteronomium krönt die Arbeit der Propheten': Gesetz und Prophetie im Deuteronomium," in *"Ich bewirke das Heil und erschaffe das Unheil" (Jes 45,7): Studien zur Botschaft der Propheten*, ed. Friedrich Diedrich and Bernd Willmes, FB 88 (Würzburg: Echter, 1998), 277–309; Christophe Nihan, "'Moses and the Prophets': Deuteronomy 18 and the Emergence of the Pentateuch as Torah," *SEÅ* 75 (2010): 21–55.

180 Eckart Otto

Deuteronomistic *Fortschreibungen* is seen from the fact that influences can be seen in both directions, as seen, for example, in Lev 26 in relation to Deut 11, so that it is too simplistic to presume only one direction of literary dependence.

3. The Post-Priestly Holiness Code in Lev 26 and the Postexilic *Fortschreibung* of Deuteronomy in Deut 10–11

Deuteronomy 10:12–11:32, which is the transition from the Mosaic narrative of the golden calf in Deut 9–10 to the promulgation of commands in Deut 12–26, contains an allusion in Deut 10:17–19 to the command to love the foreigner in Lev 19:33–34 in the Holiness Code:[50]

> For YHWH your God is God of gods and Lord of lords, the great mighty and awesome God, who shows no partiality and does not accept bribes, who works justice for the widows and orphans, and loves the foreigner, providing him with bread to eat, and clothing. Therefore you shall love the foreigner, for you were foreigners in the land of Egypt.

YHWH's love for the foreigner is manifest with the requisite provision for bread and clothing. This detail in Deuteronomy is linked to the Book of the Covenant in Exod 22:25. The social ethos of the Book of the Covenant receives a rationale in Deut 10:18 that goes beyond the Book of the Covenant: the provision for the foreigners is an expression of the love of God. This fact also grounds the demand of the addressees of Deuteronomy to love foreigners. The authors of the postexilic *Fortschreibung* of Deuteronomy found this demand to love foreigners in the Holiness Code. They combine the reception of the Book of the Covenant with the allusions to the Holiness Code in Lev 19:33–34.[51] The Hebrew Bible mentions the demand

---

50. On Deut 9–10, see Otto, *Deuteronomium 1,1–11,32*, 924–1002. On Deut 10:12–11:32, see 1011–72.

51. For Lev 19:33–34, see Christophe Nihan, "Resident Aliens and Natives in the Holiness Legislation," in *The Foreigner and the Law: Perspectives from the Hebrew Bible and the Ancient Near East*, ed. Reinhard Achenbach, Rainer Albertz, and Jakob Wöhrle, BZAR 16 (Wiesbaden: Harrassowitz, 2011), 111–34, 120–22. When Christoph Bultmann (*Der Fremde im antiken Juda: Eine Untersuchung zum sozialen Typenbegriff 'ger' und seinem Bedeutungswandel in der alttestamentlichen Gesetzgebung*, FRLANT 153 [Göttingen: Vandenhoeck und Ruprecht, 1992], 127) as well as José E. Ramirez-Kidd (*Alterity and Identity in Israel: The ger in the Old Testament*, BZAW

The Priestly Writing and Deuteronomy in the Book of Leviticus 181

to love foreigners only in Lev 19:33–34 and Deut 10:18–19. The combination of the Holiness Code in Lev 19:33–34 with the Book of the Covenant in Exod 22:20–23:9 speaks for a direction of dependence from the Holiness Code to the postexilic *Fortschreibung* of Deuteronomy in this point. This, however, does not have to be taken as evidence of different literary layers. Instead, in the postexilic interpretation in Deuteronomy, Moses is portrayed as a scribe who interprets legal texts from Sinai by combining them in a *midrash*-like manner. This process of postexilic *Fortschreibung* observed in Deuteronomy is also utilized in the postexilic Holiness Code. In Lev 19:33–34, the reception of the love command from Lev 19:18 is marked as a citation by *Numeruswechsel*.[52] Again, this does not indicate that these are different literary layers. Both in the Holiness Code as well as in the postexilic *Fortschreibung* of Deuteronomy, we are dealing with literature of the Pentateuch in which the fiction of the Mosaic *midrashic* interpretation is a firm part of the process of the formation of the text. Thus, the *midrash*-like combination of texts, with mutual interpretation in both directions, is by no means to be explained merely as evidence of different literary layers.

This also applies for another example of allusions to the Holiness Code in Lev 26 found in the postexilic *Fortschreibungen* of Deuteronomy in Deut 11:13–15:

> If you obey my statutes [מצותי], which I command you today, to love YHWH your God with your whole hear and whole strength, then I will give [ונתתי] your land rain in its time, spring rains and late rains, and you will harvest your field, your wine, and your oil. And I will grow grass for your cattle from the field, so that you will eat and be satisfied.

Both the Septuagint and Samaritan Pentateuch raise the question of the identity of the speaker in Deut 11:13, specifically, whether the first singular suffix in מצותי refers to YHWH or Moses. The Septuagint and Samaritan Pentateuch have smoothed out the text by either changing the

---

283 [Berlin: de Gruyter, 1999], 78–79), derive the command to love one's neighbor in Deut 10:19 from the hymnic predication of YHWH as a God who loves foreigners in Ps 146:9, they overlook the fact that Ps 146 is from the concluding section of the *hallal* psalms that derives from the second century BCE; see also Frank-Lothar Hossfeld and Erich Zenger, *Psalmen 101–150*, HThKAT (Freiburg: Herder, 2008), 807–10.

52. On the function of the *Numeruswechsel* to mark citations, see Otto, *Deuteronomium 1,1–11,32*, 379–80, 387–88.

182   Eckart Otto

suffix from the first singular to the third singular or by removing it, and, in doing so, they miss the meaning of the MT, which the latter preserved as a lectio difficilior and so should be seen as more original.[53] If one follows the Septuagint and sees Moses as the speaker, then one could argue that the command to love YHWH is given by YHWH in the third-person. But the following line demonstrates that this interpretation is incorrect, because it cannot be Moses who sends rain. YHWH speaks here, and he is the one to whom the suffix of the first-person מצותי refers. As in Deut 7:3–4, Moses is mentioned here in the context of his second speech in Deuteronomy again as the one who speaks on behalf of God. Also in that text, there is a prohibition against taking non-Israelite spouses which is not given by Moses, but by YHWH.[54] If Deut 11:13–14, with the change of subject from Moses to Yahweh as the speaker, transmitted what is at first glance a difficult text, which led the versions to smooth it out, then there must be reasons why the authors of the postexilic *Fortschreibung* of Deuteronomy incorporated this stumbling block as a marker in the text. Reasons for this can be found on two levels: first, on a legal-hermeneutical-literary level in order to mark the connection to Lev 26 and therefore to identify Moses as a scribal interpreter of the Sinai torah, and, second, on a hermeneutical-theological level to portray Moses as a prophetic figure.

Let us consider first the legal-hermeneutically relevant allusions of the postexilic *Fortschreibung* of Deuteronomy to the Holiness Code in Lev 26. With reference to the rain for the land, which YHWH gives at its proper time in the spring and fall, the postexilic authors of Deut 11:14 connect the triad of the blessing for the harvest, wine, and oil in Deut 7:13 to the blessing in Deut 28:12 and then connect the blessing in Deut 28:12 with YHWH's promise of blessing in Lev 26:3–4, which is then, as in Deut 11:14–15, connected to obedience to the commandments:

> If you walk in my commandments and keep my statutes [מצותי] and do them, then I will give [ונתתי] your rains in their time and the land will yield its produce and the trees of the field their fruits.

---

53. On the search for the *more* original text rather than the original text in various types of reading, see Eckart Otto, "Jenseits der Suche nach dem 'ursprünglich Text' in der Textkritik: Fortschreibungen und Textautorität in der nachexilischen Zeit," *ZAR* 18 (2012): 365–71.

54. For details on Deut 7, see Otto, *Deuteronomium 1,1–11,32*, 830–89.

The Priestly Writing and Deuteronomy in the Book of Leviticus   183

Here, the subject of the giving of the rains in the first-person singular in the speech by YHWH, according to Lev 25:1, refers to YHWH. If it is recognized that Lev 26:3–4 corresponds to the structure of Deut 11:13–15, then it is emphasized that neither מצותי in Deut 11:13 nor ונתתי is well adapted to the flow of the text in Deut 11 and so points to מצותי and ונתתי in Lev 26:3–4, where both terms smoothly fit into the characteristic style of speech by YHWH. Leviticus 26:3–4 shows how close the postexilic *Fortschreibung* of Deuteronomy in Deut 11:13–15, which in turn is linked with the blessing section of Deut 28:1–14, is intertwined with the Holiness Code in the process of the integration of Deuteronomy into the Pentateuch. With Lev 26:3–4, Deut 11 is linked to verses that are central for the structure of Lev 26. Nihan has emphasized the importance of Lev 26:3 for the post-Priestly theology of the Holiness Code: "But contrary to P, where Yahweh's covenant is still unconnected with the Sinai legislation, the restoration of the divine presence is now conditioned to Israel's obedience to the statutes (חקת) and the commands (מצות) given by Yahweh to Israel (26:3)."[55] The combination of מצות and חקות in Lev 26:3 is encountered in the Holiness Code only there and in Lev 26:14–15, and in Lev 26:14–15 it is connected with the covenant theme:[56] "If you will not listen to me and will not do all these statutes, if you spurn my statutes, and if your soul abhors my rules, so that you will not do all my commandments and therefore break my covenant." In the structuring of the promises and threats in Lev 26,[57] Lev 26:3–4 functions to introduce the promises, while Lev 26:14–15, on the other hand, introduces the threats. Although some of the individual lexemes in these two introductions of promises and threats in Lev 26 occur in the parenetic framework of the Holiness Code in Lev 18:1–5, 24–30; 19:14; 20:7–8, 22–27; 22:8, 31–33; 25:18–19, 38, 42a, 55; 26:1–2,[58] they are nowhere brought together so comprehensively as in Lev 26:3–4, 14–15. This indicates that the parenetic framework of the Holiness Code of Lev 26:3–4, 14–15 was designed from the conclusion of the Holiness Code through promise and threat. In turn, the Mosaic transition in

---

55. See Nihan, *From Priestly Torah to Pentateuch*, 539.

56. See Graham I. Davies, "Covenant, Oath, and the Composition of the Pentateuch," in *Covenant as Context: Essays in Honor of Ernest W. Nicholson*, ed. Andrew D. H. Mayes (Oxford: Oxford University Press, 2003), 82–86.

57. See Hans Ulrich Steymans, "Verheißung und Drohung: Lev 26," in Fabry and Jüngling, *Levitikus als Buch*, 263–307.

58. On this issue, see Otto, "Das Heiligkeitsgesetz," 172–76.

184   Eckart Otto

Deut 10:12–11:32 that is interwoven with Deut 28 is therefore linked to
the legal corpus in Deut 12–28. The literary connection between Lev 26:3–
4, 14–15 and Deut 11:13–15 is further marked out by lexemes unique to
both contexts. Within the command series structuring Deut 10:12–11:32
in Deut 10:12–13, 20–11:1; 11:13, 22,[59] there is a demand to observe commandments that is formulated with the verb שמר in Deut 10:13; 11:1(8),
22(, 32). But in the command series in Deut 11:13, which introduces the
section of Deut 11:13–21, the command is given irregularly with the verb
שמע. In Lev 26:14, this verb is combined with the verb עשה, which in
turn is connected in Deut 11:22(, 32) with the verb שמר in commands
that demand obedience, whereas the lexeme שמע is unique in this context. Deuteronomy 11:13–15 should be read from the perspective of the
promises and threats in Lev 26 and thus creates a bridge from Lev 26 to
Deut 28. Deuteronomy 11:16–17 then returns to the use of the verb שמר,
which had been passed over in Deut 11:13 in favor of שמע. Therefore, Deut
11:16–17 preserves the fullness of language of the command series that
structures Deut 10:12–11:32 and simultaneously marks the connection
to Lev 26:3–4, 14–15. The term יבול "produce" occurs in the Pentateuch
only in Lev 26:4, 20 and Deut 11:17(; 32:22), which indicates that Deut
11:16–17 should also be interpreted from the perspective of Lev 26:1–2.
Whereas Lev 26:3–4 promises that YHWH will give rain in its time when
his commands are observed, resulting in the ground yielding its "produce,"
Lev 26:19–20 follows on Lev 26:14–15 and takes up Deut 28:23–24 with
its threats that YHWH will make the heaven like iron and the earth like
bronze. Thus, YHWH will close the heavens and not send rain, as in Deut
11:17. Leviticus 26:20 develops the idea from Lev 26:4 and provides a
counterpoint to it: "Your strength shall be spent to no purpose: your land
shall not yield its produce, and the trees of the land shall not yield their
fruit." Deut 11:17 states this with a direct resonance: "and the land will
yield no produce." The motifs of promise and threat, which are separated
from one another in Lev 26 at verses 3–4 and verses 16–20, are brought
together in Deut 11:13–17. This indicates that Lev 26 is received in Deut
11, which also suggests that Deut 10–11 should be read in light of Leviticus. This also explains the difficulty resulting from the fact that YHWH is
addressed in the first-person in a speech by Moses in Deut 11: the material

---

59. On the literary structuring of Deut 10:12–11:32 according to these series of
interrelated commandments, see Otto, *Deuteronomium 1,1–11,32*, 1020–21.

The Priestly Writing and Deuteronomy in the Book of Leviticus   185

that does not fit well in Deut 11 nonetheless fits smoothly in a speech by YHWH in Lev 26. These incongruities are intentionally unaltered so that the connection with Lev 26 remains apparent.[60]

But this is not now to be assessed literary-critically, as if the postexilic *Fortschreibung* of Deuteronomy was literarily later than Lev 26 as a firmly integrated part of the Holiness Code. The post-Priestly formation of the Holiness Code and the postexilic *Fortschreibung* of Deuteronomy belong in the horizon of the postexilic formation of the Pentateuch, which urged its addressees in the postexilic period to interpret the references to the blessings and curses in Deut 10:12–11:32 within the horizon of the promises and threats of Lev 26, which are found preceding it in the sequential order in which the texts are read. The authors of the postexilic *Fortschreibung* of Deuteronomy take up a late wisdom motif with the warning against deception of the heart in Deut 11:16.[61] The admonition against turning away from YHWH and serving foreign gods and bowing down before them is taken up from the literary realm of the *Fortschreibungen* of the first command of the Decalogue in Deut 7:4; 8:19–20; 9:12, 16. The threat of destruction in Deut 11:17 connects the threats of YHWH from Lev 26:16–20 with the curses in Deut 28:12, 20 and with motifs from the postexilic *Fortschreibungen* of Deuteronomy in Deut 6:15 and Deut 7:4, and it also develops them by taking up the proclamations of judgment from Moses's speech in Deut 4:26: "I call heaven and earth to witness against you today that you will soon utterly perish from the land that you are crossing the Jordan to occupy."[62] This enables one to appreciate the theological perspectives in the use of the first-person for

---

60. The Septuagint and Samaritan Pentateuch no longer recognized this and smoothed the text of Deuteronomy. The proposal by Hans Ulrich Steymans, *Deuteronomium 28 und die adê zur Thronfolgeregelung Asarhaddons*, OBO 145 (Fribourg: Vandenhoeck & Ruprecht 1995), 171, that the uncorrected changes to YHWH in first-person are due to "formulaic promises with a divine subject," and thus the change to the first-person is to be understood from tradition-history as going beyond the intentions connected with the explanation.

61. See Prov 1:10; Job 31:9, 27.

62. On Deut 6:10–19 as part of the postexilic *Fortschreibung* of Deuteronomy, see Otto, *Deuteronomium 1,1–11,32*, 785–90, 812–21. On Deut 7:4, see 863–64. On Deut 4, see Otto, "Tora für eine neue Generation in Dtn 4: Die hermeneutische Theologie des Numeruswechsels im Deuteronomium," in *Deuteronomium: Tora für eine neue Generation*, ed. Georg Fischer, Dominik Markl, and Smone Paganini, BZAR 17 (Wiesbaden: Harrassowitz, 2011), 105–22; Otto, *Deuteronomium 1,1–11,32*, 508–92.

186 Eckart Otto

YHWH within a speech by Moses in Deut 11. With the connection to Lev 26 extensively interwoven with Deuteronomy, Deut 11:13–17 expressly develops Moses's authority as interpreter of the Sinai torah from Deut 1:1–5.[63] This intention goes beyond the recognition of the Mosaic reception of the Holiness Code and explains why the change in the first-person speech for YHWH in the speech of Moses is not smoothed out. This result is that the depiction of Moses as the interpreter of the law is paralleled with YHWH as the originator of the law.[64] Along with this, another role is connection to Moses, which Deuteronomy ascribes to him as his "prophetic testament." August Dillmann and, following him, Moshe Weinfeld have identified a "prophetic style of speech" in the use of the first-person for the speech of YHWH in the speech of Moses.[65] But we must make more specific distinctions here. A prophetic manner of speech is found in Moses's speeches in Deuteronomy in texts where Moses speaks of the behavior of the people after his death as well as in Deut 7:4. The parallel of YHWH as the legislator with Moses as the interpreter of the law in Deut 7:4, 12–16; 11:13–15 has a correspondence in the identification of Moses as the prophet par excellence with YHWH in Deut 34:11.[66] Deuteronomy

---

63. On this, see Eckart Otto, "Mose, der erste Schriftgelehrte: Deuteronomium 1,5 in der Fabel des Pentateuch," in *L'Écrit et l'Esprit: Études d'histoire du texte et de théologie biblique*, ed. Dieter Böhler, Innocent Himbaza, and Philippe Hugo, OBO 214 (Fribourg: Academic Press; Göttingen: Vandenhoeck & Ruprecht, 2005), 273–84; Otto, *Deuteronomium 1,1–11,32*, 298–328. On the intertwining of Deut 11 with the post-Priestly book of Numbers, see Otto, "The Book of Deuteronomy and Numbers in One Torah: The Book of Numbers Read in the Horizon of the Postexilic *Fortschreibung* in the Book of Deuteronomy; New Horizons in the Interpretation of the Pentateuch," in *Torah and the Book of Numbers*, ed. Christian Frevel, Thomas Pola, and Aaron Schaart, FAT 2/62 (Tübingen: Mohr Siebeck, 2013), 383–97.

64. On the legal-historical aspects of this juxtaposition from the perspective of the Achaemenid legal theory of the combination of *data* and *arta*, see Otto, *Deuteronomium 1,1–11,32*, 1055–58; Otto, "The Book of Deuteronomy and Its Answer to the Persian State Ideology: The Legal Implications," in *Loi et justice dans la literature du Proche-Orient ancient*, ed. Olivier Artus, BZAR 20 (Wiesbaden: Harrassowitz, 2013), 112–22.

65. See August Dillmann, *Die Bücher Numeri, Deuteronomium und Josua*, KeH 13, 2nd ed. (Leipzig: Hirzel, 1886), 273, 287; See Moshe Weinfeld, *Deuteronomy 1–11: A New Translation with Introduction and Commentary*, AB 5A (New Haven: Yale University Press, 1991), 446–47.

66. On Deut 7, see Otto, *Deuteronomium 1,1–11,32*, 872–74. On Deut 34, see Otto, *Deuteronomium 23,16–34,12*, 2284–85; cf. Otto, *Das Deuteronomium im Penta-*

The Priestly Writing and Deuteronomy in the Book of Leviticus   187

11 links to precisely such a text in the Holiness Code with Lev 26, where YHWH announces the exile and return like a prophet. Leviticus 26, for its part, is characterized by the reception of prophetic traditions, especially Ezekiel, but also Amos and Jeremiah. Leviticus 26:4, the verse to which Deuteronomy alludes, shows the interweaving of motifs from Deut 28:12 and Ezek 34:26, and Lev 26:6 shows the combination of Ezek 34:23 with Ezek 34:28.[67] The legitimation of Moses as the prophet in Deuteronomy in the horizon of YHWH's prophetic threat and promise from Sinai in Lev 26 suggests a further reason for the linking of Deut 11 to Lev 26. The authors of the postexilic *Fortschreibung* of Deuteronomy are concerned to anchor Deuteronomy as the prophetic testament of Moses[68] in YHWH's proclamations of salvation and judgment at Sinai in Lev (25:1;) 26, as they integrated it into the Pentateuch, just as Moses's interpretation of the Sinai Torah in Deuteronomy does. In Lev 26, it is YHWH, and not Moses, who speaks in the form of prophetic speech.[69]

The Mosaic prophecies in Deuteronomy as a prophetic testament in Deut 4:23–31 and Deut 29:21–28 aim at Deut 30:1–10:

> And when all these words come on you, the blessing and the curse which I have set before you, and you take them to heart wherever the Lord your God disperses you among the nations, and when you return to YHWH your God, and obey his voice as I command you today, you and all your descendants, with your whole heart and with your whole strength, then YHWH your God will restore your fortunes and will have compassion on you and turn to you and gather you from among all the people where YHWH your God has scattered you. (Deut 30:1–3)

The question arises of why it requires such an intensive textual pragmatism as developed in Deuteronomy to emphatically present the demand to obedience to commands, if the future of the addressees of Moses in the narrated time and that of the addressees of Deuteronomy in the postex-

---

teuch und Hexateuch: Studien zur Literaturgeschichte von Pentateuch und Hexateuch im Lichte des Deuteronomiumrahmens, FAT 30 (Tübingen: Mohr Siebeck, 2000), 228–29.

67. See Otto, "Das Heiligkeitsgesetz," 180–81.

68. On this, see Otto, *Deuteronomium 1,1–11,32*, 274–82.

69. In contrast to Deut 28, Lev 26 does not have *yiqtol*-x statements with a jussive function, nor morphological jussives; therein Lev 26 is not about blessings and curses but is rather a prophetic style of speech as promises and threats; so following Steymans, "Verheißung und Drohung," 273–74 n. 50.

188 Eckart Otto

ilic time of narration is already determined from primordial time by the prophecies of Moses in the land of Moab.[70] The addressees in the postexilic time of narration already have the exile and restoration from exile behind them, as described in Deut 4 and Deut 30. The circumcision of the heart, however, remains in the future for the addressees of postexilic Deuteronomy. Deuteronomy sees its addressees as being "between the times" in the time of narration, in which time Moses addresses them as he is speaking in the narrated time in the land of Moab in Deuteronomy. They have endured the catastrophe of the exile as a consequence of covenant violation at the time of narration, just as the first generation in the remote narrative time experienced the violation of the covenant with the breaking of the first commandment in the episode of the golden calf. The declarations of salvation which Moses proclaims as a prophet in Deut 4:29–31; 30:1–10 apply now to those who survive in the postexilic time of narration. However, just as the first generation in the narrative time forfeited its life during the second rebellion at Kadesh in the spy narrative in Deut 1:19–46, so also the generation addressed in the time of narration is in danger of forfeiting its life, if they break the covenant again. This explains the text-pragmatic performative emphasis of the parenesis, with which Moses as prophet connects his demands to obedience to the commands. As in Deut 4:3–4, the authors of the postexilic *Fortschreibung* of Deuteronomy (Deut 6:18; 8:1; 11:8, 22) aim beyond the addressees of Moses in the narrative time to the addressees of the book of Deuteronomy in the postexilic time of narration. They do so in that they break out of the logic of the narrative of Deuteronomy in the narrated Mosaic era by connecting the success of the conquest of the land to the condition of obedience to the preceding commandments, although up to the day that Moses dies, the act of crossing over the Jordan still stands immediately before them. In Deut 30:1–10 in the context of his declaration of salvation, Moses further develops a perspective that connects the parenetic impression to obey the commands with the prophetic announcement of salvation from Deut

---

70. On textual pragmatism to demand obedience, see Dominik Markl, *Gottes Volk im Deuteronomium*, BZAR 18 (Wiesbaden: Harrassowitz, 2012), 43–56. On the hermeneutical difference and relationship between the time of narration and narrated time in the Pentateuch, see the summary in Otto, *Das Gesetz des Mose*, 98–103. On the hermeneutical difference of the time of narration and narrated time in Deuteronomy, see Otto, *Deuteronomium 1,1–11,32*, 258–63, 311–13, 467–70, 502, 618–20, 680–81, 907–9, 923, 985–1001.

The Priestly Writing and Deuteronomy in the Book of Leviticus 189

30:6.[71] According to these verses, YHWH will circumcise the hearts of the Israelites, so that the addressees can love YHWH with their whole hearts and all their strength. This transcends the parenetic textual pragmatism of Deuteronomy: "YHWH your God will circumcise your heart and the heart of your descendants, so that you can love YHWH your God with your whole heart and whole strength, that you may live" (Deut 30:6). If their hearts are circumcised, the Mosaic demand to love YHWH and obey his voice as obliged in Deut 30:2 is ultimately fulfilled. Here the authors of the postexilic *Fortschreibung* are in conversation with the corresponding proclamations of salvation from post-exilic prophetic tradition in Ezek 36:24–28 and Jer 31:31–34.[72]

Which divine speech, however, legitimates the Mosaic prophecy in Deuteronomy? On this point we must consider Lev 26, which announces the judgment of exile and salvation by YHWH in the time of narration in the form of prophetic speech. The prophecy of Moses in Deuteronomy links to this divine speech and takes up a core motif from it. Before the promise that YHWH will remember his covenant with Jacob in Lev 26:42, Lev 26:41 introduces the motif of the uncircumcised heart. The exiles will confess their sins and humble their uncircumcised heart. The phrase לבבם הערל is notable in that it is unique in the Pentateuch. In the characteristic style of the announcement of salvation by YHWH, it points beyond Lev 26 in that the question remains open regarding whether the heart remains uncircumcised when YHWH remembers his covenant. The Holiness Code gives no further information on this. Only the Mosaic prophecy in Deuteronomy takes up the motif and develops it further. The paradoxical rationale of the love of YHWH for his people in Deut 10:15 is followed in

---

71. On the hermeneutical function of Deut 30:1–10 in the horizon of the Pentateuch, see Otto, *Deuteronomium 23,16–34,12*, 2066–77, cf. Ernst Ehrenreich, *Wähle das Leben! Deuteronomium 30 als hermeneutischer Schlüssel zur Tora*, BZAR 14 (Wiesbaden: Harrassowitz, 2011), 71ff.

72. On the dialogue between the postexilic authors of the Pentateuch and the authors of the tradents of Jeremiah-traditions, see Eckart Otto, "Scribal Scholarship in the Formation of Torah and Prophets: A Postexilic Scribal Debate between Priestly Scholarship and Literary Prophecy; The Example of the Book of Jeremiah and Its Relation to the Pentateuch," in *The Pentateuch as Torah: New Models for Understanding Its Promulgation and Acceptance*, ed. Gary N. Knoppers and Bernard M. Levinson (Winona Lake, IN: Eisenbrauns, 2007), 171–84, as well as Harald Knobloch, *Die nachexilische Prophetentheorie des Jeremiabuches*, BZAR 12 (Wiesbaden: Harrassowitz, 2009).

190   Eckart Otto

the postexilic *Fortschreibung* in Deut 10:16 by the demand for circumcising the heart.[73]

However, Deuteronomy is not content to simply maintain this motif with its parenesis, but it goes beyond it by Mosaic prophecy. The demand to circumcise the heart in Deut 10:16 points beyond this to the Mosaic prophecy in Deut 30:6, according to which YHWH himself will circumcise the hearts of the people. In this way, Moses's prophecy answers the question that remains open with the proclamation of salvation in Lev 26 with regard to the motif of the uncircumcised heart: God himself will circumcise their hearts.

In Deut 31:16–18, then, the narrator of the book of Deuteronomy comes to a conclusion with a bang: following YHWH's prophetic speech in Lev 26, YHWH again takes up the word and confirms the threats and destruction announced by his prophet Moses. The people will break the first commandment, and YHWH's wrath will be kindled so that the people will be destroyed. YHWH will hide his face because the people will have broken his covenant. YHWH will hide his face from them, even when the people wonder if God is no longer with them in their time of need and even when the people want to return to YHWH. The catastrophe will be inevitable.

Deuteronomy speaks to the people in the time of narration after the catastrophe.[74] The textual pragmatism of the parenesis applies to them. In contrast to the Mosaic prophecy in Deut 4 and Deut 29–30, any announcement of salvation by YHWH is missing. Rather, YHWH's last word is that he will hide his face. The Song of Moses in Deut 32:1–43 is to be a witness against the people according to Deut 31:19–21. But it is precisely this

---

73. See Otto, *Deuteronomium 1,1–11,32*, 1036–37. The postexilic *Fortschreibung* of Deut 10:15–16 is also oriented to Neh 9:7–8.

74. Therein Deut 34:9 is transcended with the Mosaic prophecy of Deut 4 and 30 and through YHWH's announcement of judgment on the descendants in Deut 31, which is related to the threats of Lev 26. The statement about obedience to commands in Deut 34:9 is related to the narrative time with the transition of leadership from Moses to Joshua and intends to make clear that a distinction needs to be made between the people of the narrative time and the people of the postexilic time of narration. On the theological function of Deut 34:9, see Otto, *Deuteronomium 23,16–34,12*, 2282–83. For a synchronic interpretation, see Jean-Pierre Sonnet, "Redefining the Plot of Deuteronomy—From End to Beginning: The Import of Deut 34:9," in Fischer, Markl, and Paganini *Deuteronomium*, 15–36. On the diachronic assessment of Deut 34:9, see Otto, *Deuteronomium 23,16–34,12*, 2279.

The Priestly Writing and Deuteronomy in the Book of Leviticus 191

song that serves as a witness against the covenant breaking of the people, that announces the turn to salvation.[75] The song is a collage of allusions and citations from the books of the Prophets, the Psalms, and Wisdom literature; the respective contexts of the texts are also to be included in the reading, which gives the song the character of a collage as a testimony of the theological promise of salvation of the entire canon.[76] The canon in the form of the sum of the received and allusive texts verifies and legitimates the salvation proclamations of the prophet Moses. The Song of Moses together with its frame as one of the latest additions in the Pentateuch takes the function of the word of God. This word of God in Deut 31:19–21 only proclaimed judgment and thus only confirmed one side of YHWH's own speech in Lev 26 and its interpretation in Mosaic prophecy in Deut 4 and 29–30.

Let us now return to the text-critical problem in which YHWH is suddenly described as the subject in the first-person in a speech by Moses. Here, Moses merges with YHWH in his prophetic office. But if the connection to Lev 26 is made clear in Deut 10:13–15, a distance between God and prophet is also indicated, in that the prophet Moses is characterized as mediator and interpreter of the divine threats of judgment and the promise of the turn to salvation in the time of narration. The heading in Lev 25:1, "YHWH spoke to Moses on Mount Sinai," relates to this, as Moses is characterized as the interpreter of the divine revelation from YHWH at Sinai in Deuteronomy. The versions of the Septuagint and Samaritan text have smoothed out the text in Deut 10:13–15 like modern commentators and by doing so have not been able to see the hermeneutics of its message. Here, once again, it is clear that unevenness and tensions in the text of Deuteronomy are not to be harmonized or eliminated literary-critically at any cost. Rather, we should begin with the notion that they have been left in the text for an intentional hermeneutical purpose, or, as in the case of

---

75. See Otto, *Deuteronomium 23,16–34,12*, 2130–33; see also Otto, "Singing Moses: His Farewell Song in Deuteronomy 32," in *Psalmody and Poetry in Old Testament Ethics*, ed. Drik J. Human, LHBOTS 572 (New York: T&T Clark, 2012), 169–81.

76. See Eckart Otto, "Moses Abschiedslied in Deuteronomium 32: Ein Zeugnis der Kanonsbildung in der Hebräischen Bibel," in *Die Tora*, 641–78. On the hermeneutics of the Song of Moses in Deut 32 in relation to the fourth book of Psalms, especially Pss 90–92, see Otto, "The Suffering Prophet in Deuteronomy and Psalm 90–92," in *Propheten der Epochen: Prophets of the Epochs*, ed. Viktor Kókai Nagy and László Sándor Egeresi, AOAT 426 (Münster: Ugarit, 2015), 137–49.

Deut 10:13–15, it was intentionally placed in the text with a specific meaning.[77] If this is recognized, our methodological handling of the textual and literary criticism in Deuteronomy, as well as the rest of the Pentateuch, will be significantly changed.

---

77. See Eckart Otto, "A Hidden Truth behind the Text or the Truth of the Text: At a Turning Point in Biblical Scholarship Hundred Years after de Wette's *Dissertatio critico-exegetica*," in Le Roux and Otto, *South African Perspectives on the Pentateuch*, 19–28.

The Holiness Legislation and the Pentateuch: Tradition- and Composition-Historical Aspects of Leviticus 26

Christophe Nihan

1. Leviticus 26 as Theme of Contemporary Pentateuchal Research

Since the late 1990s, the penultimate chapter of the book of Leviticus has established itself as an important theme in pentateuchal research, as a series of studies clearly demonstrates.[1] This exegetical interest in Lev 26

---

1. While studies of Lev 26 were infrequent in previous research, the situation has changed significantly in recent times. See especially Walter Groß, "'Rezeption' in Ex 31,12–17 und Lev 26,39–45: Sprachliche Form und theologisch-konzeptionelle Leistung," in *Rezeption und Auslegung im Alten Testament und in seinem Umfeld: Ein Symposion aus Anlass des 60. Geburtstags von Odil Hannes Steck*, ed. Reinhard G. Kratz and Thomas Krüger, OBO 153 (Göttingen: Vandenhoeck & Ruprecht, 1997), 45–64; Jacob Milgrom, "Leviticus 26 and Ezekiel," in *The Quest for Context and Meaning: Studies in Biblical Intertextuality in Honor of James A. Sanders*, ed. Craig A. Evans and Shemaryahu Talmon, BibInt 28 (Leiden: Brill, 1997), 57–62; Jan Joosten, "Covenant Theology in the Holiness Code," *ZAR* 4 (1998): 145–64; Norbert C. Baumgart, "Überkommene Traditionen neu aufgearbeitet und angeeignet: Lev 26,3–45: Das Heiligkeitsgesetz in Exil und Diaspora," *BZ* 43 (1999): 1–25; Hans Ulrich Steymans, "Verheißung und Drohung: Lev 26," in *Levitikus als Buch*, ed. Heinz-Josef Fabry and Hans-Winfried Jüngling, BBB 119 (Berlin: Philo, 1999), 263–307; Ariel Alvarez Valdés, "Levitico 26: una sintesis de alianzas como clave de lectura," *EstBib* 61 (2003): 155–81; Reinhard Müller, "A Prophetic View of the Exile in the Holiness Code: Literary Growth and Tradition History in Leviticus 26," in *The Concept of Exile in Ancient Israel and Its Historical Contexts*, ed. Ehud Ben Zvi and Christoph Levin, BZAW 404 (Berlin: De Gruyter, 2010), 207–28; Jeffrey Stackert, "Distinguishing Innerbiblical Exegesis from Pentateuchal Redaction: Leviticus 26 as a Test Case," in *The Pentateuch: International Perspectives on Current Research*, ed. Thomas B. Dozeman, Konrad Schmid, and Barukh Ya'aḳov Shyarts, FAT 78 (Tübingen: Mohr Siebeck, 2011), 369–86. See also

-193-

194   Christophe Nihan

is explained both by the strategic placement of this chapter at the end
of the Sinai narrative (before the subsequent and, in fact, later appendix
Lev 27) as well as by the significant intertextuality with various traditions
such as the Priestly writing, Deuteronomy, and the Prophets, in particular
Ezekiel. Both aspects have, indeed, long been recognized, but they have
played only a minor role in the discussion of the Pentateuch until recent
decades. As long as the Documentary Hypothesis was assumed to be valid,
the so-called Holiness Code in Lev 17–26 was understood to comprise an
originally independent collection of laws from the exilic (or Neo-Babylo-
nian) period, which were later placed in their current location during the
postexilic period when they were included in the Priestly writing.[2] Within
this model, the blending of Priestly and Deuteronomic or Deuteronomistic
expressions that distinguishes this corpus was regarded as being consistent
with the chronological position of this collection between the late preex-
ilic Deuteronomy and the postexilic Priestly writing. The Holiness Code
in general, and Lev 26 in particular, was thus understood—in diachronic
perspective—as a kind of missing link between these two corpuses, taking
over the language of Deuteronomy while anticipating expressions later

---

Eckart Otto, "Innerbiblische Exegese im Heiligkeitsgesetz Levitikus 17–26," in *Levi-
tikus als Buch*, ed. Heinz-Josef Fabry and Hans-Winfried Jüngling, BBB 119 (Berlin:
Philo, 1999), 176–82. For earlier research, see Norbert Lohfink, "Die Abänderung der
Theologie des priesterlichen Geschichtswerks im Segen des Heilikeitsgesetzes: Zu Lev.
26,9.1 1–13," in *Wort und Geschichte: Festschrift für Karl Elliger zum 70. Geburtstag*, ed.
Hartmut Gese and Hans Peter Rüger (Neukirchen-Vlyun: Neukirchner, 1973), 129–36;
Lohfink, *Studien zum Pentateuch*, SBAB 4 (Stuttgart: Katholisches Bibelwerk, 1988),
157–68; Baruch Levine, "The Epilogue to the Holiness Code: A Priestly Statement on
the Destiny of Israel," in *Judaic Perspectives on Ancient Israel*, ed. Jacob Neusner et al.
(Philadelphia: Wipf & Stock, 1987), 9–34; Marjo C. A. Korpel, "The Epilogue to the
Holiness Code," in *Verse in Ancient Near Eastern Prose*, ed. Johannes. C. de Moor and
Wilfred G. E. Watson, AOAT 43 (Kevelaer: Butzon & Bercker, 1993), 123–50.

2. See Julius Wellhausen, *Die Composition des Hexateuchs*, 4th ed. (Berlin: de
Gruyter, 1963), 149–72; already in his 1901 Leviticus commentary, Alfred Betholet
could present this model as being firmly established; see Alfred Bertholet, *Leviticus*,
KHC 3 (Tübingen: Mohr, 1901), X ("as already long recognized"). For a detailed his-
tory of research for the Holiness Code, see Klaus Grünwaldt, *Das Heiligkeitsgesetz
Leviticus 17–26: Ursprüngliche Gestalt, Tradition und Theologie*, BZAW 271 (Berlin: de
Gruyter, 1999), 5–22, as well as Christophe Nihan, *From Priestly Torah to Pentateuch:
A Study in the Composition of Leviticus*, FAT 2/25 (Tübingen: Mohr Siebeck, 2007),
4–11.

The Holiness Legislation and the Pentateuch   195

found in the Priestly writing.[3] In recent decades, this old consensus gradually collapsed in favor of the position initially formulated by Karl Elliger in 1959, who argued that the so-called Holiness Code had been composed from the beginning in connection with, and as a supplement to, the Priestly writing.[4] A somewhat comparable development in research occurred in North American and Israeli discussions of the Pentateuch, particularly under the influence of the models of Israel Knohl and Jacob Milgrom, who argued for a post-Priestly "Holiness School" or "Holiness Redaction" in Lev 17–26 and similar passages of the Pentateuch.[5] Today, as far as I can tell, the thesis of a pre-Priestly version of Lev 17–26 is only marginally represented. Even Klaus Grünwaldt's attempt to defend the old consensus cannot answer the basic arguments raised by Elliger and others against the

------

3. On this interpretation of the Holiness Code in earlier research, see my discussion in Christophe Nihan, "The Holiness Code between D and P: Some Comments on the Function and Significance of Leviticus 17–26 in the Composition of the Torah," in *Das Deuteronomium zwischen Pentateuch und Deuteronomistischem Geschichtswerk*, ed. Eckart Otto and Reinhard Achenbach, FRLANT 206 (Göttingen: Vandenhoeck & Ruprecht, 2004), 81–82.

4. Karl Elliger, "Heiligkeitsgesetz," *RGG* (1959): 3:175–76; see also Elliger, *Leviticus*, HAT 1.4 (Tübingen: Mohr Siebeck, 1966), 14–20 and *passim*. See further, e.g., Alfred Cholewiński, *Heiligkeitsgesetz und Deuteronomium: Eine vergleichende Studie*, AnBib 66 (Rome: Pontifical Biblical Institute, 1976); Horst Dietrich Preuss, "Heiligkeitsgesetz," *TRE* 14 (1985): 713–19.

5. Israel Knohl, *The Sanctuary of Silence: The Priestly Torah and the Holiness School* (Winona Lake, IN: Eisenbrauns, 1995); Jacob Milgrom, *Leviticus 1–16: A Translation with Introduction and Commentary*, AB 3 (New York: Doubleday, 1991); Milgrom, *Leviticus 17–22: A New Translation with Introduction and Commentary*, AB 3A (New York: Doubleday, 2000), 1327–30, 1349–52 and *passim*; Milgrom, *Leviticus 23–27: A New Translation with Introduction and Commentary*, AB 3B (New York: Doubleday, 2001). See also Milgrom, "The Changing Concept of Holiness in the Pentateuchal Codes with Emphasis on Leviticus 19," in *Reading Leviticus: A Conversation with Mary Douglas*, ed. John F. A. Sawyer, JSOTSup 227 (Sheffield: Sheffield Academic, 1996), 65–78. Knohl's thesis has been adopted by several Israeli as well as North American researchers; see, e.g., Jeffrey Stackert, *Rewriting the Torah: Literary Revision in Deuteronomy and the Holiness Legislation*, FAT 52 (Tübingen: Mohr Siebeck, 2007). For a Holiness Redaction, see in particular Milgrom in recent works: Jacob Milgrom, "HR in Leviticus and Elsewhere in the Torah," in *The Book of Leviticus: Composition and Reception*, ed. Rolf Rendtorff and Robert A. Kugler, VTSup 93 (Leiden: Brill, 2003), 24–40; see also Milgrom, *Leviticus 17–22*, 1345–47.

196 Christophe Nihan

notion of a pre-Priestly version of the Holiness Code.[6] This is all the more so since Grünwaldt must acknowledge that the so-called Holiness Code has no real introduction and is not earlier than the Priestly Grundschrift (P^G) in any event. The acknowledgment that Lev 17–26 never comprised a discrete code but that these chapters were conceived from the beginning as a legal supplement of sorts to other materials likewise means that the classical designation of this collection as a "Holiness Code" is problematic. Other designations, such as "Holiness legislation" (as proposed by Baruch Schwartz) may instead be preferred. In the following, the abbreviation "H" will be used to refer to this collection.[7]

The new assessment of Lev 17–26 as a legal corpus that was composed from the beginning as a supplement to the Priestly writing logically led to a new assessment of the coexistence of Priestly and non-Priestly traditions within this corpus. In a brief 1973 essay, Norbert Lohfink already analyzed this phenomenon using the example of the covenant theme in Lev 26. He basically argued that the first part of the chapter was distinguished by a fundamental "alteration" ("Abänderung") of the Priestly covenant theology in which this theology underwent a "Deuteronomization." But he also noticed that this Deuteronomization of the Priestly covenant theology at the end of the chapter had been reversed because the validity of the covenant with the patriarchs was reestablished after the exile.[8] After Lohfink's article, the analysis of the coexistence of Priestly and Deuteronomic or Deuteronomistic traditions continued in various studies—first in 1976 by Alfred Cholewiński—not only in regard to Lev 26 but to the entire collection.[9] Today, there appears to be a broad consensus for the view that the corpus Lev 17–26 is distinguished by a substantial reception of both

---

6. Grünwaldt, *Das Heiligkeitsgesetz Leviticus 17–26*, 127–30, 366–68, and 381–85. On this issue, see the response by Reinhard Achenbach, "Das Heiligkeitsgesetz im nachpriesterschriftlichen Pentateuch: Zu einem Buch von Klaus Grünwaldt," *ZAR* 6 (2000): 341–50, as well as my discussion in Nihan, *From Priestly Torah to Pentateuch*, 395–401.

7. Baruch J. Schwartz, "The Strata of the Priestly Writings and the Revised Relative Dating of P and H," in *The Strata of the Priestly Writings, Contemporary Debate and Future Directions*, ed. Joel Baden and Sarah Shectman, ATANT 95 (Zürich: TVZ, 2009), 1–12.

8. Lohfink, "Die Abänderung."

9. Cholewiński, *Heiligkeitsgesetz und Deuteronomium*; further, especially Otto, "Innerbiblische Exegese"; Stackert, *Rewriting the Torah*; Nihan, *From Priestly Torah to Pentateuch*, 395–575; and recently Müller, "Prophetic View of the Exile."

The Holiness Legislation and the Pentateuch   197

Deuteronomy and the Priestly writing, involving the interpretation of, and negotiation between, both traditions.[10] What remains disputed is how these findings are to be explained.

Since Elliger and Cholewiński, H has classically been interpreted as an addition to the Priestly writing *before* the latter was combined with other traditions into a single document—the Pentateuch. Within this model, H has generally been understood as representing the inner-Priestly reception of Deuteronomy, an assumption still represented by exegetes such as Jeffrey Stackert or David Carr.[11] Not least in view of Lev 26, other researchers have alternatively proposed the thesis that the inner-biblical exegesis of P and non-P explains that Lev 17–26 was composed in the context of the redaction of the Pentateuch, as argued in particular by Eckart Otto and, from a different perspective, by myself.[12] Still another position is represented by exegetes—especially Erhard Blum, Andreas Ruwe, and Alfred Marx—who describe the so-called Priestly writing as a compositional layer within the Pentateuch and who, as a rule, tend to interpret H as part of this P-composition.[13]

---

10. See, e.g., Konrad Schmid, *The Old Testament: A Literary History* (Minneapolis: Fortress, 2012), 176–77; David Carr, *The Formation of the Hebrew Bible: A New Reconstruction* (New York: Oxford University Press, 2011), 298–303: "One striking characteristic of H materials that links them to the post-D Hexateuch and subsequent expansions documented in some manuscript traditions is their frequent orientation toward coordination of various materials, in this case Priestly regulations, with materials found in Deuteronomy" (301).

11. Cholewiński, *Heiligkeitsgesetz und Deuteronomium*; for a similar view, see Preuss, "Heiligkeitsgesetz"; also Stackert, *Rewriting the Torah*; Stackert, "Distinguishing Innerbiblical Exegesis"; David Carr, "Scribal Processes of Coordination/Harmonization and the Formation of the First Hexateuch(s)," in Dozeman, Schmid, and Shyarts, *Pentateuch*, 63–83, esp. 72–73; Carr, *Formation of the Hebrew Bible*, 298–303. See also Reinhard G. Kratz, *Die Komposition der erzählenden Bücher des Alten Testaments: Grundwissen der Bibelkritik*, UTB 2157 (Göttingen: Vandenhoeck & Ruprecht, 2000), 114.

12. Eckart Otto, *Theologische Ethik des Alten Testaments*, ThW 3.2 (Stuttgart: Kohlhammer, 1994), 240–42; Otto, "Das Heiligkeitsgesetz Leviticus 17–26 in der Pentateuchredaktion," in *Altes Testament: Forschung und Wirkung: FS H. G. Reventlow*, ed. Peter Mommer and Winfried Thiel (Frankfurt am Main: Lang, 1994), 65–80; Otto, "Innerbiblische Exegese"; Otto, *Das Deuteronomium im Pentateuch und Hexateuch: Studien zur Literaturgeschichte von Pentateuch und Hexateuch im Lichte des Deuteronomiumrahmens*, FAT 30 (Tübingen: Mohr Siebeck, 2000); Nihan, *From Priestly Torah to Pentateuch*, 545–59.

13. Erhard Blum, *Studien zur Komposition des Pentateuch*, BZAW 189 (Berlin: De Gruyter, 1990); Blum, "Issues and Problems in the Contemporary Debate Regard-

198   Christophe Nihan

It is manifest that all these models presuppose different concepts not only for the Priestly writing, but also for the literary history of the Pentateuch. But in my view, this is not the main methodological problem in this discussion. The main problem is primarily related to the distinctive position of the book of Leviticus within the Pentateuch. In contrast to Genesis and Exodus, or even Numbers, the combination of P and non-P here cannot be a criterion for the classification of the diachronic development of the Priestly materials, since the book of Leviticus only contains Priestly material (intended here, of course, in a broad sense).

So, in the case of H, we come to the central difficulty: in Lev 17–26 we have a corpus where the coexistence of Priestly and non-Priestly (particularly Deuteronomic/Deuteronomistic) materials is to be grasped most clearly within the Pentateuch but where the source- and redaction-critical assessment of this result proves to be difficult. From this perspective, it is evident that Lev 17–26 stands at the center of a broader discussion about the relationship between *conceptual* and *redactional* harmonization. In a 2011 essay in conversation with Eckart Otto and me, Carr discussed in detail some key methodological issues raised by these chapters. In particular, his discussion focuses on the question whether the conceptual integration of texts like the Priestly writing and Deuteronomy, which were probably kept together for decades in the library of the Jerusalem temple, could have made headway without their redactional integration.[14] In this sense, Carr proposes that H could be a particular example of such preredactional harmonization between P and D. Carr states, "Thus, I am suggesting that H represents the sort of scribal consciousness of P and non-P just prior to the combination of those materials and possibly contributing to the move toward that combination."[15]

---

ing the Priestly Writings," in *The Strata of the Priestly Writings: Contemporary Debate and Future Directions*, ed. Sarah Shectman and Joel Baden, ATANT 95 (Zürich: TVZ, 2009), 31–44. Similarly, Frank Crüsemann, *Die Tora: Theologie und Sozialgeschichte des alttestamentlichen Gesetzes* (Munich: Kaiser, 1992); Andreas Ruwe, *"Heiligkeitsgesetz" und "Priesterschrift": Literaturgeschichtliche und rechtssystematische Untersuchungen zu Levitikus 17–26*, FAT 26 (Tübingen: Mohr Siebeck, 1999). This model is also defended by Alfred Marx in his new Leviticus commentary: Alfred Marx, *Lévitique 17–27*, CAT 3b (Geneva: Labor et Fides, 2011).

14. Cf. Carr, "Scribal Processes"; Carr, *Formation of the Hebrew Bible*, 298–303. See, similarly, the comments by Stackert, "Distinguishing Innerbiblical Exegesis," and see his methodological considerations in Stackert, *Rewriting the Torah*, 211–24.

15. Carr, "Scribal Processes," 73; emphasis mine.

The Holiness Legislation and the Pentateuch 199

In the context of the aforementioned discussion, my main concern is the question of whether, and to what extent, there are textual findings that either allow a particular model to be given preference or force us to develop other new models. For this, however, one must first take into consideration the complexity of this chapter, not least in view of the problem of its literary unity, which several recent analyses too often simply assume. Reinhard Müller, in particular, has recently offered valuable arguments that challenge traditional assumptions regarding the chapter's unity.[16] Other key questions concern the complex interrelation between the Priestly writing, Deuteronomy, and the Prophets in Lev 26, as well as the literary function of this chapter and its relationship to the legal corpus in Lev 17–25. The following essay addresses these issues, before drawing some larger conclusions.

2. Some Preliminary Comments on the Form of Lev 26 within H

I begin with some brief observations concerning the form of Lev 26 that also have significance for further analysis of the chapter. Taken formally, Lev 26 together with Lev 25 constitutes a single speech by YHWH to Moses, which is framed by the location notice בהר סיני "at Mount Sinai" in 25:1 and 26:46.[17] That these two chapters are united in this way can be explained not least by the fact that they are both oriented toward the

---

16. Müller, "Prophetic View of the Exile"; contrast, e.g., Marx, *Lévitique 17–27*, 196–211.

17. That בהר סיני in Lev 25:1 and 26:46, just as in Lev 7:38, means "at Mount Sinai," has already been demonstrated by Erhard Blum, cf. Blum, *Studien zur Komposition des Pentateuch*, 313–14; see also my comments in Nihan, *From Priestly Torah to Pentateuch*, 551–52. See recently also Christian Frevel, "Alte Stücke—späte Brücke? Zur Rolle des Buches Numeri in der jüngeren Pentateuchdiskussion," in *Congress Volume Munich 2013*, ed. Christl M. Maier (Leiden: Brill, 2014), 290 with note 129. The alternative meaning, which interprets בהר סיני as "on Mount Sinai" (so, for instance, Jean-François Lefebvre, *Le Jubilé biblique: Lv 25—exégèse et théologie*, OBO 194 [Göttingen: Vandenhoeck & Ruprecht, 2003], 32–33), leads to an impasse, since one must assume that Moses has once again gone up on the mountain in order to receive the precepts of Lev 25 and 26. But the text itself provides no evidence for this assumption, and it is explicitly contradicted by Lev 26:46. The wording of the latter passage points to a series of commands in the revelation to Moses (חקים, משפטים, and תורת), which obviously are not restricted to the precepts of chapters 25 and 26 but include other, additional laws; see below for further comments.

200　　　　　　　　　　　　Christophe Nihan

theme of the land: Lev 25:2–7, 8–54 works out in detail the instructions for how Israelites should deal with the land in the Sabbath and Jubilee years, while Lev 26:3–45 discusses the consequences of observance or nonobservance of the commandments for the Israelites in connection to life in the land.[18] At the same time, this setting of Lev 25 and 26 with reference to Mount Sinai emphasizes the significance of these two chapters, which together form a first conclusion of the Sinai revelation, before Lev 27 (cf. 27:34).[19]

The laws about the Sabbath and Jubilee years end in 25:55 with a motive clause, according to which the Israelites were freed in order to become עבדים "servants" or "slaves" of the deity on its land. The motive clause in 25:55 can legitimately be viewed as the culmination of H's interpretation of the exodus in the parenetic framework of Lev 17–26, as various scholars have already remarked.[20] There follows in Lev 26:1–2 a first, short admonition, which combines and takes up Lev 19:4 (prohibition of images) and 19:30 (Sabbath observance and reverence for the sanctuary), thereby forming a compositional framework between Lev 19 (first admonition about holiness) and Lev 25 (last law of H before the epilogue Lev 26:3–45). Additionally, the connection established in these verses between the exodus, the prohibition of images, and the observance of Sabbath also recalls the Decalogue in Exod 20. The parallel with the Decalogue is further emphasized by the formulation of Lev 26:1a (לא־תעשו לכם אלילם ופסל), which corresponds to the prohibition at the beginning of Exod 20:4a (לא תעשה־לך פסל), yet combines it with the term אלילם that already occurs within a similar context in Lev 19:4.[21]

---

18. Crüsemann, *Die Tora*, 353: "It is likely due to this common subject that both chapters are combined to form a unit in the system of the headings through 25:1f."; see also Steymans, "Verheißung und Drohung," 264–66.

19. See, e.g., John Hartley, *Leviticus*, WBC 4 (Dallas: Word Books, 1992), 433; Lefebvre, *Le Jubilé biblique*, 32–33. On the relationship between Lev 27:34 and 26:46 (and chapters 27 and 26 as a whole), see below.

20. On the exodus theme in the paraenetic framework of H, see Frank Crüsemann, "Der Exodus als Heiligung: Zur rechtsgeschichtlichen Bedeutung des Heiligkeitsgesetzes," in *Die Hebräische Bibel und ihre zweifache Nachgeschichte: Festschrift für Rolf Rendtorff zum 65. Geburtstag*, ed. Erhard Blum, Christian Macholz, and Ekkehard Stegemann (Neukirchen-Vluyn: Neukirchner, 1990), 117–29, as well as Otto, *Theologische Ethik des Alten Testaments*, 237–40.

21. See, e.g., Hartley, *Leviticus*, 450: "This commandment [scil. Lev 26:1] is an elucidation on the second commandment of the Decalogue (Exod 20:4–6 // Deut

The Holiness Legislation and the Pentateuch 201

Lev 26:1	Exod 20:4a
לא תעשו לכם אלילם ופסל ...	לא תעשה לך פסל ...
	Lev 19:4
	אל תפנו אל האלילים ואלהי מסכה
	לא יעשו אני יהוה אלהיכם
Lev 26:2	Lev 19:30
את שבתתי ישמרו	את שבתתי תשמרו
ומקדשי תיראו אני יהוה	ומקדשי תיראו אני יהוה

The combined reception of Exod 20 and Lev 19 that characterizes Lev 26:1–2 concludes the preceding Holiness legislation in Lev 17–25 by returning to the Decalogue, which marks itself the beginning of the revelation at Sinai. As such, Lev 26:1–2 aptly functions as a transition between Lev 25, ending the various laws contained in Lev 17–25, and 26:3–46, which forms the conclusion or (as Baruch Levine called it) the "epilogue," not only to H but more generally to the entire Sinai account.[22] Topically and, to some extent, linguistically as well (see below), this epilogue in 26:3–45 provides a parallel to the blessings and curses in Deut 28 that conclude the Moab covenant, as it has long been recognized. But as particularly stressed by Hans Ulrich Steymans, unlike Deut 28, Lev 26 no longer stands in the ancient Near Eastern genre of epilogues to curses or laws where an earthly ruler calls down blessings and curses on his addressees. This observation may also explain why the terminology of blessing and curse from Deut 28 (with קלל, ברך, and ארר) is completely absent in Lev 26.[23] What we

---

5:8–10)"; cf. also Grünwaldt, *Das Heiligkeitsgesetz Leviticus 17–26*, 349: "The Decalogue prohibits the production of a cult image (פסל; Exod 20:4; Deut 5:8)." The following wording of Lev 26:1 includes further traditions, which similarly pertains to the command of images or representations of YHWH or other gods, as especially Deut 16:21–22; see the summary of the evidence in Nihan, *From Priestly Torah to Pentateuch*, 536–37.

22. Levine, "Epilogue to the Holiness Code."

23. Steymans, "Verheißung und Drohung," esp. 273–74; see further Nihan, *From Priestly Torah to Pentateuch*, 535–36; Müller, "Prophetic View of the Exile," 207–8. Marx, *Lévitique 17–27*, 200, also rightly remarks that the absence of the verb ברך in Lev 26 corresponds to a theology where "Yhwh never blesses only by his word," but "his presence itself is a blessing" (200). But even if this explanation is valid for the first

202 Christophe Nihan

have here instead is an oracle to Moses that interprets the history of Israel from the perspective of the alternative between torah observance or non-observance.[24] As has been correctly observed by Müller, this prophetic character of the epilogue to H is further confirmed by the reception of several prophetic texts in Lev 26, particularly from Ezekiel.[25]

Before going further into the analysis of Lev 26, a brief word is in order regarding ancient versions of this text. Altogether, the main versions show only a few significant differences with MT. Apart from some well-known variants—such as the singular reading מקדשכם "your sanctuary" in Lev 26:31 instead of the plural form מקדשיכם "your sanctuaries"—the text of the Samaritan Pentateuch (SP) is generally close to MT. LXX, on the other hand, contains several variants, particularly in Lev 26:39–45 (see below). In general, however, it remains unlikely that the Greek translator of Leviticus worked with a Hebrew *Vorlage* that would correspond to a literary edition of Leviticus substantially different from the one preserved in MT, and this is presumably true in the case of Lev 26 as well.[26] The situation may be different with the Greek translation of Leviticus found in Qumran, but the text preserved is limited and makes a definitive conclusion regarding the underlying *Vorlage* difficult.[27] Other Qumran manuscripts preserve

---

part of Lev 26 (vv. 3–13), it cannot explain the absence of verbs such as קלל and ארר in the second part of the chapter.

24. So, rightly Wellhausen, *Die Composition des Hexateuchs*, 168: "Prophecy in lofty, poetic speech" (see also Wellhausen, *Prolegomena zur Geschichte Israels*, 2nd ed. [Berlin: De Gruyter, 1883], 388); also Christoph Levin, *Die Verheißung des neuen Bundes in ihrem theologiegeschichtlichen Zusammenhang ausgelegt*, FRLANT 137 (Göttingen: Vandenhoeck & Ruprecht, 1985), 223–24; Steymans, "Verheißung und Drohung," 273: "Lev 26 thus belongs to the *Gattung* of prophetic speech." See also Ralf Rothenbusch, "Zur Ausgestaltung der Sinaiperikope durch die Priesterliche Gebotsmitteilung," in *"Ich werde meinen Bund mit euch niemals brechen!" (Ri 2,1): Festschrift für Walter Groß zum 70. Geburtstag*, ed. Erasmus Gaß and Hermann-Josef Stipp, HBS 62 (Freiburg i.B.: Herder, 2011), 4–5.

25. Müller, "Prophetic View of the Exile," 208: "The prophetic character of Lev 26 is not only due to the form; it results also from many quotations of or allusions to prophetic oracles, mainly from the book of Ezekiel."

26. For the expression *literary edition*, see, e.g., the methodological remarks by Philippe Hugo, "Text History of the Books of Samuel: An Assessment of the Recent Research," in *Archaeology of the Books of Samuel: The Entangling of the Textual and Literary History*, ed. Philippe Hugo and Adrian Schenker, VTSup 132 (Leiden: Brill, 2010), 7–10.

27. The Greek version of Leviticus that was found at Qumran contains a column

The Holiness Legislation and the Pentateuch 203

fragments of Hebrew versions of Lev 26, which do not show substantial differences vis-à-vis of MT.[28]

3. Tradition- and Composition-Historical Aspects of Lev 26:3–13

It is widely recognized that the concluding parenesis Lev 26:3–45 that follows the short exhortation in 26:1–2 consists of two main parts, 26:3–13 and 26:14–45, and this view requires no new demonstration. Each section begins with a protasis (vv. 3, 14) and ends with a reference to the exodus (vv. 13, 45).[29] The protasis in 26:3, which opens the first part of the epilogue, takes up the formula from Deut 28:1, 15.[30] The following apodoses in verses 4–13 describe the fullness of the prosperity that will be granted to the land and the Israelites if they keep YHWH's statutes (חקת) and com-

---

with Lev 26:2–16 that presents some variants with the LXX version of Leviticus. These variants have generally been understood as corresponding to a free translation of a Hebrew *Vorlage* close to the MT, cf., e.g., Esther Eshel, "Leviticus, Book of," in *Encyclopedia of the Dead Sea Scrolls*, ed. Lawrence H. Schiffman and James C. VanderKam (Oxford: Oxford University Press, 2000), 491. Recently, however, Innocent Himbaza, "What Are the Consequences If 4QLXXLev[a] Contains Earliest Formulation of the Septuagint?," in *Die Septuaginta—Orte und Intentionen: 5. Internationale Fachtagung veranstaltet von Septuaginta Deutsch (LXX.D), Wuppertal 24.–27. Juli 2014*, ed. Siegfried Kreuzer et al. (Tübingen: Mohr Siebeck, 2016), 294–308, has argued that the Greek fragments of Leviticus from Qumran may point to an edition of Leviticus distinct from the one used in other LXX witnesses. The whole issue is interesting but would require a longer discussion than can be provided here.

28. 4QLev-Num[a] preserves some lines in frag. 21, col. I that correspond to Lev 26:26–33 (cf. DJD XII, 161). The paleo-Hebrew Leviticus scroll (11QpaleoLev) contains lines in col. V that correspond to Lev 26:17–26 (see David N. Freedman and Kenneth A. Mathews, *The Paleo-Hebrew Leviticus Scroll (11QpaleoLev)* [Philadelphia: Eisenbrauns, 1985], 46–47). In both passages, the variants with MT, SamP, and LXX are mostly orthographic. The text of Lev 26 is not included in the other Leviticus scrolls from Qumran (4QLev[b, g]).

29. As Crüsemann, *Die Tora*, 354, rightly observes.

30. See the wording of Lev 26:3: אם־בחקתי תלכו ואת־מצותי תשמרו ועשיתם אתם with Deut 28:15 לשמר לעשות את־כל־, and Deut 28:1 לשמר לעשות את־כל־מצותיו וחקתיו מצותיו. The parallels with Deut 28:15 are quite obvious, as חקה and מצוה with שמר and עשה only occur together in these two places within the Pentateuch; outside the Pentateuch, this motif is found in some late- and post-Dtr passages in the book of Kings: 1 Kgs 6:12 MT (a passage that is missing from the LXX); 11:38; 2 Kgs 17:19, although in all these passages the wording is slightly closer to Deut 28:15 than to Lev 26:3. On the parallels with Deut 28, see Otto, "Innerbiblische Exegese," 179.

204 Christophe Nihan

mandments (מצות). This passage contains a fairly clear structure: verses 4–6 describe the prosperity of the land, verses 7–10 that of the people. In verses 11–13 there follows a representation of the divine presence in the midst of Israel, which concludes the entire passage. Verse 8, which is characterized by the *Wiederaufnahme* (resumptive repetition) of verse 7b in verse 8b, as well as verse 10, which further interprets the theme of 5bα and thus interrupts the connection between verses 9 and 11, are presumably later additions within 26:3–13.[31]

As often noted, this description has a clear parallel in two passages of Ezekiel announcing a future "covenant of peace" (ברית שלום) between YHWH and his people after the exile (Ezek 34:25–29 and 37:25–28), as well as in some key passages of the covenant theology of P, which speak of the consequences of the covenant with Abraham and his offspring.[32]

Lev 26:4–13	Exod 34:25–29
	... 26
4 ונתתי גשמיכם בעתם	והורדתי הגשם בעתו גשמי ברכה יהי
ונתנה הארץ יבולה	
ועץ השדה יתן פריו	27a ונתן עץ השדה את־פריו
5 והשיג לכם דיש את־בציר	והארץ תתן יבולה
ובציר ישיג את זרע	והיו על־אדמתם לבטח

---

31. So also Elliger, *Leviticus*, 365; Levin, *Die Verheißung*, 223; Müller, "Prophetic View of Exile," 211–12. These authors would also explain v. 5a as secondary, but their arguments are, in my opinion, not very strong, and v. 5a fits well between vv. 4 and 5b. The assumption that 26:11b and 12aα are later additions because of the repetition of בתוככם in 26:11a and 12aα (so Levin, *Die Verheißung*, 223; Müller, "Prophetic View of Exile"), is, indeed, possible but remains similarly unfounded.

32. For these parallels, see the detailed discussion by Bruno Baentsch, *Das Heiligkeits-Gesetz Lev XVII–XXVI: Eine historisch-kritische Untersuchung* (Erfurt: Güther, 1893), 121–24, as well as Levin, *Die Verheißung*, 224–26; also, e.g., Grünwaldt, *Das Heiligkeitsgesetz Leviticus 17–26*, 349–52; most recently, Müller, "Prophetic View of Exile," 209–12. See also Milgrom, "Leviticus 26 and Ezekiel," as well as Michael Lyons, *From Law to Prophecy: Ezekiel's Use of the Holiness Code*, LHBOTS 507 (London: T&T Clark, 2009), who both argue for the chronological priority of Lev 26 over Ezekiel. For the parallels with the key texts of the Priestly writing, which are all devoted to the covenant promise, cf. Lohfink, "Die Abänderung," 131, 133; see further Blum, *Studien zur Komposition des Pentateuch*, 326–27.

ואכלתם לחמכם לשבע	28b וישבו לבטח ואין מחריד
וישבתם לבטח בארצכם	וכרתי להם ברית שלום
6 ונתתי שלום בארץ	והשבתי חיה רעה מן הארץ
ושכבתם ואין מחריד	
והשבתי חיה רעה מן הארץ	
וחרב לא תעבר בארצכם	
7 ורדפתם את איביכם	
ונפלו לפניכם לחרב	
8 ורדפו מכם חמשה מאה	
ומאה מכם רבבה ירדפו	
ונפלו איביכם לפניכם לחרב	
9 ופניתי אליכם	Ezek 36:9 כי הנני אליכם ופניתי אליכם
והפריתי אתכם והרביתי אתכם	Gen 28:3 ואל שדי יברך אתך ויפרך וירבך
והקימתי את־בריתי אתכם	
10 ואכלתם ישן נושן	Gen 17:19b והקמתי את בריתי אתו
וישן מפני חדש תוציאו	לברית עולם לזרעו אחריו
	Ezek 37:25–28
11 ונתתי משכני בתוככם	26 וכרתי להם ברית שלו
ולא־תגעל נפשי אתכם	ברית עולם יהיה אותם ...
12 והתהלכתי בתוככם	ונתתי את מקדשי בתוכם לעולם
והייתי לכם לאלהים	27 והיה משכני עליהם
ואתם תהיו־לי לעם	והייתי להם לאלהים
	והמה יהיו־לי לעם
13 אני יהוה אלהיכם	
אשר הוצאתי אתכם מארץ מצרים	Ezek 34:27 וידעו כי אני יהוה
מהית להם עבדים	בשברי את מטות עלם
ואשבר	

The relationship between Lev 26 and Ezekiel can, in my opinion, be seen most clearly in Lev 26:9–13: Lev 26:9: "I will make you fruitful and increase you," with פרה and רבה, both in the *hiphil*, is characteristic for P but not for H or Ezekiel. The formulation with the *hiphil* corresponds instead to the promise to Abraham and his offspring in Gen 17:20; 28:3, and 48:4, which is also to be read against the background of Gen 1:22, 28, and 9:1, 7. In the same verse, the reference to the establishment or maintenance of the covenant with the people (with קום *hiphil*) similarly refers to the covenant with Abraham. However, the statement introduced in verse 9 that YHWH will devote himself to the Israelites—with ופניתי אליכם—has no parallel in P but corresponds word for word to Ezek 36:9.[33] Likewise, the promise that YHWH will establish his dwelling place "in the midst of the people" (Lev 26:11) corresponds to Ezek 37:26bβ (ונתתי את־מקדשי בתוכם), as Christoph Levin rightly remarks.[34] On the other hand, the replacement of מקדש with the word משכן in Lev 26:11 may be an allusion to the P passages in Exod 25:8 and 29:45–46.[35] The formulation of 26:11 (YHWH will erect his dwelling in the midst of the people, if they follow his commandments) implies a clear revision of the P-conception of Exod 40:34–35 where the promise of Exod 29:45 (and 25:8) is introduced as already realized—but it corresponds to the new definition of P's covenant theology in Lev 26 (see below).[36] Apparently, the word משכן in the context of Lev 26:11 describes not only the physical building but contains a more abstract meaning—something in the sense of "my (divine) presence."[37] This meaning of משכן is hardly prepared for in the prior narrative, where משכן always and exclusively describes the material sanctuary, but corresponds to Ezek 37:27a, where משכן already appears in parallel to אלהים.[38] As in Exod 29:45, the reference to the sanctuary in Lev 26:11 is followed by the covenant formula (והייתי לכם לאלהים) in verse 12, but, as in Ezek 37:27 already, this formula is now supplemented by the statement ואתם תהיו־לי לעם and thus corrects the more unilateral outlook that defines P's covenant theology.

---

33. Levin, *Die Verheißung*, 225; see also Grünwaldt, *Das Heiligkeitsgesetz Leviticus 17–26*, 352; Otto, "Innerbiblische Exegese," 181.

34. Levin, *Die Verheißung*, 224–225; see also, e.g., Grünwaldt, *Das Heiligkeitsgesetz Leviticus 17–26*, 352.

35. So also Müller, "Prophetic View of Exile," 210–11. Also, Levin, who argues for the priority of Lev 26 over P, must recognize that in this passage "the Ezekielian expression מקדש 'sanctuary' was replaced with the Priestly משכן 'dwelling'" (*Die Verheißung*, 225).

36. Nihan, *From Priestly Torah to Pentateuch*, 539–40.

37. As Milgrom, *Leviticus 23–27*, remarks.

38. See Ezek 37:27aα: והיה משכני עליהם with 37:27a: והייתי להם לאלהים.

The Holiness Legislation and the Pentateuch   207

Finally, Lev 26:13a takes up Lev 25:55, so that the first part of the epilogue is framed with the exodus motif. But in 26:13b, the quote from 25:55 is continued and supplemented with a reference to the "breaking" (שבר) of the "bars" (מטה) of the yoke, which likewise has a parallel in Ezek 34:27b.[39]

The way in which Lev 26:9–13 takes up and develops central P passages, but combines them with Ezek 37:25–28, already suggests that Ezek 37 is here the source for Lev 26. Otherwise, one would have to assume that the author of Ezek 37 carefully excised the majority of references to P, as he received his *Vorlage*, which seems rather implausible.[40] Ezekiel 37:25–28, for its part, can be explained without any reference to H, as I have argued elsewhere in detail, which confirms the chronological priority of this passage over Lev 26:9–13.[41] In contrast, the relationship between Lev 26 and Ezek 34 is more difficult to evaluate. With the exceptions of Lev 26:13b and Ezek 34:27b, the parallels with Ezek 34 are concentrated in Lev 26:4–6: Lev 26:4a corresponds to Ezek 34:26bα and Lev 26:4b with Ezek 34:27aα. Leviticus 26:5b repeats—in a slightly variant form—Lev 25:19, but the linking of ישב לבטח ("to dwell safely") with ואין מחריד ("and no one will terrify you") in 26:5b and 6a is also reminiscent of Ezek 34:28b. Finally, Lev 26:6b corresponds to the promise from Ezek 34:25a that YHWH will remove wild animals from the land, whereas the promise that the sword will no longer pass through the land has no parallel in Ezek 34, but is reminiscent of the court oracle of Ezek 14:17.[42] While some form of literary dependence between the two passages seems likely in view of these parallels, the relationship between Lev 26 (especially vv. 4–6) and Ezek 34:25–30 remains difficult to evaluate. Some observations may suggest that Ezek 34 presupposes Lev 26, rather than the other way round.[43] If so,

---

39. Otto, "Innerbiblische Exegese," 181. The expression עול + מטות is found only in these two passages.

40. Against Milgrom, "Leviticus 26 and Ezekiel," esp. 61–62; cf. also Milgrom, *Leviticus 23–27*, 2348–49. See also Hartley, *Leviticus*, 459–62.

41. Christophe Nihan, "Ezekiel and the Holiness Legislation: A Plea for Non-linear Models," in *The Formation of the Pentateuch: Bridging the Academic Cultures of Europe, Israel and North America*, ed. Jan C. Gertz et al., FAT 111 (Tübingen: Mohr Siebeck, 2016), 1029–34.

42. See Lev 26:6b: וחרב לא־תעבר בארצכם with Ezek 14:17: ואמרתי חרב העׁרב בארץ; also Levin, *Die Verheißung*, 225; Müller, "Prophetic View of Exile," 210.

43. In particular, while both Ezek 34:26 and Lev 26:4 contain a similar reference to the sending of rain by YHWH, Ezek 34 adds over Lev 26 an explicative comment, יהיו ברכה גשם (rendered as ὑετὸν εὐλογίας in G), "they will be rains of blessing." The

208   Christophe Nihan

this conclusion would correspond to the fact that Ezek 34:25–30 rewrites and expands Ezek 37:25–28, including features from Lev 26, which itself derives from Ezek 37 (reflecting the chronological sequence Ezek 37 → Lev 26 → Ezek 34).[44]

It appears, therefore, that the first part of the epilogue (Lev 26:3–13) takes up and revises various traditions from P and Ezekiel. In Lev 26, the promises contained in these Priestly and Ezekiel traditions are now rephrased as part of the apodoses that follow the protase in verse 3, with the resulting implication that the fulfillment of these promises is now made conditional upon Israel's compliance with YHWH's laws revealed at Mount Sinai: "If you observe my statutes and obey my commandments" (v. 3). The reinterpretation of earlier promises involved here does not merely impact P's covenant theology—as it has been generally recognized following Lohfink's seminal essay[45]—but also Ezekiel's covenant theology, particularly the oracle about the covenant of peace in Ezek 37. Like the covenant with Noah already, the covenant with Abraham in P comes with

---

presence of this explicative comment is easier to explain if one assumes that the reference to the sending of rain did not originate in Ezek 34 but was taken from Lev 26, so that the author of Ezek 34 felt the need to explain the meaning of this statement. Also, both in Ezek 34 and in Lev 26 a connection is made between YHWH's breaking of Israel's yoke and the deliverance from slavery, with the root עבד (see Lev 26:13a; Ezek 34:27b). The reference to the Israelites as the slaves of the nations and, correspondingly, the comparison of the return from exile as a deliverance from slavery are never found otherwise in Ezekiel, unlike in the other prophetic books. It is apparent that this concept is much more at home in Lev 26:13, where the reference is explicitly to YHWH delivering Israel from Egypt (see אשר הוצאתי אתכם מארץ מצרים, v. 13a). For these and other observations supporting the priority of Lev 26 over Ezek 34, see my discussion in Nihan, "Ezekiel and the Holiness Legislation," 1026–29.

44. For the view that Ezek 34:25–30 presupposes and rewrites 37:25–28, see, e.g., Karl-Friedrich Pohlmann, *Der Prophet Hesekiel/Ezechiel: Kapitel 20–48*, ATD 22.2 (Göttingen: Vandenhoeck & Ruprecht, 2001), 468. For the opposite view, see, especially Anja Klein, *Schriftauslegung im Ezechielbuch: Redaktionsgeschichtliche Untersuchungen zu Ez 34–39*, BZAW 391 (Berlin: De Gruyter, 2008), 175–79. But the argument for this thesis does not seem particularly plausible to me. Even the remark that against Ezek 34:23–24 the parallel passage 37:24–25 exclusively uses the title נשיא, whereas Ezek 37 has both נשיא and מלך, is best explained if Ezek 34 harmonized the earlier oracle in Ezek 37 (cf. also the LXX, which always reads ἄρχων = נשיא). For the chronological priority of Ezek 37:25–28 over 34:25–30, see further my discussion in Nihan, "Ezekiel and the Holiness Legislation," 1036–38.

45. Lohfink, "Die Abänderung"; see also above.

The Holiness Legislation and the Pentateuch   209

ethical conditions (cf. Gen 17:1b, התהלך לפני והיה תמים). Yet it remains, nevertheless, an "everlasting covenant" (ברית עולם), which can apparently not be unilaterally destroyed by Abraham and his offspring—a conception which also corresponds to P's distinct covenant formula.[46] Similarly— although this time from a more decidedly utopian perspective—the covenant of peace in Ezek 37 is declared an "everlasting covenant," as the formula in 37:26a makes clear (cf. וכרתי להם ברית שלום ברית עולם). However, this conception is now clearly revised in Lev 26. The covenant is no longer characterized as ברית עולם, and the possibility that the Israelites could "break" it (with פדר hiphil) is explicitly mentioned in 26:15–33. Correspondingly, Lev 26:12 supplements (cf. 26:12b, ואתם תהיו-לי לעם) and explicitly corrects P's unilateral covenant formula. The speech is also no longer about a covenant of peace as in Ezek 37:26 (and 34:25). Instead, the promise of peace within the land (Lev 26:6a) connects the instructions given at Sinai (v. 3) to Israel's obedience.[47]

The view that Lev 26 represents a substantial revision of the Priestly concept of covenant, is, however, questioned by those authors who interpret this chapter as an integral part of the Priestly writing. For these authors, particularly Blum and more recently Marx (who develops an argument similar to Blum's), the differences in the conceptions of covenant should rather be understood from the perspective of the narrative logic of the Priestly texts from Gen 1 to Lev 26: With Lev 26, which concludes the Sinai revelation, we reach a climax, so to speak. For Blum, this climax concerns the gradual "restitution" of God's imminence in Israel, for Marx, the return of a cosmic order, which is characterized by peace between human-

---

46. Specifically, it means that covenant offenses are punished individually, as Gen 9:5–6 makes clear (see also Gen 17:14), but they will not break the covenant itself between YHWH and Israel; see also Walter Groß, *Zukunft für Israel: Alttestamentliche Bundeskonzepte und die aktuelle Debatte um den Neuen Bund*, SBS 176 (Stuttgart: Katholisches Bibelwerk, 1998), 45–70; as well as my comments in Christophe Nihan, "The Priestly Covenant, Its Reinterpretations, and the Composition of 'P,'" in *The Strata of the Priestly Writings: Contemporary Debate and Future Directions*, ATANT 95, ed. Sarah Shectman and Joel Baden (Zürich: TVZ, 2009), 86–134, esp. 95–103.

47. For this comment, cf. esp. Otto, "Innerbiblische Exegese," 181. Further, as rightly noted by Otto, Ezek 34 and 37 combine the covenant of Israel with YHWH with the (re)instatement of David (cf. Ezek 34:23–24—in continuation of Jer 23:1–6— and 37:24–25); a perspective that is decidedly corrected in Lev 26: "The time for healing is not a result of the instatement of a new royal shepherd, but only Israel's obedience to the law" (Otto, "Innerbiblische Exegese," 182).

210   Christophe Nihan

ity and animals.[48] This climax produces new conditions in terms of the covenant that had not yet been given to the patriarchs, which then would explain the placement of Lev 26 at the end of the Sinai pericope.

Certainly, the assumption is correct that the observance of the law in Lev 26:3–13 leads to a new order, which is distinguished by a cosmic fullness like that approached by the Priestly worldview prior to the flood. This does not mean, however, that the remaining Priestly narrative in Genesis to Exodus was conceived from the beginning for such a climax in Lev 26, so that this chapter becomes an "absolutely necessary component" (so Blum) of this narrative.[49] In particular, this reading comes upon the difficulty that—in contrast to the conclusion of the narrative of the construction of the sanctuary in Exod 39–40—the allusions to the beginning of the Priestly narrative are very limited. Instead, the description of the fullness and the prosperity of the land in Lev 26 is much closer to Ezek 34 and 37, as observed above. The main connection between Lev 26:3–13 and Gen 1–11 concerns the expression והתהלכתי בתוככם in Lev 26:12a, which Blum interprets as alluding to the motif of the "walking" (also with הלך, hithpael) of the righteous Enoch and Noah with God before the flood (Gen 5:22, 24; 6:9).[50] Yet it is unclear whether this connection is so evident. The inversion of the subjects (in Gen 5–6 the righteous ones, in Lev 26 YHWH himself) cannot be so easily explained, and many exegetes have preferred seeing in Lev 26:12 a reference to 2 Sam 7:6, not without good reasons.[51] Apparently, this was already the interpretation of the Greek translator of Leviticus, since he renders הלך hithpael in 26:12 with the rare verb ἐμπεριπατέω, as also in 2 Sam 7:6.[52] At any rate, whether or not Lev

---

48. Blum, *Studien zur Komposition des Pentateuch*, 287–332; with regard to Lev 26, esp. 325–26; Marx, *Lévitique 17–27*, 198–200.

49. Blum, *Studien zur Komposition des Pentateuch*, 328.

50. Blum, *Studien zur Komposition des Pentateuch*, 326, and on this motif, 291–92.

51. See Lohfink, "Die Abänderung," 133; further, e.g., Grünwaldt, *Das Heiligkeitsgesetz Leviticus 17–26*, 352; Otto, "Innerbiblische Exegese," 179. Particularly the connection in 2 Sam 7:6 of "dwelling" (משכן, YHWH's "wandering" with the Israelites (with הלך hithpael) and Exodus corresponds to the motif of Lev 26:11–13. Additionally, Grünwaldt rightly remarks: "The idea of God walking in the midst of his people (v. 12aα) has its closest parallel in 2 Sam 7:6–7. where the dwelling of God with his people in a tent or a dwelling (משכן) contrasts with the dwelling in the temple" (*Das Heiligkeitsgesetz Leviticus 17–26*, 352).

52. In addition to 2 Sam 7:6, there could possibly be an allusion to Deut 23:15 in the LXX—where YHWH "walks" in the midst of the Israelite camp. Otherwise, the

The Holiness Legislation and the Pentateuch   211

26:12a alludes to Gen 5–6, it seems rather doubtful that such an observation can prove the assumption that the Priestly origins story in Gen 1–11 was designed from the outset to climax in Lev 26. Furthermore, this model cannot account for the obvious tensions between Lev 26 and the Priestly writing. How can it be explained, for example, that the giving of the משכן "in the midst of the people" is introduced as a promise, whereas it is presented as something already realized in Exod 40? Similarly, the assumption that the same Priestly writer would use the one-sided covenant formula in Genesis and Exodus and then move to a two-sided covenant formula in Lev 26 hardly seems convincing to me.[53] The alternative interpretation, which sees in Lev 26 a distinct—and consequently later—revision of the Priestly tradition regarding the covenant, seems more compelling.

4. Tradition- and Composition-Historical Aspects of Lev 26:14–46

The second and, in fact, largest part of the epilogue deals with the threats that the Israelites will encounter if they do not keep the commandments. These threats are organized in five successive penalties (26:16–17, 18–20, 21–22, 23–26, and 27–33), which—corresponding to the main theme of Lev 26 (see above)—culminate in the devastation of the land and the dispersion of the people. After the first punishment (vv. 16–17) each following sanction is introduced by the refrain that YHWH will punish the Israelites "sevenfold" for their sins (חטאת). The last two punishments are characterized by the use of the formula והלכתם עמי קרי or בקרי, "if you walk in hostility against me," in order to describe the disobedience of the people (vv. 23b, 27b). The same formula is found in the description of the fifth punishment (v. 28), where is it supplemented with the word חמה and describes YHWH's reaction against the Israelites (והלכתי עמכם בחמת־קרי), which formally signals the climax of the pattern. Overall, this pattern of escalation of the plagues or punishments forms a thematically coherent and—on the whole—literarily unified composition, which, on the one hand, portrays the negative counterpart to the various promises of 26:3–13 but, on the other hand, takes up further threats from Deut 28 and prophetic texts—especially Ezekiel. The fact that several of these threats belong to the genre of ancient Near Eastern treaties or laws—such as the

---

only other passages where the verb הלך hithpael is rendered as ἐμπεριπατέω in the LXX are Job 1:7 and 2:2.

53. See also the comments by Otto, *Theologische Ethik des Alten Testaments*, 237.

212   Christophe Nihan

motif of the ten women in 26:26, who have to bake bread in a single oven, which also appears in the inscription of Tell Fekheriye and Bukan[54]—does not change this picture. In the context of this essay, I can only mention the most important parallels with Deuteronomy and the prophetic corpus.[55]

With the phrase את־השפת ואת־הקדחת מכלות עינים ומדיבת נפש, Lev 26:16a takes up Deut 28:22 (קדחת and שחפת) as well as 28:65 (וכליון עינים ודאבון נפש),[56] and so the beginning and the end of the curse section of Deut 28. Leviticus 26:17a corresponds to Deut 28:25 (נגף לפני איביך), but introduces this quote with a formula (ונתתי פני בכם) that recalls Ezek 14:8.[57] Leviticus 26:17b, for its part, is a clear inversion of the promise of 26:7. Leviticus 26:19b "I will make your sky like iron and your land like copper" takes up Deut 28:23 (with inversion of the adjective), whereas the expression "strong pride" (גאון עז) in the first part of the verse otherwise only occurs in Ezekiel.[58] The end of the second punishment in 26:20 inverts the deliverance formula of 26:4.[59] The third punishment in 26:22—the sending of wild animals by YHWH, who will destroy humans and livestock—has several parallels with Ezekiel and seemingly combines Ezek 5:17 with 14:12–23.[60] The reference in the fourth punishment (Lev 26:25–26) to the triad of sword, plague, and hunger corresponds to a common

---

54. See also Jonas C. Greenfield and Aaron Schaffer, "Notes on the Curse Formulae of the Tell Fekherye Inscription," *RB* 92.1 (1985): 47–59; and the general remarks by Marx, *Lévitique 17–27*, 202–4.

55. For a detailed analysis of these parallels, cf. Grünwaldt, *Das Heiligkeitsgesetz Leviticus 17–26*, 355–64, and recently Müller, "Prophetic View," 213–16.

56. Grünwaldt, *Das Heiligkeitsgesetz Leviticus 17–26*, 355; and see Bruno Baentsch, *Exodus—Leviticus—Numeri*, HKAT 1.2 (Göttingen: Vandenhoeck & Ruprecht, 1903), 431; Elliger, *Leviticus*, 375.

57. So also, e.g., Müller, "Prophetic View from Exile," 214.

58. See Ezek 7:24; 24:21; 30:6, 18, and 33:28.

59. Compare ונתנה הארץ יבולה ועץ השדה יתן פריו (Lev 26:4b) with the wording of Lev 26:20b: ולא־תתן ארצכם את־יבולה ועץ הארץ לא יתן פריו.

60. On the parallels between Lev 26:22 and Ezekiel, see in detail, Baentsch, *Exodus—Leviticus—Numeri*, 431. For the combination, see rightly Müller, "Prophetic View from Exile," 215. The "sending" (with שלח) of wild animals (חיה), which "bereave" (שכל), is found only in Lev 26:22 and Ezek 5:17. The "destruction" (כרת) of cattle as well as the "devastation" (root: שמם) of the land recalls especially the oracle in Ezek 14:12–23; compare Ezek 14:15, 17, 19, 21. Müller, "Prophetic View from Exile," sees a further parallel with Ezek 33:28, although this does not seem particularly obvious to me.

The Holiness Legislation and the Pentateuch

motif in Jeremiah and Ezekiel (although the order is usually different).[61] But the formulation of Lev 26:25–26 again particularly recalls Ezekiel. The "sending" of the sword with בוא *hiphil* and חרב is characteristic for Ezekiel.[62] That the plague is mentioned as a single object of the verb שלח in Lev 26:25b is not typical for Jeremiah, since in Jer דבר only occurs as part of the triad, "sword, hunger, plague," but it does have a parallel in Ezekiel (see especially Ezek 14:19; 28:23).[63] The picture of the breaking of the bread pole (Lev 26:26aα) also occurs verbatim in some passages in Ezekiel.[64] In contrast, the announcement at the end of verse 25 (ביד־ ונתתם אויב "you will be given into the hand of your enemy") is reminiscent of a recurring formula in Jeremiah.[65] The combination of Deut 28, Ezekiel, and other prophetic texts is continued in the fifth and final punishment (Lev 26:27–33). Leviticus 26:29—the Israelites will eat the flesh of their sons and daughters—corresponds to Deut 28:53 (cf. also Jer 19:9).[66] The following verse (26:30) is parallel to Ezek 6:3bβ–5a (according to the MT),[67] as the following synopsis shows:

Lev 26:30	Ezek 6:3bβ–5a
והשמדתי את במתיכם	ואבדתי במותיכם
והכרתי את חמניכם	ונשמו מזבחותיכם ונשברו חמניכם
ונתתי את פגריכם על פגרי גלוליכם	והפלתי חלליכם לפני גלוליכם
וגעלה נפשי אתכם	ונתתי את פגרי בני ישראל לפני גלוליהם

---

61. See also Milgrom, *Leviticus 23–27*, 2313; Nihan, *From Priestly Torah to Pentateuch*, 543 n. 585.

62. Ezek 5:17; 6:3; 11:8; 14:17; 29:8; 33:2; otherwise only in a later passage of the book of Jeremiah (Jer 49:37 MT). Müller, "Prophetic View from Exile," 215, sees a specific reference to Ezek 14:17, but this view seems questionable to me.

63. Müller, "Prophetic View from Exile," sees Lev 26:25bα as a quote from Ezek 14:19, but the two passages are, in my opinion, formulated too distinctively to confirm this conclusion.

64. Ezek 4:16; 5:16; 14:13, elsewhere Ps 105:16; see also Grünwaldt, *Das Heiligkeitsgesetz Leviticus 17–26*, 359.

65. Cf. esp. Jer 20:5; 34:20, 21; 44:30; etc., and also Grünwaldt, *Das Heiligkeitsgesetz Leviticus 17–26*, 359; Müller, "Prophetic View from Exile," 215.

66. Although the same motif appears in other places (2 Kgs 6:28–29; Ezek 5:10 Lam 2:20; 4:10), the wording of Lev 26:29 is particularly close to Deut 28:53 (and Jer 19:9); see also Grünwaldt, *Das Heiligkeitsgesetz Leviticus 17–26*, 360.

67. Ezek 6:5a is missing from the LXX and could be a later addition.

214   Christophe Nihan

The last phrase (v. 30b) וגעלה נפשי אתכם is the only one without parallel in Ezek 6, because it is the counterimage to the positive phrase in Lev 26:11b (cf. 26:15, further 26:43).[68] Particularly interesting in this parallel between Lev 26:30 and Ezek 6:3bβ–5a are two comments. On the one hand, the sequence of the cultic places, whose destruction is announced, is almost identical in both passages: במות (high places), חמנים (possibly "incense altars" [?]), and, finally, גלולים (idols).[69] But on the other hand, the formula from Lev 26:30aβ, which corresponds to Ezek 6:5a, introduces a new expression: פגרי גלוליכם, literally, "the corpses of your idols."[70] This expression, which otherwise never occurs in the Hebrew Bible (!), is evidently to be understood as an explanatory update vis-à-vis the parallel passages in Ezekiel, whose function is to identify the idols (גלולים) with the dead (cf. Jer 16:18). So here is yet another example of the reception of Ezekiel in Lev 26.[71] This reception is further continued in the following verses (Lev 26:31–33): Lev 26:31aα (ונתתי את־עריכם חרבה) corresponds to a frequent formula from Ezekiel,[72] whereas Lev 26:31aβ recalls Ezek 6:4a (ונשמו מזב־חותיכם) and Amos 7:9. The announcement in Lev 26:32a, YHWH himself will "devastate" (שמם) the land of Israel, recalls the language of Ezekiel (cf.

---

68. Grünwaldt, *Das Heiligkeitsgesetz Leviticus 17–26*, 360.

69. Only the reference to the destruction of the altars at the beginning of Ezek 6:4 is not mentioned in the list of Lev 26:30, but this motif has a parallel in Lev 26:31aβ, cf. Nihan, *From Priestly Torah to Pentateuch*, 544 n. 590. The meaning of חמנים is unclear; often it is translated as "incense altar," but there is a reason to accept that חמן describes a structure that was different from an altar. Compare especially 2 Chr 34:4: "In his presence, they pulled down the altars of the Baals; the חמנים, which stood above them, he shattered." See also Milgrom, *Leviticus 23–27*, 2318: the Aramaic Inscription from Palmyra, where the word חמן appears next to "altar" (ḥmn' dnh w'lt' dnh), is compatible with this meaning, as Milgrom rightly remarks. Often it is assumed that גלולים refers to a stela, which is at least partly correct, but—especially in the context of the book of Ezekiel—there is a reason for the assumption that the word could include other cultic or ritual platelets, like, e.g., amulets; see also J. Schoneveld, "Ezekiel XIV 1–8," *OTS* 15 (1969): 193–204, as well as Daniel Bodi, *The Book of Ezekiel and the Poem of Erra*, OBO 104 (Fribourg: Vandenhoeck & Ruprecht, 1991), 314 n. 17. The meaning of גלולים as amulets is especially supported by Ezek 14:3, 4, 7, where the גלולים are placed "on the heart" (על לב).

70. Compare LXX: τα κῶλα τῶν εἰδώλων ὑμῶν.

71. Against Milgrom, *Leviticus 23–27*, 2319.

72. See Ezek 5:14; 25:13; 29:10; 30:12; see also Jer 25:18. In Ezek 5:14 and Jer 25:18, however, the syntactic construction represents a small variant, since the verb נתן before the object (חרבה) takes a *lamed*.

The Holiness Legislation and the Pentateuch   215

esp. Ezek 6:14; 33:28). The same goes for the announcement of the exile of the people (v. 33a), which culminates with the threats of Lev 26:27–33: The expression "draw the sword against you/them" (with ריק *hiphil* + אחר) is found otherwise only in Ezekiel (!), and the announcement that YHWH will "scatter" (זרה) his people "among the nations" (בגוים)—once again— has its closest parallel in Ezekiel.[73]

Admittedly, the literary unity of verses 30–33 has been questioned at times, especially in the case of verses 30–31.[74] But those arguments are not necessarily compelling, and this solution creates some difficulties. Verses 30–31 represent the counterpart for the promise of 26:11–12, namely, that YHWH will establish his dwelling "in the midst" of Israel (v. 11a) and walk himself "in the midst" of his people (v. 12a). In light of the central-ity of this promise—and, further, of the sanctuary theology of H!—the absence of any reference to the sanctuary and the cult in the second part of Lev 26 would be surprising. Verse 32 follows logically after this. As a matter of fact, it is simpler to understand why verse 32 emphasizes the total destruction of the land by YHWH himself: והשמתי אני את הארץ, if one reads this verse after verses 30–31: instead of appeasing YHWH, the Israelites' sacrifices irritated him. Apparently, this is because the Israelite sanctuaries mixed Yahwistic and non-Yahwistic customs to such an extent that the deity itself will devastate the entire land in response to these sac-rifices (v. 32)—a description which represents a complete and deliberate inversion of the traditional function of the cult. These observations shed light on the structure and logic of the passage and suggest that the text of verses 30–33 follows a clear line from cult to land, which fits well within H's theology. Verse 30 foretells the dispersion of the cultic institutions, where YHWH was worshiped together with other gods; verse 31, the dis-persion of the cities and their sanctuaries dedicated to YHWH; and verse 32, the devastation of the land itself. Finally, verse 33a culminates with the announcement of the dispersion of the Israelites among the nations, while verse 33b functions as a short summary of the whole passage.[75] Based on

---

73. For "draw the sword," see Ezek 5:2, 12; 12:14. Regarding "scatter … among the nations," the book of Ezekiel consistently uses a longer form, including פוץ *hiphil* + בגוים followed by זרה *piel* + בארצות; see Ezek 12:15; 20:23; 22:15; 29:12; 30:23, 26; 36:19.

74. Among recent scholars, see, especially, Müller, "Prophetic View from Exile," 216–17.

75. The identification of this structure thus accounts for the apparent difficulties

216   Christophe Nihan

these observations, I consider the literary unity of verses 30–33 quite possible and even probable.

More complicated is the formulation of verses 34–36, the rest of the second part of the epilogue. Leviticus 26:34–35 mention the restoration of the land after the exile, since the land will enjoy its Sabbaths. The description is clearly formulated as an allusion to the law of the Sabbath year (Lev 25:2–7), since the construction with ארץ as the subject of the verb שבת is found only in Lev 25:2 and 26:34 (and also once in 2 Chr 36:21). There follows in 26:36–38 a mention of the situation of the exiled Israelites in the land or in their enemies' land, which again clearly frames the description of the salvation in 26:3–13: cf. 26:36b (ונפלו ואין רדף) and 26:37a with 26:7, as well as 26:37b (ולא־תהיה לכם הקומה) with 26:13bβ (ואולך אתכם קוממיות). With the assertion in verse 38: "You will perish [with אבד] among the nations and your enemy's land will consume you," clearly a new climax is reached. But a perspective of restoration, which stands in marked contrast with the previous disasters in verses 14–38, begins with verse 39 (and not only with v. 40, as is often assumed).[76] The wording of this last unit includes several difficulties, which also partially explains the variations in the text of the LXX and therefore requires a more detailed analysis.

Verses 39 and 40a were designed as a contrast. Verse 39 MT mentions how the remaining Israelites will rot (מקק) because of their "guilt" (עון) as well as because of the guilt of their fathers. The wording is prob-

---

raised by the description in vv. 30–33, on the basis of which Müller wants to identify vv. 30–31 as a later addition ("Prophetic View from Exile," 216–17). Thus, the repetition of the destruction of the cities in v. 33b after v. 31a corresponds to the summary function of v. 33. Likewise, the emphasis in v. 32 on the destruction of the land by YHWH himself does not come "too late" after vv. 30–31 but corresponds on the contrary to the logic of this passage. I also do not find Müller's other arguments particularly persuasive: The repetition of the form והשמותי in vv. 31a and 32a is not redundant, since the object of the verb is different (in v. 31 the sanctuaries, in v. 32 the land); and the destruction of the sanctuaries is certainly not a simple "digression" after v. 29 but a necessary theme of the second part of Lev 26, as discussed above.

76. See recently, e.g., John W. Wevers, *Notes on the Greek Text of Leviticus*, SCS 44 (Atlanta: Scholars Press, 1997), 460 ("With v. 40 begins a message of hope"); Milgrom, *Leviticus 23–27*, 2329–30; Marx, *Lévitique 17–27*, 206–7; on the contrary, other commentators rightly think that the restoration perspective already begins with v. 39, see, e.g., Elliger, *Leviticus*, 372; Baruch Levine, *Leviticus: The Traditional Hebrew Text with the New JPS Translation*, JPSTC (Philadelphia: The Jewish publication Society, 1989), 190; Steymans, "Verheißung und Drohung," 282 n. 71; Grünwaldt, *Das Heiligkeitsgesetz Leviticus 17–26*, 361; Müller, "Prophetic View from Exile," 221.

The Holiness Legislation and the Pentateuch 217

ably taken from Ezek 4:17 and 33:10, whereas the idea that the Israelites languish because of their fathers' guilt implies a correction of Ezek 18.[77] The repetition of the verb מקק at the end of verse 39 is not sufficient to regard the mention of the fathers' guilt as evidence of its literary-critical secondary nature, not least because the motif is mentioned again in verse 40 (see below).[78] This observation also suggests that the LXX, which is missing the reference to the fathers' guilt in verse 39b, does not automatically preserve the older reading here.[79] The omission of the fathers' guilt in the Greek versions of Lev 26:39 probably goes back to a textual change and not an older version. As already seen in Ezek 33:10, the mention of the "wasting away" of the Israelites immediately leads to a proclamation of salvation. But while Ezek 33:11 calls the Israelites to "turn" (שוב), Lev 26:40a announces that the Israelites will "confess" (ידה hithpael) their iniquity and the iniquity of their fathers (40a). Against many exegetes, the syntax provides no reason to understand verse 40a as the beginning a new protasis (namely, "if they will confess their iniquity").[80] The confession of the Israelites is clearly announced as a future event, which is also how the LXX understands it.[81] The Israelites' confession of iniquity follows, then, in verses 40b–41a. The wording that is used here clearly takes up the beginning and the end of the last punishment (Lev 26:27–33), which is now summarized, in a certain sense, in the confession of the people found in verses 40b–41a: The claim that the Israelites have "walked" against YHWH

---

77. See Ezek 18:20a: הנפש החטאת היא תמות; on the contrast between Lev 26:39 and Ezek 18, see also Levine, *Leviticus*, 190; Grünwaldt, *Das Heiligkeitsgesetz Leviticus 17–26*, 362. For the connection with Ezek 4 and 33, see Grünwaldt, *Das Heiligkeitsgesetz Leviticus 17–26*, 361–62.

78. Müller, "Prophetic View from Exile," 222, explains, to the contrary, the reference to the guilt of the fathers in v. 39 as an addition because of the repetition of מקק, but this solution forces him to make the phrase ואת עון אבתם in v. 40a also secondary, for which I see no compelling reason.

79. However, it is unclear whether the omission of the fathers in the LXX of Lev 26:39 is to be explained as intentional or unintentional; Wevers, *Notes on the Greek Text of Leviticus*, 459, understand it as a homoeoteleuton—the Greek translator skipped from איביהם to אתם—but this explanation does not seem obvious to me.

80. So recently Milgrom, *Leviticus 23–27*, 2330; see also, e.g., Hartley, *Leviticus*, 453, 469.

81. The slightly different wording of the LXX at the end of v. 40a is explained by the fact that the Greek translator rendered the complicated Hebrew expression במעלם אשר מעלו in the MT and SamP with two different phrases; for more detail, see Wevers, *Notes on the Greek Text of Leviticus*, 460.

218 Christophe Nihan

in hostility (ואף אשר־הלכו עמי בקרי), so that YHWH himself must "walk" in hostility against the Israelites (ואף אני אלך עמם בקרי) corresponds to Lev 26:27b–28a (cf. 26:21, 23, 24),[82] while the claim that YHWH has brought them into their enemy's land corresponds to 26:34, 38.

This future scenario is then completed in verse 41b with a further statement, which is introduced with the unique expression או אז. Against the assumption of some commentators, there are, in my opinion, few reasons to translate או אז here with "if then."[83] It is more probable that או here is to be interpreted as "or," as most commentators assume.[84] In this case, it must be understood that verse 41b describes another alternative scenario alongside verses 40–41a. This interpretation is, indeed, possible, but it does not really explain why או is here combined with אז. It is possible that the construct או אז results from a textual corruption (dittography), since the LXX only reads τότε = אז at the beginning of verse 41b.[85] However, it is equally possible that LXX simplifies here the difficult Hebrew text. If one wishes to retain the Hebrew text as it is, arguably the best solution is Levine's assumption that או אז should be rendered here as "only then."[86] In this case, verse 41b is not an alternative scenario but a further—and, in fact,

---

82. The *yiqtol* is to be interpreted here as a modal. Although the statement that the Israelites have "walked" in hostility against YHWH, with הלך עם + קרי, is already found in Lev 26:21, 23, 24, it appears with בקרי (and not only קרי), only at the beginning of the fifth and final punishment in Lev 26:27b. Marx, *Lévitique 17–27*, 207, who wants to see in 26:40b–41a a specific reference to the fourth punishment (vv. 23b–24a), unfortunately ignores this point.

83. So Rashi, and compare, e.g., Milgrom, *Leviticus 23–27*, 2332; recently also Müller, "Prophetic View from Exile," 224. 1 Sam 20:10 points to the fact that in the context of an indirect interrogative clause או can introduce a conditional clause; cf. also GKC §150i. But the context of Lev 26:41 is clearly different, and—against Elliger, *Leviticus*, 362–63—there is no reason here to understand Lev 26:41b as an indirect interrogative clause. The parallel with Exod 21:36 (so Rashi) is not very clear, since in this passage the protasis, which is introduced with או follows another protasis in 21:35, which is classically introduced with כי; the same particle is probably presupposed in v. 36.

84. So, e.g., Hartley, *Leviticus*, 455; Marx, *Lévitique 17–27*, 194.

85. So, e.g., Wevers, *Notes on the Greek Text of Leviticus*, 461. See also Steymans, "Verheißung und Drohung," 282, who notes: "Perhaps, one should not, however, over interpret the particle או at this point, because the Septuagint does not translate it."

86. Levine, *Leviticus*, 191. According to Levine, the unique construct או אז may be compared with כי אז, a construct that clearly has the meaning "only then" in Josh 1:8 and other passages (e.g., Zeph 3:9).

The Holiness Legislation and the Pentateuch   219

necessary!—consequence of the scenario initiated in verses 40–41: "(only) then [אז או] will their uncircumcised hearts be humbled, and then [אז] will the Israelites make amends for their iniquity." The motif of the people's "uncircumcised heart" recalls, of course, Jeremiah and Ezekiel,[87] while the "payment" for iniquity in a quasi-juristic sense (with רצה and עון) sets the epilogue of the Sinai revelation in parallel to Isa 40:2 (the beginning of Deutero-Isaiah!).[88] At the same time, the situation of the exiled Israelites parallels the situation of the land, which "enjoys" (also with רצה, v. 34a) its Sabbaths during the exile.[89]

Starting with verse 42, the consequences of the confession of iniquity are no longer described for the Israelites but for Yahweh himself: According to verse 42, YHWH will remember (זכר) his ברית with Jacob, Isaac, and Abraham (in this order) together with the land.[90] Remembering the covenant with the patriarchs is clearly further reception of P's covenant theology. It is combined here in a unique way with the motif of "remembering the land," which corresponds to the overall theme of Lev 25–26. Additionally, one may also see in the motif of the remembering of the land an allusion to the motif of the ברית with the earth in Gen 9:13. In 26:43–44, then, YHWH's remembrance of the covenant (and the land) is justified by the fact that even if the Israelites were exiled because they "rejected" (מאס) and "detested" (געל) YHWH's משפטים and חקת (v. 43)—a

---

87. See Jer 4:4; 9:25; Ezek 44:7, 9; see also Deut 10:16; 30:6. In Lev 26:41, however, this motif is used in connection with the verb כנע niphal, which is without parallel in the Hebrew Bible. Müller, "Prophetic View from Exile," 224, rightly remarks that this use of כנע niphal with the sense "humble themselves" is characteristic especially for the language of the book of Chronicles: 2 Chr 7:14; 12:6–7, 12; 30:11; 32:26; 33:12, 19, 23; 34:27; 36:12.

88. The parallel with Isa 40:2 is unavoidable, since this expression only appears in these two passages; cf., e.g., Groß, *Zukunft für Israel*, 94–95. The assumption of a root רצה II (so Groß and others) seems questionable to me, but this point may be passed over for now.

89. Marx, *Lévitique 17–27*, 208–9.

90. The wording of the MT and SamP with בריתי + PN (Jacob, Isaac, Abraham), is syntactically difficult but should be maintained despite various proposals to emend the text; compare Jer 33:20 and see also my detailed discussion in Nihan, *From Priestly Torah to Pentateuch*, 541 n. 576. The order of the patriarchs is best explained as an intentional literary-exegetical technique of the scribes, a "'Zurückschreiten' in der Geschichte" (="a 'retrogression' in the story"), so Thomas Römer, *Israels Väter: Untersuchungen zur Väterthematik im Deuteronomium und in der deuteronomistischen Tradition*, OBO 99 (Göttingen: Vandenhoeck & Ruprecht, 1990), 549.

220   Christophe Nihan

clear reference to Lev 26:15 (beginning of the threats!)[91]—YHWH will nevertheless not "break" his covenant with them (v. 44). Quite clearly, the reinterpretation of P's covenant theology here, which characterized the first part of the epilogue, goes one step further: namely, the one-sidedness of the Priestly covenant is reconfirmed after the exile, but the restoration of the covenant is nevertheless dependent upon the fact that the remaining Israelites confess their iniquity. Nonetheless, this confession of guilt in Lev 26 is not formulated as a condition but as a future event, as argued above. This reinterpretation of the Priestly covenant theology in the final verses of the epilogue culminates, then, in verse 45, where YHWH's remembrance of the covenant is mentioned once again, but this time with the formula ברית ראשים, "covenant with the forefathers (or ancestors)" (26:45a). In the relative clause of the second half of the verse, these ראשנים are characterized by the following words: "whom I brought out of the land of Egypt before the eyes of the nations to be their God" (26:45b). For that reason, ראשנים hardly describes the patriarchs but rather the exodus generation, whose covenant with YHWH is now coordinated with the patriarchal covenant at the end of the Sinai revelation.[92] Thus, here the covenant with the exodus generation is integrated in a coherent "covenant remembrance of YHWH," which goes back to Abraham—at least if 26:45 is read in connection with 26:42.

---

91. In the Hebrew Bible, the combination מאס משפט and נעל הקה is found only in these two passages: Lev 26:15 and 26:43.

92. For the position that ראשנים denotes the patriarchs, see especially Groß, *Zukunft für Israel*, 97–99; see also also Steymans, "Verheißung und Drohung," 275. The difficulties that this interpretation raises are shown by the fact that Groß must remove the construction ברית ראשנים from its context in his translation of Lev 26:45 in order to move it to the end of the verse (!), which hardly corresponds to the syntax of the MT (and SamP) (*Zukunft für Israel*, 98). Additionally, in Groß's interpretation, Lev 26:45 is simply redundant in light of Exod 2:24. For a further discussion, see Milgrom, *Leviticus 23–27*, 2338–39, as well as my comments in Nihan, *From Priestly Torah to Pentateuch*, 542 n. 580. For the position that Lev 26:45 refers to the Sinai covenant, see also recently Rothenbusch, "Ausgestaltung," 5. For a detailed argument that Lev 26:45 can only refer to the exodus generation, see my discussion in Christophe Nihan, "Leviticus 26:39–46 and the Post-Priestly Composition of Leviticus: Some Remarks in Light of the Recent Discussion," in *The Post-Priestly Pentateuch: New Perspectives on its Redactional Development and Theological Profiles*, ed. Frederico Giuntoli and Konrad Schmid, FAT 101 (Tübingen: Mohr Siebeck, 2015), 321–22.

The Holiness Legislation and the Pentateuch 221

5. Lev 26:39–46 and the Post-Priestly Redaction of H

It is no coincidence that the thesis that Lev 26 should be assigned to a post-Priestly Pentateuch redaction was first proposed (if I am not mistaken) by Thomas Römer, with reference to Lev 26:42–45.[93] That the covenant to which Lev 26:45 refers can only be the Sinai covenant is clear from the context—at least if one accepts that the "ancestors" (ראשנים) in this verse describe the exodus generation (see above). But, as has long been recognized, the conclusion of a covenant with the exodus generation is narrated nowhere in P. On the contrary, P understands both exodus and Sinai as realizations of the Abrahamic covenant, as the comparison between Exod 6:2–8, 25:8 and 29:45–46 with Gen 17 already demonstrates.[94] The most

---

93. Römer, *Israels Väter*, 549–50: "Damit kommen wir in der Nähe einer nach-priesterlichen Pentateuch-(End-)Redaktion in 'dtr' Gewand." For this position in reference to Lev 26:42–45, see esp. Otto, *Theologische Ethik des Alten Testaments*, 237; Groß, *Zukunft für Israel*, 99–101; Christophe Nihan, "The Priestly Covenant, Its Reinterpretations, and the Composition of 'P,'" in *The Strata of the Priestly Writings: Contemporary Debate and Future Directions*, ed. Sarah Shectman (Zürich: TVZ, 2009), 106–15.

94. See the classic essay by Walther Zimmerli, "Sinaibund und Abrahambund: Ein Beitrag zum Verständnis der Priesterschrift," in *Gottes Offenbarung. Gesammelte Aufsätze zum Alten Testament*, TB 19 (Munich: Kaiser, 1963), 205–16. The attempt by Jeffrey Stackert to identify a P covenant tradition in Exod 31:12–17 is, in my view, not convincing, despite Stackert's detailed argumentation; see Jeffrey Stackert, "Compositional Strata in the Priestly Sabbath: Exodus 31:12–17 and 35:1–3," *JHS* 11 (2011): 1–21, and see also Stackert, "Distinguishing Innerbiblical Exegesis," 378 n. 28. Although he recognizes that Exod 31:12–17 in its present form is post-Priestly ("H"), Stackert reconstructs a P-Grundlage in vv. 12, 13aα, 15*, 16–17. On the one hand, the criteria for this reconstruction are rather questionable; so, e.g., Stackert must remove the words שבתון and קדש in v. 15 in order to identify a "P" stratum in this verse, although there are no literary-critical arguments for this operation; on the other hand, it should be noted that even when the text is reconstructed in this way, it still shows clear parallels to the HC; see, e.g., the beginning of v. 15 ששת ימים יעשה מלאכה וביום השביעי שבת—which Stackert identifies as "P" material within Exod 31:12–17—with Lev 23:3a! As before, I remain closer to the opinion that Exod 31:12–17 is *in toto* a later, post-Priestly text; compare Klaus Grünwaldt, *Exil und Identität: Beschneidung, Passa und Sabbat in der Priesterschrift*, BBB 85 (Frankfurt am Main: Vandenhoeck & Ruprecht, 1992), 173–77; and recently Alexandra Grund, *Die Entstehung des Sabbats: Seine Bedeutung für Israels Zeitkonzept und Erinnerungskultur*, FAT 75 (Tübingen: Mohr Siebeck, 2011), 273–87. For a detailed statement, cf. now my discussion in Christophe Nihan, "Das Sabbatgesetz Exodus 31,12–17, die Priesterschrift und das

222 Christophe Nihan

likely—if not the only possible—explanation is thus the position that here Lev 26 refers to a covenant whose development is narrated only in the non-Priestly traditions. The position of Jan Joosten, who identifies this covenant with the exodus itself, seems unlikely to me, as Joosten must interpret this verse in the following way: "I will remember the covenant with the first ones, in that [אשר] I led them out of the land of Egypt," an interpretation, which in principle is grammatically possible, but is not natural and, as far as I can tell, is also not confirmed by any of the ancient versions.[95]

In order to advocate a reading of Lev 26 within the mere context of the Priestly narrative, which knows no covenant at Sinai, the main alternative is to assume that the covenant to which Lev 26:45 refers corresponds to the Holiness legislation itself, a solution that was already argued by Cholewiński in particular.[96] Cholewiński rightly remarked that Lev 26:45 and 46 are connected by the reference to the Sinai covenant, of which the subscription in verse 46 would form the conclusion.[97] Yet he errs when he assumes that the laws mentioned in the subscription of verse 46 are identical with the Holiness legislation itself. As Elliger already observed, the terminology that is used for these laws in Lev 26:46 is quite unusual for H.[98] The phrase אלה החקים והמשפטים והתורת has a parallel in Deut 12:1, the introduction to the Deuteronomic Code proper (Deut 12–26), except that Lev 26:46 adds the mention of תורת (more on this below); a further parallel can be found in Deut 4:45. The combined use of חקים and משפטים to describe the entirety of the divine laws is likewise characteristic of the

---

Heiligkeitsgesetz: Eine Auseinandersetzung mit neueren Interpretationen," in *Wege der Freiheit: Zur Entstehung und Theologie des Exodusbuches; Die Beiträge eines Symposions zum 70. Geburtstag von Rainer Albertz*, ed. Reinhard Achenbach et al., ATANT 104 (Zürich: TVZ, 2014), 131–49.

95. See Joosten, "Covenant Theology in the Holiness Code," 143–64. For the identification of the covenant in Lev 26:45 with the (non-Priestly) Sinai covenant, see also my discussion in Nihan, "Leviticus 26:39–46," 322–24.

96. See Cholewiński, *Heiligkeitsgesetz und Deuteronomium*, 126–27, 138–39: The redactor of H—against the Priestly writing—returned "its character of a covenant conclusion" to the Sinai event and understood H itself as a "Zeichen" (= "sign") of this covenant (p. 139). This view was recently defended by Joosten, "Covenant Theology," 152 with note 34 and *passim*.

97. Cholewiński, *Heiligkeitsgesetz und Deuteronomium*, 126.

98. Elliger, *Leviticus*, ad. loc.; compare Steymans, "Verheißung und Drohung," 265–66.

The Holiness Legislation and the Pentateuch 223

Deuteronomic legislation; in effect, outside of Deuteronomy, Lev 26:46 is the *only* occurrence of the phrase החקים והמשפטים in the Tetrateuch.[99] In fact, as noted by several scholars, the term חקים is entirely unusual in H or, for that matter, in Leviticus as a whole.[100] As a term referring to the divine laws, or statutes, it never occurs previously within Lev 17–26, where only the feminine form, חקה, is used.[101] It only occurs once within Lev 1–16, in Lev 10:11—a passage which, moreover, could derive from Lev 26:46.[102] The third term listed in Lev 26:46, תורת, is likewise unusual for H, since it never occurs in Lev 17–26 prior to this verse. As suggested by various commentators, it is presumably a reference to the rituals described in Lev 1–16, which are consistently referenced as תורה (although the plural, תורת, is never used).[103] At the same time, the plural תורת also occurs, in combination with other legal terms, in some late non-Priestly traditions.[104] This perspective is continued in the LXX, where תורת in Lev 26:46 is rendered with ὁ νόμος, possibly a reference to the Mosaic legislation as a whole.[105]

These observations appear to indicate that the divine laws which, in Lev 26:46, comprise the contents of the ברית with the exodus generation to which 26:45 refers, are not restricted to H, or even to a combined narrative comprising P and H, but include both Priestly and non-Priestly legal traditions.[106] Against Carr's aforementioned assumption, it is thus not about

---

99. See Deut 4:1, 5, 8, 14, 45; 5:1, 31; 6:1, 20; 7:11; 11:32; 12:1; 26:16, 17. It also occurs three times in some (late) passages of the book of Kings, see 1 Kgs 8:58; 9:4; 2 Kgs 17:37.

100. For this observation, see already Elliger, *Leviticus*, 371; further, e.g., Milgrom, *Leviticus 23–27*, 2342; similarly Thomas Hieke, *Levitikus*, HKAT (Freiburg i.B.: Herder, 2014), 1098–99.

101. In Lev 24:9, the term חק is used with the meaning of "assigned portion (of an offering)," which is its usual meaning in P.

102. For a detailed discussion, see Nihan, *From Priestly Torah to Pentateuch*, 590–93.

103. See Lev 7:37–38; 11:46; 12:7; 13:59; 14:2, 32, 54, 57; 15:32. For this idea, see, e.g., Milgrom, *Leviticus 23–27*, 2342; Hieke, *Levitikus*, 1099.

104. See Gen 26:5; Exod 16:28; 18:16, 20; outside of the Pentateuch, this usage is also found in some late passages of the Dtr literature, like especially 1 Kgs 2:3. For this observation, see Otto, "Innerbiblische Exegese," 179.

105. See the discussion by Wevers, *Notes on the Greek Text of Leviticus*, 464–65. In my view, the shift from the plural to the singular has a precedent in Deut 4:8, where we already find the combination of חקים and משפטים with תורה (in the singular), instead of תורת as in Lev 26:46.

106. For this view, with regard to the language of Lev 26:46, see already the

224 Christophe Nihan

conceptual coherence but more fundamentally about *narrative* coherence. The covenantal theology of Lev 26 is not to be construed as a preredactional adaptation or harmonization of Priestly and non-Priestly materials within a still independent Priestly Document, but instead Lev 26 seems to already presuppose the redactional integration of the Priestly narrative with the non-Priestly tradition of the Sinai covenant.

The conclusion presented here, however, is valid for the current form of Lev 26:39–45. Before I discuss further implications of these results for the Holiness legislation and its relationship to Leviticus, first the question of the literary unity of this material as well as how it fits with the rest of the chapter needs to be briefly addressed. H. Louis Ginsberg and Levine in particular have advocated the thesis that Lev 26 originally ended with the reference to the perishing of the Israelites in verse 38, in the same way as in Deut 28 (cf. Deut 28:64–68).[107] Müller has recently reaffirmed this position in his essay.[108] In my opinion, however, the arguments in favor of this reconstruction are not decisive and the alleged tensions between verses 36–38 and 39–45 may have been overemphasized, especially as regards the transition between verses 38 and 39.[109] For instance, there is no need to see a contradiction between the reference to the "disappearance" (with אבד *qal*) of the Israelites "among the nations" (בגוים) in verse 38 and the mention of "survivors" (הנשארים) in verse 39; in other contexts where the verb אבד *qal* is used to describe the catastrophe striking the Israelites, such catastrophe leaves nonetheless a number of survivors.[110] It is true that verse 39 MT now mentions "the *lands* of your enemies" (ארצת איביכם), in the plural, whereas other passages in Lev 26 refer to "the land of your

---

remarks by Otto, "Innerbiblische Exegese," 179–80. See also my earlier discussion in Nihan, *From Priestly Torah to Pentateuch*, 551–52.

107. Harold Louis Ginsberg, *The Israelian Heritage of Judaism*, Texts and Studies of the Jewish Theological Seminary of America 24 (New York: The Jewish Theological Seminary of America, 1982), 80–81; Levine, "Epilogue to the Holiness Code," esp. 19; see also Levine, *Leviticus*, 275–81.

108. Müller, "Prophetic View from Exile," 218–22.

109. The following discussion takes up and continues the argument I have already developed in Nihan, "Leviticus 26:39–46," 314–17.

110. See especially Deut 4:26–27, with the same sequence comprising אבד *qal* and שאר *niphal*; compare also, e.g., Deut 28:51 and 28:62. It should be noted that אבד does not mean only "to perish," as it is usually translated, but has a broader meaning of "to be lost, dispersed" (see, e.g., Isa 27:13); compare also the comments by Milgrom, *Leviticus 23–27*, 2326.

The Holiness Legislation and the Pentateuch 225

enemies" (ארץ איביכם), in the singular (Lev 26:34, 38, 43). However, the phrase "in the lands (pl.) of their enemies" already occurs in verse 36, and besides it is entirely consistent with earlier references to the scattering of the Israelites "among the *nations* [בגוים]" in 26:33aα, which is repeated in 26:38a. It seems difficult, therefore, to regard the alternation between the singular and the plural reference to the land(s) of the enemies as a valid redactional criterion. Presumably, the plural has in view a broader diaspora, whereas the singular refers to a specific group of exiles—most likely the Babylonian *golah*.[111] A similar observation applies with regard to the alternation between the second-person plural and the third-person plural in the reference to the Israelites. As cogently argued by Norbert Baumgart, the fact that Lev 26 consistently uses the address in the second-person plural up to verse 35, but then turns exclusively to the third-person plural in verses 40–45, matches in fact the distinction between two groups in the narrative logic of H. The direct plural address is oriented toward the community of Israel as a whole—namely, the community gathered at Mount Sinai—whereas the third-person plural refers to the small minority who, in a distant future, will survive the exile and who are aptly designated in verses 36 and 39 as "the survivors of/among *you*" (והנשארים בכם!).[112] Furthermore, the transition from one group to the other is aptly affected in verses 36–39, which describes the dramatic situation of the exiles, through a combination of both forms (2pl. and 3pl.).[113] Here also, therefore, it is

---

111. As perceptively observed by Müller, "Prophetic View from Exile," 221. Surprisingly enough, few commentators appear to have paid attention to this distinction within Lev 26.

112. Baumgart, "Überkommene Traditionen," 11: "Über die Exilsgemeinde spricht das Kapitel in der 3. Person Plural: *Sie, Ihrer, Ihnen.* Das beginnt mitten in Vers 36. In bezug auf die 2. und 3. Person gibt es zwar nach Vers 36 noch Überlappungen, aber der Wechsel der Person geschieht unübersehbar. *Eine neue Adressatenschaft des Heiligkeitsgesetzes soll deutlich werden*" (my emphasis). This observation also accounts for the alleged tension between the divine statement in vv. 30 and 44 (Müller, "Prophetic View from Exile," 221). While YHWH, in effect, will "loathe" the Israelites for their disloyalty (v. 30), he will no longer act in the same way with respect to the survivors of the exile (v. 44).

113. *Pace* Müller, "Prophetic View from Exile," 221, the second-person plural address does not end in v. 38 but continues in v. 39 through the reference to "the lands of your (pl.) enemies" (איביכם), another indication that the alternation between second-person plural and third-person plural cannot be used here as a valid redactional criterion for sorting between "earlier" and "later" passages within vv. 36–39. With regard to "the lands of your enemies" in v. 39, Milgrom, *Leviticus 23–27*, 2327,

226   Christophe Nihan

unwarranted to see the use of a different address in verses 40–45 as signaling a later hand at work in this chapter: this usage is, in fact, perfectly consistent with the internal logic of Lev 26. Arguably the only possible indication of a tension between verses 36–38 and 39–46 concerns the observation that the beginning of verse 39 repeats the beginning of verse 36. If this is indeed a case of *Wiederaufnahme* (resumptive repetition), it may indicate that verses 36–38 were introduced by a later scribe, who wanted to describe in more detail the dire situation of the exiles (in which case v. 39 would have followed directly after vv. 33, 34–35).[114] While possible, this conclusion is also not necessary. After the development concerning the situation of the exiles in verses 36–38, a mention of the survivors of Israel was required anyway at the beginning of verse 39, since they are in effect the subject of the following verses.

In short, there is no compelling reason to consider that verses 39, 40–45 have been added after verses 36–38. On the contrary, the previous discussion already implies that certain features within verses 36–39, such as the alternation between second-person plural and third-person plural, can only be understood if Lev 26 did not end with a description of the exile, as per Deut 28, but included a continuation. This conclusion can, in effect, be supported by some additional observations. In particular, some commentators have rightly observed that the repeated use of the verb יסר (twice in the *piel* [26:18, 28] and once in the *niphal* [26:23]) in the enumeration of the punishments inflicted by YHWH upon the Israelites indicates that these punishments actually have a *pedagogical* function. While in some contexts יסר can take the specific meaning of "punish," its more general meaning is "discipline, educate" and even (by extension) "instruct."[115] This basic meaning is clearly reflected in Lev 26 as well, especially in Lev 26:23 where יסר can only be translated with "to discipline" and not just

---

aptly observes: "This is the final second person in this chapter, *referring to all the exiles, including those who will not survive*" (emphasis added).

114. It should be recalled here that the scribal technique of *Wiederaufnahme* can be used in the Hebrew Bible to introduce new material *before* the passage that is repeated and not only after. I leave aside here the question of whether vv. 34–35 are integral to the composition of Lev 26. I tend to think so, but this point is not significant for the present discussion.

115. See on this R. Branson (with a contribution by G. J. Botterweck), "יסר *yāsar*," *TDOT* 6: 127–34, esp. 129–31. With regard to the first two mentions of this verb in Lev 26:18, 23, Branson notes: "Twice God seeks through harsh treatment to correct the people's error."

The Holiness Legislation and the Pentateuch   227

"to punish."[116] As such, the divine punishments do not merely serve to sanction the disloyal Israelites but are simultaneously intended to educate them.[117] This notion also applies, as it appears, to the exile, since the same verb יסר also occurs at the beginning of the fifth and last threat (v. 28). This observation is difficult to reconcile with the view that Lev 26 would have originally ended with the complete destruction of the Israelites in verses 36–38. Instead, it is consistent with the view developed in verses 39–45, where the exile clearly functions to lead the Israelites to some sort of internal transformation (referred in v. 41b as the "humbling of their uncircumcised hearts").[118]

All in all, there are good reasons to assume that at least a first form of verses 39–46 belongs to the base layer of Lev 26. I cannot discuss in detail here the literary-critical issues of verses 39–46 but can only mention a few important aspects.[119] I see no literary-critical reason to divide verses 39–41, as already argued above.[120] The same applies to verses 44–45, which com-

---

116. See 26:23a: ואם באלה לא תוסרו לי, "If, with these (i.e., previous disasters) you are not disciplined for me."

117. See, e.g., Hartley, *Leviticus*, 458: "This verb [i.e., יסר, C.N.] signifies that the curses are disciplines designed to awaken the people to their wrongful ways." Similarly Marx, *Lévitique 17–27*, 201–2: "Les maux que Yhwh envoie ont *d'abord* une fonction pédagogique. *Ils sont uniquement destinés à obtenir son repentir*. Certes, Israël est châtié pour ses manquements.... Mais ce châtiment n'est pas une fin en soi." However, I would dispute the notion that the punishments sent by YHWH are exclusively ("uniquement") meant to educate the people.

118. Müller, "Prophetic View from Exile," 224, perceptively notes that the exile is presented in vv. 40–41 as "Yahweh's final attempt to lead Israel to repentance," but he misses the point that this notion runs in fact throughout all of the section enumerating the divine threats for covenantal disloyalty that begins in v. 14. The notion that the exile was meant to "discipline" or "educate" the community of Israel is seldom attested, yet not entirely unique: see, e.g., Jer 31:18 in the case of Ephraim; further Jer 30:10–11 (MT) and 46:27–28 in the context of Judah's exile.

119. See also my earlier discussion in Nihan, *From Priestly Torah to Pentateuch*, 535–45.

120. The tension that Ginsberg (*Israelian Heritage of Judaism*, 80–81) and Levine ("Epilogue to the Holiness Code," 19) see between vv. 40a and 40b (see also now Müller, "Prophetic View from Exile," 223), hardly seems concrete to me. That v. 41a mentions the "land of the enemy" (sing.), while v. 39 has the plural form, is explained, in my opinion, by the fact that v. 41a refers to the deportation to Babylon in v. 38, where the singular form is already used, and not to the situation of the worldwide diaspora in v. 39 (cf. above). Müller's position that vv. 40b and 41a were inserted and

228 — Christophe Nihan

mentators assign to the base layer of the chapter.[121] I would also argue for the originality of the postscript in verse 46, not least in regard to the frame with Lev 25:1 previously discussed (§2). Without the postscript in 26:46, the mention of Mount Sinai in Lev 25:1 is nothing more than a blind motif. Consequently, authors who consider 26:46 secondary must also interpret בהר סני in 25:1 as secondary,[122] but there is no literary-critical reason for this. Furthermore, without verse 46 the contents of the ברית mentioned in the previous verse (v. 45) remain likewise unknown and unspecified. The two verses are in fact complementary: verse 45 introduces the concept of a covenant concluded with the generation of the exodus, whereas verse 46 details the contents of that covenant.[123] By contrast, it is possible that verse 42 is a later addition, since the beginning of verse 43, "But the land will be abandoned by them," can only refer to the Israelites (who are mentioned at the end of v. 41) and not to the three patriarchs mentioned in verse 42.[124] In this case, one must assume that the motif of remembering the covenant with the patriarchs was inserted in verse 42 by a glossator, who wanted to include the remembrance of the exodus covenant in verse 45 in a line that reaches back to Abraham.

---

that v. 41b originally followed v. 40a, does not account for the inner logic and coherence of vv. 40–41; see above for my discussion of these two verses.

121. See, e.g., Elliger, *Leviticus*, 369–370; this remark also applies to the authors who attribute vv. 39–45 in their entirety to a later redaction of Lev 26; cf. Levine, "Epilogue to the Holiness Code," as well as Müller, "Prophetic View from Exile," 222–27. One exception is Milgrom, *Leviticus 23–27*, 2364–65, who attributes vv. 40–42, 45 and vv. 43–44 to two different layers. But a division between vv. 44 and 45 is unlikely, as is a transition from v. 42 to v. 45.

122. See, e.g., Levin, *Die Verheißung*, 227 with note 111; Grünwaldt, *Das Heiligkeitsgesetz Leviticus 17–26*, 126.

123. On the interconnection between Lev 26:45 and 46 and its implications from a compositional perspective, see also my discussion in Nihan, "Lev 26:39–46," 324–25.

124. So also rightly Müller, "Prophetic View from Exile," 225. The contrasting function of vv. 43 and 44 speaks against a division between the two verses; see also especially Grünwaldt, *Das Heiligkeitsgesetz Leviticus 17–26*, 373: "V.44 knüpft kontrastierend an V.43 an. Indem H die Verben מאס und געל nicht nur aus den Bedingungssätzen V.14f, sondern auch aus V.43 aufgreift, stellt es klar: Mögen auch die Menschen den Bund übertreten, für JHWH ist der Bund ein niemals gekündigter und auch niemals zu kündigender Bund. Die Strafe ... war zwar gerecht und auch (im Hinblick auf das Land) notwendig, doch bedeutet die Bestrafung keinesfalls eine Kündigung des Bundesverhältnisses." See also Baumgart, "Überkommene Traditionen," 13–14.

The Holiness Legislation and the Pentateuch 229

6. Lev 26 and the Composition of Leviticus as a Book

I come now in conclusion to the redaction-critical and compositional implications of this analysis of Lev 26. The core of the epilogue to H is portrayed as an oracle to Moses at the conclusion of the Sinai narrative, which provides a certain interpretation of Israel's history from the perspective of the basic alternatives of observance or nonobservance of the torah. This prophetic interpretation of Israel's history contains a complex and far-reaching interpretation of the Priestly and non-Priestly covenant. In spite of various attempts, this text is not to be read within the sole context of the Priestly writing but already presupposes the narrative— and simultaneously redactional—connections between the Priestly and non-Priestly narratives in Genesis to Exodus. In this sense, Lev 26 forms a frame with Exod 19 around the post-Priestly Sinai narrative. This frame with the beginning of the Sinai narrative corresponds not only to the reference to the Sinai covenant in Lev 26:45–46, but also to the reception of the Decalogue in 26:1–2, so that the reference to Exod 19–20 frames both the beginning and the end of the epilogue to the Sinai revelation in Lev 26. Moreover, as Otto in particular already observed, the epilogue to the post-Priestly Sinai account (Lev 26) implies a particular view of the relationship between the Sinai and Moab covenants, on the one hand, and between torah and Prophets (*Nebi'im*), on the other, which is reflected in the reception of the Priestly writing, Deuteronomy, and the Prophets, especially Ezekiel.[125] Differently from Otto, however, the position of Lev 26 over against the Prophets cannot be simply described as "antiprophetic."[126] What is at stake here is, instead, a reception of the Prophets within the Sinai revelation, which acknowledges the authority of these Prophets but at the same time attempts to subordinate them under the authority of Moses as the first prophet. A further question, which cannot be discussed here but would require a separate analysis, concerns the interpretation of Deuteronomy within this legal-prophetic hermeneutics. Contrary to what Otto asserts, the notion that Deuteronomy would

---

125. For this phenomenon of the reception of the Priestly writing, Deuteronomy, and the Prophets, see the previous discussion and recently Müller, "Prophetic View from Exile."

126. So particularly Otto in some earlier essays: see, e.g., Otto, "Innerbiblische Exegese," esp. 182: "This redaction of the Pentateuch is thus not only anti-monarchic, but even more so anti-prophetic to the bone."

230 Christophe Nihan

have been transformed into a sheer interpretation of the torah at Sinai when Lev 26 became the conclusion to the Sinai revelation seems too simplistic.[127] In the post-Priestly Pentateuch, the narrative setting of Deuteronomy, with Moses's address to the *second* generation of the exodus, does not merely function as an elaborate comment on the Sinaitic laws delivered to the first generation in Exodus and Leviticus; it also serves simultaneously to introduce new, additional laws, which likewise claim the authority of the Sinai/Horeb revelation (cf. Deut 5:2) and therefore have a status comparable to, if not identical with, the laws of Exodus and Leviticus. But this question would require further discussion.[128]

The previous interpretation implies, at any rate, that Lev 26 was composed for a narrative context in which the Priestly (P) traditions had already been merged with some other, non-Priestly texts. This conclusion has already been argued by various scholars, but the question remains of the larger compositional model in which it can be accounted for. Some scholars have argued that Lev 26 was originally the conclusion of a "Triateuch" comprising Genesis to Leviticus, to which the book of Numbers was added later as a bridge of sorts toward Deuteronomy.[129] This model does

---

127. See, e.g., Eckart Otto, "Wie 'synchron' wurde in der Antike der Pentateuch gelesen?," in *"Das Manna fällt auch heute noch": Beiträge zur Geschichte und Theologie des Alten, Ersten Testaments*, ed. Frank-Lothar Hossfeld and Ludger Schwienhorst-Schönberger, HBS 44 (Freiburg: Herder, 2004), 470–85; Otto, "Mose, der erste Schriftgelehrte: Deuteronomium 1,5 in der Fabel des Pentateuch," in *L'Ecrit et l'Esprit: Études d'histoire du texte et de théologie biblique*, ed. Dieter Böhler, Innocent Himbaza, and Philippe Hugo, OBO 214 (Fribourg: Academic Press; Göttingen: Vandenhoeck & Ruprecht, 2005), 273–84. With respect to Deut 1:5, however, see Georg Braulik and Norbert Lohfink, "Deuteronomium 1,5 ראב ידרותזד־חא: 'er verlieh dieser Tora Rechtskraft,'" in *Textarbeit: Studien zu Texten und ihrer Rezeption aus dem Alten Testament und der Umwelt Israels*, ed. Klaus Kiesow and Thomas Meurer, AOAT 294 (Münster: Ugarit, 2003), 35–51.

128. See my preliminary comments in Nihan, *From Priestly Torah to Pentateuch*, 553–57.

129. So especially Thomas Römer, "Das Buch Numeri und das Ende des Jahwisten: Anfragen zur 'Quellenscheidung' im vierten Buch des Pentateuch," in *Abschied vom Jahwisten: Die Komposition des Hexateuch in der jüngsten Diskussion*, ed. Jan C.Gertz et al., BZAW 315 (Berlin: De Gruyter, 2002), 215–31; cf. also A. Graeme Auld, "Leviticus: After Exodus and Before Numbers," in *The Book of Leviticus: Composition and Reception*, ed. Rolf Rendtorff and Robert A. Kügler, VTSup 93 (Leiden: Brill, 2003), 41–54. Most recently, and most comprehensively, Rainer Albertz, *Pentateuchstudien*, FAT 117 (Tübingen: Mohr Siebeck, 2018), esp. 251–26. I also previously considered

The Holiness Legislation and the Pentateuch   231

justice to the strategic function of Lev 26 as the conclusion or epilogue to the Sinai account. Yet the assumption that the book of Numbers *in its entirety* would have been added to an already existing collection comprising Genesis to Leviticus is too simple. The account of the exodus requires a continuation in Numbers through the narration of the wilderness journey, so that in all likelihood a portion of Numbers (Num 10–25*) must have been part of the narrative combining Priestly and non-Priestly traditions. Others have located Lev 26 within a pentateuchal redaction, which ranged from Genesis to Deuteronomy (although it did not yet include all the materials now found in the canonical Pentateuch) and whose purpose would have been, among others, to mediate between the various legal collections preserved in the Pentateuch.[130] This model does justice to the sort of complex legal hermeneutics that is apparent in Lev 26—and more generally in H (see above). On the other hand, it fails to account for the distinctive features of Lev 26. Both the theology and the language of Lev 26 are unique within the Pentateuch: for instance, the focus on the Sabbath of the land can be related to other passages in H (i.e., especially, Lev 18:24–30; 20:22–26, and, of course, Lev 25), but hardly elsewhere in the Pentateuch. The same conclusion applies to various idioms used in Lev 26, such as the גָּעַל נֶפֶשׁ, which appears several times in Lev 26 (see vv. 11, 15, 30, 43) but nowhere else in the Pentateuch.[131] Even the substantial reception of Ezekiel in Lev 26 (and again elsewhere in H) presents a comparable phenomenon and can be seen as a distinctive feature of this legislation, which sets it apart from other legal (or, for that matter, nonlegal) traditions within the Pentateuch.

In this regard, the theory of Knohl and Milgrom of a post-Priestly Holiness school or redaction, operating across the Pentateuch (and thus sharing some common features with the notion of a pentateuchal redaction) but with a distinct language and theology centered on the Holiness legislation in Lev 17–26 offers in some ways a better model to account for the interpretation of Lev 26 I have proposed here. Yet even this model is

----

this position in part, see Nihan, "Holiness Code between D and P," 121–22, and my criticism of this thesis in Nihan, *From Priestly Torah to Pentateuch*, 555 n. 617.

130. So, especially, Otto, "Innerbiblische Exegese."

131. This point was correctly noted by Otto, "Innerbiblische Exegese," 178, although he did not draw further conclusions regarding the phraseological and theological coherence of his "pentateuchal redaction."

232   Christophe Nihan

not without problems, which I have discussed elsewhere in more details.[132] In particular, the amount of materials *outside* of Lev 17–26 that can be safely assigned to this Holiness layer is arguably too limited to warrant the assumption of a proper school (however the latter concept, which is notoriously fuzzy, may be defined).[133] It would be more appropriate to speak of a limited process of redactional coordination, in which some laws, primarily in the first part of Leviticus (Lev 1–16), were aligned with the Holiness legislation of Lev 17–26. Such redactional alignment shows that the composition of the Holiness legislation had an impact on the shaping of the Pentateuch, but it remains too limited to warrant the identification of H with something like the "redaction of the Pentateuch."

In order to explain the function of Lev 26, and of H in general, within the post-Priestly Pentateuch, a more promising perspective in my view is to relate the composition of H with the delineation of Leviticus as a discrete book within the Pentateuch. As the subscription in Lev 26:46 makes clear, *it is only with the introduction of the Holiness legislation in Lev 17–26 that Leviticus was identified as a separate book.*[134] This point was apparently already recognized by the later scribe who introduced Lev 27 and who was forced to repeat the subscription of Lev 26:46 in 27:34 (albeit

---

132. See Christophe Nihan, "The Priestly Laws of Numbers, the Holiness Legislation, and the Pentateuch," in *Torah and the Book of Numbers*, ed. Christian Frevel et al., FAT 2/62 (Tübingen: Mohr Siebeck, 2013), 109–37.

133. For a discussion of H materials outside of Lev 17–26 and of the criteria that can be used to identify such materials, see Nihan, *From Priestly Torah to Pentateuch*, 562–75; further my discussion in Nihan, "Priestly Laws." For the thesis of a post-Priestly adaptation of the Priestly laws with H, see also Reinhard Achenbach, "Das Heiligkeitsgesetz und die sakralen Ordnungen des Numeribuches im Horizont der Pentateuchredaktion," in *The Books of Leviticus and Numbers*, ed. Thomas Römer, BETL 215 (Leuven: Peeters, 2008), 145–75.

134. The term *book*, as I use it here, refers primarily to a compositional unit and is not identical with the separation of the Pentateuch into various scrolls; this point is consistent with the distinction between ספר and מגלה in biblical and postbiblical Hebrew. The relationship between the formation of the Pentateuch and its division into discrete books is an issue that has only recently been addressed, and which requires more work in the future. See, provisionally, the remarks by Thomas Römer, "De la périphérie au centre: Les livres du Lévitique et des Nombres dans le débat actuel sur le Pentateuque," in Römer, *Books of Leviticus and Numbers*, 23; Christoph Levin, "On the Cohesion and Separation of Books within the Enneateuch," in *Pentateuch, Hexateuch, or Enneateuch? Identifying Literary Works in Genesis through Kings*, ed. Thomas Dozeman et al., AIL 8 (Atlanta: Society of Biblical Literature, 2011), 127–54.

The Holiness Legislation and the Pentateuch 233

with a distinct legal phraseology), thereby acknowledging the existence of a conceptual break between Leviticus and the following book of Numbers.[135] Furthermore, the composition of Lev 17–26 and, correspondingly, the delineation of Leviticus as a discrete book appear to be related to a process of revision, through which various laws in the first part of Leviticus, Lev 1–16, were aligned with Lev 17–26.[136] In light of these findings, it appears that the composition of Lev 17–26 is part of a redactional process which is somehow related to the emergence of Leviticus as a discrete book—a "Leviticus redaction" so to speak. This Leviticus redaction was presumably related to similar redactional and revisional enterprises in other books of the Pentateuch, but it also had its own distinct profile and agenda. This conclusion, in turn, can account for the twofold observation made above that the composition of H partakes in a larger legal hermeneutics within the post-Priestly Pentateuch, while simultaneously evincing a distinct phraseological and theological profile.

---

135. As correctly observed by Milgrom, *Leviticus 23–27*, 2401–02, Lev 27 ends in v. 34 with a subscript which partially repeats 26:46 but now uses the term מצות, because this legal term was the only term that had not yet been used in the prior postscript 26:46.

136. See, especially, Lev 3:17; 7:22–27; 11:43–45; 16:29–34a, and on this my discussion in Nihan, *From Priestly Torah to Pentateuch*, 569 and *passim*.

Bibliography

Achenbach, Reinhard. "Das Heiligkeitsgesetz im nachpriesterschriftlichen Pentateuch: Zu einem Buch von Klaus Grünwaldt." *ZAR* 6 (2000): 341–50.

———. "Das Heiligkeitsgesetz und die sakralen Ordnungen des Numeribuches im Horizont der Pentateuchredaktion." Pages 145–75 in *The Books of Leviticus and Numbers*. Edited by Thomas Römer. BETL 215. Leuven: Peeters, 2008.

———. *Die Vollendung der Tora*. BZAR 3. Wiesbaden: Harrassowitz, 2003.

———. "Zur Systematik der Speisegebote in Lev 11 und in Deuteronomium 14." *ZAR* 17 (2011): 161–210.

Aejmelaeus, Anneli, and Ludwig Schmidt. *The Traditional Prayer in the Psalms / Literarische Studien zur Josephsgeschichte*. BZAW 167. Berlin: De Gruyter 1986.

Albertz, Rainer. "The Canonical Alignment of the Book of Joshua." Pages 287–303 in *Judah and the Judeans in the Fourth Century B.C.E.* Edited by Oded Lipschits, Gary N. Knoppers, and Rainer Albertz. Winona Lake, IN: Eisenbrauns, 2007.

———. "Die Josephsgeschichte im Pentateuch." Pages 11–37 in *Diasynchron: Beiträge zur Exegese, Theologie und Rezeption der hebräischen Bibel; Walter Dietrich zum 65. Geburtstag*. Edited by Thomas Naumann and Regine Hunziker-Rodewald. Stuttgart: Kohlhammer, 2009.

———. *Ex 1–18*. Vol. 1 of *Exodus*. ZBK.AT 2.1. Zürich: TVZ, 2012.

———. *Pentateuchstudien*. FAT 117. Tübingen: Mohr Siebeck, 2018.

Arneth, Martin. *'Durch Adams Fall ist ganz verderbt …': Studien zur Entstehung der alttestamentlichen Urgeschichte*. FRLANT 217. Göttingen: Vandenhoeck & Ruprecht, 2007.

Astruc, Jean. *Conjectures sur les mémoires originaux Dont il paroit que Moyse s'est servi pour composer le livre de la Genese: Avec des remarques, qui appuient ou qui éclaircissent ces Conjectures*. Paris: Fricx, 1753.

Auld, A. Graeme. "Leviticus: After Exodus and Before Numbers." Pages 41–54 in *The Book of Leviticus: Composition and Reception*. Edited by Rolf Rendtorff and Robert A. Kügler. VTSup 93. Leiden: Brill, 2003.

236 Bibliography

Baden, Joel S. *The Composition of the Pentateuch: Renewing the Documentary Hypothesis.* AYBRL. New Haven: Yale University Press, 2012.

———. *J, E, and the Redaction of the Pentateuch.* FAT 68. Tübingen: Mohr Siebeck, 2009.

Baden, Joel S., and Jeffrey Stackert, eds. *The Oxford Handbook of the Pentateuch.* Oxford: Oxford University Press, 2021.

Baentsch, Bruno. *Das Heiligkeits-Gesetz Lev XVII–XXVI: Eine historisch-kritische Untersuchung.* Erfurt: Güther, 1893.

———. *Exodus—Leviticus—Numeri.* HKAT 1.2. Göttingen: Vandenhoeck & Ruprecht, 1903.

Bauks, Michaela. "Das Dämonische im Menschen: Einige Anmerkungen zur priesterschriftlichen Theologie (Ex 7–14)." Pages 239–53 in *Die Dämonen—Demons: Die Dämonologie der israelitisch-jüdischen und frühchristlichen Literatur im Kontext ihrer Umwelt.* Edited by Armin Lange, Hermann Lichtenberger, and K.F. Diethard Römheld. Tübingen: Mohr Siebeck, 2003.

———. "Die Begriffe מוֹרָשָׁה und אֲחֻזָּה in Pᵍ: Überlegungen zur Landkonzeption in der Priestergrundschrift." *ZAW* 116 (2004): 171–88.

Baumgart, Norbert C. "Überkommene Traditionen neu aufgearbeitet und angeeignet: Lev 26,3–45; Das Heiligkeitsgesetz in Exil und Diaspora." *BZ* 43 (1999): 1–25.

Berge, Käre. *Reading Sources in a Text: Coherence and Literary Criticism in the Call of Moses.* ATAT 54. Saint Ottilien: EOS Verlag, 1997.

Berner, Christoph. "Der Sabbat in der Mannaerzählung Ex 16 und in den priesterlichen Partien des Pentateuch." *ZAW* 128 (2016): 562–78.

———. *Die Exoduserzählung: Das literarische Werden einer Ursprungslegende Israels.* FAT 73. Tübingen: Mohr Siebeck, 2010.

———. "Gab es einen vorpriesterlichen Meerwunderbericht?" *Bib* 95 (2014): 1–25.

———. "*Moses vs. Aaron: The Clash of Prophetic and Priestly Concepts of Leadership in the Pentateuch.*" Pages 31–44 in *Debating Authority: Concepts of Leadership in the Pentateuch and the Former Prophets.* Edited by Katharina Pyschny and Sarah Schulz. BZAW 507. Berlin: De Gruyter, 2018.

Berner, Christoph, and Harald Samuel, eds. *Book-Seams in the Hexateuch I.* FAT 120. Tübingen: Mohr Siebeck, 2018.

Bertholet, Alfred. *Leviticus.* KHC 3. Tübingen: Mohr, 1901.

Blenkinsopp, Joseph. "The Structure of P." *CBQ* 38 (1976): 275–92.

Bibliography

Blum, Erhard. "Das exilische deuteronomistische Geschichtswerk." Pages 269–94 in *Das deuteronomistische Geschichtswerk*. Edited by Hermann-Josef Stipp. ÖBS 39. Frankfurt am Main: Lang, 2011.

———. *Die Komposition der Vätergeschichte*. WMANT 57. Neukirchen-Vluyn: Neukirchener Verlag, 1984.

———. "Die literarische Verbindung von Erzvätern und Exodus." Pages 119–56 in *Abschied vom Jahwisten: Die Komposition des Hexateuch in der jüngsten Diskussion*. Edited by Jan Christian Gertz, Konrad Schmid, and Markus Witte. BZAW 315. Berlin: De Gruyter, 2002. Repr. in *Textgestalt und Komposition*. By Erhard Blum. FAT 69. Tübingen: Mohr Siebeck, 2010.

———. "Esra, die Mosetora und die persische Politik." Pages 231–56 in *Religion und Religionskontakte im Zeitalter der Achämeniden*. Edited by Reinhard G. Kratz. VGTh 22. Gütersloh: Gütersloher, 2002.

———. "Issues and Problems in the Contemporary Debate Regarding the Priestly Writings." Pages 31–44 in *The Strata of the Priestly Writings: Contemporary Debate and Future Directions*. Edited by Sarah Shectman and Joel S. Baden. ATANT 95. Zürich: TVZ, 2009.

———. "Pentateuch-Hexateuch-Enneateuch? Or: How Can One Recognize a Literary Work in the Hebrew Bible?" Pages 43–72 in *Pentateuch, Hexateuch, or Enneateuch? Identifying Literary Works in Genesis through Kings*. Edited by Thomas B. Dozeman, Thomas Römer, and Konrad Schmid. AIL 8. Atlanta: Society of Biblical Literature, 2011.

———. *Studien zur Komposition des Pentateuch*. BZAW 189. Berlin: De Gruyter, 1990.

———. "Zwischen Literarkritik und Stilkritik: Die diachrone Analyse der literarischen Verbindung von Genesis und Exodus—im Gespräch mit Ludwig Schmidt." *ZAW* 124 (2012): 492–515.

Bodi, Daniel. *The Book of Ezekiel and the Poem of Erra*. OBO 104. Fribourg: Vandenhoeck & Ruprecht, 1991.

Bosshard-Nepustil, Erich. *Vor uns die Sintflut: Studien zu Text, Kontexten und Rezeption der Fluterzählung Genesis 6–9*. BWANT 165. Stuttgart: Kohlhammer, 2005.

Braulik, Georg, and Norbert Lohfink. "Deuteronomium 1,5 ראב ידרו תזדחא: 'er verlieh dieser Tora Rechtskraft.'" Pages 35–51 in *Textarbeit: Studien zu Texten und ihrer Rezeption aus dem Alten Testament und der Umwelt Israels*. Edited by Klaus Kiesow and Thomas Meurer. AOAT 294. Münster: Ugarit, 2003.

238 Bibliography

Budde, Karl. *Das Buch der Richter erklärt*. KHC 7. Tübingen: Mohr Siebeck, 1897.

———. *Die Biblische Urgeschichte (Gen. 1–12, 5) untersucht*. Gießen: Ricker, 1883.

———. *Die Bücher Richter und Samuel, ihre Quellen und ihr Aufbau*. Gießen: Ricker, 1890.

———. *Die Bücher Samuel erklärt*. KHC 8. Tübingen: Mohr Siebeck, 1902.

———. "Ellä toledoth." *ZAW* 34 (1914): 241–53.

Bultmann, Christoph. *Der Fremde im antiken Juda: Eine Untersuchung zum sozialen Typenbegriff 'ger' und seinem Bedeutungswandel in der alttestamentlichen Gesetzgebung*. FRLANT 153. Göttingen: Vandenhoeck & Ruprecht, 1992.

Buttmann, Phillip. *Mythologus oder gesammelte Abhandlungen über die Sagen des Alterthums*. Vol. 1. Berlin: Mylius, 1828.

Carr, David. "Βίβλος γενέσεως Revisited: A Synchronic Analysis of Patterns in Genesis as Part of the Torah." *ZAW* 110 (1998): 159–72, 327–47.

———. *The Formation of the Hebrew Bible: A New Reconstruction*. New York: Oxford University Press, 2011.

———. "The Moses Story: Literary-Historical Reflections." *HeBAI* 1 (2012): 7–36.

———. *Reading the Fractures of Genesis: Historical and Literary Approaches*. Louisville: John Knox, 1996.

———. "Scribal Processes of Coordination/Harmonization and the Formation of the First Hexateuch(s)." Pages 63–83 in *The Pentateuch: International Perspectives on Current Research*. Edited by Thomas B. Dozeman, Konrad Schmid, and Barukh Ya'aḳov Shvarts. FAT 78. Tübingen: Mohr Siebeck, 2011.

———. "What Is Required to Identify Pre-Priestly Narrative Connections between Genesis and Exodus? Some General Reflections and Specific Cases." Pages 159–80 in *A Farewell to the Yahwist? The Composition of the Pentateuch in Recent European Interpretation*. Edited by Thomas B. Dozeman and Konrad Schmid. SymS 34. Atlanta: Society of Biblical Literature, 2006.

Catanzaro, Carmino Joseph de. *A Literary Analysis of Genesis I–XI*. MA thesis. University of Toronto, 1957.

Childs, Brevard S. *The Book of Exodus*. OTL. London: Westminster John Knox, 1974.

———. "Deuteronomic Formulae of the Exodus Traditions." Pages 30–39 in *Hebräische Wortforschung: Festschrift zum 80. Geburtstag von Walter Baumgartner.* Edited by Benedikt Hartmann et al. VTSup 16. Leiden: Brill, 1967.

Cholewiński, Alfred. *Heiligkeitsgesetz und Deuteronomium: Eine vergleichende Studie.* AnBib 66. Rome: Pontifical Biblical Institute, 1976.

Collins, John. "Changing Scripture." Pages 23–45 in *Changes in Scripture: Rewriting and Interpreting Authoritative Traditions in the Second Temple Period.* Edited by Hanne von Weissenberg, Juha Pakkala, and Marko Martilla. BZAW 419. Berlin: De Gruyter, 2011.

Couroyer, Bernard. "Le 'doigt de Dieu' (Exode, VIII, 15)." *RB* 63 (1956): 481–95.

Cross, Frank Moore. *Canaanite Myth and Hebrew Epic: Essays in the History of the Religion of Israel.* Cambridge, MA: Harvard University Press, 1973.

———. *From Epic to Canon: History and Literature in Ancient Israel.* Baltimore: Johns Hopkins University Press, 1998.

———. "The Priestly Work." Pages 293–325 in *Canaanite Myth and Hebrew Epic: Essays in the History of the Religion of Israel.* Cambridge, MA: Harvard University Press, 1973.

Crüsemann, Frank. "Der Exodus als Heiligung: Zur rechtsgeschichtlichen Bedeutung des Heiligkeitsgesetzes." Pages 117–29 in *Die Hebräische Bibel und ihre zweifache Nachgeschichte: Festschrift für Rolf Rendtorff zum 65. Geburtstag.* Edited by Erhard Blum, Christian Macholz, and Ekkehard Stegemann. Neukirchen-Vluyn: Neukirchner, 1990.

———. *Die Tora: Theologie und Sozialgeschichte des alttestamentlichen Gesetzes.* Munich: Kaiser, 1992.

Dahse, Johannes. "P in Genesis 12–50." Pages 144–74 in *Textkritische Materialien zur Hexateuchfrage.* Vol. 1. Gießen: Töpelmann 1912.

Davies, Graham I. "Covenant, Oath, and the Composition of the Pentateuch." Pages 71–90 in *Covenant as Context: Essays in Honor of Ernest W. Nicholson.* Edited by Andrew D. H. Mayes. Oxford: Oxford University Press, 2003.

Dillmann, August. *Die Bücher Numeri, Deuteronomium und Josua.* KeH 13. 2nd ed. Leipzig: Hirzel, 1886.

———. *Die Genesis.* KeH 11.6. 6th ed. Leipzig: Hirzel, 1892.

Donner, Herbert. "Der Redaktor: Überlegungen zum vorkritischen Umgang mit der Heiligen Schrift." *Hen* 2 (1980): 1–29.

Dozeman, Thomas B. *Exodus.* ECC. Grand Rapids: Eerdmans, 2009.

240 Bibliography

Dozeman, Thomas B., Konrad Schmid, and Baruch J. Schwartz, eds. *The Pentateuch: International Perspectives on Current Research*. FAT 78. Tübingen: Mohr Siebeck, 2011.

Duhm, Bernhard. *Das Buch Jeremia*. KHC 11. Tübingen: Mohr Siebeck, 1901.

Ede, Franziska. *Die Josefsgeschichte: Literarkritische und redaktionsgeschichtliche Untersuchungen zur Entstehung von Gen 37–50*. BZAW 485. Berlin: De Gruyter, 2016.

Eerdmans, Bernardus D. *Die Komposition der Genesis*. Vol. 1 of *Alttestamentliche Studien*. Gießen: Töpelmann, 1908.

Ehrenreich, Ernst. *Wähle das Leben! Deuteronomium 30 als hermeneutischer Schlüssel zur Tora*. BZAR 14. Wiesbaden: Harrassowitz, 2011.

Eichhorn, Johann Gottfried. *Einleitung ins Alte Testament*. 3 vols. Leipzig: Weidmann & Reich, 1780–1783.

Eißfeldt, Otto. *Hexateuch-Synopse: Die Erzählung der fünf Bücher Mose und des Buches Josua mit dem Anfange des Richterbuches*. Leipzig: Hinrichs, 1922. Repr., Darmstadt: Wissenschaftliche Buchgesellschaft, 1962.

Elliger, Karl. "Heiligkeitsgesetz." *RGG* (1959): 3:175–76.

———. *Leviticus*. HAT 1.4. Tübingen: Mohr Siebeck, 1966.

———. "Sinn und Ursprung der priesterlichen Geschichtserzählung." *ZTK* 49 (1952): 121–43.

Engnell, Ivan. *Gamla Testamentet: En traditionshistorisk inledning*. Vol 1. Stockholm: Svenska Kyrkans Diakonistyrelses Bokförlag, 1945.

———. "The Pentateuch." Pages 50–67 in *A Rigid Scrutiny: Critical Essays on the Old Testament*. Nashville: Vanderbilt University Press, 1969.

Eshel, Esther. "Leviticus, Book of." Pages 488–93 in *Encyclopedia of the Dead Sea Scrolls*. Edited by Lawrence H. Schiffman and James C. VanderKam. Oxford: Oxford University Press, 2000.

Etz, Donald V. "The Numbers of Genesis V:3–31: A Suggested Conversion and Its Implications." *VT* 43 (1993): 171–89.

Ewald, Heinrich. *Die Komposition der Genesis kritisch untersucht*. Braunschweig: Ludwig Lucius, 1823.

———. *Geschichte des Volkes Israels bis Christus*. 3rd ed. Göttingen: Dieterich, 1864.

Fischer, Georg. "Keine Priesterschrift in Ex 1–15?" *ZKT* 117 (1995): 203–11.

———. "Zur Lage der Pentateuchforschung." *ZAW* 115 (2003): 283–92.

Freedman, David N., and Kenneth A. Mathews. *The Paleo-Hebrew Leviticus Scroll (11QpaleoLev)*. Philadelphia: Eisenbrauns, 1985.

Frevel, Christian. "Alte Stücke—späte Brücke? Zur Rolle des Buches Numeri in der jüngeren Pentateuchdiskussion." Pages 255–99 in *Congress Volume Munich 2013*. Edited by Christl M. Maier. Leiden: Brill, 2014.

———. "Die Wiederkehr der Hexateuchperspektive: Eine Her- ausforderung für die These vom deuteronomistischen Geschichtswerk." Pages 13–53 in *Das deuteronomistische Geschichtswerk*. Edited by Hermann-Josef Stipp. ÖBS 39. Frankfurt am Main: Lang, 2011.

———. *Mit Blick auf das Land die Schöpfung erinnern*. HBS 23. Freiburg: Herder, 2000.

Fritz, Volkmar. *Tempel und Zelt: Studien zum Tempelbau in Israel und zu dem Zelthei- ligtum der Priesterschrift*. WMANT 47. Neukirchen-Vluyn: Neukirchener Verlag, 1977.

Gabler, Johann Philipp. *Neuer Versuch über die Mosaische Schöpfungsgeschichte aus der höhern Kritik: Ein Nachtrag zum ersten Theil seiner Ausgabe der Eichhorn'schen Urgeschichte*. Altdorf: Monath & Kußler, 1795.

Gane, Roy E. *Cult and Character: Purification Offerings, Day of Atonement, and Theodicy*. Winona Lake, IN: Eisenbrauns, 2005.

Germany, Stephen. "The Literary Relationship between Genesis 50–Exodus 1 and Joshua 24–Judges 2." Pages 385–400 in *Book-Seams in the Hexateuch I*. Edited by Christoph Berner, and Harald Samuel. FAT 120. Tübingen: Mohr Siebeck, 2018.

Gertz, Jan Christian. "Beobachtungen zum literarischen Charakter und zum geistesgeschichtlichen Ort der nichtpriesterschriftlichen Sintfluterzählung." Pages 41–57 in *Auf dem Weg zur Endgestalt von Genesis bis II Regum: Festschrift Hans-Christoph Schmitt*. Edited by Martin Beck and Ulrike Schorn. BZAW 370. Berlin: De Gruyter, 2006.

———. *Das erste Buch Mose (Genesis): Die Urgeschichte Gen 1–11*. ATD 1. Göttingen: Vandenhoeck & Ruprecht, 2018.

———. "The Formation of the Primeval History." Pages 107–36 in *The Book of Genesis: Composition, Reception, and Interpretation*. Edited by Craig A. Evans, Joel N. Lohr, and David L. Petersen. VTSup 152. Leiden: Brill, 2012.

———. "Hams Sündenfall und Kanaans Erbfluch: Anmerkungen zur kompositionsgeschichtlichen Stellung von Gen 9:18–29." Pages 81–95 in *'Gerechtigkeit und Recht zu üben' (Gen 18:19): Studien zur altori-*

242 Bibliography

entalischen und biblischen Rechtsgeschichte, zur Religionsgeschichte Israels und zur Religionssoziologie. Festschrift für Eckart Otto zum 65. Geburtstag. Edited by Rinhard Achenbach and Martin Arneth. BZAR 13. Wiesbaden: Harrassowitz, 2009.

———. "Source Criticism in the Primeval History of Genesis: An Outdated Paradigma for the Study of the Pentateuch?" Pages 169–80 in *The Pentateuch: International Perspectives on Current Research.* Edited by Thomas B. Dozeman, Konrad Schmid, and Baruch J. Schwartz. FAT 78. Tübingen: Mohr Siebeck, 2011.

———. *Tradition und Redaktion in der Exoduserzählung: Untersuchungen zur Endredaktion des Pentateuch.* FRLANT 186. Göttingen: Vandenhoeck & Ruprecht, 2000.

———. "Tora und Vordere Propheten." Pages 193–312 in *Grundinformation Altes Testament: Eine Einführung in Literatur, Religion, und Geschichte des Alten Testaments.* Edited by Jan Christian Gertz, Angelika Berlejung, Konrad Schmid, and Markus Witte. 6th ed. UTB 2745. Göttingen: Vandenhoeck & Ruprecht, 2019.

———. "The Transition between the Books of Genesis and Exodus." Pages 73–87 in *A Farewell to the Yahwist? The Composition of the Pentateuch in Recent European Interpretation.* Edited by Thomas Dozeman and Konrad Schmid. SymS 34. Atlanta: Society of Biblical Literature, 2006.

Gertz, Jan Christian, Angelika Berlejung, Konrad Schmid, and Markus Witte, eds. *T&T Clark Handbook of the Old Testament: An Introduction to the Literature, Religion and History of the Old Testament.* London: T&T Clark, 2012.

Gesundheit, Shimon. *Three Times a Year.* FAT 82. Tübingen: Mohr Siebeck, 2012.

Ginsberg, Harold Louis. *The Israelian Heritage of Judaism.* Texts and Studies of the Jewish Theological Seminary of America 24. New York: The Jewish Theological Seminary of America, 1982.

Gosse, Bernard. "Exode 6,8 comme réponse à Ezéchiel 33,24." *RHPR* 74 (1994): 241–47.

———. "Le livre d'Ezéchiel et Ex 6,2–8 dans le cadre du Pentateuque." *BN* 104 (2000): 20–25.

Graf, Karl Heinrich. "Die Bestandtheile der geschichtlichen Bücher von Genes. 1 bis 2 Reg. 25 (Pentateuch und Prophetae priores)." Pages 1–113 in *Die geschichtlichen Bücher des Alten Testaments: Zwei historisch-kritische Untersuchungen.* Leipzig: Weigel, 1866.

Bibliography 243

———. "Die s. g. Grundschrift des Pentateuchs." Pages 466–77 in *Archiv für wissenschaftliche Erforschung des Alten Testamentes*. Edited by Adalbert Merx. Vol. 1. Halle: Buchhandlung des Waisenhauses, 1869.

Greenberg, Moshe. *Understanding Exodus*. New York: Behrman, 1969.

Greenfield, Jonas C., and Aaron Schaffer. "Notes on the Curse Formulae of the Tell Fekherye Inscription." *RB* 92.1 (1985): 47–59.

Groß, Walter. "Die Wolkensäule in Ex 13 + 14." Pages 142–65 in *Biblische Theologie und Gesellschaft im Wandel*. Edited by Georg Braulik, Seán McEvenue, and Norbert Lohfink. Freiburg: Herder, 1993.

———. "'Rezeption' in Ex 31,12–17 und Lev 26,39–45: Sprachliche Form und theologisch-konzeptionelle Leistung." Pages 45–64 in *Rezeption und Auslegung im Alten Testament und in seinem Umfeld: Ein Symposion aus Anlass des 60. Geburtstags von Odil Hannes Steck*. Edited by Reinhard G. Kratz and Thomas Krüger. OBO 153. Göttingen: Vandenhoeck & Ruprecht, 1997.

———. *Zukunft für Israel: Alttestamentliche Bundeskonzepte und die aktuelle Debatte um den Neuen Bund*. SBS 176. Stuttgart: Katholisches Bibelwerk, 1998.

Grund, Alexandra. *Die Entstehung des Sabbats: Seine Bedeutung für Israels Zeitkonzept und Erinnerungskultur*. FAT 75. Tübingen: Mohr Siebeck, 2011.

Grünwaldt, Klaus. *Das Heiligkeitsgesetz Leviticus 17–26: Ursprüngliche Gestalt, Tradition und Theologie*. BZAW 271. Berlin: de Gruyter, 1999.

———. *Exil und Identität: Beschneidung, Passa und Sabbat in der Priesterschrift*. BBB 85. Frankfurt am Main: Vandenhoeck & Ruprecht, 1992.

Gunkel, Hermann. *Genesis*. HKAT 1.1. 3rd ed. Göttingen: Vandenhoeck & Ruprecht, 1910. 9th ed. Göttingen: Vandenhoeck & Ruprecht, 1977.

———. *Genesis Translated and Interpreted*. Translated by Mark E. Biddle. Macon, GA: Mercer University Press, 1997.

Hartley, John. *Leviticus*. WBC 4. Dallas: Word Books, 1992.

Hendel, Ronald S. *The Text of Genesis 1–11: Textual Studies and Critical Edition*. Oxford: Oxford University Press, 1998.

Hezel, Wilhelm Friedrich. *Ueber die Quellen der Mosaischen Urgeschichte*. Lemgo: Meyer, 1780.

Hieke, Thomas. *Die Genealogien der Genesis*. HBS 39. Freiburg: Herder, 2004.

———. *Levitikus*. HKAT. Freiburg i.B.: Herder, 2014.

Himbaza, Innocent. "What Are the Consequences If 4QLXXLevᵃ Contains Earliest Formulation of the Septuagint?" Pages 294–308 in *Die Septua-*

244   Bibliography

ginta—Orte und Intentionen: 5. Internationale Fachtagung veranstaltet von Septuaginta Deutsch (LXX.D), Wuppertal 24.–27. Juli 2014. Edited by Siegfried Kreuzer et al. Tübingen: Mohr Siebeck, 2016.

Hoffmann, David. *Leviticus*. 2 vols. Berlin: Poppelauer, 1905.

Holzinger, Heinrich. *Genesis*. KHC 1. Freiburg: Mohr, 1898.

Hossfeld, Frank-Lothar, and Erich Zenger. *Psalmen 101–150*. HThKAT. Freiburg: Herder, 2008.

Hughes, Jeremy. *Secrets of the Times: Myth and History in Biblical Chronology*. JSOTSup 66. Sheffield: Sheffield Academic, 1990.

Hugo, Philippe. "Text History of the Books of Samuel: An Assessment of the Recent Research." Pages 1–19 in *Archaeology of the Books of Samuel: The Entangling of the Textual and Literary History*. Edited by Philippe Hugo and Adrian Schenker. VTSup 132. Leiden: Brill, 2010.

Hupfeld, Hermann. *Die Quellen der Genesis und die Art ihrer Zusammensetzung*. Berlin: Wiegandt & Grieben, 1853.

Hutzli, Jürg. "Tradition and Interpretation in Gen 1:1–2:4a." *JHS* 10/12 (2010): 1–22.

Ilgen, Karl David. *Die Urkunden des Jerusalemischen Tempelarchivs in ihrer Urgestalt*. Vol. 1. Halle: Hemmerde & Schwetschke, 1798.

Jacob, Benno. *Das Buch Genesis*. Repr. Stuttgart: Calwer, 2000.

Janowski, Bernd. *Sühne als Heilsgeschehen: Studien zur Sühnetheologie der Priester- schrift und zur Wurzel KPR im Alten Orient und im Alten Testament*. WMANT 55. Neukirchen-Vluyn: Neukirchener Verlag, 1982.

Jeon, Jaeyoung. *The Call of Moses and the Exodus Story: A Redactional-Critical Study in Exodus 3–4 and 5–13*. FAT 2/60. Tübingen: Mohr Siebeck, 2013.

———. "The Promise of the Land and the Extent of P." *ZAW* 130 (2018): 513–28.

———. "A Source of P? The Priestly Exodus Account and the Book of Ezekiel." *Semitica* 58 (2016): 77–92.

Jepsen, Alfred. "Zur Chronologie des Priesterkodex." *ZAW* 47 (1929): 251–55.

Joosten, Jan. "Covenant Theology in the Holiness Code." *ZAR* 4 (1998): 145–64.

Jülicher, Adolf. "Die Quellen von Exodus I–VII,7." *JPTh* 8 (1882): 79–127, 272–315.

Kaiser, Otto. *Einleitung in das Alte Testament: Eine Einführung in ihre Ergebnisse und Probleme*. 5th ed. Gütersloh: Gütersloher Verlaghaus, 1984.

Kegler, Jürgen. "Die Berufung des Mose als Befreier Israels: Zur Einheitlichkeit des Berufungsberichts in Exodus 3–4." Pages 162–88 in *Freiheit und Recht: Festschrift für Frank Crüsemann zum 65. Geburtstag.* Edited by Christof Hardmeier, Rainer Kessler, and Andreas Ruwe. Gütersloh: Gütersloher Verlagshaus, 2003.

Keil, Carl Friedrich. *Lehrbuch der historisch-kritischen Einleitung in die kanonischen und apokryphischen Schriften des Alten Testaments.* 2nd ed. Frankfurt: Heyder & Zimmer, 1859. 3rd ed. Frankfurt: Heyder & Zimmer, 1873.

Klein, Anja. *Schriftauslegung im Ezechielbuch: Redaktionsgeschichtliche Untersuchungen zu Ez 34–39.* BZAW 391. Berlin: De Gruyter, 2008.

Klein, Ralph W. "Archaic Chronologies and the Textual History of the Old Testament." *HTR* 67 (1974): 255–63.

———. "The Message of P." Pages 57–66 in *Die Botschaft und die Boten: Festschrift für Hans Walter Wolff zum 70. Geburtstag.* Edited by Jörg Jeremias and Lothar Perlitt. Neukirchen-Vluyn: Neukirchener, 1981.

Klostermann, August. *Der Pentateuch: Beiträge zu seinem Verständnis und seiner Entstehungsgeschichte.* Leipzig: Deichert, 1893.

Knobel, August. *Die Genesis erklärt.* Leipzig: Hirzel, 1852.

Knobloch, Harald. *Die nachexilische Prophetentheorie des Jeremiabuches.* BZAR 12. Wiesbaden: Harrassowitz, 2009.

Knohl, Israel. *The Sanctuary of Silence: The Priestly Torah and the Holiness School.* Winona Lake, IN: Eisenbrauns, 1995.

Knauf, Ernst Axel. "Der Exodus zwischen Mythos und Geschichte: Zur priesterschriftlichen Rezeption der Schilfmeer-Geschichte in Ex 14." Pages 73–84 in *Schriftauslegung in der Schrift: Festschrift für Odil Hannes Steck zu seinem 65. Geburtstag.* Edited by Reinhard G. Kratz, Thomas Krüger, and Konrad Schmid. Berlin: de Gruyter, 2000.

———. "Die Priesterschrift und die Geschichten der Deuteronomisten." Pages 101–18 in *The Future of the Deuteronomistic History.* Edited by Thomas Römer. BETL 147. Leuven: Peeters, 2000.

———. *Josua.* ZBKAT 6. Zürich: Theologischer Verlag, 2008.

Koch, Klaus. *Die Priesterschrift von Exodus 25 bis Leviticus 16: Eine überlieferungsgeschichtliche und literarkritische Untersuchung.* FRLANT 53. Göttingen: Vandenhoeck & Ruprecht, 1959.

———. "Die Toledot-Formeln als Strukturprinzip des Buches Genesis." Pages 183–92 in *Recht und Ethos im Alten Testament: Gestalt und Wirkung, FS H. Seebass.* Edited by Stefan Beyerle et al. Neukirchen-Vluyn: Neukirchner, 1999.

246   Bibliography

———. "P—kein Redaktor! Erinnerung an zwei Eckdaten der Quellenscheidung." *VT* 37 (1987): 446–67.

———. "Sabbatstruktur der Geschichte: Die sogenannte Zehn-Wochen-Apokalypse (I Hen 93,1–10; 91,11–17) und das Ringen um die alttestamentlichen Chronologien im späten Israelitentum." *ZAW* 95 (1983): 403–30.

Köckert, Matthias. "'Land' als theologisches Thema im Alten Testament." Pages 503–22 in *Ex oriente Lux: Studien zur Theologie des Alten Testaments: Festschrift für Rüdiger Lux zum 65. Geburstag*. Edited by Angelika Berlejung and Raik Heckl. ABG 39. Leipzig: Evangelische Verlagsanstalt, 2012.

———. "Leben in Gottes Gegenwart. Zum Verständnis des Gesetzes in der priesterschriftlichen Literatur." *JBT* 4 (1989): 29–61.

Kohata, Fujiko. *Jahwist und Priesterschrift in Exodus 3–14*. BZAW 166. Berlin: De Gruyter, 1986.

Korpel, Marjo C. A. "The Epilogue to the Holiness Code." Pages 123–50 in *Verse in Ancient Near Eastern Prose*. Edited by Johannes. C. de Moor and Wilfred G. E. Watson. AOAT 43. Kevelaer: Butzon & Bercker, 1993.

Kratz, Reinhard Gregor. *The Composition of the Narrative Books of the Old Testament*. Translated by John Bowden. London: T&T Clark, 2005.

———. *Die Komposition der erzählenden Bücher des Alten Testaments: Grundwissen der Bibelkritik*. UTB 2157. Göttingen: Vandenhoeck & Ruprecht, 2000.

Krüger, Thomas. "Erwägung zur Redaktion der Meerwundererzählung (Exodus 13,17–14, 31)." *ZAW* 108 (1996): 519–33.

Kuenen, Abraham. "Dina en Sichem." *TT* 14 (1880): 257–81.

———. *An Historical-Critical Inquiry into the Origin and Composition of the Hexateuch*. Translated by Philip H. Wicksteed. London: Macmillan, 1886. Translation of *De Thora en de historische boeken des Ouden Verbonds*. Vol. 1 of *Historisch-critisch onderzoek naar het ontstaan en de verzameling van de boeken des Ouden Verbonds*. 2nd ed. Leiden: Engels, 1885.

———. *Historisch-kritische Einleitung in die Bücher des Alten Testaments*. Vols. 1–2. Leipzig: Schulze, 1885.

Kurtz, Johann Heinrich. *Beiträge zur Vertheidigung und Begründung der Einheit des Pentateuchs*. Nachweis der Einheit von Genesis I–IV. Königsberg: Gräfe & Unzer, 1844.

Bibliography 247

———. *Die Einheit der Genesis: Ein Beitrag zur Kritik und Exegese der Genesis.* Berlin: Justus Albert Wohlgemuth, 1846.

Le Boulluec, Alain, and Pierre Sandevoir. *L'Exode.* BA 2. Paris: Cerf, 1989.

Lefebvre, Jean-François. *Le Jubilé biblique: Lv 25—exégèse et théologie.* OBO 194. Göttingen: Vandenhoeck & Ruprecht, 2003.

Lee, Kyong-Jin. *The Authority and Authorization of Torah in the Persian Period.* CBET 64. Leuven: Peeters, 2011.

Levin, Christoph. *Der Jahwist.* FRLANT 157. Göttingen: Vandenhoeck & Ruprecht, 1993.

———. "Die Priesterschrift und die Geschichte." Pages 189–225 in *Congress Volume Göttingen.* Edited by Walter Zimmerli. VTSup 29. Göttingen: Brill, 1977.

———. "Die Redaktion R^JP in der Urgeschichte." Pages 59–79 in *Auf dem Weg zur Endgestalt von Genesis bis II Regum: Festschrift Hans-Christoph Schmitt.* Edited by Martin Beck and Ulrike Schorn. BZAW 370. Berlin: De Gruyter, 2006.

———. *Die Verheißung des neuen Bundes in ihrem theologiegeschichtlichen Zusammenhang ausgelegt.* FRLANT 137. Göttingen: Vandenhoeck & Ruprecht, 1985.

———. "Jahwe und Abraham im Dialog: Genesis 15." Pages 237–57 in *Gott und Mensch im Dialog: Festschrift Otto Kaiser.* Edited by Markus Witte. BZAW 345.1. Berlin: De Gruyter, 2004.

———. "On the Cohesion and Separation of Books within the Enneateuch." Pages 127–54 in *Pentateuch, Hexateuch, or Enneateuch? Identifying Literary Works in Genesis through Kings.* Edited by Thomas Dozeman et al. AIL 8. Atlanta: Society of Biblical Literature, 2011.

———. "Source Criticism: The Miracle at the Sea." Pages 39–61 in *Method Matters: Essays on the Interpretation of the Hebrew Bible in Honor of David L. Petersen.* Edited by Joel M. LeMon and Kent Harold Richards. RBS 56. Atlanta, GA: Society of Biblical Literature, 2009.

———. "Tatbericht und Wortbericht in der priesterschriftlichen Schöpfungserzählung." *ZTK* 91 (1994): 115–33.

———. "The Yahwist and the Redactional Link Between Genesis and Exodus." Pages 131–41 in *A Farewell to the Yahwist? The Composition of the Pentateuch in Recent European Interpretation.* Edited by Thomas B. Dozeman and Konrad Schmid. SymS 34. Atlanta: Society of Biblical Literature, 2006.

Levine, Baruch. "The Epilogue to the Holiness Code: A Priestly Statement on the Destiny of Israel." Pages 9–34 in *Judaic Perspectives on Ancient*

248   Bibliography

Israel. Edited by Jacob Neusner, Baruch A. Levine, Ernest S. Frerichs, and Caroline McCracken-Flesher. Philadelphia: Wipf & Stock, 1987.

———. *Leviticus: The Traditional Hebrew Text with the New JPS Translation.* JPSTC. Philadelphia: The Jewish publication Society, 1989.

Levinson, Bernard M. *Deuteronomy and the Hermeneutics of Legal Innovation.* Oxford: Oxford University Press, 1997.

Levinson, Bernard M., and Jeffrey Stackert. "Between the Covenant Code and Esarhaddon's Succession Treaty: Deuteronomy 13 and the Composition of Deuteronomy." *JAJ* 3 (2012): 123–40.

Lohfink, Norbert. "Die Abänderung der Theologie des priesterlichen Geschichtswerks im Segen des Heilikeitsgesetzes: Zu Lev. 26,9.1 1–13." Pages 129–36 in *Wort und Geschichte: Festschrift für Karl Elliger zum 70. Geburtstag.* Edited by Hartmut Gese and Hans Peter Rüger. Neukirchen-Vlyun: Neukirchner, 1973.

———. "Die Priesterschrift und die Geschichte." Pages 189–225 in *Congress Volume: Göttingen 1977.* Edited by J. A. Emerton. VTSup 29. Leiden: Brill, 1978.

———. "Die priesterschriftliche Abwertung der Tradition von der Offenbarung des Jahwenamens an Mose." *Bib* 49 (1968): 1–8.

———. *Studien zum Pentateuch.* SBAB 4. Stuttgart: Katholisches Bibelwerk, 1988.

———. "Zum 'kleinen geschichtlichen Credo' Dtn 26,5–9." *TP* 46 (1971): 19–39.

Löhr, Max. *Der Priesterkodex in der Genesis.* Vol. 1 of *Untersuchungen zum Hexateuchproblem.* BZAW 38. Gießen: Töpelmann, 1924.

López, Félix García. *El Pentateuco: Introducción a la lectura de los cinco primeros libros de la Biblia.* Introducción al estudio de la Biblia 3a. Estella: Verbo Divino, 2003.

Lowth, Robert. *De sacra poesi Hebræorum prælectiones academicæ Oxonii habitæ.* Oxford: Clarendon, 1753.

Lust, Johan. *Traditie, redactie en kerygma bij Ezechiel: Een analyse van Ez., xx, 1–26.* Brussel: Paleis der Academiën, 1969.

Lux, Rüdiger. "Geschichte als Erfahrung, Erinnerung und Erzählung in der priesterschriftlichen Rezeption der Josefsnovelle." Pages 147–80 in *Erzählte Geschichte: Beiträge zur narrativen Kultur im alten Israel.* Edited by Rüdiger Lux. BThSt 40. Neukirchen-Vluyn: Neukurchner, 2000.

Lyons, Michael. *From Law to Prophecy: Ezekiel's Use of the Holiness Code.* LHBOTS 507. London: T&T Clark, 2009.

Markl, Dominik. *Gottes Volk im Deuteronomium*. BZAR 18. Wiesbaden: Harrassowitz, 2012.

Marx, Alfred. *Lévitique 17–27*. CAT 3b. Geneva: Labor et Fides, 2011.

Michaeli, Franck. *Le livre de l'Exode*. CAT 2. Neuchâtel: Delachaux et Niestlé, 1974.

Milgrom, Jacob. "The Changing Concept of Holiness in the Pentateuchal Codes with Emphasis on Leviticus 19." Pages 65–78 in *Reading Leviticus: A Conversation with Mary Douglas*. Edited by John F. A. Sawyer. JSOTSup 227. Sheffield: Sheffield Academic, 1996.

———. "HR in Leviticus and Elsewhere in the Torah." Pages 24–40 in *The Book of Leviticus: Composition and Recaption*. Edited by Rolf Rendtorff and Robert A. Kugler. VTSup 93. Leiden: Brill, 2003.

———. *Leviticus 1–16: A Translation with Introduction and Commentary*. AB 3. New Haven: Yale University Press, 1991.

———. *Leviticus 17–22: A New Translation with Introduction and Commentary*. AB 3A. New York: Doubleday, 2000.

———. *Leviticus 23–27: A New Translation with Introduction and Commentary*. AB 3B. New York: Doubleday, 2001.

———. "Leviticus 26 and Ezekiel." Pages 57–62 in *The Quest for Context and Meaning: Studies in Biblical Intertextuality in Honor of James A. Sanders*. Edited by Craig A. Evans and Shemaryahu Talmon. BibInt 28. Leiden: Brill, 1997.

Müller, Reinhard. "A Prophetic View of the Exile in the Holiness Code: Literary Growth and Tradition History in Leviticus 26." Pages 207–28 in *The Concept of Exile in Ancient Israel and Its Historical Contexts*. Edited by Ehud Ben Zvi and Christoph Levin. BZAW 404. Berlin: De Gruyter, 2010.

Murtonen, A. E. "On the Chronology of the Old Testament." *ST* 8 (1954): 133–37.

Najman, Hindy. *Seconding Sinai. The Development of Mosaic Discourse in Second Temple Judaism*. JSJSup 77. Leiden: Brill, 2003.

Nihan, Christophe. "Das Sabbatgesetz Exodus 31,12–17, die Priesterschrift und das Heiligkeitsgesetz: Eine Auseinandersetzung mit neueren Interpretationen." Pages 131–49 in *Wege der Freiheit: Zur Entstehung und Theologie des Exodusbuches; Die Beiträge eines Symposions zum 70. Geburtstag von Rainer Albertz*. Edited by Reinhard Achenbach et al. ATANT 104. Zürich: TVZ, 2014.

———. "Ezekiel and the Holiness Legislation: A Plea for Non-linear Models." Pages 1015–39 in *The Formation of the Pentateuch: Bridging*

250 Bibliography

the Academic Cultures of Europe, Israel and North America. Edited by Jan C. Gertz, Bernard M Levinson, Dalit Rom-Shiloni, and Konrad Schmid. FAT 111. Tübingen: Mohr Siebeck, 2016.

———. *From Priestly Torah to Pentateuch: A Study in the Composition of the Book of Leviticus.* FAT 2/25. Tübingen: Mohr Siebeck, 2007.

———. "The Holiness Code between D and P: Some Comments on the Function and Significance of Leviticus 17–26 in the Composition of the Torah." Pages 81–122 in *Das Deuteronomium zwischen Pentateuch und Deuteronomistischem Geschichtswerk.* Edited by Eckart Otto and Reinhard Achenbach. FRLANT 206. Göttingen: Vandenhoeck & Ruprecht, 2004.

———. "Israel's Festival Calendars in Leviticus 23, Numbers 28–29 and the Formation of 'Priestly' Literature." Pages 177–231 in *The Books of Leviticus and Numbers.* Edited by Thomas Römer. BETL 215. Leuven: Peeters, 2008.

———. "Leviticus 26:39–46 and the Post-Priestly Composition of Leviticus: Some Remarks in Light of the Recent Discussion." Pages 305–29 in *The Post-Priestly Pentateuch: New Perspectives on its Redactional Development and Theological Profiles.* Edited by Frederico Giuntoli and Konrad Schmid. FAT 101. Tübingen: Mohr Siebeck, 2015.

———. "'Moses and the Prophets': Deuteronomy 18 and the Emergence of the Pentateuch as Torah." *SEÅ* 75 (2010): 21–55.

———. "The Priestly Covenant, Its Reinterpretations, and the Composition of 'P.'" Pages 87–134 in *The Strata of the Priestly Writings: Contemporary Debate and Future Directions.* Edited by Sarah Shectman. Zürich: TVZ, 2009.

———. "The Priestly Laws of Numbers, the Holiness Legislation, and the Pentateuch." Pages 109–37 in *Torah and the Book of Numbers.* Edited by Christian Frevel et al. FAT 2/62. Tübingen: Mohr Siebeck, 2013.

———. "Resident Aliens and Natives in the Holiness Legislation." Pages 111–34 in *The Foreigner and the Law: Perspectives from the Hebrew Bible and the Ancient Near East.* Edited by Reinhard Achenbach, Rainer Albertz, and Jakob Wöhrle. BZAR 16. Wiesbaden: Harrassowitz, 2011.

Nöldeke, Theodor. "Die s. g. Grundschrift des Pentateuchs." Pages 1–144 in *Untersuchungen zur Kritik des Alten Testaments.* Kiel: Schwers'sche Buchhandlung, 1869.

Noth, Martin. *The Chronicler's History.* Translated by Hugh G. M. Williamson. JSOTSup 50. Sheffield: JSOT Press, 1987. Translated from *Überlieferungsgeschichtliche Studien* Halle: Niemeyer, 1943.

———. *Das Zweite Buch Mose: Exodus.* ATD 5. Göttingen: Vandenhoeck & Ruprecht, 1958.

———. *A History of Pentateuchal Traditions.* Translation by Bernhard W. Anderson. Chico, CA: Scholars Press, 1981.

———. *Überlieferungsgeschichte des Pentateuch.* Stuttgart: Kohlhammer, 1948. 2nd ed. Stuttgart: Kohlhammer, 1960.

Otto, Eckart. "The Book of Deuteronomy and Its Answer to the Persian State Ideology: The Legal Implications." Pages 112–22 in *Loi et justice dans la literature du Proche-Orient ancient.* Edited by Olivier Artus. BZAR 20. Wiesbaden: Harrassowitz, 2013.

———. "The Book of Deuteronomy and Numbers in One Torah: The Book of Numbers Read in the Horizon of the Postexilic *Fortschreibung* in the Book of Deuteronomy; New Horizons in the Interpretation of the Pentateuch." Pages 383–97 in *Torah and the Book of Numbers.* Edited by Christian Frevel, Thomas Pola, and Aaron Schaart. FAT 2/62. Tübingen: Mohr Siebeck, 2013.

———. "Das Buch Levitikus im Pentateuch." *TRu* 74 (2009): 470–79.

———. "Das Buch Levitikus zwischen Priesterschrift und Pentateuch." Pages 107–142 in *Die Tora: Studien zum Pentateuch; Gesammelte Aufsätze.* BZAR 9. Wiesbaden: Harrassowitz, 2009.

———. *Das Deuteronomium: Politische Theologie und Rechtsreform in Juda und Assyrien.* BZAW 284. Berlin: De Gruyter, 1999.

———. *Das Deuteronomium im Pentateuch und Hexateuch: Studien zur Literaturgeschichte von Pentateuch und Hexateuch im Lichte des Deuteronomiumrahmens.* FAT 30. Tübingen: Mohr Siebeck, 2000.

———. "'Das Deuteronomium krönt die Arbeit der Propheten': Gesetz und Prophetie im Deuteronomium." Pages 277–309 in *"Ich bewirke das Heil und erschaffe das Unheil" (Jes 45,7): Studien zur Botschaft der Propheten.* Edited by Friedrich Diedrich and Bernd Willmes. FB 88. Würzburg: Echter, 1998.

———. *Das Gesetz des Mose: Die Literatur- und Rechtsgeschichte der Mosebücher.* Darmstadt: Wissenschaftliche Buchgesellschaft, 2007.

———. "Das Heiligkeitsgesetz Leviticus 17–26 in der Pentateuchredaktion." Pages 65–80 in *Altes Testament: Forschung und Wirkung: FS H. G. Reventlow.* Edited by Peter Mommer and Winfried Thiel. Frankfurt am Main: Lang, 1994.

252   Bibliography

———. "Das Heiligkeitsgesetz zwischen Priesterschrift und Deuteronomium." *ZAR* 6 (2000): 330–40.

———. *Deuteronomium 1,1–11,32*. HKAT. Freiburg: Herder, 2012.

———. *Deuteronomium 12,1–23,15*. HKAT. Freiburg: Herder, 2016.

———. *Deuteronomium 23,16–34,12*. HKAT. Freiburg: Herder, 2017.

———. "Die nachpriesterschriftliche Pentateuchredakton im Buch
Exodus." Pages 61–111 in *Studies in the Book of Exodus*. Edited by
Marc Vervenne. BETL 126. Leuven: Peeters, 1996.

———. "Die Paradieserzählung Genesis 2–3: Eine nachpriesterschriftliche
Lehrerzählung in ihrem religionshistorischen Kontext." Pages 167–92
in *'Jedes Ding hat seine Zeit...': Studien zur israelitischen und altorientalischen Weisheit; Festschrift für Diethelm Michel zum 65. Geburtstag*.
Edited by Anja A. Diesel et al. BZAW 241. Berlin: De Gruyter, 1996.

———. "*Ersetzen* oder *Ergänzen* von Gesetzen in der Rechtshermeneutik
des Pentateuch." Pages 248–56 in *Die Tora: Studien zum Pentateuch;
Gesammelte Aufsätze*. BZAR 9. Wiesbaden: Harrassowitz, 2009.

———. "*Ersetzen* oder *Ergänzen* von Gesetzen in der Rechtshermeneutik
des Pentateuch: Zu einem Buch von Jeffrey Stackert." *ZAR* 14 (2008):
434–42.

———. "Forschungen zur Priesterschrift." *TRu* 62 (1997): 1–50.

———. "A Hidden Truth behind the Text or the Truth of the Text: At a
Turning Point in Biblical Scholarship Hundred Years after de Wette's
Dissertatio critico-exegetica." Pages 19–28 in *South African Perspectives
on the Pentateuch between Synchrony and Diachrony*. Edited by Jurie
Le Roux and Eckart Otto. LHBOTS 463. New York: T&T Clark, 2007.

———. "Innerbiblische Exegese im Heiligkeitsgesetz Levitikus 17–26."
Pages 125–96 in *Levitikus als Buch*. Edited by Heinz-Josef Fabry and
Hans-Wilfried Jüngling. BBB 119. Berlin: Philo, 1999.

———. "Jenseits der Suche nach dem 'ursprünglich Text' in der Textkritik:
Fortschreibungen und Textautorität in der nachexilischen Zeit." *ZAR*
18 (2012): 365–71.

———. "Kritik der Pentateuchkomposition." *TRu* 60 (1995): 163–91.

———. "Mose, der erste Schriftgelehrte: Deuteronomium 1,5 in der Fabel
des Pentateuch." Pages 273–84 in *L'Écrit et l'Esprit: Études d'histoire du
texte et de théologie biblique*. Edited by Dieter Böhler, Innocent Himbaza, and Philippe Hugo. OBO 214. Fribourg: Academic Press; Göttingen: Vandenhoeck & Ruprecht, 2005.

———. "Moses Abschiedslied in Deuteronomium 32: Ein Zeugnis der
Kanonsbildung in der Hebräischen Bibel." Pages 641–78 in *Die Tora:*

Studien zum Pentateuch; Gesammelte Aufsätze. BZAR 9. Wiesbaden: Harrassowitz, 2009.

——. "The Pivotal Meaning of Pentateuch Research for a History of Israelite and Judean Religion and Society." Pages 29–54 in *South African Perspectives on the Pentateuch between Synchrony and Diachrony.* Edited by Jurie Le Roux and Eckart Otto. LHBOTS 463. New York: T&T Clark, 2007.

——. "The Pre-exilic Deuteronomy as a Revision of the Covenant Code." Pages 112–22 in *Kontinuum und Proprium: Studien zur Sozial- und Rechtsgeschichte im Alten Orient und im Alten.* Orientalia Biblica et Christiana 8. Wiesbaden: Harrassowitz, 1996.

——. "Rechtshermeneutik in der Hebräischen Bibel: Die innerbiblischen Ursprünge halachischer Bibelauslegung." *ZAR* 5 (1999): 75–98.

——. Review of *J, E, and the Redaction of the Pentateuch,* by Joel Baden. *ZAR* 15 (2009): 451–55.

——. "Scribal Scholarship in the Formation of Torah and Prophets: A Postexilic Scribal Debate between Priestly Scholarship and Literary Prophecy; The Example of the Book of Jeremiah and Its Relation to the Pentateuch." Pages 171–84 in *The Pentateuch as Torah: New Models for Understanding Its Promulgation and Acceptance.* Edited by Gary N. Knoppers and Bernard M. Levinson. Winona Lake, IN: Eisenbrauns, 2007.

——. "Singing Moses: His Farewell Song in Deuteronomy 32." Pages 169–81 in *Psalmody and Poetry in Old Testament Ethics.* Edited by Drik J. Human. LHBOTS 572. New York: T&T Clark, 2012.

——. "The Suffering Prophet in Deuteronomy and Psalm 90–92." Pages 137–49 in *Propheten der Epochen: Prophets of the Epochs.* Edited by Viktor Kókai Nagy and László Sándor Egeresi. AOAT 426. Münster: Ugarit, 2015.

——. *Theologische Ethik des Alten Testaments.* ThW 3.2. Stuttgart: Kohlhammer, 1994.

——. "Tora für eine neue Generation in Dtn 4: Die hermeneutische Theologie des Numeruswechsels im Deuteronomium." Pages 105–22 in *Deuteronomium: Tora für eine neue Generation.* Edited by Georg Fischer, Dominik Markl, and Smone Paganini. BZAR 17. Wiesbaden: Harrassowitz, 2011.

——. "Vom Bundesbuch zum Deuteronomium: Die deuteronomische Redaktion in Dtn 12–26." Pages 260–78 in *Biblische Theologie und*

254 Bibliography

Gesellschaft im Wandel. Edited by Georg Braulik, Seán McEvenue, and Norbert Lohfink. Freiburg: Herder, 1993.

———. "Wie 'synchron' wurde in der Antike der Pentateuch gelesen?" Pages 420–85 in *"Das Manna fällt auch heute noch": Beiträge zur Geschichte und Theologie des Alten Testaments/Ersten Testaments.* Edited by Frank-Lothar Hossfeld and Ludger Schwienhorst-Schönberger. HBS 44. Freiburg: Herder, 2004.

Perlitt, Lothar. "Priesterschrift im Deuteronomium?" *ZAW* 100 (1988): 44–88.

Pohlmann, Karl-Friedrich. *Der Prophet Hesekiel/Ezechiel: Kapitel 20–48.* ATD 22.2. Göttingen: Vandenhoeck & Ruprecht, 2001.

Pola, Thomas. *Die ursprüngliche Priesterschrift: Beobachtungen zur Literarkritik und Traditionsgeschichte von Pg.* WMANT 70. Neukirchen-Vluyn: Neukirchener Verlag, 1995.

Preuss, Horst Dietrich. "Heiligkeitsgesetz." *TRE* 14 (1985): 713–19.

Pury, Albert de. "Der priesterschriftliche Umgang mit der Jakobsgeschichte." Pages 33–60 in *Schriftauslegung in der Schrift: FS O. H. Steck.* Edited by R. G. Kratz et al. BZAW 300. Berlin: De Gruyter, 2000.

———. "The Jacob Story and the Beginning of the Formation of the Pentateuch." Pages 51–72 in *A Farewell to the Yahwist?* Edited by Thomas Dozeman and Konrad Schmid. SymS 34. Atlanta: Society of Biblical Literature, 2006.

———. "Pg as the Absolute Beginning." Pages 99–128 in *Les dernières rédactions du Pentateuque, de l'Hexateuque et de l'Ennéateuque.* Edited by Thomas Römer and Konrad Schmid. BETL 203. Leuven: Peeters, 2007.

Rad, Gerhard von. *Die Priesterschrift im Hexateuch untersucht und theologisch bewertet.* BWANT 65. Stuttgart: Kohlhammer, 1934.

———. "The Form-Critical Problem of the Hetateuch." Pages 1–58 in *From Genesis to Chronicles: Explorations in Old Testament Theology.* Edited by E. W. Trueman Dicken. Minneapolis: Fortress, 2005.

Ramirez-Kidd, José E. *Alterity and Identity in Israel: The ger in the Old Testament.* BZAW 283. Berlin: de Gruyter, 1999.

Reindl, Joseph. "Der Finger Gottes und die Macht der Götter: Ein Problem des ägyptischen Diasporajudentums und sein literarischer Niederschlag." Pages 49–60 in *Dienst der Vermittlung: Festschrift Priesterseminar Erfurt.* Edited by Wilhelm Ernst, Konrad Feiereis, and Fritz Hoffmann. Erfurter Theologische Studien 37. Leipzig: St. Benno Verlag, 1977.

Bibliography   255

Rendtorff, Rolf. *Das überlieferungsgeschichtliche Problem des Pentateuch.* BZAW 147. Berlin: De Gruyter, 1976.

———. "L'histoire biblique des origines (Gen 1–11) dans le contexte de la redaction 'sacerdotale' du Pentateuque." Pages 83–94 in *Le Pentateuque en question: Les origines et la composition des cinq premiers livres de la Bible à la lumière des recherches récentes.* Edited by Albert de Pury and Thomas Römer. MdB 19. Geneva: Labor et Fides, 1989.

———. *Leviticus 1–10.* BKAT 3.1. Neukirchen-Vluyn: Neukirchener Verlag, 1985.

Richter, Wolfgang. "Beobachtungen zur theologischen Systembildung in der alttestamentlichen Literatur anhand des 'Kleinen geschichtlichen Credo.'" Pages 175–212 in *Wahrheit und Verkündigung: Michael Schmaus zum 70. Geburtstag.* Edited by Leo Scheffczyk et al. Vol. 1. Munich: Schöningh, 1967.

Römer, Thomas. "Competing Magicians in Exodus 7–9: Interpreting Magic in Priestly Theology." Pages 12–22 in *Magic in the Biblical World: From the Rod of Aaron to the Ring of Solomon.* Edited by Todd E. Klutz. JSNTSup 245. London: T&T Clark, 2003.

———. "Das Buch Numeri und das Ende des Jahwisten: Anfragen zur 'Quellenscheidung' im vierten Buch des Pentateuch." Pages 215–31 in *Abschied vom Jahwisten: Die Komposition des Hexateuch in der jüngsten Diskussion.* Edited by Jan C.Gertz et al. BZAW 315. Berlin: De Gruyter, 2002.

———. "De la périphérie au centre: Les livres du Lévitique et des Nombres dans le débat actuel sur le Pentateuque." Pages 3–34 in *The Books of Leviticus and Numbers.* Edited by Thomas Römer. BETL 215. Leuven: Uitgeveru Peeters, 2008.

———. "Deux repas 'en miroir' dans l'histoire de Joseph (Gn 37–50)." *RHPR* 93 (2013): 15–27.

———. "Egypt Nostalgia in Exodus 14–Numbers 21." Pages 66–86 in *Torah and the Book of Numbers.* Edited by Christian Frevel, Thomas Pola, and Aaron Schart. FAT 2/62. Tübingen: Mohr Siebeck, 2013.

———. "The Exodus Narrative according to the Priestly Document." Pages 157–74 in *The Strata of the Priestly Writings: Contemporary Debate and Future Directions.* Edited by Sarah Shectman and Joel S. Baden. ATANT 95. Zürich: Theologischer Verlag, 2009.

———. "From the Call of Moses to the Parting of the Sea: Reflections on the Priestly Version of the Exodus Narrative." Pages 121–50 in *The Book of Exodus: Composition, Reception, and Interpretation.* Edited by Thomas Dozeman, Craig A. Evans, and Joel N. Lohr. VTSup 164. Leiden: Brill, 2014.

———. *Israels Väter: Untersuchungen zur Väterthematik im Deuteronomium und in der deuteronomistischen Tradition.* OBO 99. Göttingen: Vandenhoeck & Ruprecht, 1990.

———. "Israel's Sojourn in the Wilderness and the Construction of the Book of Numbers." Pages 419–45 in *Reflection and Refraction: Studies in Biblical Historiography in Honour of A. Graeme Auld.* Edited by Robert Rezetko. VTSup 113. Brill: Leiden, 2007.

———. "Tracking Some 'Censored' Moses Traditions inside and outside the Hebrew Bible." *HeBAI* 1 (2012): 64–76.

Rösel, Martin. *Übersetzung als Vollendung der Auslegung: Studien zur Genesis-Septuaginta.* BZAW 223. Berlin: De Gruyter, 1994.

Rost, Leonhard. "Das kleine geschichtliche Credo." Pages 11–25 in *Das kleine Credo und andere Studien zum Alten Testament.* Heidelberg: Quelle & Meyer, 1965.

Rothenbusch, Ralf. "Zur Ausgestaltung der Sinaiperikope durch die Priesterliche Gebotsmitteilung." Pages 3–28 in *"Ich werde meinen Bund mit euch niemals brechen!" (Ri 2,1): Festschrift für Walter Groß zum 70. Geburtstag.* Edited by Erasmus Gaß and Hermann-Josef Stipp. HBS 62. Freiburg i.B.: Herder, 2011.

Rudolph, Wilhelm. *Der "Elohist" von Exodus bis Josua.* BZAW 68. Berlin: Töpelmann, 1938.

———. "Die Josefsgeschichte." Pages 143–83 in *Der Elohist als Erzähler: Ein Irrweg der Pentateuchkritik? An der Genesis erläutert.* Edited by Paul Volz and Wilhelm Rudolph. BZAW 63. Giessen: Alfred Töpelmann, 1933.

Ruwe, Andreas. *"Heiligkeitsgesetz" und "Priesterschrift": Literaturgeschichtliche und rechtssystematische Untersuchungen zu Levitikus 17–26.* FAT 26. Tübingen: Mohr Siebeck, 1999.

Shectman, Sarah, and Joel S. Baden, eds. *The Strata of the Priestly Writings. Contemporary Debate and Future Directions.* ATANT 95. Zürich: TVZ, 2009.

Schmid, Konrad. "Der Abschluss der Tora als exegetisches und historisches Problem." Pages 159–84 in *Schriftgelehrte Traditionsliteratur.* FAT 77. Tübingen: Mohr Siebeck, 2011.

———. "Differenzierungen und Konzeptualisierungen der Einheit Gottes in der Religions- und Literaturgeschichte Israels." Pages 11–39 in *Der eine Gott und die Götter: Polytheismus und Monotheismus im antiken*

Israel. Edited by Manfred Oeming and Konrad Schmid. ATANT 82. Zürich: Theologischer Verlag, 2003.

———. *Erzväter und Exodus.* WMANT 81. Neukirchen-Vluyn: Neukirchener, 1999.

———. *Literaturgeschichte des Alten Testaments: Eine Einführung.* Darmstadt: Wissenschaftliche Buchgesellschaft, 2008.

———. *The Old Testament: A Literary History.* Minneapolis: Fortress, 2012.

———. "The Neo-Documentarian Manifesto: A Critical Reading." *JBL* 140 (2021): 461–79.

———. "Persische Reichsauthorisation und Tora." *TRu* 71 (2006): 494–506.

Schmidt, Ludwig. *Beobachtungen zu der Plagenerzählung in Exodus VII 14–XI 10.* StudBib 4. Leiden: Brill, 1990.

———. "Die vorpriesterliche Verbindung von Erzvätern und Exodus durch die Josefsgeschichte (Gen 37; 39–50*) und Exodus 1." *ZAW* 124 (2012): 19–37.

———. *Studien zur Priesterschrift.* BZAW 214. Berlin: De Gruyter, 1993.

Schmidt, Werner H. *Exodus.* BKAT 2. Neukirchen-Vluyn: Neukirchner, 1974. Repr. 1995.

Schmitt, Hans-Christoph. "Erzvätergeschichte und Exodusgeschichte als konkurrierende Ursprungslegenden Israels—Ein Irrweg der Pentateuchforschung." Pages 241–66 in *Die Erzväter in der biblischen Tradition: Festschrift für Matthias Köckert.* Edited by Anselm C. Hagedorn and Henrik Pfeiffer. BZAW 400. Berlin: de Gruyter, 2009.

———. "'Priesterliches' und 'prophetisches' Geschichtsverständnis in der Meerwundererzählung Ex 13,17–14,31." Pages 203–19 in *Theologie in Prophetie und Pentateuch.* BZAW 310. Berlin: De Gruyter, 2001.

———. "Wie deuteronomistisch ist der nichtpriesterliche Meerwunderbericht von Ex 13,17–14,31?" *Bib* 95 (2014): 26–48.

Schoneveld, J. "Ezekiel XIV 1–8." *OTS* 15 (1969): 193–204.

Schrader, Eberhard. *Studien zur Kritik und Erklärung der biblischen Urgeschichte.* Zürich: Meyer & Zeller, 1863.

Schwartz, Baruch J. "How the Compiler of the Pentateuch Worked: The Composition of Genesis 37." Pages 263–78 in *The Book of Genesis: Composition, Reception, and Interpretation.* Edited by Craig A. Evans, Joel N. Lohr, and David L. Petersen. VTSup 152. Leiden: Brill, 2012.

———. "The Strata of the Priestly Writings and the Revised Relative Dating of P and H." Pages 1–12 in *The Strata of the Priestly Writings, Contemporary Debate and Future Directions.* Edited by Joel Baden and Sarah Shectman. ATANT 95. Zürich: TVZ, 2009.

258 Bibliography

Schüle, Andreas. *Der Prolog der hebräischen Bibel: Der literar- und theologiegeschichtliche Diskurs der Urgeschichte (Gen 1–11)*. ATANT 86. Zürich: Theologischer Verlag, 2006.

Seebass, Horst. *Genesis I: Urgeschichte (1:1–11:26)*. Neukirchen-Vluyn: Neukirchener, 1996.

———. *Genesis II: Vätergeschichte II (23,1–36,43)*. Neukirchen-Vluyn: Neukirchner, 1999.

Seebass, Horst. "Josua." *BN* 28 (1985): 53–65.

Seidel, Bodo. *Karl David Ilgen und die Pentateuchforschung im Umkreis der sogenannten Älteren Urkundenhypothese*. BZAW 213. Berlin: De Gruyter, 1993.

Seidel, Theodor. "Levitikus 16: 'Schlussstein' des priesterlichen Systems der Sündenvergebung." Pages 219–48 in *Levitikus als Buch*. Edited by Heinz-Josef Fabry and Hans-Wilfried Jüngling. BBB 119. Berlin: Philo, 1999.

Ska, Jean Louis. "El Relato des Diluvio: Un Relato Sacerdotal y Algunos Fragmentos Redaccionales Posteriores." *EstBib* 52 (1994): 37–62.

———. *Introduction à la lecture du Pentateuque: Clés pour l'interprétation des cinque premiers livres de la Bible*. Brüssel: Lessius, 2000.

———. "La sortie d'Egypte (Ex 7–14) dans le récit sacerdotal et la tradition prophétique." *Bib* 60 (1979): 191–215.

———. *Le passage de la mer: Etude sur la construction du style et de la symbolique d'Ex 14,1–31*. AnBib 109. Rome: Pontifical Institute, 1986.

———. "Le récit sacerdotal: Une 'histoire sans fin'?" Pages 631–53 in *The Books of Leviticus and Numbers*. Edited by Thomas Römer. BETL 215. Leuven: Peeters, 2008.

———. "Les plaies d'Egypte dans le recit sacerdotal." *Bib* 60 (1979): 23–35.

———. "Quelques remarques sur Pg et la dernière rédaction du Pentateuque." Pages 95–125 in *Le Pentateuque en question: Les origines et la composition des cinq premiers livres de la Bible à la lumière des recherches récentes*. Edited by Albert de Pury and Thomas Römer, MdB 19. 3rd ed. Geneva: Labor et Fides, 2002.

———. "The Story of the Flood: A Priestly Writer and Some Later Editorial Fragments." Pages 1–22 in *The Exegesis of the Pentateuch: Exegetical Studies and Basic Questions*. FAT 66. Tübingen: Mohr Siebeck, 2009.

Smend, Rudolf. "Das alte Israel im Alten Testament." Pages 1–14 in *Bibel und Wissenschaft: Historische Aufsätze*. Tübingen: Mohr Siebeck, 2004.

———. *Die Erzählung des Hexateuch auf ihre Quellen untersucht*. Berlin: Reimer, 1912. 4th ed. Stuttgart: Kohlhammer, 1989.

Sonnet, Jean-Pierre. "The Fifth Book of the Pentateuch. Deuteronomy in Its Narrative Dynamic." *JAJ* 3 (2012): 197–234.

———. "Redefining the Plot of Deuteronomy—From End to Beginning: The Import of Deut 34:9." Pages 15–36 in *Deuteronomium: Tora für eine neue Generation*. Edited by Georg Fischer, Dominik Markl, and Smone Paganini. BZAR 17. Wiesbaden: Harrassowitz, 2011.

Specht, Herbert. "Von Gott enttäuscht—Die priesterschriftliche Abrahamsgeschichte." *EvT* 47 (1987): 395–411.

Stackert, Jeffrey. "Compositional Strata in the Priestly Sabbath: Exodus 31:12–17 and 35:1–3." *JHS* 11 (2011): 1–21.

———. "Distinguishing Innerbiblical Exegesis from Pentateuchal Redaction: Leviticus 26 as a Test Case." Pages 369–86 in *The Pentateuch: International Perspectives on Current Research*. Edited by Thomas B. Dozeman, Konrad Schmid, and Barukh Ya'aḳov Shvarts. FAT 78. Tübingen: Mohr Siebeck, 2011.

———. *A Prophet Like Moses: Prophecy, Law, and Israelite Religion*. Oxford: Oxford University Press, 2014.

———. *Rewriting the Torah: Literary Revision in Deuteronomy and the Holiness Legislation*. FAT 52. Tübingen: Mohr Siebeck, 2007.

Steck, Odil Hannes. *Der Schöpfungsbericht der Priesterschrift*. FRLANT 115. 2nd ed. Göttingen: Vandenhoeck & Ruprecht, 1981.

Steins, Georg. "Sie sollen mir ein Heiligtum machen": Zur Struktur und Entstehung von Ex 24,12–31,18." Pages 145–67 in *Vom Sinai zum Horeb: Stationen alttestamentlicher Glaubensgeschichte*. Edited by Frank-Lothar Hossfeld. Würzburg: Echter, 1989.

Steymans, Hans Ulrich. *Deuteronomium 28 und die adê zur Thronfolgeregelung Asarhaddons*. OBO 145. Fribourg: Vandenhoeck & Ruprecht 1995.

———. "Verheißung und Drohung: Lev 26." Pages 263–307 in *Levitikus als Buch*. Edited by Heinz-Josef Fabry and Hans-Wilfried Jüngling. BBB 119. Berlin: Philo, 1999.

Tengström, Sven. *Die Toledotformel und die literarische Struktur der priesterlichen Erweiterungsschicht im Pentateuch*. ConBOT 17. Lund: CWK Gleerup, 1981.

Tigay, Jeffrey H. *The Evolution of the Gilgamesh Epic*. Philadelphia: University of Pennsylvania Press, 1982.

Tuch, Friedrich. *Kommentar über die Genesis*. Halle: Buchhandlung des Waisenhauses, 1838.

260 Bibliography

Utzschneider, Helmut. *Das Heiligtum und das Gesetz*. OBO 77. Göttingen: Vandenhoeck & Ruprecht, 1988.

Utzschneider, Helmut, and Wolfgang Oswald. *Exodus 1–15*. IEKAT. Stuttgart: Kohlhammer, 2013.

Valdés, Ariel Alvarez. "Levitico 26: una sintesis de alianzas como clave de lectura." *EstBib* 61 (2003): 155–81.

Van Seters, John. *Abraham in History and Tradition*. New Haven: Yale University Press, 1975.

———. "A Contest of Magicians? The Plague Stories in P." Pages 569–80 in *Pomegranates and Golden Bells: Studies in Biblical, Jewish, and Near Eastern Ritual, Law, and Literature in Honor of Jacob Milgrom*. Edited by David P. Wright, David Noel Freedman, and Avi Hurvitz. Winona Lake, IN: Eisenbrauns, 1995.

———. *The Life of Moses*. CBET 10. Kampen: Kok, 1994.

———. "The Patriarchs and the Exodus: Bridging the Gap between Two Origin Traditions." Pages 1–15 in *The Interpretation of Exodus: Studies in Honour of Cornelis Houtman*. Edited by Riemer Roukema. CBET 44. Leuven: Peeters, 2006.

———. *The Pentateuch: A Social-Science Commentary*. Trajectories 1. Sheffield: Sheffield Academic, 1999.

Vermeylen, Jacques. *La formation du Pentateuque: Bref historique de la recherche et essai de solution cohérente, pro manu scripto*. Brüssel: CETP, 1990.

Vervenne, Marc. "The 'P' Tradition in the Pentateuch." Pages 67–90 in *Pentateuchal and Deuteronomistic Studies*. Edited by Christian Brekelmans and Johan Lust. BETL 94. Leuven: Leuven University Press, 1990.

Volz, Paul. "Anhang: P ist kein Erzähler." Pages 135–42 in *Der Elohist als Erzähler: Ein Irrweg der Pentateuchkritik? An der Genesis erläutert*. Edited by Paul Volz and Wilhelm Rudolph. BZAW 63. Gießen: Töpelmann, 1933.

Volz, Paul, and Wilhelm Rudolph. *Der Elohist als Erzähler: Ein Irrweg der Pentateuchkritik? An der Genesis erläutert*. BZAW 63. Gießen: Töpelmann, 1933.

Watts, James W., ed. *Persia and the Torah: The Theory of the Imperial Authorization of the Pentateuch*. SymS 17. Atlanta: Society of Biblical Literature Press, 2001.

Wevers, John W. *Notes on the Greek Text of Leviticus*. SCS 44. Atlanta: Scholars Press, 1997.

Weimar, Peter. "Die Toledotformel in der priesterschriftlichen Geschichtsdarstellung." Pages 151–84 in *Studien zur Priesterschrift*. FAT 56. Tübingen: Mohr Siebeck, 2008.

———. "'Nicht konnten die Magier vor Mose hintreten' (Exod 9:11)." Pages 97–117 in *Berühungspunkte: Studien zur Sozial- und Religionsgeschichte Israels und seiner Umwelt*. Edited by Ingo Kottsieper, Ruediger Schmitt, Jakob Wöhrle, and Ruth Ebach. AOAT 350. Münster: Ugarit Verlag, 2008.

———. *Untersuchungen zur priesterschriftlichen Exoduserzählung*. FB 9. Würzburg: Echter-Verlag, 1973.

Weinfeld, Moshe. *Deuteronomy 1–11: A New Translation with Introduction and Commentary*. AB 5A. New Haven: Yale University Press, 1991.

———. "Sabbath, Temple and the Enthronement of the Lord: The Problem of the Sitz im Leben of Genesis 1:1–2:3." Pages 501–12 in *Mélanges bibliques et orientaux en l'honneur de M. Henri Cazelles*. Edited by André Caquot and Mathias Delcor. AOAT 212. Neukirchen-Vluyn: Neukirchener, 1981.

Wellhausen, Julius. "Die Composition des Hexateuchs." *JDT* 21 (1876): 392–450; *JDT* 22 (1877): 407–79.

———. *Die Composition des Hexateuchs*. Berlin: Reimer, 1885. 3rd ed. Berlin: Reimer, 1899. 4th ed. Berlin: de Gruyter, 1963.

———. "Julius Wellhausen to Adolf Jülicher, 8 November 1880." Page 78 in *Briefe*. Edited by Rudolf Smend. Translated by Margaret Kohl. Tübingen: Mohr Siebeck, 2013.

———. "Julius Wellhausen to William Robertson Smith, 30 December 1883." Page 138 in *Briefe*. Edited by Rudolf Smend. Translated by Margaret Kohl. Tübingen: Mohr Siebeck, 2013.

———. *Prolegomena to the History of Ancient Israel*. Translated by J. Sutherland Black and Allan R. Menzies. Edinburgh: Black, 1885.

———. *Prolegomena zur Geschichte Israels*. 2nd ed. Berlin: De Gruyter, 1883. 6th ed. Berlin: Reimer, 1905.

———. *Der Text der Bücher Samuelis*. Göttingen: Vandenhoeck & Ruprecht, 1871.

Welte, Benedikt. *Nachmosaisches im Pentateuch*. Karlsruhe: Herder'sche Verlagshandlung, 1841.

Wenham, Gordon J. *The Book of Leviticus*. NICOT. London: Hodder, 1979.

Westermann, Claus. *Genesis 1–11*. Darmstadt: Wissenschaftliche Buchgesellschaft, 1972.

———. *Genesis 37–50*. BKAT 1.3. Neukirchen-Vluyn: Neukirchener, 1982.

262   Bibliography

Wette, Wilhelm Martin Leberecht de. *Kritik der Mosaischen Geschichte*. Vol. 2 of *Beiträge zur Einleitung in das Alte Testament*. Halle: Schimmelpfennig, 1807.

Whybray, Robert N. *The Making of the Pentateuch: A Methodological Study*. JSOTSup 53. Sheffield: Sheffield Academic, 1987,

Witte, Markus. *Die biblische Urgeschichte: Redaktions- und theologiegeschichtliche Beobachtungen zu Genesis 1,1–11,26*. BZAW 265. Berlin: De Gruyter, 1998.

Wöhrle, Jakob. *Fremdlinge im eigenen Land: Zur Entstehung und Intention der priesterlichen Passagen der Vätergeschichte*. FRLANT 246. Göttingen: Vandenhoeck & Ruprecht, 2012.

———. "The Un-empty Land: The Concept of Exile and Land in P." Pages 189–206 in *The Concept of Exile in Ancient Israel and its Historical Contexts*. Edited by Ehud Ben Zvi and Christoph Levin. BZAW 404. Berlin: de Gruyter, 2010.

Wolff, Hans Walter. "Das Kerygma des Jahwisten." Pages 345–73 in *Gesammelte Studien zum Alten Testament*. 2nd ed. TB 22. Munich: Kaiser, 1973.

Zakovitch, Yair. "The Synonymous Word and Synonymous Name in Name-Midrashim" [Hebrew]. *Shnaton* 2 (1977): 100–15.

Zenger, Erich. *Gottes Bogen in den Wolken*. SBS 112. 2nd ed. Stuttgart: Kohlhammer, 1987.

———. "Priesterschrift." *TRE* 27 (1997): 435–46.

Ziegler, Werner Carl Ludewig. "Kritik über den Artikel von der Schöpfung nach unserer gewöhnlichen Dogmatik." Pages 1–113 in *Magazin für Religionsphilosophie, Exegese und Kirchengeschichte*. Edited by Heinrich Philipp Conrad Henke. Vol. 2. Helmstädt: Fleckeisen, 1794.

Ziemer, Benjamin. "Erklärung der Zahlen von Gen 5 aus ihrem kompositionellen Zusammenhang." *ZAW* 121 (2009): 1–18.

Zimmerli, Walther. *1. Mose 12–25: Abraham*. ZBK 1.2. Zürich: TVZ, 1976.

———. "Sinaibund und Abrahambund: Ein Beitrag zum Verständnis der Priesterschrift." Pages 205–16 in *Gottes Offenbarung. Gesammelte Aufsätze zum Alten Testament*. TB 19. Munich: Kaiser, 1963.

Zvi, Ehud Ben. "Observations on Prophetic Characters, Prophetic Texts, Priests of Old, Persian Period Priests and Literati." Pages 19–30 in *The Priests in the Prophets: The Portrayal of Priests, Prophets and Other Religious Specialists in the Latter Prophets*. Edited by Lester L. Grabbe and Alice Ogden Bellis. JSOTSup 408. London: T&T Clark, 2004.

Contributors

Christoph Berner is Professor of Old Testament at Christian-Albrechts University of Kiel.

Erhard Blum is Professor Emeritus of Old Testament at Eberhard-Karls University of Tübingen.

Jan Christian Gertz is Professor of Old Testament at Ruprecht-Karls University of Heidelberg.

Friedhelm Hartenstein is Professor of Old Testament at Ludwig-Maximilians University of Munich.

Christoph Levin is Professor Emeritus of Old Testament at Ludwig-Maximilians University of Munich.

Christophe Nihan is Professor of Hebrew Bible at Westfälische-Wilhelms University of Münster.

Eckart Otto is Professor Emeritus of Old Testament at Ludwig-Maximilians University of Munich.

Thomas Römer is the chairman of the Collège de France and holds the chair of "The Hebrew Bible and Its Contexts."

Konrad Schmid is Professor of Hebrew Bible at the University of Zurich.

Ancient Sources Index

Hebrew Bible/Old Testament

Genesis	1–3, 5, 7, 12, 14–15, 19, 22, 28, 46–48, 51, 65, 86–88, 146, 149, 198, 229–31
1	14, 72, 148, 162–63, 209
1ff.	12
1–5	77–78
1–11	11, 19, 31, 66, 68, 210–11
1:1	75
1:1–2:3	71, 76–77, 81, 85, 163
1:1–2:4	70
1:6	163
1:9	67
1:9–10	163
1:12	67
1:17	163
1:18	67
1:21	67
1:22	206
1:25	67
1:26	76–77
1:26–27	77
1:26–28	88
1:27	76
1:27–28	76
1:28	76–77, 138, 206
1:31	67
2–3	81
2–4	78
2:1	169
2:3	67, 74–75
2:3–4	74
2:4	22, 69, 71, 74–77, 82
2:4–7	69, 75

2:4–3:24	20
2:4–4:26	81
2:5	23
2:17	77
3:5	77
3:8	74
3:17	68
3:22	77
4	82, 88
4:3–4	23
4:4	83
4:17–24	82–83
4:24	90–91
4:25	68, 78, 82
4:25–26	83
4:26	23, 82–83
5	63, 67, 69–70, 73–74, 82–85, 91
5–6	210–11
5:1	71, 75–77, 82, 88
5:1–2	76, 78
5:1–3	69, 74, 76, 78
5:1–31	86
5:1–32	76, 85
5:2	76–77, 88
5:3	68, 76–77, 82, 88
5:6	82
5:21	85
5:22	69, 74, 88, 210
5:24	69, 74, 210
5:29	68
5:31	78
5:32	68–69, 78–80
6	74
6–9	19–20, 25
6:1–4	81

-265-

266   Ancient Sources Index

Genesis (cont.)

6:1–8	67
6:5–8	71
6:9	68, 71, 74–75, 85, 88, 210
6:9–10	78–79
6:9–13	81
6:9–22	71
6:10	69
6:11	67, 80
6:11–13	80–81
6:12	81, 85
6:13	67, 80–81
6:17	80
7–8	162
7:2	23
7:6	69, 71, 79–80, 87–88
7:11	69, 80, 163
8:3	205
8:4	80
8:5	80
8:6	20
8:13	80
8:14	80
8:20	23
8:20–22	71
8:21–22	69
9:1	206
9:1–7	138
9:1–17	69, 71
9:4	178
9:7	206
9:9	22
9:11	22
9:13	219
9:28	71
9:28–29	79
10:1	22, 71, 75
10:1–32	76
10:32	71
10:33	71
11	85, 89, 97
11:1–9	12
11:10	71, 75–76, 79, 89
11:10–26	85
11:26	79

11:26–27	79–80
11:27	37, 42, 71, 75, 79
11:27–28	36
11:27–50:13	53–60
11:31–32	36
11:32	79
12	4, 49
12ff.	92
12–50	16, 25, 66, 96
12:1–4	36
12:4	21, 36, 42
12:4–5	36
12:5	20–21, 37
12:7–8	23
12:10–20	104
12:15	36
13:6	20–21, 36
13:11	36
13:11–12	20–21
13:12	36–37
13:18	23
14	25
15	23, 25
16	36, 49
16:1	36
16:3	36–37
16:15	36
16:15–16	36
16:16	18
17	5, 23, 36–37, 49, 143, 148–51, 162–63, 221
17–19	37
17:1	23, 74, 209
17:7	22
17:7–8	150
17:8	151
17:14	209
17:15–16	45
17:19	205
17:19–21	148
17:20	206
18	25
19:29	18, 20–21, 37
20	49
20–22	25

Ancient Sources Index

21	49	31:13	44, 221
21:1–5	37	31:15	221
21:3	36	31:16–17	221
21:5	18, 36	31:17	31
21:22–32	49	31:17–18	31, 32, 35
23	5, 25, 53	31:18	18, 31–32
23:4	178	32	43
24	104	32:22–33	44
25	31	33	4
25–50	35	33:18	50
25:9–10	40	34	25
25:11	40	35	43–45, 61
25:12	75	35:1–5	43
25:12–17	40	35:6	43, 45, 50
25:18	40	35:7	43
25:19	40–41, 75	35:9	43–44
25:20	18, 31, 79	35:9–10	45–46
25:26	18, 31, 36	35:9–11	45
26	42	35:9–15	5, 43–44
26:5	223	35:10	43, 50
26:27–32	76	35:10–13	50, 148
26:34–35	36, 46, 48	35:11	23, 43, 45, 50
27	36, 39, 43, 46	35:11–12	44
27:46–28:9	36, 46	35:11–13	43
28	43–45, 61	35:11–15	43, 45–46
28:1–5	45	35:12	45
28:1–9	45	35:13	45
28:3	23, 206	35:14	43–45
28:3–4	45	35:15	44–45
28:9	31, 48	35:16–19	34
28:11–12	44	35:16–20	32, 34, 50
28:11–19	23, 43	35:22–26	31–32, 46, 99
28:44	13	35:26	32
28:13–15	43	36	53
28:16–17	44	36:1	75
28:18	44	36:2–5	48
28:19	44	36:5	40
29	104	36:8	33, 40
29:24	31	36:9	22, 75
29:28	31	37	41
29:29	31	37–50	101
30:4	29	37:1	33–34, 40
30:9	31	37:1–2	32
31:12	221	37:2	18, 32, 35, 42, 75, 79
31:12–17	221	38	4, 25

268 Ancient Sources Index

Genesis (cont.)

41:8	161
41:24	161
41:45	32
41:46	18, 32–33, 35–36
43:14	23
45:19	32
45:21	32
45:27	32
45:28	32
46:1–5	32
46:2ff.	5
46:5	32, 35
46:5–7	32
46:6–7	18, 32, 32, 35
46:8–27	32
47:1	33
47:5–6	32
47:5–11	32
47:7	33
47:7–10	32–33
47:7–11	32
47:8–10	33
47:9	35
47:11	32–33
47:27	33
47:27–28	18, 33–34
48	25
48:1–7	5
48:2	34
48:3	23
48:3–7	33–35, 50
48:4	206
48:5	33
48:6	33
48:7	33–34
48:8–27	99
49	25
49:1	34
49:25	23
49:29–33	5, 34
49:31	34
49:33	34–35, 100
50	99
50:7–11	108

50:12	5
50:12–13	34, 108
50:13	5
50:14	34–35, 108
50:21	101, 149
50:22	18, 34–35, 40, 60, 99–100
50:22–23	101
50:26	60, 100

Exodus   8, 28, 36, 47–48, 50–51, 65, 95, 142, 149, 198, 210, 229–30

1	99
1–2	99, 105
1–14	95–97, 101, 133
1–15	92, 161
1:1	98
1:1–4	98
1:1–5	38, 98–99, 101, 132
1:1–7	97
1:2–4	98
1:5	98–99
1:6	100–101, 149
1:7	38, 98–101, 132
1:8	99
1:8–9	101
1:8–10	149
1:9	101
1:10	101
1:11–12	101–2, 105, 108
1:11–13	102
1:11–14	108
1:12	99, 102
1:13	98–100, 102, 105, 111, 133
1:13–14	20–21, 38, 80, 97, 100, 102, 105, 108, 147
1:14	97–100, 102, 105, 111, 133
1:20	99
1:22	101–2
2	39, 49, 104–5
2:1–10	102, 107, 111
2:1–4:10	111
2:11	104–5
2:11–15	102
2:12	105
2:15	104–5

Ancient Sources Index

2:15–22   102
2:16–22   104
2:19   104
2:22   103–4
2:24   148
2:23   97–100, 102–5, 114, 133, 145, 147
2:23–24   108
2:23–25   20–21, 38–39, 97–98, 105, 141, 144–47
2:24   98–100, 102–5, 107, 111, 133, 146
2:25   39, 97–98, 105, 145–46, 155
3   46, 96, 98, 108–10, 146–47, 163
3–4   144–46
3:1   103, 146
3:1ff.   145
3:1–10   110
3:1–4:18   103, 144–45
3:7   98, 145
3:7–9   145
3:8   98, 104
3:15   109, 147
3:16   109
3:18   109
4:1–17   146
4:18   110
4:19   103
4:19–20   102
4:20   110, 111
5:1   110
5:1–2   110
6   19, 96, 108, 110, 142, 144–45, 147–49, 155, 163, 173
6–7   160–61
6:1   144, 147
6:1–8   144
6:1–12   145, 154–56
6:2   19, 23, 39, 107, 109–10, 143, 146–47, 155
6:2ff.   20
6:2–3   21
6:2–5   49, 106, 108
6:2–6   38
6:2–8   46, 106, 109, 141–44, 146–47, 150, 221

6:2–9   38
6:2–12   110, 144, 146
6:2–23   39
6:2–7:7   97–98, 105–7, 109–10
6:2–7:13   111, 133
6:3   23, 39, 146, 155
6:3–4   143, 148
6:4   144, 148, 150–51, 178
6:5   98
6:5–7   22
6:6   108, 144, 155
6:6–7   108, 155
6:6–8   106, 108–9, 111
6:7   108, 110, 153
6:7–9   163
6:8   109, 143–44, 150–54
6:9   109, 142, 155
6:9–12   106, 109, 144
6:10–12   39
6:12–30   106
6:13   39
6:13–30   132
6:14–27   39
6:26–27   39
6:27   106
6:28–30   39, 144
7–9   155, 160, 163
7:1   107, 159–60
7:1–2   106
7:1–6   39, 106, 109, 111, 133
7:1–7   144, 155
7:1–13   110, 157–58
7:2   106, 109
7:3   106, 156, 160
7:4   106, 109, 113, 125, 155–56, 160
7:4–5   106
7:5   103, 110
7:6   106, 111
7:7   106
7:8–13   106–7, 109–10, 112–13, 118, 122, 155
7:8–11:10   112
7:8–9:12   112
7:9   157
7:9–10   156

270 Ancient Sources Index

Exodus (cont.)

7:10	115, 157
7:11	107, 157
7:12	107, 115
7:13	109, 156, 157
7:14	111, 156
7:14ff.	111
7:14–25	110
7:14–8:11	112–14, 118–19
7:14–8:15	118
7:14–8:28	133
7:14–9:12	114
7:17	117
7:17–23	114–15
7:18	116–17
7:19	115, 117, 156–57
7:19–20	155
7:19–22	158
7:20	115, 117, 157
7:21	115–17, 155, 157
7:22	117, 155–57, 160
7:23	117
7:27	116
7:28	116
8:1	115–16, 157–58
8:1–3	116, 155
8:2	115–16, 157
8:2–3	115
8:3	20, 116, 157, 160
8:6–7	158
9:8–12	160
8:11	20, 115–16, 155–59
8:12	157
8:12–15	112–14, 117–19, 155, 158
8:13	115, 157
8:14	157
8:14–15	157, 160
8:15	156–57, 160
8:16–28	118
8:28	156
9	97
9:7	156
9:8–9	157
9:8–12	112–13, 118–19, 122, 132, 155, 158

9:10	115, 157
9:12	113, 156–57, 160
9:13–10:27	113–14
9:13–11:10	113
9:22	151
9:22–25	113
9:34	156
9:35	113, 156
10:1	156
10:12–15	113
10:20	113, 156
10:21–23	113
10:27	113, 156
11:10	113, 118, 121–22, 132, 156, 159–60
12	119, 121, 123–24, 133, 160
12:1	109, 111
12:1–13	120–25, 133
12:1–20	119, 121
12:8	124
12:12	124
12:12–13	121–22, 125
12:12–27	125
12:13	133
12:14–20	120, 125, 132
12:14–41	120, 122
12:17	120
12:21–23	121
12:21–27	120
12:24–27	121
12:27	121
12:28	119–25, 133
12:29	122–24
12:29–33	120, 123–25, 133
12:29–39	121
12:34–39	120
12:37	130–31
12:40	120, 132
12:40–41	120–22
12:41	120, 122, 132
12:42	119, 121
12:42–51	125
12:43–50	119–21
12:43–51	132
12:51	120

Ancient Sources Index

271

13:3–10	125	14:28	131
13:11–16	125	14:29	131–32, 163
13:20	129	14:30	131, 162
13:21–22	127	16	132
14	19, 25, 96, 108, 122, 125, 127–28,	16:28	223
	130–33, 156, 160–63	18:10	104
14:1	131	18:16	223
14:1–4	125	18:20	223
14:1–10	161	19–20	229
14:1–29	162	19–24	25
14:2	127, 129, 131	19–40	140
14:2–3	129	19:1	140, 153
14:2–4	131–32	20	176, 200–201
14:3	129	20:4	200–201
14:4	110, 129, 131, 160, 162	20:4–6	200
14:5	128, 130–31	20:5	155
14:6	130–31	21	125, 178
14:8	127–28, 131–32, 160, 162	21:2–11	178
14:8–10	125	21:35	218
14:9	127, 131–32, 162	21:36	218
14:10	128–32, 162	22–23	125
14:13	130–31, 162	22:20–23:9	181
14:13–14	126, 129	22:24	177
14:14	130–31	22:25	180
14:15	128–29, 131–32	22:30	178–79
14:15–18	125	23	178
14:15–23	162	23:10–12	178
14:16	131–32, 163	24:15	140
14:17	129	24:15–18	170
14:17–18	131–32	24:16–17	140
14:18	110, 162	24:18	140
14:19	162	25–29	170
14:19–20	126	25–31	163, 170
14:20	162	25:1	140
14:21	126, 130–31, 163	25:8	140, 206, 221
14:22	131, 163	25:8–9	169–70
14:22–23	163	25:9	140
14:23	131–32	25:22	146
14:24	127, 130–31, 162	26	125, 169
14:24–25	126, 129	26:1–27:19	169
14:25	130–31, 162	26:7–11	169
14:26	131	26:12	169
14:26–29	162	26:14	169
14:27	126, 129–31, 163	27	125
14:27–28	130	27:1–19	169

Ancient Sources Index

Exodus (cont.)

28	172
28–29	125
28:1–41	169
28:1–29:46	170
28:36–37	172
29	52, 140, 170–72
29:5	172
29:6	172
29:42	146
29:42–46	140, 169–71, 177
29:45	206
29:45–46	22, 140, 153, 206, 221
29:46	110
30	170
30–31	170–72
30:6	146
30:36	146
32–34	25
33:7–11	46
34:25–29	204–5
35–39	169–70
35–40	163, 170–72
39–40	210
40	52, 139, 141
40:16	140, 170
40:16–17	169
40:16–33	172
40:17	140, 170
40:33	140, 169–70
40:34	172
40:35	172

Leviticus 48, 168, 171, 193, 198, 202, 230–31, 233

1–3	172–75
1–7	140, 172
1–8	172
1–10	174
1–15	175–76
1–16	140, 223, 232–33
1:1	172
3:17	233
4–7	173–75
6:13	77

7:16	77
7:22–27	233
7:36	77
7:37–38	223
7:38	77, 199
8	171–72
8–9	172–75
8:7	172
8:9	172
8:10–11	173
9	140, 172–73
9:7	172
9:22–24	173
9:23	172
10	172–74
10:1–7	173
10:8–10	173
10:8–11	175
10:8–12	174
10:8–15	173–75
10:10	174
10:10–11	173
10:11	223
10:16–20	173
11	174
11–15	173–75
11–16	175
11:43–45	174, 233
11:46	223
12:7	223
13–14	174
13:59	223
14:2	223
14:32	223
14:54	223
14:57	223
15	172
15:31	174
15:32	223
16	140, 174–75
16:29–34	233
17	176, 178–79
17–25	199–201
17–26	175–76, 178–79, 194–98, 200, 223, 231–33

Ancient Sources Index

17:3–14	178	25:38	177–78, 183
17:11	178	25:39–55	177
17:14	178	25:42	177–78, 183
17:15	178	25:55	177–78, 183, 200, 207
17:22–27	178	26	176, 179–87, 189–91, 193–
18	172, 179	94, 196–97, 199–211, 214–16, 220,
18–26	179	222, 224–31
18:1–5	177, 183	26:1	200–201
18:2–5	179	26:1–2	177, 183–84, 200–201, 203,
18:6–23	177	229
18:21	179	26:1–13	210
18:24–30	177, 183, 231	26:3	183, 203, 208
19	176, 200–201	26:3–4	182–84
19:1–4	177	26:3–13	202–3, 208, 210–11, 216
19:4	200–201	26:3–45	200–201, 203
19:14	183	26:3–46	201
19:18	181	26:4	184, 187, 207, 212
19:30	200–201	26:4–6	207
19:33–34	180–81	26:5	207
19:36	177	26:6	187, 207, 209
20:2–5	179	26:7	212, 216
20:6	179	26:9	205–6
20:7–8	177, 183	26:9–13	205, 207
20:22–26	231	26:11	206, 214–15, 231
20:22–27	177, 183	26:11–12	215
20:25	174	26:11–13	210
21:11	173	26:12	206, 208, 210–11, 215
22–24	172	26:13	177, 203, 207–8, 216
22:8	177	26:14	184, 203, 227
22:31	177	26:14–13	204–5
22:31–33	177	26:14–15	183–84
23	176–77	26:14–38	216
23:3	221	26:14–45	203
24:9	223	26:14–46	211
25	176–78, 199–201, 231	26:15	214, 220, 231
25–26	219	26:16	212
25:1	183, 187, 191, 199, 228	26:16–17	211
25:2	216	26:16–20	184–85
25:2–7	178, 200, 216	26:17	212
25:8–54	200	26:17–26	203
25:18	177	26:18	226
25:18–19	177, 183	26:18–20	211
25:23–24	177–78	26:19	212
25:27	187	26:19–20	184
25:35–38	177	26:20	184, 212

274 Ancient Sources Index

Leviticus (cont.)

26:21	218
26:22	212
26:23	211, 218, 226–27
26:23–24	218
26:23–26	211
26:24	218
26:25	213
26:25–26	212–13
26:26	212–13
26:26–33	203
26:27	211, 218
26:27–28	218
26:27–33	211, 213, 215, 217
26:28	211, 226–27
26:29	213, 216
26:30	213–15, 225, 231
26:30–31	215–16
26:30–33	215–16
26:31	202, 214–16
26:31–33	214
26:32	214–16
26:33	215–16, 225–26
26:34	216, 219, 225
26:34–35	216, 226
26:34–36	215
26:35	225
26:36	216, 225–26
26:36–38	216, 224, 226–27
26:36–39	225–26
26:37	216
26:38	216, 224–25, 227
26:39	216–17, 224–27
26:39–41	227
26:39–45	202, 224, 227–28
26:39–46	221, 226–27
26:40	216–17, 227–28
26:40–41	217–19, 227–28
26:40–45	225–26, 228
26:41	189, 218–19, 228
26:42	189, 219–20, 228
26:42–45	221
26:43	214, 219–20, 225, 228, 231
26:43–44	219, 228
26:44	220, 225

26:44–45	227
26:45	177, 203, 220–23, 228
26:45–46	229
26:46	52, 199–200, 222–23, 228, 232–33
27	52, 194, 200, 232–33
27:34	200, 232–33
28	172

Numbers	28, 51–52, 141, 198, 230–31, 233
1–4	120
1–12	146
6:13	77
7:10	77
9:15	77
10–25	231
13–14	152
20	51, 152
20:23–29	40
25:23–24	151
26:4	184
26:20	184
27	139, 152
27:12–23	52, 139
32–36	152

Deuteronomy	52, 146, 152, 165–68, 174–83, 185–90, 194, 197–98, 229–31
1:1–5	174, 186
1:5	230
1:8	152
1:19–46	188
4	185, 188, 190–91
4:1	223
4:3–4	188
4:5	223
4:8	223
4:14	223
4:23–31	187
4:26	185
4:26–27	224
4:29–31	188
4:45	222–23
5	176

5:1	223	11:14–15	182
5:2	230	11:16	185
5:8–10	201	11:16–17	184
5:31	223	11:17	184–85
6:1	223	11:21	151
6:10–19	185	11:22	184, 188
6:15	185	11:32	184, 223
6:18	188	12	176, 178
6:20	223	12–26	166, 176, 178, 180, 222
6:20–24	16	12–28	184
7	186	12:1	222–23
7:3–4	182	12:10–11	177
7:4	185–86	12:13–14	23
7:11	223	12:23	178
7:12–16	186	12:29	179
7:13	182	12:29–31	177, 179
8:1	188	12:31	179
8:19–20	185	14	174
9–10	180	14:21	178–79
9:12	185	15	178
9:16	185	15:4–6	177
10–11	180, 184	15:7–11	177
10:11	151	15:12–18	177
10:12–13	184	15:15	177
10:12–11:32	180, 184–85	16	176–77
10:13	184	16:21–22	201
10:13–15	191–92	18:9–13	179
10:15	189	18:9–14	177
10:15–16	190	18:10	179
10:16	190, 219	20:1–4	162
10:17–19	180	23:15	210
10:18	180	23:20	177
10:18–19	181	24:8	174
10:19	181	26:2–16	203
10:20–11:1	184	26:5–9	16
11	180, 183–87	26:7	145
11:1	184	26:11	204
11:8	184, 188	26:12	204
11:9	151–52	26:16	223
11:13	181, 183–84	26:17	223
11:13–14	182	28	176, 184, 187, 201, 203, 211–13, 224, 226
11:13–15	181, 183–84, 186	28:1	203
11:13–17	184, 186	28:1–4	183
11:13–21	184	28:4	204
11:14	182		

Ancient Sources Index

Deuteronomy (*cont.*)

28:4–6	204	34:11	186
28:4–13	203	**Joshua**	
28:5	204	1–24	70
28:7	204	1:8	218
28:7–10	204	4:19	138
28:8	204	5:10–12	138
28:9	204	18:1	138
28:10	204	19:51	138
28:11	204	24:2–13	16
28:11–13	204	24:29	138
28:12	182, 185, 187		
28:15	203	**Judges**	22
28:20	185		
28:22	212	**1 Samuel**	22
28:23	212	2:30	74
28:23–24	184	20:10	218
28:25	212		
28:51	224	**2 Samuel**	22
28:53	213	7:6	210
28:62	224	7:6–7	210
28:64–68	224	23:16	44
28:65	212		
29–30	190–91	**1 Kings**	22, 203, 223
29:21–28	187	2:3	223
30	188, 190	6:12	203
30–31	52	8:58	223
30:1–3	187	9:4	223
30:1–10	187–89	11:38	203
30:2	188		
30:6	188–90, 219	**2 Kings**	22, 203, 223
30:20	152	6:28–29	
31:7	151	17:19	203
31:14–34:9	70	17:37	223
31:16–18	190		
31:19–21	190–91	**1 Chronicles**	29
32	191		
32:1–43	190	**2 Chronicles**	29, 219
32:22	184	7:4	219
32:48–52	52	12:6–7	219
33:4	153	12:12	219
34	52, 139, 186	30:11	219
34:7–9	139	32:26	219
34:8	139	33:12	219
34:9	139, 190	33:19	219

Ancient Sources Index

33:23	219	49:37	213
34:4	214		
34:27	219	**Lamentations**	
36:12	219	2:20	213
		4:10	213
Nehemiah			
8:8	14	**Ezekiel**	152, 155–56, 202, 204–5, 208,
9:7–8	190	211–15, 219, 229, 231	
		2:7	156
Psalms		3:7	156
90–92	191	4	217
90:4	77	4:16	213
105:16	213	4:17	217
146	181	5:2	215
146:9	181	5:10	213
		5:12	215
Proverbs		5:14	214
1:10	185	5:16	213
		5:17	212–13
Job		6:3	213
1:7	211	6:3–5	213–14
2:2	211	6:4	214
31:9	185	6:5	213–14
31:27	185	6:8	153
		6:14	215
Isaiah		7:24	212
27:13	224	11:5	153
40:2	219	11:16–17	143
		11:18	213
Jeremiah	213, 219	12:14	215
4:4	219	12:15	215
9:25	219	12:23	143
16:18	214	12:28	143
19:9	213	14:3	214
20:5	213	14:4	214
23:1–6	209	14:7	214
25:18	214	14:8	212
30:10–11	227	14:12–23	212
31:18	227	14:13	213
31:31–34	189	14:15	212
33:20	219	14:17	207, 212–13
34:20	213	14:19	212–13
34:21	213	14:21	212
44:30	213	18	217
46:27–28	227	18:20	217

278 Ancient Sources Index

Ezekiel (cont.)

19:13	153
20	140, 153–55
20:5	155
20:8	155
20:23	143, 215
20:24	140
20:42	152
22:15	215
24:21	212
25:4	153
25:10	153
25:13	214
28:23	213
28:25	155
29–32	156
29:2–6	156
29:8	213
29:10	214
29:12	215
30:6	212
30:18	212
30:23	215
30:26	215
31:12	214
32:1–8	156
33	217
33:2	213
33:10	217
33:11	217
33:24	153, 155
33:25	143
33:28	212, 215
34	207–10
34:23	187
34:23–24	208–9
34:25	207, 209
34:25–28	208
34:25–29	204
34:25–30	207–8
34:26	187, 207
34:27	205, 207–8
34:28	187, 207
36:2	153
36:5	153

36:9	205–6
36:19	215
36:22	143
36:24–28	189
37	207–10
37:24–25	208–9
37:25	155
37:25–28	204–5, 207
37:26	206, 208–9
37:27	206
44:7	219
44:9	219

Daniel

1:20	161
2:2	161

Amos

7:9	214

Zephaniah

3:0	218

Ancient Near East

Gilgamesh	142

Early Jewish Literature

4QLev-Num[a]	203
21 I	203
4QLev[b]	203
4QLev[g]	203
11QpaleoLev	203
V	203
Josephus, *Antiquitates judaicae*	29
Jubilees	22
4.30	77

Bereshit Rabbah
22:1 77

Early Christian Literature

Tatian, *Diatessaron* (gospel harmony) 5

Modern Authors Index

Achenbach, Reinhard 97, 172–76, 196
Aejmelaeus, Anneli 34
Albertz, Rainer 28, 96, 100, 141, 154, 230
Arneth, Martin 71, 75
Astruc, Jean 1–4
Auld, A. Graeme 230
Baden, Joel S. 95, 127, 136, 166
Baentsch, Bruno 39, 204, 212
Bauks, Michaela 151, 159
Baumgart, Norbert C. 193, 225. 228
Berge, Käre 147
Berlejung, Angelika 166
Berner, Christoph 28, 63, 98–99, 101, 103, 106, 110, 114–15, 118, 121, 123, 125, 129–30, 132–33, 136, 141, 144–45, 149, 159, 162
Bertholet, Alfred 194
Blenkinsopp, Joseph 138
Blum, Erhard 3, 13, 16, 20–21, 26–28, 32–35, 38–40, 43, 46, 49, 51–52, 63–64, 69, 72–73, 76, 78, 80, 88, 92, 96, 98–103, 107–8, 113, 130, 142, 145, 160, 167–68, 175, 179, 197, 199, 204, 209–10
Bodi, Daniel 214
Bosshard-Nepustil, Erich 71
Botterweck, G. J. 226
Branson, R. 226
Braulik, Georg 230
Budde, Karl 11–12, 20, 42, 82, 85–86
Bultmann, Christoph 180
Buttmann, Phillip 82
Carr, David 32, 34, 75–76, 88, 136, 149–50, 197–98, 223

Catanzaro, Carmino Joseph de 68, 70
Childs, Brevard S. 17, 98
Cholewiński, Alfred 176–77, 195–97, 222
Collins, John 167
Couroyer, Bernard 160
Cross, Frank Moore 15–16, 28, 39, 64, 68, 80, 95, 141
Crüsemann, Frank 198, 200, 203
Dahse, Johannes 14
Davies, Graham I. 183
Dillmann, August 39, 44, 186
Donner, Herbert 8
Dozeman, Thomas B. 24, 95, 136
Duhm, Bernhard 26
Ede, Franziska 101
Eerdmans, Bernardus D. 14, 42
Ehrenreich, Ernst 189
Eichhorn, Johann Gottfried 2–4, 19–20
Eißfeldt, Otto 12–13, 15, 31, 127
Elliger, Karl 150, 171, 176, 195, 197, 204, 216, 218, 222–23, 228
Engnell, Ivan 28
Eshel, Esther 203
Etz, Donald V. 86
Ewald, Heinrich 5, 9, 65, 172
Fischer, Georg 137
Freedman, David N. 203
Frevel, Christian 109, 139, 167–68, 199
Fritz, Volkmar 170
Gabler, Johann Philipp 4
Gane, Roy E. 174
Germany, Stephen 101
Gertz, Jan Christian 19, 35, 63–64, 71, 75, 78, 82, 92, 99, 101, 103,

-280-

Modern Authors Index

Gertz, Jan Christian (*cont.*)
107, 109, 113, 120–22, 125, 127, 144, 146, 154–57, 159, 166
Gesundheit, Shimon 121
Ginsberg, Harold Louis 224, 227
Gosse, Bernard 144, 153
Graf, Karl Heinrich 13, 27, 36–39, 66, 68–69
Greenberg, Moshe 118
Greenfield, Jonas C. 212
Groß, Walter 127, 193, 209, 219–20
Grund, Alexandra 221
Grünwaldt, Klaus 176, 194–96, 201, 206, 201, 212–14, 217, 221, 228
Gunkel, Hermann 12, 20, 32, 45, 78
Hartley, John 200, 207, 217–18, 227
Hendel, Ronald S. 86, 88–89
Hezel, Wilhelm Friedrich 74
Hieke, Thomas 79, 82, 223
Himbaza, Innocent 203
Hoffmann, David 179
Holzinger, Heinrich 76
Hossfeld, Frank-Lothar 181
Hughes, Jeremy 84, 86, 88, 91
Hugo, Philippe 202
Hupfeld, Hermann 6–9, 20, 24, 34, 65
Hutzli, Jürg 160
Ilgen, Karl David 3–4
Jacob, Benno 33
Janowski, Bernd 169
Jeon, Jaeyoung 148, 152–53, 156
Jepsen, Alfred 84
Joosten, Jan 193, 222
Jülicher, Adolf 10, 122
Kaiser, Otto 27
Kegler, Jürgen 145
Keil, Carl Friedrich 67–68, 80
Klein, Anja 208
Klein, Ralph W. 86, 150
Klostermann, August 13–14, 70
Knauf, Ernst Axel 138, 162, 164
Knobel, August 5–6
Knobloch, Harald 189
Knohl, Israel 28, 172, 176, 195, 231
Koch, Klaus 39, 41, 84, 109, 168–69

Köckert, Matthias 141, 151
Kohata, Fujiko 113, 116, 144
Korpel, Marjo C. A. 194
Kratz, Reinhard Gregor 64, 75, 96, 99–100, 103, 107, 125, 141, 149, 156, 197
Krüger, Thomas 127, 162
Kuenen, Abraham 8, 12–13, 25, 39, 65, 167, 171
Kurtz, Johann Heinrich 67–68
Le Boulluec, Alain 145
Lee, Kyong-Jin 73
Lefebvre, Jean-François 199–200
Levin, Christoph 4, 19–20, 23, 25, 63, 65–66, 76, 79, 95, 99–100, 113, 121, 125–29, 149, 157, 161, 202, 204, 206, 228, 232
Levine, Baruch 194, 201, 216–18, 224, 227–28
Levinson, Bernard M. 165–66
Lohfink, Norbert 17, 27, 41, 47, 138, 148, 194, 196, 204, 208, 201, 230
Löhr, Max 15
López, Félix García 139, 166
Lowth, Robert 1
Lust, Johan 152, 154
Lux, Rüdiger 32–33
Lyons, Michael 204
Markl, Dominik 188
Marx, Alfred 197–99, 209–10, 212, 216, 218–19, 227
Mathews, Kenneth A. 203
Michaeli, Franck 147–48
Milgrom, Jacob 172, 174, 193, 195, 204, 206–7, 213–14, 216–18, 220, 223–25, 228, 231, 233
Müller, Reinhard 193, 196, 199, 201–2, 204, 206, 212–13, 215–19, 224–25, 227–29
Murtonen, A. E. 84
Najman, Hindy 167
Nihan, Christophe 63, 97, 141, 151, 171–77, 179–80, 183, 194–99, 201, 206–9, 213–14, 219–24, 227–28, 230–33

Modern Authors Index

Nöldeke, Theodor   8, 18, 27, 32, 35, 37–39, 63

Noth, Martin   16–17, 19, 30–33, 37, 50–51, 53, 64–65, 74, 76, 98, 103, 113, 116, 121, 125, 139, 150, 167–68, 171

Oswald, Wolfgang   96, 106

Otto, Eckart   18, 63, 66, 69, 95, 103, 108, 110, 140, 144, 166–79, 181–92, 194, 196–98, 200, 203, 206–7, 209–11, 221, 223–24, 229–31

Perlitt, Lothar   52, 139, 169

Pohlmann, Karl-Friedrich   208

Pola, Thomas   22, 64, 75, 139–40, 153, 169–70, 172

Preuss, Horst Dietrich   195, 197

Pury, Albert de   45, 148

Rad, Gerhard von   16, 74, 88

Ramirez-Kidd, José E.   180

Reindl, Joseph   160

Rendtorff, Rolf   28, 36, 64, 68, 68–70, 95, 141, 179

Richter, Wolfgang   16

Römer, Thomas   97, 109, 146, 149, 152–53, 155–56, 219, 221, 230, 232

Rösel, Martin   82–85, 89, 91

Rost, Leonhard   16

Rothenbusch, Ralf   202, 220

Rudolph, Wilhelm   2, 17, 33

Ruwe, Andreas   176, 197–98

Samuel, Harald   99

Sandevoir, Pierre   145

Schaffer, Aaron   212

Schmid, Konrad   17, 73, 95, 103, 137, 145–47, 166, 197

Schmidt, Ludwig   34, 101, 108, 117, 122, 139, 149

Schmidt, Werner H.   38, 97–98, 112, 139, 146, 149, 154

Schmitt, Hans-Christoph   130, 149

Schoneveld, J.   214

Schrader, Eberhard   20

Schüle, Andreas   71, 88

Schwartz, Baruch J.   95, 136, 196

Seebass, Horst   43, 76, 82, 88, 138

Seidel, Bodo   3

Seidel, Theodor   174

Shectman, Sarah   95

Ska, Jean Louis   20, 71, 96, 110, 125, 139, 160, 162, 165

Smend, Rudolf   1, 10–12, 21–22, 150

Smith, William Robertson   12

Sonnet, Jean-Pierre   168, 190

Specht, Herbert   37

Stackert, Jeffrey   136, 165–66, 178, 193, 195–98, 221

Steck, Odil Hannes   75–76

Steins, Georg   169

Steymans, Hans Ulrich   183, 185, 187, 193, 200–202, 216, 218, 220, 222

Tengström, Sven   69

Tigay, Jeffrey H.   142

Tuch, Friedrich   5–6, 65–67, 71

Utzschneider, Helmut   96, 106

Valdés, Ariel Alvarez   193

Van Seters, John   28, 64, 96, 104, 116, 122, 141, 149, 156, 159

Vermeylen, Jacques   70

Vervenne, Marc   129

Volz, Paul   2, 15, 17, 72–73

Watts, James W.   73

Weimar, Peter   75–77, 97, 112, 126–27, 129, 154

Weinfeld, Moshe   140, 186

Wellhausen, Julius   8–13, 18, 21, 30, 39, 42, 44, 65, 70, 75, 90, 112, 136, 166–67, 170–72, 194, 202

Welte, Benedikt   67

Wenham, Gordon J.   179

Westermann, Claus   33, 74

Wette, Wilhelm Martin Leberecht de   4–5, 11, 65

Wevers, John W.   216–18, 223

Whybray, Robert N.   138

Witte, Markus   75, 77–78, 80–81, 166

Wöhrle, Jakob   28, 92, 101, 151

Wolff, Hans Walter   17

Zakovitch, Yair   45

Zenger, Erich   74–75, 80, 140, 181

Ziegler, Werner Carl Ludewig   4, 74

Ziemer, Benjamin   77, 78, 94

Zimmerli, Walther	41, 221
Zvi, Ehud Ben	164

Printed in the USA
CPSIA information can be obtained
at www.ICGtesting.com
JSHW080500291223
54427JS00003B/81